Peter R. Martin:

Historical Vocabulary of Addiction

Design and Artwork
By
Carlos A. Morra

INHN Publisher
2022
Cordoba, Argentina

ISBN: 978-987-47722-9-9

INHN Publisher

Fundación Morra

Av. Sagrada Familia S/N, X5009 Córdoba

centraloffice@inhnpublishers.org

DEDICATION

To Thomas Arthur Ban, my dear friend, mentor and almost father or older brother, who inspired me to undertake the task of writing *Historical Vocabulary of Addiction*. He sensed that writing this book would be good for me. This book could become the work of a lifetime, allowing me to reflect on my academic interest in addiction psychiatry and to uncover unique insights through exploring the historical development of the field.

Contents

Preface

Patients who suffer from a loss of control over alcohol and/or drug use, or the compulsive seeking and taking of alcohol/drugs despite adverse consequences, have not typically interested psychiatrists. Even though a significant proportion of all psychiatric patients actually possess such *self-destructive* and *out-of-control* behaviors, either as their primary psychopathology or as a consequence of their underlying psychiatric disorder (Regier, Farmer, Rae 1990), alcohol and/or drug use disorders have been viewed by psychiatrists as orphan conditions, not of fundamental importance compared to "pure" psychiatric diagnoses uncomplicated by alcohol/drug use disorders. However, this viewpoint of "nosological purity" becomes untenable if it is recognized that so many patients thought to have a unique psychiatric diagnosis may have a co-occurring drug/alcohol use disorder of which the treating psychiatrist is unaware; hence, the manifest psychopathology in such patients may actually be influenced by neuropsychopharmacologic effects of the substance(s) they use in an uncontrolled manner. Such patients may not respond to "appropriate" treatment of their "pure" disorder if the alcohol/drug use disorders are not identified and also addressed.

Substances that are commonly self-administered in an out-of-control manner must always be considered in psychiatry and neuropsychopharmacology not only because they can co-occur with all psychiatric conditions but also because: 1) they have yielded some compelling clues about the pathophysiology of many psychiatric disorders; and 2) they are increasingly recognized as potential "lead compounds" in the search for novel pharmacotherapies, especially for patients who are not responsive to standard treatments. For example, stimulant-induced psychosis has long been considered a heuristic model of the psychopathology of schizophrenia and other psychoses (Snyder, Banerjee, Yamamura, Greenberg 1974; Kety 1959). More recently, cannabis use has emerged as a fundamentally important etiologic factor in development of schizophrenia in young people (Andreasson, Engstrom, Allebeck, Rydberg 1987). Moreover, despite the recognized abuse liability of opioids (Carlson, Simpson 1963) and stimulants (Hare, Dominian, Sharpe 1962) both classes of drugs have a long history of use in treatment of major depressive disorder. The most recent advance has been the investigation of a potential role of dissociative anesthetics, also with significant abuse liability, in treatment of depressed patients (Berman, Cappiello, Anand et al. 2000) due to their glutamatergic actions. This perspective has greatly expanded the scope of our understanding of the pathogenesis of depression beyond the biogenic amines (Paul, Nowak, Layer et al. 1994).

Accordingly, it seems justified that the pathogenesis, nosology and treatment of substance-related and addictive disorders *per idem* should be seriously considered in our conceptualization of the field of neuropsychopharmacology. Indeed, the presence of co-occurring alcohol/drug use disorders may actually represent the *typical course* of some psychiatric disorders characterized by mood instability, and hence, the so-called "pure" form is the exception rather than the rule and their pathogenesis and treatment may not truly be possible without a firm grasp of the alcohol/drug use component of such disorders (Rich, Martin 2014).

The logical rapprochement of the study of alcohol/drug use and other psychiatric disorders within the realm of psychiatry and neuropsychopharmacology should lead to a more complete understanding by psychiatrists of the vocabulary of addiction. This involves an appreciation not only of the meaning of the words used to convey our understanding of alcohol/drug use and related disorders but also their historical origins and evolution. My goal in this *Historical Vocabulary of Addiction* has been to prepare "vignettes" of the words that are commonly used in addiction psychiatry, encompassing their origins, historical development as well as the common usage as independent entries.

It continues to be a joy to work on these vignettes for posting on the International Network for the History of Neuropsychopharmacology (INHN) website as the task is fulfilling and almost endless as this field evolves. This process has allowed me to examine from whence addiction psychiatry, including the related neuroscience and therapeutics, have come and also anticipate where they may be going. I plan to incorporate future entries on the INHN website as they accumulate into further volumes of the *Historical Vocabulary of Addiction* which I hope will continue to be of value in education of psychiatrists.

Nashville, Tennessee

May 6, 2022

Acupuncture

According to the current electronic version of the Oxford English Dictionary (OED), the noun *acupuncture* is a borrowing from the Latin *acupunctura* which is derived from the classical Latin *acū* and the post-classical Latin *punctura*. The former is the ablative of *acus* needle, which is from the noun *acicula* as used in Zoology and Botany ("A slender spine, prickle, or other needle-like structure; [in polychaete annelids] a chitinous rod forming an internal support for a parapodium"). The latter is derived from the classical Latin *punct-*, the past participial stem of *pungere* ("to prick, puncture, [of insects] to sting, in post-classical Latin also to cause to smart") and the suffix *-ūra* ("action or process, the result or product of this").

The noun *puncture* is the modern derivative, meaning "penetration by a pointed object…, wound made by perforation, pricking sensation or pain…, compunction." According to OED, the noun *puncture* has its "first element being after Japanese *hari* needle (8th century), acupuncture needle (11th century), acupuncture (late 16th century) and also (written with the same kanji) *shin-* needle." There are multiple other references related to *acupuncture* in OED, such as *moxibustion* (Alternative Medicine: "The therapeutic practice of burning moxa or another substance on or next to the skin.") in both Chinese and Japanese.

The definition of *acupuncture* in OED is: "A method of medical treatment, originating in China, in which fine needles are inserted into the skin at specific points on the body surface; the performance of this." The definition continues: "Acupuncture, used in China for several thousand years, became the object of scientific study in the west in the latter part of the 20th century, and is now increasingly accepted as a therapeutic technique by western physicians, especially for pain relief." This supports the relevance of acupuncture as a potential treatment of addiction through the evolving connections of addiction with pain (see Pain) and various other co-occurring disorders (see Self-medication).

The first use of the word *acupuncture* in the English language via translation appeared in the compendium *A guide to the practical physician* by Theophile Bonet (1620-1689). Known as the Physician of Geneva (Anonymous 1969), Bonet wrote a yearbook of medical practice compiled from reports sent to him by physicians of the day which included observations and recent discoveries in the basic sciences. He quoted Willem ten Rhijne (1647–1700), a Dutch physician and botanist who had been sent by the Dutch East India Company in 1674 to the trading post Dejima in Japan, where he collected materials on Japanese medicine, especially on acupuncture and moxibustion: "Among themselves, they [sc. the

Japanese] have, by the guidance of China, adapted a two-fold method of Cure to the foresaid Diseases, namely, Acupuncture [L. acuum puncturam], and burning with their Moxa" (Bonet 1686).

Daniel Turner (1667–1740), an English physician who started his medical career as a surgeon/barber and subsequently was awarded the first ever M.D. degree in the U.S. by Yale College in 1723 (Anonymous 1970), published the first English textbook on dermatology, *De Morbis Cutaneis*. In this book, he argued that surgeons/barbers, who for centuries had been relegated by physicians to treating external diseases, should be given the right to also administer medicines internally, since the medicines they were applying externally to the skin were also producing internal effects. Acupuncture, no doubt, represented an illustration of this inconsistency to Turner — a "surgical" technique with the potential to treat illnesses that are typically viewed as "medical" problems: "A great Part of the World, viz. China and Japan, give very few, and those very simple ones, laying their chief Stress, and undertaking to cure almost all Distempers, by Acupuncture and Inustion" (Turner 1723).

According to the understanding of physiology in Asia, specific external body locations are linked with body organs by pathways called *meridians* along which vital energy, or *qi (chi)*, is said to flow and each of a set of twelve such pathways are associated with specific organ systems (Lawson-Wood 1959). In health, flow of vital energy along these meridians is in a dynamic balance of opposing, interdependent qualities, namely the *yin* and *yang*, whereas disturbances of this balance result in disease. It has been held for millennia that disease could be alleviated by restoring the balance of vital energy by stimulation, usually by needle insertion or by other means, of *specific* locations along the relevant meridians. According to Chen (2011), mechanistic understanding of pain, especially the symptoms and signs of nociceptive and inflammatory pain, as an imbalance of *yin* and *yang* that could be restored by treatment has been central in traditional Chinese medicine, first described in the 3000-year-old medical book *Huang Di Nei Jing*.

Scholars of medicine in the West were aware of these therapeutic techniques and quite ambivalent about their efficacy as suggested by an editorial in the *Edinburgh Medical Surgical Journal* (Anonymous 1827):

> "Those of our readers who have perused the essay of Mr. Churchill on acupuncture [James Morss Churchill (1796—1863) was a British physician, surgeon and botanist who wrote the first article on acupuncture in England (1821)] … and who are aware that investigations have been lately made on the same subject in

various parts of the Continent, may be surprised that hitherto no notice has been taken of it in this *Journal*. One reason has been, that the first accounts given of the virtues of the new remedy were so marvellous, and therefore seemed to savour so much of quackery, that, coming, as they did, from persons not of the highest authority, we could not but follow the general example, and decline giving implicit credit to their assertions. But these assertions have been re-echoed from almost every quarter of Europe; observations have been made on the subject at many continental schools of eminence; the several accounts given by unconnected writers agree very remarkably in every essential particular; the alleged facts have at length been put to the test of a full and minute train of experiments by one of the most scientific of the Parisian physicians, in a great public hospital, and under the eyes of its pupils; the results of these experiments, as published by his hospital assistants, harmonize exactly with the statements made by those who introduced the remedy into Europe; and under such circumstances we cannot any longer delay presenting a summary of the interesting information which has been accumulated in its favour.

"It must be confessed, however, that after all we cannot approach this singular topic without hesitation. It is true, that, in the hands of M. Cloquet (Jules Germain Cloquet [1790–1883]), a French physician and surgeon who was a skilled artist and anatomist with a keen interest in alternative medical practices such as mesmerism and acupuncture (Morand 1825), the remedial virtues of acupuncture have passed triumphantly through an ordeal, to which no remedy, whose claims were false, could be submitted without detection. But, at the same time, the utmost ingenuity of its favourers has been unable to discover, in a long course of minute inquiries, any rational way of accounting for its effects; and, what is perhaps of more consequence, they have been unable to detect any physiological change or phenomenon co-ordinate with its operation. There is in short a total want of every sort of evidence in its favour as a remedy, except that most treacherous kind, the evidence of succession; and consequently, a philosophical mind, especially considering the diseases in which the greatest success has been obtained, will naturally feel inclined to attribute the cures which have been accomplished to the influence of the imagination, and to sentence acupuncture to banishment from regular practice, as being nothing else than a variety of animal magnetism."

All the same, despite the ambivalence about acupuncture in western medicine, historical and philosophical interest in the contributions of acupuncture as the mainstay of traditional Chinese medicine to Asian understanding of the role of Man in the Universe continued unabated to the present day (Veith 1962).

To be accepted as a reputable treatment in western medicine for treatment of pain and other distressing conditions, the theoretical foundation of the acupuncture technique had to be reconceptualized within a construct that is compatible with the western perspective of the structure of the body (Detwiler 1929) and of the sensory transmission of pain in the nervous system (Brown-Sequard 1859), both of which were distinctly different from ideas in Asia. Additionally, as mentioned above, a dichotomy of interests and tension between practitioners of surgery and medicine (Stienen, Scholtes, Samuel et al. 2018) may also have contributed to the reasons it has been so challenging to establish objective evidence for efficacy of acupuncture and to accept a role for this technique in healing by western practitioners.

Although Western fascination with Chinese medicine has been longstanding (Penfield 1963), widespread interest in the therapeutic potential of acupuncture in the United States seems to date to an article in the July 26, 1971 edition of the *New York Times* in which the columnist James Reston described his experience with acupuncture anesthesia during his surgery for acute appendicitis while in China. Subsequently, as part of President Nixon's rapprochement with China, influential American physician groups began visiting that country. Curiosity was generated in the capacity of acupuncture to manage pain, and this provided the impetus for understanding the technique within the traditions of Western medicine. Opinions at this time about acupuncture varied widely, but mostly the technique was viewed as no more than placebo-like in its actions, akin to hypnosis, and effective mostly in "strong reactors" (Mann 1974; Gaw, Chang and Shaw 1975). In short order, scientists developed explanatory anatomic and physiological theories for acupuncture that were compatible with Western scientific principles and its lexicon (Melzack and Wall 1965; Dornette 1975; Watkins and Mayer 1982).

The interest in acupuncture for treatment of drug use disorders originated from the role of this technique in the field of anesthesia (Cheng and Ding 1973) and early reports in high quality scientific journals that electro-acupuncture, indeed, did elevate pain threshold in the great majority of patients

(Andersson, Ericson, Holmgren and Lindqvist 1973). The mechanistic relationship between pain and addiction received further support from the reported effectiveness of acupuncture for treatment of opioid withdrawal (Tseung 1974). The potential of acupuncture in treatment of addictive disorders seemed a *hypothesis* worthy of investigation for two very important reasons: 1) the pathogenesis of addiction and pain are now understood to be profoundly interdigitated; and 2) treatment of addiction has been on a less solid footing in Western medicine than that many other common disorders (Martin, Weinberg and Bealer 2007) suggesting an opportunity for improvement.

Initial experience with acupuncture resulted in a position paper from a professional organization that concluded the technique was not a reputable medical treatment (National Council Against Health Fraud 1991). In response to the controversy concerning the efficacy of acupuncture, the National Institute of Drug Abuse (NIDA) conducted a technical review of the role of acupuncture in the treatment of alcohol and drug use disorders (McLellan, Grossman, Blaine and Haverkos 1993). The NIDA committee identified a need to clarify and define the terms and methodologies of acupuncture in an operational manner before robust research was possible. (These issues related to standardization of the acupuncture techniques are not at all surprising or dissimilar from research in all treatment approaches practiced in medicine—whether pharmacological, surgical or psychosocial.)

Moreover, the committee proposed defining with greater granularity the goals of acupuncture treatment with respect to the clinical course of alcohol and drug use disorders (see Recovery) —whether the treatment was intended for *detoxification* (initial phase of treatment, lasting 3-7 days after stopping use, when a patient is suffering from direct effects of the abused substance); *rehabilitation* (the second stage of treatment, typically lasting 15-90 days, beginning after the completion of detoxification/stabilization); or *relapse prevention* (the third stage of treatment, beginning near the end of the rehabilitation phase, with the goals to maintain the gains achieved in the earlier phases of treatment and to actively develop strategies to avoid relapse).

Over the years, there have been reports of employing acupuncture in treatment of many drug use disorders, and Moner (1996) concluded that efficacy of the technique is "very encouraging" as it has positive attributes of being "quick, inexpensive, and relatively safe" so that "acupuncture treatment may establish itself as an important addition to addiction services in the future." Accordingly, acupuncture has been viewed by most as an integrated adjunct to the pharmacopsychosocial elements of addiction treatment (Martin, Weinberg and Bealer 2007) rather than as a stand-alone medical/psychiatric/surgical technique which can "cure" the disorder.

Consistent with this complementary role, acupuncture has been demonstrated to have broader therapeutic effects than analgesia alone, including treatment of insomnia, depression and anxiety (Spence, Kayumov, Chen et al. 2004; Lee, Kim, Kim et al. 2020; Yu, Wei, Chang et al. 2021), symptoms that are mechanistically interconnected with alcohol and drug use disorders and contribute to morbidity of these conditions (see Sleep, Pain and Self-medication). Moreover, acupuncture has been reported to possibly benefit behavioral addictions like overeating manifested as obesity (Zhong, Luo, Chen et al. 2020).

The mechanism of action of acupuncture and related techniques is thought to be based on frequency of electrostimulation resulting in stimulation of the release of diverse neuropeptides such as endorphins, neuropeptide Y, oxytocin, substance P, neurokinin, (Han 2003). β-endorphin, endomorphin and encephalin are released with low frequency electrostimulation, which then interact with mu-opioid receptors and delta-opioid receptors as supported by antagonism of these effects with naloxone. By contrast, high-frequency electroacupuncture (100 Hz) accelerates the release of dynorphin, which binds preferentially to kappa-opioid receptors.

Acupuncture has been found to have a somatotopic distribution in its release of brain-gut peptides and anti- and pro-inflammatory responses in the rat, including in a model of Parkinson's disease (Liu, Wang, Su et al. 2020; Yu, Min, Bai et al. 2020). As research progresses, acupuncture has been reported to activate a remarkable number of neuroreceptors and neuromediators involved in pain control and related physiological actions (Trento, Moré, Duarte and Martins 2021), suggesting the potential for important, though not yet harnessed, therapeutic effects.

Similar caveats that were voiced over the past two centuries have continued in recent years as studies of the role of acupuncture in management of alcohol/drug use disorders and a plethora of medical/surgical/psychiatric conditions have continued. Advances in neuroimaging studies have allowed dissection of brain mechanisms involved in the therapeutic actions of acupuncture by determining connectivity among specific limbic brain regions in depressed humans (Duan, He, Pang et al. 2020). The consensus seems to be that there is significant efficacy compared to placebo/sham conditions, but the quality of the available evidence remains low and the therapeutic potential of acupuncture warrants further investigations as a "promising" adjunctive treatment for alcohol/drug and related disorders.

Of course, the question that must be answered is whether these data are any different from other widely used components that comprise an integrated pharmacopsychosocial approach to addiction treatment. At this stage, it is predicted that there may be a particular role for acupuncture in treating stimulant use disorders and possibly behavioral addictions, disorders for which there are no current good pharmacological approaches available (Gates, Smith and Foxcroft 2006; Kim, Zhao, Lee et al. 2020; Ronsley, Nolan, Knight et al. 2020; Yang, Yao, Wang et al. 2020; Zhong et al. 2020).

Addiction

According to the latest electronic version of the Oxford English Dictionary (OED), the word *addiction* is a borrowing from the classical Latin *addictiōn-*, *addictiō* ("assignment [of disputed property], assigning of a debtor to the custody of his creditor"). The past participial stem of *addīcere*, namely *addict-*, is combined with the suffix *-iō* *-ion* ("Forming nouns of action from verbs") to form *addiction*. The medical meaning of the word corresponds to one of the definitions of addiction in OED ("Immoderate or compulsive consumption of a drug or other substance; specifically, a condition characterized by regular or poorly controlled use of a psychoactive substance despite adverse physical, psychological, or social consequences, often with the development of physiological tolerance and withdrawal symptoms; an instance of this").

Specific reference to a pathological neurobehavioral interaction between an individual and a self-administered (exogenous) neuropsychopharmacologic agent is not the primary meaning of *addiction* in OED, nor is it the earliest use of the word in history. The earliest recorded written reference in the English language, according to OED, was from *Glasse of Truthe* a book written in support of Henry VIII of England in his desire to seek annulment of his marriage to Catherine of Aragon (Henry 1532): "An ouermoche addiction to priuate appetites, mixed with to moche heedinesse and obstinacy"), where the term was used in its original meaning (" The state or condition of being dedicated or devoted *to* a thing, especially an activity or occupation; adherence or attachment, especially of an immoderate or compulsive kind").

The first written reference to *addiction* as it is commonly understood in medicine today comes from the English political writer William Pittis (1673/4–1724) in *Dr. Radcliffe's Life & Letters* (Pittis 1716): "The Doctor…made a Forfeit of them, by his too great Addiction to the Bottle, after a very uncourtly manner." This is a different emphasis of the original meaning of the word ("dedication or devotion to a thing"), as the thing is "the Bottle," which represents its contents, namely alcohol, clearly understood to be self-administered for recognized neuropharmacological actions, hence, alcohol addiction. First mention of addiction to another neuropsychopharmacologic agent tobacco was in reference to the chain-smoking 18th century English poet John Philips (1676–1709) by author, biographer and lexicographer Samuel Johnson (1709 –1784) in his *Prefaces, Biographical and Critical, to the Works of the English poets* (Johnson 2018): "His addiction to tobacco is mentioned by one of his biographers." Thereby, addiction came to include another commonly used psychoactive agent, suggesting that very diverse substances could share the specific attribute of out-of-control self-administration. Generalizability of the term beyond alcohol and tobacco is significant because it signals that the agent alone is perhaps less important than the out-of-control and self-destructive manner in which it is self-administered, as suggested by the first appearance of the term *drug addiction* in *The Medical and Surgical Reporter* (Kane 1881): "A clerk, aged forty-two years, a widower, no family history of alcoholism, drug addiction, insanity, marked nervous disease, or syphilis".

Use of the word *addiction* to specify a medical disorder, according to OED, seems to date to an entry in the *Journal of the American Medical Association* (Jelliffe 1906): "It matters little whether one speaks of the opium habit, the opium disease or the opium addiction." Addiction also acquired scientific meaning as evidenced by entries in pharmacology textbooks and the scientific literature. For example, the following definition can be found in *Pharmacology and Therapeutics: a Textbook for Students and Practitioners of Medicine* (Grollman 1951): "Addiction refers to that condition induced by a drug which necessitates the continuation of the drug and without which physical and mental derangements result." Whereas in the scientific journal *Nature*, discussion of the mechanistic underpinnings of addiction became an important topic of discussion (Snyder 1975): "Most people consider opiate addiction to comprise three major elements: tolerance, physical dependence, and compulsive craving".

By the 20th century, a syndrome of self-destructive and out-of-control self-administration of various neuropsychopharmacologic agents had been described by many of the leaders of modern scientific psychiatry (Nathan, Conrad, and Skinstad 2016). Nevertheless, it was believed that these disorders were caused by or were associated with other psychiatric disorders, including melancholia, mania and schizophrenia. In fact, the word *toxicomanie*, still widely used in the French language synonymously with addiction, possibly reflects this early confounding of what was considered the primary cause of the observed psychopathology in this syndrome, which due to its self-destructive nature seemed only explicable based on insanity of some form. With elucidation of reward mechanisms in the brain that could shape behavior such as out-of-control self-administration of psychoactive agents, it became feasible to conceptualize *addiction* as a psychiatric disorder in its own right (Olds 1958).

Even though the word *addiction* had become associated by usage with a well-recognized medical/psychiatric syndrome, debate continued about whether it was, indeed, the best word to describe the behaviors characterized by out-of-control and self-destructive alcohol/drug use (Jaffe 1975): "It is possible to describe all known patterns of drug use without the terms addict or addiction. In many respects this would be advantageous, for the term addiction, like the term abuse, has been used in so many ways that it can no longer be employed without further qualification or elaboration. However, since it is not likely that the term will be dropped from the language, it is appropriate to make an effort to delimit its meaning." Additionally, the most appropriate way to refer to, yet not to stigmatize, those diagnosed with what had slowly become accepted as a medical condition rather than a bad habit, has been a continuing discussion to the present day (Botticelli and Koh 2016). Deliberations have focused on which term most accurately captures the essence of these behaviors, describing the characteristics of use as abuse (or misuse), non-medical, problematic, pathological, harmful, hazardous, illicit and compulsive, among many others. The World Health Organization (WHO) Expert Committee attempted throughout the 1950s to define addiction applicable to drugs, trying to differentiate *addiction* from *habituation* without successful application to clinical practice. In 1964, the WHO Expert Committee introduced the term *dependence* to replace the terms addiction and habituation. The rationale was that dependence could be used generally with reference to the entire range of psychoactive drugs (e.g., drug dependence, chemical dependence, substance use dependence) or with specific reference to a particular drug or class of drugs (e.g., alcohol dependence, opioid dependence), the term could be dichotomized into complementary components (*psychic* or *physical* dependence) and it did not carry a connotation of the degree of health risk or need for legal control of the drug in question. The current *WHO International Statistical Classification of Diseases and Related Health Problems 10th Revision* (ICD-10) still describes dependence in terms applicable across drug classes with differences in the characteristic dependence symptoms for different drugs (World Health Organization 2016).

On the other hand, the American Psychiatric Association (APA) initially conceptualized addiction in the realm of abnormal personality development and sociopathic personality disturbances (Nathan, Conrad and Skinstad 2016). For the first time, in the *Diagnostic and Statistical Manual of Mental Disorders, Third Edition* (DSM III), the disorder emerged as a primary diagnosis as *abuse* or *dependence*, not fully resonating with the WHO diagnostic system with its unitary focus on dependence, but nevertheless unifying the disease construct in medicine and as a psychiatric disorder (American Psychiatric Association 1980). It was not until DSM-III-R that the notion of the generic substance dependence syndrome for all drugs of abuse received confirmation, however, the construct of abuse and dependence persisted (Kosten, Rounsaville, Babor et al. 1987). More recently, APA has settled, after many decades of employing abuse and dependence on conceptualizing the breadth of the disorder, on the single term drug use disorder with designation by degrees of severity (mild, moderate and severe based on numbers of criteria satisfied) in the *Diagnostic and Statistical Manual of Mental Disorders, Fifth Edition* (DSM-5) (American Psychiatric Association 2013).

An important advance in recent years is recognition that various behaviors, such as gambling, problematic hypersexuality, overeating, etc., can also "hijack" brain reward pathways and thus share similar mechanistic underpinnings and essential clinical features of drug use disorders (Martin, Weinberg, and Bealer 2007). In the context of these *behavioral* or *context addictions*, the word addiction seems to have returned to its original meaning in OED, namely a habit and inclination towards an out-of-control repetitive behavior, which is endogenous to the organism and does not involve self-administration of an exogenous agent. The APA Task Force describes these as addictive disorders and includes gambling disorder in the same chapter of the DSM-5 as the substance-related disorders (American Psychiatric Association 2013). Nevertheless, questioning whether behaviors other than gambling with comparable psychopathological features merit inclusion in DSM-5 seems to be a continuation of the polemics that seem to haunt the nosology of these disorders (p. 481): "Thus, groups of repetitive behaviors, which some term behavioral addictions, with such subcategories as sex addiction, exercise addiction, or shopping addiction, are not included because at this time as there is insufficient peer-reviewed evidence to establish the diagnostic criteria and course descriptions needed to identify these behaviors as mental disorders."

Acceptance in the APA diagnostic terminology of addictive disorders may well suggest that the word addiction has returned to acceptability in medicine; but that seems not to be the case at this stage, as DSM-5 clearly states (p. 485) that "the word addiction is not applied as a diagnostic term in this classification, although it is in common usage in many countries to describe severe problems related to compulsive and habitual use of substances. The more neutral term substance use disorder is used to describe the wide range of the disorder, from a mild form to a severe state of chronically relapsing compulsive drug taking. Some clinicians will choose to use the word addiction to describe more extreme presentations, but the word is omitted from the official DSM-5 substance use disorder diagnostic terminology because of its uncertain definition and its potentially negative connotation" (American Psychiatric Association 2013).

In conclusion, the concept denoted by the word *addiction* has a history as long as mankind. However, society continues to struggle with the paradox that another human can be engaged in out-of-control and self-destructive behavior without being insane and what to call this condition despite its acceptance as a brain disorder for some time (Leshner 1997). This conundrum makes it unacceptable to some to call a well-characterized disorder by its original name and hence, a more acceptable terminology may be needed (Botticelli and Koh 2016) in order to assuage our guilt for not treating these patients without prejudice, simply as humans suffering from an all-too-common condition.

Aggression

According to the current electronic version of the Oxford English Dictionary (OED), the noun *aggression* is partly a borrowing from French and Latin. The French *aggression* is derived from the classical Latin *aggressiōn-, aggressiō*. Both of these were formed originally as the combination of the past participial stem of *aggredī* ("to attack") and *-iō -ion* (a suffix which is used to form a noun from a verb). The first use in the English language of the word *aggress* which is found in both noun and verb forms preceded that of the noun *aggression*.

The noun *aggress* was first used in the English language as exemplified by an entry in *The Acts of the Lords Auditors of Causes & Complaints* dating originally to 1475, edited by Thomas Thomson (1773–1852), a Scottish physician and chemist (Thomson 1839): "In the mein tyme he to haue aggress [to] Malcom Fleming for quham he is bundin." This meaning of the noun *agress* ("access, approach") is now obsolete, replaced by one that designates motivated antagonism ("An attack, an act of aggression") as in (Fletcher 1677): "The 3d. and last aggress was managed by Salmanasser… who in the 9th of Hoshea sweeped the Land of its inhabitants." An example of the first appearance of the verb *aggress* occurred in a book by Thomas Preston (1537–1598), playwright and college head (Preston 1569): "Beholde I see him now agresse and enter into place." This meaning ("To approach, march forward; to progress") is also considered obsolete; it has been supplanted by one that denotes ferocious fighting ("To make an attack; to commit the first act of violence, to provoke conflict."), as for example by Edmund Arwaker the elder (?1660–1730), an Irish poet and cleric (Arwaker 1708): "The Man's Son, thro' Wantonness, aggress'd, And with a rude Assault provok'd the Beast."

The original meaning of *aggression* in the English language ("An unprovoked attack; the first attack in a dispute or conflict; an assault, an inroad") is exemplified by (Sheldon 1611): "Who is ignorant how that same furious aggression and censure of Boniface the VIII. upon Philip the Faire, how little it profited?" Then the meaning of *aggression* shifted ("The practice of attacking another or others; the making of an attack or assault"), as for example (Lord 1630): "They renewed their battell by fresh Aggression and Onset, till darknesse did prohibit the use of Armes." The progression of meanings evolved from military to more political contexts until *aggression* came to be viewed as an attribute ("Feeling or energy displayed in asserting oneself, or in showing drive or initiative; aggressiveness, assertiveness, forcefulness"). An example is from Gustav Adolf Lindner (1828–1887), the Czech pedagogue, sociologist, psychologist and philosopher, in his book *Manual of Empirical Psychology as an*

Inductive Science (Lindner and De Garmo 1890): "The great secret of their aggression and efficiency is to be found in the fact that they [sc. the Herbartian school] have a vital psychology."

Eventually, the word *aggression* came to be used in psychology having the meaning, "Behaviour intended to injure another person or animal; an instance of this." An example of this sense of the word was in a paper entitled *The Gambling Impulse* (France 1902): "[In gambling] we find arising emulation, aggression, the instinct of domination, with the love of humiliating one's opponent." Analogously, *aggression* became closely linked in the psychodynamic literature with sexuality as for example by Freud (1910): "The sexuality of most men shows a taint of aggression." Also, *aggression* emerged as having a substantial role in neuroticism, whereby physical force is not needed or practiced but domination is accomplished with the emotional quality of profound passivity (Adler 1917): "The neurotic succeeds in... this new line so skillfully as to manage to set up an aggression which enables him to dominate and torture others." Eventually, the blending of *pleasure* and *aggression* evolved such that these constructs could be discussed in very similar terms by Charles Anthony Storr (1920–2001), an English psychiatrist and psychoanalyst, in his book *Human Aggression* (Storr 1968):

> "Once we can bring ourselves to abandon the pleasure principle, it is easy to accept the idea that the achievement of dominance, the overcoming of obstacles, and the mastery of the external world, for all of which aggression is necessary, are as much innate human needs as sexuality or hunger."

This quotation seems to predict that *aggression* could be considered a vital *drive* with the potential to go awry and manifest characteristics of an addictive disorder.

Aggression has long been recognized as a common *consequence* of alcohol/drug use (Spain, Bradess and Eggston 1951; MacAndrew and Edgerton 1969; Virkkunen 1974; Kalant and Kalant 1975; Nurco and DuPont 1977). Even recreational use of drugs and alcohol has been directly linked to aggression and violence, mediated by personality characteristics (Tomlinson, Brown and Hoaken 2016), especially in those with a previous history of aggressive behavior (Ritter, Lookatch, Schmidt and Moore 2019). However, out-of-control use of drugs/alcohol in those suffering from addiction is additionally punctuated by the pressure of distressing symptoms of craving and withdrawal. Attempts to overcome such urges by obtaining, often from illicit sources at hard-to-afford cost, the substance(s) to which an individual is addicted, frequently involves *criminality* and *aggressive behavior*, albeit mediated by personality, sex, family history, other psychiatric diagnoses and multiple socioeconomic factors (Guze, Woodruff and Clayton 1974; Cloninger, Christiansen, Reich and Gottesman 1978). When the addicted individual succeeds in obtaining the abused substance, *intoxication* can often wreak havoc, implicated in a large proportion of all assaults, rapes, homicides and violent deaths.

Aggressive behavior is a distinct response to self-administration of alcohol/drugs influenced by interindividual genetic and experiential differences, much as is susceptibility to other manifestations of intoxication such as sedation, ataxia and blackout (Brown, Goodwin, Ballenger et al. 1979; Schuckit 1980; Pihl, Smith and Farrell 1984; Lappalainen, Long, Eggert et al. 1998; Moeller, Dougherty, Lane et al. 1998; Hingson, Simons-Morton and White 2016). Intoxication may release deep-seated anger, the basis of aggression, that would otherwise be distressing and incompatible with one's personality (Snell, Rosenwald and Robey 1964); repeated use under these circumstances can eventually progress to alcohol/drug use disorder. This situation is quite analogous to *self-medication* of pain (see Pain), insomnia (see Sleep) or anxiety/depression (Martin, Weinberg and Bealer 2007; see Self-medication). Nevertheless, the significant association between *aggression* and *substance use disorders* does not specify direction of any putative linkage.

Aggression may have an *etiologic* role in addiction beyond simply an *association* with phenomenology of the *addiction syndrome* that characterizes substance use disorders. This concept originates from Thompson (1963) demonstrating that aggression can serve as a *positive reinforcer* in its own right in male Siamese fighting fish (*Betta splendens*). Subsequently, it was shown that access to aggression can be *conditioned* (see Conditioning) using the paradigm of nose pokes in mice as an operant response on ratio- and time-based reinforcement schedules (May and Kennedy 2009) and heightened by various agents such as alcohol (Fish, DeBold and Miczek 2002b) and the neurosteroid allopregnanolone (Fish, De Bold and Miczek 2002a) but diminished by NMDA antagonists. Delineation of modulators of aggressive behaviors have led to predictions of the underlying neural circuits (Covington, Newman, Leonard and Miczek 2019). Furthermore, in non-human primates, McClintick and Grant (2016) demonstrated that baseline aggressive temperament and behavior were associated with increased risk of higher ethanol *self-administration* and *intoxication* when ethanol and water were concurrently made available. The interaction between alcohol and aggression seems to be recapitulated across the animal kingdom as alcohol potentiates pheromone signaling tied to nutrition and reproduction in the fruit fly *Drosophila melanogaster* (Park, Tran, Scheuermann et al. 2020). The breadth of these convergent findings has lent support to the substantial contribution of operant conditioning to aggression, along with other fundamental drives.

The well-accepted and robust association between addiction and aggression that so profoundly affects society, previously examined primarily from ethological (Dollard, Miller, Doob et al. 1939) and social (MacAndrew and Edgerton 1969) perspectives might, therefore, be further elucidated using theories of conditioning, a heuristic model for understanding addiction (see Conditioning). Accordingly, disturbances in the biological drive of aggression may join the family of addictive disorders termed *behavioral addictions*, e.g., gambling disorder and perhaps problematic hypersexuality and over-eating (Ragan and Martin 2000; Martin and Petry 2005; American Psychiatric Association 2013). Although aggression seems to stoke the fires of substance use disorders and *vice versa*, under this conceptualization, *pathological aggression* may progress to an addictive disorder *per se* with or without co-occurring drug/alcohol use disorder. A transitory episode of an all-encompassing emotion like aggression can serve as a distraction, a reprieve from or a manner of coping with potentially distressing symptoms of an underlying medical or psychiatric disorder. Thereby, aggressive behaviors can be used in an analogous manner to *self-medication*, frequently employed to avoid feeling primary medical or psychiatric symptoms such as pain or anxiety/depression (see Self-medication). If this means of coping is momentarily beneficial and repeatedly practiced, it may eventually progress to development of pathological aggression.

Current pathogenetic, phenomenological and nosological concepts related to out-of-control aggressive behavior manifest striking lacunae with respect to the potentially rewarding nature of these behaviors. Classically, aggression has been described as defensive, premeditated or predatory and impulsive or non-premeditated; only impulsive and predatory aggression are considered pathological (Coccaro 2012). Attempts to understand and classify *impulsive* aggression have culminated in the DSM-5 term *intermittent explosive disorder* (American Psychiatric Association 2013). Beginning in adolescence or early adulthood in about 5% of the population, this disorder consists of either infrequent very intense outbursts of aggression or repeated less severe outbursts. Nosological conceptualization of this disorder has swung over time between attributing these *impulsive* aggressive outbursts either to a psychological response style based on *personality* structure or to disruption of neurobiological underpinnings of the *expression* of anger (Coccaro 2012). These developments in clinical phenomenology and classification have focused predominantly on *impulsiveness* and resultant harm to the self and others, paying little attention to *compulsiveness* based on reinforcement and learning.

As impulsive aggression became clinically more reliably characterized (Coccaro 2012), etiopathogenesis drifted towards establishing an association with abnormal metabolism of brain biogenic amines, predominantly serotonin (Brown, Goodwin, Ballenger et al. 1979; Linnoila, Virkkunen, Scheinin et al. 1983; Kolla and Bortolato 2020). This idea originated from observations by Åsberg, Träskman and Thorén (1976) that a subgroup of depressed patients with low concentrations of 5-hydroxyindoleacetic acid (the major metabolite of serotonin) in the cerebrospinal fluid (CSF) were more likely than depressed patients with normal 5-HIAA to have attempted or completed suicide using particularly violent means. This observation was eventually generalized to a trait in various disorders such as intermittent explosive disorder, personality and other psychiatric disorders which frequently co-occur with impulsive aggression (Coccaro, Lee and Kavoussi 2010). Of relevance to addiction, low CSF 5-HIAA was also found associated with a tendency to repeated, impulsive violent behavior which can be directed towards oneself (suicide) as well as others (murder) and with early onset alcohol use disorder (Lappalainen, Long, Eggert et al. 1998). Nevertheless, the route to intense impulsive episodes of aggression can be via other than serotonergic mechanisms, e.g., temporal lobe seizures (Bach-Y-Rita, Lion and Ervin 1970; Woermann, van Elst LT, Koepp et al. 2000), mood disorder and various other neurocognitive causes (Blair 2001).

Unravelling the neurobiological foundations of pathological aggression has led to mechanisms relevant to salience (see Salience), conditioning (see Conditioning) and learning and emergence of the term *compulsive aggression*. This perspective allows specific forms of pathological aggression to be viewed as a behavioral addiction. Golden, Jin, Heins and colleagues (2019) investigated *appetitive aggression* using a novel mouse model of aggression self-administration and relapse, in combination with immunohistochemistry, *in situ* hybridization, and chemogenetic manipulations to examine how nucleus accumbens cells are recruited for, and control, operant aggression self-administration and aggression seeking in early abstinence. They found dopamine receptor 1-expressing neurons that act as a critical modulator of operant aggression reward and aggression-seeking suggesting involvement of addiction-related reward circuits. Labonté, Abdallah, Maussion et al. (2020) identified and characterized a novel long noncoding RNA, acting as a regulator of the monoamine oxidase A gene in the brain of suicide completers, regulated by a combination of epigenetic mechanisms, suggesting that variations in DNA methylation regulate impulsive-aggressive behaviors. This mechanism of modulating aggressive behavior parallels previous findings showing the role of epigenetic modifications following stress exposure (Guillemin, Provençal, Suderman et al. 2014) and in expression of addiction- and depression-related behaviors (Heller, Cates, Peña et al. 2014). These most recent findings are compatible with the proposal that appetitive forms of pathological aggression are neurobiologically closely related to out-of-control and self-destructive drug self-administration as well as other behaviors that characterize alcohol/drug use disorders and behavioral addictions, respectively.

Alcoholism

The noun *alcoholism* according to the latest electronic version of the Oxford English Dictionary (OED) was formed within the English language by derivation from a combination of the noun *alcohol* ("a colourless volatile flammable liquid which is naturally produced in aqueous solution by the fermentation of sugars, and which is the intoxicating constituent of drinks such as beer, wine, and spirits [in which it is concentrated by distillation]. Also called *ethanol, ethyl alcohol.*") with the suffix, *-ism* (Forming a simple noun of action…, naming the process, or the completed action, or its result…). Hence, the original definition of *alcoholism* in OED is: "consumption of alcohol (ethanol), [especially] when excessive and producing drunkenness or illness; acute or chronic intoxication from alcohol." In later use, the meaning had evolved to: "the condition of being dependent upon or addicted to alcohol, and unable to limit its consumption to a level which does not produce deleterious physical, mental, or social effects."

Considerably before the Swedish physician Magnus Huss (1807—1890) first employed scientific Latin to coin the term *alcoholismus* for "a diseased condition produced by consumption of alcohol" (Huss 1849), the adverse consequences of alcohol had been recognized and described. According to a quote attributed to Lucius Annaeus Seneca (*c.* 4 BC—65 AD), the Roman statesman and philosopher, *chronic alcohol intoxication* was considered a form of insanity: "Drunkenness is nothing but voluntary madness." Beginning in the 18th century, physicians depicted the characteristic medical challenges associated with drunkenness and the acute and chronic complications of drinking alcohol (Rush, Thomas, and Andrews 1790; Trotter 1804; Woodward 1838). In literature, the term *alcoholism* had been used in a non-medical sense, as in the famous ode to temperance *First & Last Days of Alcohol the Great* (Cowen 1848): "He came out a decided foe to all Alcoholism." Ultimately, within a few years after Huss, most languages had incorporated an equivalent and easily recognizable term for alcoholism, e.g., the Swedish *alkoholism*, German *Alkoholismus*, and French *alcoolisme*. However, the dynamic tension between considering alcoholism a pathological condition under the purview of medicine or a construct reflecting troubles of man within society have remained to the present day (Chaudron and Wilkinson 1988).

Even after introduction of the term *alcoholism* in the scientific/medical literature uptake of its use was not immediate. The noun *inebriety* ("The state or habit of being inebriated; drunkenness, intoxication, inebriation; now chiefly applied to habitual drunkenness, especially when regarded as a disease") seems to have been the more popular of the two terms in the 19th century, even though their meanings were interchangeable. According to OED an early example of use of *inebriety* was found in *The Medical and Physical Journal* (Anonymous 1801): "Driven to the slower suicide of habitual inebriety." *The Quarterly Journal of Inebriety* (1876-1914) was published by the American Association for the Study and Cure of Inebriety, formed in 1870, to improve practice at residential treatment institutions. Its sole editor for 38 years was T.D. (Thomas Davison) Crothers (1842-1918), superintendent at the Walnut Hill Asylum in Hartford, Connecticut, and a leading advocate of the medical treatment of inebriety until his death. The central principle advocated in the journal was the *disease concept* of inebriety with a commitment to medical knowledge to be used by physicians in the medical treatment of this disorder (Weiner and White 2007). The two competing terms were even combined in the title of an important book of the era *Alcoholic Inebriety* by Norman Kerr (1834–1899), a Scottish physician known for his work in the British temperance movement (Kerr 1894). Importantly, Kerr states in the preface of the first edition of his book: "The present volume has been written in the hope that it may aid, however feebly, through the medium of the attending practitioner, who I trust will be among my readers, in the enlightenment of the patient, his sorely-tried relatives, and the community, in the great truth that Inebriety is a disease, as curable as most other diseases, calling for medical, mental and moral treatment." This phrase strongly supports a significant role for the treating physician in healing those suffering from alcoholism.

After the Second World War, the World Health Organization (1955) undertook to define alcoholism and to classify it as a medical condition. In short order, the American Medical Association (AMA) House of Delegates declared (1956, p. 32): "All excessive users of alcohol are not diagnosed as alcoholics, but all alcoholics are excessive users. When, in addition to this excessive use, there are certain signs and symptoms of behavioral, personality and physical disorder or of their development, the syndrome of alcoholism is achieved." Despite such circumlocution of what it was to be alcoholic, the conclusion of the AMA declaration was unequivocal: "…alcoholism must be regarded as within the purview of medical practice. The Council on Mental Health, its Committee on Alcoholism, and the profession in general recognizes this syndrome of alcoholism as illness which justifiably should have the attention of physicians (American Medical Association, 1956, p. 32)." Considering alcoholism as a medical illness is still not universal due to the stigma associated with addiction, namely a belief that the affected person brings his suffering upon himself and is the one primarily at fault (see Addiction). This conundrum has not been fully resolved despite major advances in neuroscience that support the status of addiction as a *bone fide* brain disorder (Leshner 1997).

The AMA declaration implied that some drinkers can safely drink alcohol whereas others cannot and only those who developed complications actually have the illness. Explicating why there might be such differences in sensitivity to drinking alcohol required elucidation of at least two important research issues. The first concerned understanding hereditary risk for developing alcoholism, a natural application of the rapidly burgeoning genetic revolution in medicine (Begleiter, Porjesz, Bihari and Kissin 1984; Omenn and Motulsky, 1972). The second emerged when it became apparent that much better characterizations of alcoholic phenotype(s) were required beyond the seminal work of Jellinek (Jellinek 1960) in order to understand the genetic underpinnings of the disorder and ultimately its pharmacological treatment (Cloninger 1987; Lesch, Kefer, Lentner et al. 1990).

A major advance in conceptualizing the essential underpinnings of alcoholic phenotypes was description of the *dependence syndrome* (Edwards and Gross 1976), applicable to all drugs of abuse, including *alcohol dependence*. The *alcohol dependence syndrome*, as articulated, is characterized by narrowing of the drinking repertoire, salience of drink-seeking behavior, increased tolerance, repeated withdrawal symptoms, relief and avoidance of withdrawal symptoms, subjective awareness of a compulsion to drink, and reinstatement (of drinking) after abstinence (Edwards and Gross 1976). This conceptualization of the dependence syndrome became the diagnostic essence of what was previously known as alcoholism and by the end of the 20th century the official term became alcohol dependence as promulgated by both the World Health Organization in the International Classification of Diseases (1978) and subsequently the American Psychiatric Association Diagnostic and Statistical Manual (1987). Of note, behavioral characteristics had come to be required for diagnosis of alcohol dependence rather than toxic injury by alcohol to organs of the body which characterized earlier conceptualizations of the disease of alcoholism. Finally, the accepted term for alcoholism became alcohol use disorder as specified in the most recent version (DSM-5) of the American Psychiatric Association nomenclature (2013). Nevertheless, the noun alcoholism is an acceptable term, interchangeably used with both alcohol dependence and alcohol use disorder, for what is widely considered a mental illness, commonly associated with diverse medical complications due to the toxicity of alcohol consumption and associated lifestyle.

Blackout

The noun *blackout*, according to the electronic version of Oxford English Dictionary (OED), was formed within English from the phrasal verb *to black out*, which means "To obliterate with black, especially as form of censorship or protection." The first use in the English language according to OED dates to 1913, when the Irish playwright, critic, polemicist and political activist George Bernard Shaw (1856-1950) referred to *blackout* as a theatre production technique in his *Letters to Granville Barker* (Shaw 1956): "The more I think of that revolving business the less I see how it can be done... There will have to be a black-out."

Since this initial use, the noun has been employed in various other ways which are interesting to explore to clearly understand the use in addiction which is subtly different. All early uses of *blackout* related to altering the source of sensory stimulation so as to reduce sensory input: "The failure of an electricity supply (especially with respect to lighting) and the resulting darkness"; "Loss of radio reception (as a result of fading, jamming, an electrical storm, etc.)"; "The deliberate suppression of news or information and (also) a dearth of news reporting"; and "The action of extinguishing or obscuring lights, especially by covering the windows in a building, as a precaution during air raids, the resulting darkness, and the time or period of compulsory extinguishing or covering of lights." Other uses of *blackout* refer to environmental changes that compromise sensory capacity. The first of these is: "Temporary loss of vision experienced when a person is subjected to strong accelerative forces, especially during flying, attributed to decreased blood flow in the central retinal artery." Another, presumably fanciful example refers to a *blackout cake*: "A type of moist, rich chocolate layer cake with chocolate filling and soft chocolate icing, typically dusted with chocolate cake crumbs." (It is recognized that any similarity in meaning of *blackout cake* to other uses discussed here is figurative in that ingestion of a tasty morsel might overwhelm and seemingly detract from other sensory inputs).

It is not difficult to see how *blackout* might be employed to describe a severe state of intoxication with a self-administered pharmacologic agent, typically alcohol. The meaning of *blackout* in this context is distinctly different from those discussed above, namely, sensory input and capacity are both undiminished but incorporation of the sensory experience in the nervous system as a memory trace that can be recalled is disturbed by the effects of the self-administered pharmacologic agent. Thus, the OED definition of *blackout* used in the field of addiction is: "A (usually temporary) loss of memory; an amnesic gap, especially for events occurring during a period of alcohol intoxication." However, this meaning of *blackout* is not straightforward as the second portion of this OED definition is: "Also: a momentary or brief loss of consciousness, especially when caused by reduced blood flow to the brain; a faint."

There is a clear pathophysiological distinction between the two parts of this OED definition of *blackout* although they are typically used interchangeably in the vernacular of patients. Therefore, diagnosis can be challenging — it is essential to distinguish the meaning used in addiction from the term *syncope* ("Failure of the heart's action, resulting in loss of consciousness, and sometimes in death"). For example, one need only look at a very early description of the vascular causes of blackout published in *The Medico-Chirurgical Journal and Review* to appreciate these differences (Johnson 1817): "Dr. Parr, in his *London Medical Dictionary*, states it as his opinion, that, 'the cause is most probably a *spasm* or convulsion' and denies that ossification of the coronary arteries is any thing but a concomitant symptom, or rather an effect of angina pectoris." Brain electrophysiological changes have also been considered in pathogenesis of syncopal forms of *blackout* (Redlich 1946).

Importantly, whereas impairment of memory *may* occur due to vascular and electrophysiological causes of *syncope*, the "amnesic gap" is the *sine qua non* of *blackout* associated with ingestion of alcohol or other central nervous system depressants (Goodwin, Crane and Guze 1969). The association of cognitive disturbances with alcohol consumption, including amnesia, have been recognized by clinicians for two centuries (Sutton 1813; Courville 1955; Butters and Cermak 1980). The studies of Korsakoff between 1887 and 1900 were the first to focus attention on primarily memory disorders in alcoholism (Víctor and Yakovlev 1955). Korsakoff suggested that the paucity of interest in amnesia *per se* was because it tended to co-occur with or complicated other diseases that were of greater concern due to their disabling global neurocognitive deficits (Levin, Peters and Hulkonen 1983). The more subtle presentation of memory deficit in isolation often requires repeated observations using focused techniques to differentiate it from global impairments of dementia and may easily be overshadowed by other clinical features (Martin, Adinoff, Weingartner et al. 1986).

Formal investigations of memory functioning in alcoholism followed closely after publication in 1885 of the ground-breaking volume *Memory: A Contribution to Experimental Psychology* by German psychologist Hermann Ebbinghaus (1850-1909) who recognized that memory is a brain function subject to experimental study (Ebbinghaus 1913):

> "Mental states of every kind, -- sensations, feelings, ideas, -- which were at one time
> present in consciousness and then have disappeared from it, have not with their

disappearance absolutely ceased to exist. Although the inwardly turned look may no longer be able to find them, nevertheless they have not been utterly destroyed and annulled, but in a certain manner they continue to exist, stored up, so to speak, in the memory. We cannot, of course, directly observe their present existence, but it is revealed by the effects which come to our knowledge with a certainty like that with which we infer the existence of the stars below the horizon. These effects are of different kinds."

While Ebbinghaus introduced systematic investigation of memory functioning and Korsakoff clinically identified its dysfunction in a unique clinical syndrome (see Wernicke Korsakoff syndrome), the pathogenesis, psychopathology and nosology of the memory disturbances associated with alcohol ingestion and alcohol use disorder remains an active topic of investigation to the present day.

The first issue is the clinical presentation and duration of memory deficits in relation to alcohol ingestion (Goodwin, Crane and Guze 1969; Butters and Cermak 1980). Acute amnesia (disrupted memory traces) limited to the period of intoxication, is the characteristic feature of a *blackout*, as discussed above. On the other hand, the classical chronic amnestic condition first described clinically by Korsakoff, now termed the Wernicke-Korsakoff syndrome since recognition that it is a complication, or the chronic phase of the acute life-threatening Gayet-Wernicke's encephalopathy, is unrelated to acute ingestion of alcohol but rather is due to neuropathologic findings resulting from thiamine deficiency associated with malnutrition from chronic alcohol consumption (Victor, Adams and Collins 1971). This chronic syndrome is characterized by *anterograde* memory deficits, namely, the inability to encode/recall ongoing memories after the period when the brain insult from malnutrition was sustained (Victor, Adams and Collins 1971; Butters and Cermak 1980). The individual with Wernicke-Korsakoff syndrome, however, may have a surprising degree of knowledge of the distant past, which is often incorporated in interpretation of present experiences (*confabulation*) and distinguishes it from neurodegenerative disorders characterized by global neurocognitive decline (Martin, Adinoff, Weingartner et al. 1986). Therefore, a blackout represents only a short period of impaired memory functioning (encoding/recall) that resolves once alcohol leaves the bloodstream, whereas the Wernicke-Korsakoff syndrome can be an enduring deficit with neuropathologic residua that typically alter the course of a patient's life and severely limits its quality. Ryback (1971) proposed that the acute and chronic toxic effects of alcohol consumption on memory resemble each other, specifically that short-term memory alone, rather than immediate memory or long-term memory, is disrupted in alcoholism but to varying degrees on a continuum, least in alcoholic blackout ("cocktail-party drinking") and most severely in the Wernicke-Korsakoff syndrome. This heuristically useful idea, based purely on observation of clinical phenomena rather than pathological underpinnings, has nevertheless guided researchers in the field to the present.

The next issue is when blackouts typically occur during the course of alcoholism and their clinical implications with respect to the tempo of illness progression. Goodwin, Crane and Guze (1969) and Goodwin, Othmer, Halikas and Freemon (1970) reported that more than one-third of hospitalized alcoholics had never experienced a blackout and that, among those who did report the experience, blackouts generally began relatively late during alcoholism and possibly were precursors of chronic alcoholism-associated brain dysfunction. Blackouts were associated with severity and duration of alcoholism as well as the intensity of alcohol consumption in each drinking episode, capacity for drinking large amounts including "loss of control," neglect of meals, gulping drinks and a history of head trauma. However, Tarter and Schneider (1976) concluded that alcohol-induced blackouts and memory capacity in the sober state were unrelated. Nevertheless, "blackout is tied to the history and onset of heavy drinking, and usually manifests most frequently in persons who drink until there is a loss of consciousness and exhibit a craving for alcohol." Since early onset alcoholism is associated with precipitous acceleration of alcohol consumption with few periods of extended abstinence, once such drinking begins, it is not surprising that blackout can serve as a signal of a particularly malignant alcoholism course (Parks, Dawant, Riddle et al. 2002; Marino and Fromme 2016).

Hartzler and Fromme (2003) found two forms of blackouts in young adult volunteers: *fragmentary blackouts* (episodes for which retrieval of experiences is facilitated by provision of memory cues) and *en bloc blackouts* (occurrence of full and permanent memory loss for events during intoxication). They found that the less severe, fragmentary form, was threefold more prevalent than full blackouts. However, blood alcohol concentrations were not correlated with the most severe blackout type, suggesting interindividual differences in susceptibility. One explanation for this finding may have been that most *en bloc* blackouts in these young drinkers involved concurrent use of illicit substances, which may have had an additive or synergistic effect with alcohol in compromising neuronal circuits that subserve memory functioning.

Nelson, Heath, Bucholz et al. (2004) examined the genetic epidemiology of lifetime blackouts among young adults in the Australian Twin Register and reported substantial genetic contributions to liability for alcohol-induced blackouts as well as for frequency of intoxication experienced. Wetherill,

Castro, Squeglia and Tapert (2013) prospectively demonstrated that substance-naïve adolescents who subsequently experience alcohol-induced blackouts required greater neural activation, or effort, for inhibitory processing determined by fMRI with a go/no-go task compared to adolescents who go on to drink at similar levels without experiencing blackouts and nondrinking controls. These findings suggest mechanisms underlying blackout and susceptibility to alcohol use disorder and its complications. For example, worse performance on a response inhibition task, a demonstrated risk factor for development of alcohol use disorder, and in particular, early-onset alcoholism, may also represent neurobiological vulnerability to development of alcohol-induced blackout (Begleiter, Porjesz, Bihari and Kissin 1984; Tarter, Hegedus, Goldstein et al. 1984; Cloninger 1987). These observations complement those of Schuckit (1980) who reported that young men with a family history positive for alcoholism rated themselves less intoxicated than did controls without family histories of alcoholism, despite comparable blood alcohol levels. Hence, young individuals with genetic loading for alcoholism may feel they can drink more and thus be more likely to develop both blackouts and alcoholism. When Hingson, Zha, Simons-Morton and White (2016) examined the incidence, predictors and behavioral correlates of blackouts, they concluded that blackouts were phenomenologically important in alcoholism, as having blackouts was the strongest independent *predictor* of most other alcohol problems.

The final issue is our understanding of the neurobiological substrate of a blackout. The alcoholic blackout provides insights about alcoholism as indicated above, but also offers mechanistic understanding of the phenomena that constitute memory functioning (Berglund, Prohovnik and Risberg 1989). The memory impairment in a blackout occurs concurrently with a rapid rise in brain alcohol levels, which diminishes alertness and attention to the surrounding environment (arousal) by its effects on the major inhibitory ($GABA_A$ receptors) and excitatory (NMDA receptors) neurotransmitter systems in the brain (Goodwin, Crane and Guze 1969; Martin and Patel 2017). (This resetting of the balance in inhibitory/excitatory neurotransmission also explains why other central nervous system depressants such as barbiturates, nonbarbiturate hypnosedatives and benzodiazepines can also cause blackouts [Bixler, Scharf, Soldatos et al. 1979] and act synergistically with alcohol). While not related to memory functioning in the sober state (Tarter and Schneider 1976), memory disturbances during blackout are demonstrably *anterograde* in nature and *state-dependent* (Goodwin, Powell, Bremer et al. 1969). These observations are consistent with the hypothesis proposed by Hebb (1949) that the relationship between the efficiency of learning and the level of alertness, namely, the arousal of the nervous system at the moment learning occurs, is fundamentally important. Thus, learning can be inefficient during intoxication and, consequently, recall of material that was learned may be disturbed. Therefore, the conditions at the moment of learning and testing recall are critical — memory performance is enhanced if the condition of the nervous system at the time of learning (intoxication) is identical to that during testing for recall.

Clinical and neuropsychological characterization of alcohol-associated amnesia eventually advanced to neuroimaging studies to investigate the brain mechanisms involved. In patients with Wernicke-Korsakoff syndrome, regional cerebral blood flow (rCBF) was unexpectedly elevated above levels observed in comparison groups with neurocognitive compromise, i.e., dementia (Simard, Olesen, Paulson et al. 1971) or alcoholics (Berglund and Ingvar 1976). Additionally, Berglund, Prohovnik and Risberg (1989) reported a large increase in mean rCBF during blackout in an alcoholic patient compared with values during abstinence, not unexpected based on the effects of alcohol on rCBF (Battey, Heyman and Patterson 1953). Thus, rCBF similarities in acute blackout and in the chronic state of Wernicke-Korsakoff syndrome are compatible with the proposal of Ryback (1971). Techniques permitting more granular neuroanatomic brain mapping (positron emission tomography, PET) or during performance of memory-related tasks (functional magnetic resonance imaging, fMRI) identified disruptions of related brain circuits in Wernicke-Korsakoff syndrome and in alcoholic blackout (Martin, Rio, Adinoff et al. 1992). As discussed above, atypical brain responses during inhibitory processing may be a neural risk factor for the occurrence of alcohol-induced blackouts. Wetherill, Schnyer and Fromme (2012) examined whether neural activation during a contextual memory task differed between individuals who experienced fragmentary blackouts with drinking and those who did not. While contextual memory was not different in the two groups, acute alcohol consumption affected dorsolateral prefrontal cortex and posterior parietal cortex neural activation differentially, suggesting that frontoparietal abnormalities are a potential biomarker for vulnerability to alcohol-induced memory impairments. Interestingly, related, though perhaps not identical circuits can be compromised in neurocognitive disorders that resemble Wernicke-Korsakoff syndrome (Welch et al. 1996). As research in learning and memory progresses, these findings may advance to the cellular level in the relevant neuronal circuits (Josselyn and Tonegawa 2020).

Cannabis

According to the current electronic version of the Oxford English Dictionary (OED), the noun *cannabis* is a borrowing from the Latin word for *hemp,* originally from ancient Greek κάνναβις. The noun *cannabis* is defined in OED as: "A herbaceous flowering plant, *Cannabis sativa* (family Cannabaceae), having serrated digitate leaves, fibrous stems, and glandular hairs, native to central Asia and widely cultivated for its fibre (hemp) and for use as a recreational drug." Of note, "Cannabis has three subspecies, *C. sativa indica, C. sativa ruderalis,* and *C. sativa sativa,* which are sometimes treated as separate species." The noun *hemp* is from Old English *hęnep, hænep* and related forms of old European languages. The noun *hemp* is defined in OED as: "An annual herbaceous plant, *Cannabis sativa,* of the N.O. [natural order of plants], Urticaceæ, a native of Western and central Asia, cultivated for its valuable fibre." The noun *marijuana* is the typically used word in the vernacular for *cannabis.* The word is a borrowing from Mexican Spanish, *mariguana, marihuana,* of uncertain origin.

The first use of the word *cannabis* in the English language is from the translation of *The Travels of Monsieur de Thevenot into the Levant…* by Jean de Thévenot (1633-1667), a French traveler in the East and also a linguist, natural scientist and botanist (de Thévenot and Archibald 1687): "We found by the way, many plants called Agnus Castus, or Canabis [French *Canabis*]; for they grow three foot high, and have the leaves divided by fives, like a hand." As to be expected, the word *hemp* appears in the English language in approximately 1000, well before *cannabis* (Wright and Wülcker 1884): "*Cannabum,* hænep." On the other hand, *marijuana* was first used in English in the book, *The native races of the Pacific states of North America,* by Hubert Howe Bancroft (1832-1918), an American historian and ethnologist (Bancroft 1874): "The bride's parents then send round to the houses of their friends a bunch of mariguana, a narcotic herb, which signifies that all are to meet together at the bride's father's on the next night."

The definition of *cannabis* that is relevant to the field of addiction is: "a dried preparation of the flowering tops or other parts of the cannabis plant, or a resin extracted from it, smoked or consumed, especially as a recreational drug, for the feelings of relaxation and euphoria it induces." This meaning was first used in the English language in an article in the *Public Advertiser,* a London newspaper in the 18th century (Anonymous 1793): "Plumbum, 'tis true, when taken inwardly, has in general been found to be fatal to those Creatures; but Cannabis has a much better Effect." An example of popular usage of the word is from Kathryn Marie Lette (1958—), an Australian-British bestselling author (Lette 1989): "I mean, he couldn't have smoked it all on his own. Anyone who could consume that amount of cannabis would be a total social-reject, a bong-brain addict, wouldn't he?" The relevant definition of *marijuana* is: "(A preparation of) the plant, used as an intoxicating and hallucinogenic drug; especially, a crude preparation of the dried leaves, flowering tops, and stem of the plant in a form for smoking." It is noted in OED that: "The currency of the word increased greatly in the United States in the 1930s in the context of the debate over the use of the drug, the term being preferred as a more exotic alternative to the familiar words *hemp* and *cannabis*." An example of a variant of the word is in John Steinbeck's novel *Tortilla Flat* (Steinbeck 1935): "His eyes were as wide and pained as the eyes of one who smokes marihuana." Steinbeck (1902-1968) was an American author who won the 1962 Nobel Prize in Literature.

Cannabis has likely been used in folk healing and for socio-religious purposes prior to recorded history. There is archeological evidence of use of cannabis as a mind-altering drug in Eurasia and Africa (Abel 1982). The earliest written reference to the drug dates to the 15th century BCE in the Chinese pharmacopeia, the *Rh-Ya* (Cohen 1977). Herodotus (*c.* 484—425 BCE), the ancient Greek historian referred to the central Eurasian Scythians, nomadic Eurasians of Iranian origin, taking cannabis steam baths in his *Histories* (Herodotus, Rawlinson and Blakeney 1970):

> "The Scythians, as I said, take some of this hemp-seed [presumably, flowers], and, creeping under the felt coverings, throw it upon the red-hot stones; immediately it smokes, and gives out such a vapour as no Greek vapour-bath can exceed; the Scyths, delighted, shout for joy."

There is additional historical evidence in India, Vietnam, Cambodia and the Middle East of cannabis use in various forms as folk medicine, ritual potion, condiment and for its intoxicating effects. Cannabis seems to have been imported to the Americas by the Spaniards for its fiber, but then was used for its psychoactive properties.

It was not until the 19th century that interest in cannabis spread to the European medical community and its "newly-discovered" role in therapeutics were endorsed in the medical journals of the era as a significant addition to the existing *Materia medica*. *The British and Foreign Medical Review* published an editorial about the observations of William Brooke O'Shaughnessy (1809-1889), an Irish physician, then Professor of Chemistry in the Medical College, Calcutta, whose research in India led to introduction of *Cannabis sativa* to Western medicine (Anonymous 1840):

"This pamphlet contains a detail of facts of a very important kind, which, we doubt not, will cause a great sensation among the members of the profession throughout the world…It will appear clearly from what we shall state that Dr. O'Shaughnessy has the merit of having added to *our* materia medica a drug of great and unequivocal powers, and, probably, a remedy of marked efficacy in diseases hitherto the most unmanageable. For the sake of accuracy, in a matter of so much consequence, we shall avail ourselves, as much as possible, of the author's own words…"

Dr. O'Shaughnessy begins as follows:

"The narcotic effects of hemp are popularly known in the south of Africa, South America, Turkey, Egypt, Asia Minor, India, and the adjacent territories of the Malays, Burmese, and Siamese. In all these countries hemp is used in various forms, by the dissipated and depraved, as the ready agent of a pleasing intoxication. In the popular medicine of these nations we find it extensively employed for a multitude of affections. But in western Europe its use either as a stimulant or as a remedy is equally unknown… Much difference of opinion exists on the question, whether the hemp so abundant in Europe, even in high northern latitudes, is identical in specific characters with the hemp of Asia Minor and India. The extraordinary symptoms produced by the latter depend on a resinous secretion with which it abounds, and which seems totally absent in the European kind. The closest physical resemblance or even identity exists between both plants; difference of climate seems to me more than sufficient to account for the absence of the resinous secretion and consequent want of narcotic power in that indigenous in colder countries…"

Dr. O'Shaughnessy proceeded to review the chemical properties, popular uses, and the results of his own experiments in laboratory animals. He then described how the resinous extract is prepared into a tincture appropriate for administration to patients and the doses employed in various treatment applications. For *Rheumatism*, he describes:

"alleviation of pain in most, remarkable increase of appetite in all, unequivocal aphrodisia, and great mental cheerfulness. In no one case did these effects proceed to delirium, nor was there any tendency to quarrelling. The disposition developed was uniform in all, and in none was headache or sickness of stomach a sequel of the excitement."

John Clendinning (1798-1848), an English physician recognized as first prescribing cannabis for migraine headaches, was very familiar with O'Shaughnessy's findings and thoughtfully examined the effects of cannabis compared to opium, then the most common medicine in the pharmacopeia (1843):

"The objects I have had in view in the trials of the hemp... [and the] cases in which I have experienced beneficial effects from the new remedy… are these:

1. To determine as nearly as I could, the question, whether the hemp narcotic be in reality possessed of medicinal properties sufficiently energetic and uniform to entitle the drug to admission into our pharmacopoeia; and,

2. To determine how far the extract could be used with advantage as a substitute for opium in various important diseases, acute and chronic.

"In answer to the former question, I have no hesitation in affirming that in my hands its exhibition has usually, and with remarkably few substantial exceptions, been followed by manifest effects as a soporific or hypnotic in conciliating sleep; as an anodyne in lulling irritation; as an antispasmodic in checking cough and cramp; and as a nervine stimulant in removing languor and anxiety, and raising the pulse and spirits; and that these effects have been observed in both acute and chronic affections, in young and old, male and female.

"In reply to the latter question, I should say that these useful, and in several cases most salutary effects have been obtained without any important drawback or deduction on account of indirect or incidental inconveniences… The only class of cases in which I have found the hemp not to act as a competent substitute for opium, is in the intestinal fluxes, such as the diarrhaeas… In such cases, opium is the great controlling remedy of the narcotic class, and admits of no deputy…"

Due to the effects of cannabis as "soporific or hypnotic in conciliating sleep" (Clendinning 1843) it was only a matter of time before this agent was administered to psychiatric patients as described by Sir Thomas Smith Clouston (1840-1915), a Scottish psychiatrist (Clouston 1870):

"…with the view of obtaining more accuracy as to the immediate and remote effects of bromide of potassium and its combinations, as compared with opium, on maniacal excitement…I had amongst other things been giving both bromide of potassium and tincture of *cannabis Indica* to procure sleep in this case, which was one of melancholia, with great excitement and hallucinations, and by way of experiment I gave the patient a combination of the two. I found the effects to be so very wonderful in this case that I employed the bromide alone, and in conjunction with Indian hemp very largely thereafter in similar cases."

It is with nostalgia that one views this work, as by the next century, cannabis was found mostly to be ineffective as an antidepressant (Pond 1948) and recognized as a cause, not a treatment for psychosis (Hollister 1964). All the same, cannabis remained an agent of wonderment and experimentation with palpable effects on consciousness as described by Edward Wheeler Scripture (1864 –1945), an American physician and psychologist who was a founder of the American Psychological Association (Scripture 1893):

"The statement is generally made that the extract of *Cannabis Indica*…causes time and space greatly lengthened in consciousness. Wishing to know what is meant by these statements I obtained the prescription…"

Further understanding of the role of cannabis in pharmacotherapy required identification of the active principle of *Cannabis indica* resin (Work, Bergel and Todd 1939), an arduous task due to the very many compounds with diverse pharmacological actions found in this plant. Decades of chemistry research culminated in the synthesis of *dl*-cannabidiol (CBD) and *dl*-delta-3,4-tetrahydrocannabinol (THC), "the psychotomimetically active constituents" of marijuana (Mechoulam and Gaoni 1965), and eventually the stereochemical requirements of the major psychoactive constituent, THC (Mechoulam and Gaoni 1967). Of note, THC and CBD seem to have dissimilar actions; the major difference seems to be the lesser psychotomimetic action, and hence, abuse liability, of CBD (Babalonis, Hane, Malcolm et al. 2017). Identification of receptors in the brain that specifically bind these agents and synthesis of specific cannabinoid receptor agonists and antagonists ensued (Devane, Dysarz, Johnson et al. 1988). Arachidonoylethanolamide, or anandamide, an arachidonic acid derivative in porcine brain, was then identified as an endogenous ligand of the cannabinoid receptors, termed an endocannabinoid (Devane, Hanus, Breuer et al. 1992). The endocannabinoid system is in striking analogy to endogenous opioids (Barinaga 1992). These discoveries led to elucidation of the complexity of the cannabis plant and widened therapeutic horizons (Hollister 1986; Iversen 1993). Whether cannabis has a role in medicine, so-called "medical marijuana," continues to be examined and debated (National Academies of Sciences, Engineering, and Medicine 2017). Evidence for beneficial effects of cannabis exist but the multitude of compounds in the plant make such research pharmaceutically daunting. An exciting research direction has been the potential beneficial role of CBD over THC in treatment of psychiatric disorders (Hindley, Beck, Borgan et al. 2020).

The potential for self-harm from the use of cannabis, especially addiction, had been a source of greater concern in the U.S. than any possibility of its use for healing. This was the rationale for passing of the U.S. Marihuana Tax Act in 1937, prohibiting the production, importation, possession, use and dispersal of cannabis, rendering cannabis an illicit drug, despite widespread recreational use. By the 20th century, toxicity of cannabis became a subject of investigation (Forney 1971) superseding its potential in therapeutics. How to view cannabis use has remained a conundrum in the U.S. and throughout the world. The range of viewpoints on marijuana are exemplified by the film *Reefer Madness*. This morality tale, filming of which was financed by a church group, was intended to teach parents about the dangers of cannabis use. Ultimately, the film became an unintentional satire among advocates of decriminalization of the drug (Peary 1982). The counterpoint in the debate is disimpassioned examination of cannabis use by a committee of experts, which pronounced the drug as near harmless compared to alcohol or nicotine, which are legalized (LeDain 1970; Nutt, King, Saulsbury et al. 2007).

The controversy pertaining to the safety of cannabis as a recreational drug continues unresolved. It is well documented that cannabis is a drug of abuse and cannabis use disorder is highly prevalent, particularly in those with other psychiatric and drug use disorders (Martin, Weinberg and Bealer 2007; Schiff, Zweig, Benbenishty and Hasin 2007; Mitchell, Bhatia and Zebardast 2020). Chronic use of cannabis may be correlated with psychological withdrawal symptoms, such as irritability or insomnia, but cannabis withdrawal symptoms are typically mild and are not life-threatening (Fraser 1949; Bahji, Stephenson, Tyo et al. 2020). Due to the high lipid solubility of THC and very slow elimination from the brain, the withdrawal syndrome was mostly theoretical, until it could be demonstrated to be precipitated by cannabinoid receptor antagonists (Budney and Hughes 2006). Chronic use of cannabis is associated with medical (Page, Allen, Kloner et al. 2020) and behavioral (Andreae 2018) toxicity. However, the sale and use of cannabis in various formulations has become legalized in many jurisdictions in the U.S. and around the world with mixed results (Abuhasira, Shbiro and Landschaft 2018; Smart and Pacula 2019; McBain, Wong, Breslau et al. 2020). Only time will tell what the effects on human health and societal consequences will be if cannabis becomes as negligibly regulated as alcohol and tobacco.

Cocaine

According to the current electronic version of the Oxford English Dictionary (OED), the noun *cocaine* was formed within English by combination of the noun *coca* and the suffix *-ine* ("used unsystematically in forming names of extractive principles and chemical derivatives of various kinds"). The noun *coca* from Spanish corresponds to *cuca* (Peruvian) and is defined in OED as: "The name in Bolivia of *Erythroxylon coca*, a shrub six or eight feet high; hence, applied to its dried leaves, which have been employed from time immemorial, with powdered lime, as a masticatory, appeaser of hunger, and stimulant of the nervous system." The definition of the noun *cocaine* is: "An important alkaloid obtained from the leaves and young twigs of the coca plant, valuable as a local anæsthesiant, and also used as a stimulant."

The noun *coca* was used in the English language before *cocaine* as exemplified in a book by John Bullokar (1574–1627), an English physician and lexicographer (Bullokar 1616): "Coca, an hearbe of India, the leaues whereof being bruised and mixt with the powder of Cockles or Oysters in their shelles burnt the Indians [so-called because Christopher Columbus never clearly renounced his belief that he had reached the Far East and named the indigenous peoples he encountered "indios"] use in little balles to carry in their mouthes to preserve them from famine and great dryth."

For at least a thousand years, from the pre-Inca period, the Andean peoples of Peru, Bolivia, Ecuador, Colombia, northern Argentina and Chile chewed or brewed tea from the leaves of *Erythroxylon coca*, a plant that contains nutrients as well as the powerful stimulating alkaloid *cocaine* (Blejer-Prieto 1965). There is archeological evidence of the remains of *coca* leaves in ancient Peruvian mummies and early pottery found in the region depicts humans with bulged cheeks, presumably chewing *coca* leaves (Gay, Inaba, Sheppard et al. 1975). The *coca* plant was chewed by indigenous people to maintain their energy to work harder, longer, and with less food in brutally strenuous conditions at high altitudes as noted by Samuel Purchas (1577–1626), an English geographical editor and clergyman and Richard Hakluyt (1553–1616) a writer active in colonization of the New World (Purchas and Hakluyt 1625): "An herbe... Coca, which they carrie continually in their mouthes." The Spanish initially ignored native claims that the *coca* leaf gave them strength and energy, and forbade its use for religious reasons. After discovering the great demand for *coca*, the Spaniards taxed the value of these crops. In addition, the *coca* leaf was used among the indigenous Andean people for various medicinal purposes such as reducing inflammation and treatment of infections. There is also evidence that a mixture of *coca* leaves and saliva were used as an anesthetic for trephination.

The properties and unusual effects of the *coca* leaf became known in Europe with Spanish exploration of the New World (Mortimer 1901). Amerigo Vespucci (1454–1512), a Florentine merchant, explorer, and navigator after whom the New World was named, is said to have been the first European to discover the *coca* plant (Vespucci and Medici 1503). The first European publication on *coca* was by Nicolás Monardes (1493–1588), a Seville physician and botanist who described the aboriginal practice of chewing a mixture of tobacco and *coca* leaves to induce: "great contentment…When they wished to make themselves drunk and out of judgment, they chewed a mixture of tobacco and coca leaves which make them go as they were out of their wittes (Monardes 1569)." In 1753, Joseph de Jussieu (1704–1779), a French botanist and explorer, was the first to classify the *coca* plant according to its botanical name *Erythroxylon coca* (Blejer-Prieto 1965).

The cocaine alkaloid was first isolated from the plant by the German chemist Friedrich Gaedcke (1828–1890), who named it "erythroxyline" (Gaedcke 1855). The German chemist Albert Niemann (1834–1861) isolated and called the alkaloid "cocaine," derived from "coca" (Niemann 1860). The German chemist Carl Schorlemmer (1834–1892) described the relationship between *coca* and its derivative *cocaine* in his text *A manual of the chemistry of the carbon compounds, or, Organic chemistry* (1874): "Cocaine ($C_{17}H_{21}NO_4$) is the active principle of the coca-leaves." Richard Willstätter (1872–1942), the German who was awarded the 1915 Nobel Prize for Chemistry for studies of the structure of plant pigments, first synthesized and elucidated the structure of the cocaine molecule (Willstätter and Ettlinger 1903).

Vassily von Anrep (1852-1927), a professor of forensic medicine and a Russian statesman, had a major early influence in development of cocaine as a local anesthetic by describing its pharmacology through detailed studies in different species. The contribution of von Anrep tends to be forgotten among other notables as Koller, Freud and Halstead who published in either German or English instead of Russian and were practicing clinicians (Yentis and Vlassakov 1999). Von Anrep was the first to inject cocaine subcutaneously into humans (he injected himself) and report the anesthetic effect produced (von Anrep 1880; Liljestrand 1967):

> "It had been my intention after the animal experiments also to make experiments
> on man. Other engagements have hitherto prevented this and the animal

experiments do not permit any practical conclusions. In spite of this, I would like to recommend cocaine as a local anesthetic as well as for melancholics."

The introduction of the syringe and hypodermic needle (Rynd 1845) and von Anrep's preliminary observations presented an opportunity to extend attempts to produce local surgical anesthesia with cocaine, the logical extension to prior experiments conducted with agents as morphine, chloroform, water, and hypertonic salt solutions.

Sigmund Freud (1856-1939) was inspired to examine the stimulating effects of cocaine on mood and energy after reading the paper, "The Physiological Effect and the Importance of Cocaine" (Bernfeld 1953) by Theodor Aschenbrandt, a German army physician, who administered cocaine to Bavarian Army soldiers in 1883 during their maneuvers. Aschenbrandt reported that the drug reduced fatigue and enhanced the soldiers' endurance during drills, including such phrases as: ". . .increase of all mental powers. . . increase of the capacity to endure strain. . . suppression of hunger." As a result, Freud began studying the effects of cocaine in a different manner than surgeons would subsequently, primarily focusing on the effects of the drug on the emotional realm, using himself and others he knew and loved as his subjects (Freud 1884; Bernfeld 1953; Yentis and Vlassakov 1999). He describes his findings in *Über Coca*, a paper promoting cocaine as a treatment of everything from depression to morphine addiction (Freud 1884):

> ". . . exhilaration and lasting euphoria, which in no way differs from the normal euphoria of the healthy person... You perceive an increase of self-control, possess more vitality and capacity for work... In other words, you are simply normal; and it is soon difficult to believe that one is under the influence of any drug... Long-lasting, intensive mental or physical labor is performed without fatigue... You are able – on demand – to eat well and without disgust, but you have the clear impression that the meal was not required... This effect of hardening you against work... is enjoyed without any of the unpleasant aftermaths which accompany exhilaration through alcoholic means. Absolutely no craving for further use of cocaine appears after the first, or repeated, taking of the drug; rather you feel a certain unmotivated aversion to it."

The last sentence now seems apocryphal in the context of current understanding of addiction (Martin, Weinberg and Bealer 2007).

The introduction of cocaine as a local anesthetic was in ophthalmology by Carl Koller (1857–1944), a young physician in Vienna, whose interest dates to the spring of 1884 when his friend and colleague Freud invited him to collaborate on studies of the effect of cocaine on muscular strength and fatigue using the hand dynamometer (Liljestrand 1967). Work on cocaine quickly progressed to pioneering studies that involved giving the drug to others for putatively therapeutic effects. A friend of Freud and Koller, the eminent physiologist Ernst von Fleischl-Marxow (1846–1891) had an amputation of his thumb and subsequent unbearable pains at the site. Fleischl-Marxow started to use and became addicted to morphine and heroin. His friends were convinced that cocaine would be useful as a treatment for Fleischl-Marxow's morphine addiction. The result was that he proceeded to fall even deeper into the abyss of addiction and eventually relapsed and began using morphine again until his premature death at the age of 45 (Liljestrand 1967). A rival psychiatrist Friedrich Albrecht Erlenmeyer (1849–1926) described cocaine as the "third (presumably after morphine and alcohol) scourge of mankind" as sad outcomes occurred in many others (Goldberg 1984).

The well-known American surgeon William Stewart Halsted (1852–1922), one of the four founding professors of Johns Hopkins Hospital, accomplished pioneering surgical research with cocaine soon after he discovered the work of Koller. Within two years, Halsted performed nearly 2,000 operations using cocaine as a local anesthetic, having established the principle of nerve block anesthesia (Olch 1975). In the process of experimenting on himself, Halsted became addicted. On one occasion, according to myth, as Halsted was attempting to demonstrate an operation to colleagues, his tremor was so severe that he could not continue the procedure and was forced to leave the operating room in disgrace (Goldberg 1984). Despite needing periodic admissions to Butler Hospital in Providence, Rhode Island, for withdrawal therapy, Halsted had a distinguished career in academic surgery, implementing creative and innovative surgical procedures and training subsequent leaders of the field (Bett 1952; Blalock 1952). Fortunately, William H. Welch (1850–1934), the first dean of the Johns Hopkins Medical School, was able to take Halsted under his wings and into his Baltimore house and thereby allowed him to continue to contribute to American surgery. Halsted turned to daily morphine use in a futile attempt to "cure" his cocaine addiction as he had ready, unrestricted access to inexpensive, high-grade morphine in the surgical operating room (Martin and Finlayson 2012). The historical lessons from the lives of Fleischl-Marxow and Halsted emphatically convey the simplistic and fallacious conceptualizations of addiction historically, namely that the disorder was caused by the drug alone, not the person who self-administers the drug and their circumstances (Martin, Weinberg and Bealer 2007).

A quotation from the *British and Colonial Druggist* (Anonymous 1886) encapsulates the significance of cocaine in modern surgery: "The valuable alkaloid cocaine, whose properties as a local anæsthetic have created almost a revolution in ophthalmic and other branches of surgery." However, the debate about whether cocaine was otherwise beneficial or harmful has continued, exemplified by the following discussion (Bosworth 1895):

"…. I only venture to ask the question, Is there a cocaine habit, and, if there is, how dangerous a habit is it and how great a slavery? …I have used it indiscriminately and on a very large number of cases… I have made a pretty large and thorough investigation of the action of cocaine, by way of experiment on myself… I have failed to see anything in the action of cocaine which produced that peculiar craving which is necessary to constitute the habit. There are certain things which are characteristic of enslaving drugs. One is universal… that it creates a tolerance. Opium, hashish, and arsenic, as is well known, create such a tolerance that, as the habit increases on one, increased doses become necessary to procure the desired effect. …more noticeable in cocaine… is that its use creates a susceptibility – the more one takes cocaine the less cocaine it requires to produce the desired effect. Another characteristic action of an enslaving drug is that its intoxicating effects are followed by a reaction. This is not characteristic of cocaine, although I should say that in my own experience, after experimenting with it for some months, I found that the stimulating effects which it first produced were followed by a sense of depression afterward, but only after I had experimented for quite a while. Another feature of an enslaving drug is that it creates a craving, an appetite which cannot be resisted. This, I think, is not a characteristic of cocaine… A still further feature in regard to cocaine… is that if one does acquire a liking for the drug the continued use of it will serve to overcome the appetite… the pleasurable stimulation decreases in amount, and sooner or later the time comes when the use of the drug ceases to be a pleasure – I mean by this the use of the drug in large amount… The prolonged use of small quantities of cocaine may, perhaps, not produce this effect… Among my own patients I know of a number of instances where it has been used in moderation through periods of five, eight, and even ten years, without producing unpleasant effects and without creating a habit. …many persons addicted to morphinism took up the use of cocaine with the hope for relief. …my experience would suggest that the combination of opium and cocaine creates a far more dangerous habit than opium alone, and I am disposed to think that many so-called cases of cocaine habit are the result of a combination of the two drugs.

"Whether its use hypodermically is attended with any additional changes, I cannot say."

Thus, despite clear behavioral toxicity from cocaine in some who conducted scientific experiments with the alkaloid, few believed that cocaine truly represented a serious risk to mental health and research turned to the pharmacology of cocaine to understand its efficacy in surgical anesthesia.

Langley and Dickinson (1890) showed that cocaine directly applied reduces the irritability of nerve fibers and Dixon (1904) proposed its selective effects: "Cocaine locally applied to nerve fibres picks out and paralyses some fibres before others; sensory before motor, vagal fibres conducting upwards, before those conducting downwards, vaso-constrictor fibres before vaso-dilator, broncho-constrictor before broncho-dilator." Cocaine was found to affect electrochemical conduction between neural cells (Dale 1935) and specifically altered effects of adrenaline (Burn and Tainter 1931).

Concern about behavioral consequences of cocaine use did not cease; both acute and chronic toxicity were reported, including hallucinations (Anonymous 1889), addiction (Anonymous 1925) and "its demoralizing effects" (Bose 1902). The mixed emotions concerning this drug were conveyed in the 1977 lyrics made famous by Eric Clapton who thought he had kicked a serious heroin habit and was heavily using cocaine and alcohol with the attitude that he could manage his addiction and quit at any time – he just didn't want to – so he could sing objectively about a drug that was consuming him, before the associated dangers were eventually recognized:

"If you want to hang out/ You've got to take her out/ Cocaine/ If you want to get down/ Down on the ground/ Cocaine/ She don't lie/ She don't lie/ She don't lie/ Cocaine// If you got bad news/ You want to kick the blues/ Cocaine/ When your day is done/ And you wanna ride on/ Cocaine/ She don't lie/ She don't lie/ She don't lie/ Cocaine" (Cale 1977)

Even the authorative pharmacology textbook of its time asserted (Jaffe 1970): "Cocaine abuse is now uncommon in Western countries, although the chewing of coca leaves is still common among Peruvian Indians of the Andes."

In the early 1980s, the romance concerning this "sophisticated" drug vanished in a "snowstorm" of white powder overwhelming the western world (Byck 1987). The American Psychiatric Association had not listed *cocaine dependence* in the third edition of their *Diagnostic and Statistical Manual of Mental Disorders* (APA 1980) because it was believed that neither tolerance nor withdrawal was characteristic of its use. With the rapid increase in prevalence of pathological use of cocaine in the 1980s and striking association with other psychiatric disorders, it became apparent that this decision was sadly mistaken (Gawin and Kleber 1986; Grant 1995).

Research on cocaine changed precipitously from its original focus on anesthetic properties to the neuroscience of cocaine-induced euphoria, the powerful rewarding effects of self-administration, influence on learning and physical and behavioral toxicity (Drake and Scott 2018). It was demonstrated that presynaptic neuronal reuptake of dopamine by the specific dopamine transporter correlated with the reinforcing effects determined by self-administration of the drug (Ritz, Lamb, Goldberg and Kuhar 1987; Kilty, Lorang and Amara 1991). Cocaine became central to neuroscience research during the "Decade of the Brain" from 1990 to 1999, so designated as part of an effort of the National Institute of Mental Health to enhance the public awareness of brain research, which culminated in recognizing addiction as a brain disease (Leshner 1997). The impetus for investigating the brain effects of cocaine have continued as a particularly destructive member of the *stimulant* class of drugs (Cassidy, Carpenter, Konova et al. 2020; see Stimulants).

Coffee

According to the current electronic version of the Oxford English Dictionary (OED), the noun *coffee* is derived from the Arabic *qahwah*, pronounced *kahveh* in Turkish. The etymology of the word is described in OED as: "Arabic *qahwah*, in Turkish pronounced *kahveh*, the name of the infusion or beverage; said by Arab lexicographers to have originally meant 'wine' or some kind of wine, and to be a derivative of a verb-root *qahiya* 'to have no appetite.' Some have conjectured that it is a foreign, perhaps African, word disguised, and have thought it connected with the name of *Kaffa* in the south Ethiopian highlands, where the plant appears to be native. But of this there is no evidence, and the name *qahwah* is not given to the berry or plant, which is called *bunn*, the name in Shoa being *būn*. The European languages generally appear to have got the name from Turkish *kahveh*, about 1600, perhaps through Italian *caffè*…" The widespread popularity of this beverage is reflected by the fact that a word closely related to *coffee* is found in all Western languages and is understood around the world.

The noun *coffee*, in an early foreign form, was first used in the English language in a translation of *Iohn Hvighen van Linschoten: his discours of voyages into ye Easte & West Indies* (Linschoten 1598): "The Turkes holde almost the same manner of drinking of their Chaoua [printed Chaona], which they make of a certaine fruit… by the Egyptians called Bon or Ban." The meaning of the word in this quotation as defined in OED is: "A drink made by infusion or decoction from the seeds of a shrub (…a species of *Coffea*, chiefly *C. arabica*, a native of Ethiopia and Arabia, but now extensively cultivated throughout the tropics… [bearing] fragrant white flowers… succeeded by red fleshy berries resembling small cherries), roasted and ground or (in the East) pounded; extensively used as a beverage, and acting as a moderate stimulant." As demonstrated in *The true travels, adventures and observations of Captaine J. Smith* (1630) written by John Smith (1580-1631), an early Governor of Virginia, use of the word in English literature evolved: "Their [Turkes'] best drinke is Coffa of a graine they call Coava." Gideon Harvey, the Elder (*c.*1636–1702), a Dutch-educated physician, appointed early in the reign of William and Mary, "their majesties physician of the Tower" despite his open derision of the English College of Physicians, employed the modern version of *coffee* purporting medicinal value in *A Discourse of the Plague… with several waies for purifying the air in houses, streets* (1665): "Coffee is recommended against the Contagion." There are many mentions of *coffee* subsequently and not only as a pleasant beverage. Coffee has played an exceedingly interesting role in world history as a part of the medical pharmacopeia and with mentions in economics and politics, sociology and anthropology, among other disciplines (Pendergrast 2019).

Historical accounts of coffee's health benefits are plentiful. The Islamic physician and astronomer Rhazes (852–932) described the qualities of a plant known as *bunn* and the beverage *buncham* in his medical text *Al-Haiwi* (The Continent) as "hot and dry and very good for the stomach" (Fischer, Victor, Robinson et al. 2019). Later, the Islamic doctor Avicenna (980–1037) included an entry for *buncham* in his text *Al-Ganum fit-Tebb* (The Canon of Medicine) and described coffee as coming from Yemen and, expanding on Rhazes, explained that it "fortifies the members, cleans the skin, and dries up the humidities that are under it, and gives an excellent smell to all the body." Coffee use spread widely as a stimulant in this part of the world, in part because Islamic dietary laws strictly forbade the use of alcohol and other intoxicants.

The German physician and botanist Leonhard Rauwolf (1535–1596), who journeyed through the Levant and Mesopotamia in 1573–75 to search for herbal medicines, became the first European to write about coffee. By the 17th century, coffee was widely seen as the preferred alternative to alcohol and was viewed by many doctors as a viable treatment for a very wide range of ailments. This dynamic relationship between coffee, considered a gently stimulating component of the refined diet, and alcohol, the primary intoxicant available to the common man, has been a recurring theme in European history. Nevertheless, medical and moral concerns began to emerge around fears of over-consumption of coffee. In 1674, women in London called coffee a "drying and enfeebling liquor," thus protesting the rise in coffee consumption among their men for whom the newly established coffeehouses were popular places of business and social activities, a distraction from duties in the home (Pendergrast 2019).

Understanding the chemical composition of coffee was necessary to proceed with investigations of its actions in the human body and the putative health benefits and hazards. The modern characterization of coffee began when the Swedish physician and botanist Carolus Linnaeus (1707–1778), renowned for his research on biological taxonomy, named the species *Coffea arabica* in 1737 (Fischer, Victor, Robinson et al. 2019). Friedlieb Ferdinand Runge (1794–1867), a German analytic chemist who identified the mydriatic effects of belladonna, determined that *caffeine* was the major constituent of coffee. His interest was stimulated by a gift of coffee beans from Wolfgang von Goethe (1749–1832), considered the greatest German literary figure of the modern era, who was a great connoisseur and admirer of the effects of coffee. This was the beginning of much scientific work on the physiologic effects of coffee, not in the least because of the interest of many of the researchers in the field due to their personal experience with coffee drinking.

The French physician Francois Magendie (1783–1855), a pioneer of experimental physiology, considered coffee as a remedy for infections (Magendie 1835). Claude Bernard (1813–1878), the French physiologist who laid the foundation for experimental medicine by proposing blinded clinical trials and the notion of the *milieu intérieur*, conducted some of the earliest experiments to determine the effects of coffee on blood pressure (Bernard, Atlee and Robin 1854). (Of note, Bernard's concept of the *milieu intérieur* is the founding principle upon which the field of addiction is based, evolving into the term *homeostasis* coined in 1929 (Dale 1947) by the eminent American physiologist Walter Bradford Cannon (1871–1945) and subsequently, transformed conceptually (Koob and Le Moal 2006) into the idea of *allostasis*.) The German chemist Emil Fischer (1852–1919) synthesized caffeine in 1895, derived its structural formula in 1897 and for this and related work in chemistry won the 1902 Nobel Prize (Fischer, Victor, Robinson et al. 2019).

With a recorded history spanning centuries documenting the health benefits and medical uses of coffee, the notion that this beverage was addictive and harmful emerged and became widespread. For example, an editorial entitled "Coffee Inebriety" appeared in the influential academic journal *Science* exemplifying a common viewpoint at the turn of the 20th century (Anonymous 1890):

"Dr. Mendel of Berlin has lately published a clinical study of this neurosis; his observations being made upon the women of the working population in and about Essen. He found large numbers of women who consumed over a pound of coffee in a week; and some men drank considerably more, besides beer and wine. The leading symptoms were profound depression of spirits, and frequent headaches, with insomnia. A strong dose of coffee would relieve this for a time, then it would return. The muscles would become weak and trembling, and the hands would tremble when at rest. An increasing aversion to labor and any steady work was noticeable. The heart's action was rapid and irregular, and palpitations and a heavy feeling in the precordial region were present. Dyspepsia of an extreme nervous type was also present. Acute rosacea was common in these cases. These symptoms constantly grow worse, and are only relieved by large quantities of coffee…The victims suffer so seriously that they dare not abandon it, for fear of death. Where brandy is taken, only temporary relief follows. The face becomes sallow, and the hands and feet cold; and an expression of dread and agony settles over the countenance, only relieved by using strong doses of coffee… Melancholy and hysteria are present in all cases. Coffee inebriates are more common among the neurasthenics, and are more concealed because the effects of excessive doses of coffee are obscure and largely unknown. A very wide field for future study opens up in this direction."

This clinical description of coffee inebriety shares many features of *addiction* (Martin, Weinberg and Bealer 2007). For example, individuals who drink very large quantities of coffee, are *a priori* considered to have a *mental disorder*, termed a "neurosis." The magnitude of drinking is portrayed as *out-of-control use,* which is readily combined "with beer and wine," indicating a *co-occurring* alcohol use disorder, as often occurs with many other drugs of abuse. Interestingly, coffee is portrayed as a *gateway drug* for other drug use disorders, with "neurasthenics" being particularly predisposed to its use. "Many opium and alcoholic cases have an early history of excessive use of coffee, and are always more degenerate and difficult to treat." A *withdrawal syndrome* from coffee drinking is described as "profound depression of spirits, and frequent headaches, with insomnia…[t]hese symptoms constantly grow worse, and are only relieved by large quantities of coffee…" The *complications* of harmful coffee drinking include: "muscles… become weak and trembling… the hands… tremble when at rest… increasing aversion to labor… heart's action was rapid and irregular… palpitations and a heavy feeling in the precordial region… dyspepsia of an extreme nervous type…" The editorial emphasizes how coffee drinking is initially characterized by *self-medication* to assuage neurasthenia and eventually becomes toxic to health and well-being.

Presumably the association between coffee inebriety and neurasthenia may be related to the pharmacological actions of caffeine, as suggested by Lewis Lewin (1850–1929), a German pharmacologist, known for systematically classifying the psychoactive actions of plants based on their pharmacological and toxicological effects. He suggested in his *Phantastica: Narcotic and Stimulating Drugs* (1931) that coffee is a stimulant, causing: "…an excessive state of brain-excitation which becomes manifest by a remarkable loquaciousness sometimes accompanied by accelerated association of ideas." So, in addition to the social and moral fears about *caffeism* (addiction to coffee/caffeine), and beyond the psychopharmacological effects of caffeine, early studies of coffee's effects on humans up to the last decades of the 20th century, focused on its impact as an addictive drug and its proclivity for concurrent use with other drugs of abuse, primarily alcohol or tobacco. In fact, concurrent coffee and alcohol drinking and cigarette smoking are likely due to pharmacological and social reasons and alcoholics have been found to increase their coffee intake to cope with alcohol abstinence (Aubin, Laureaux, Tilikete and Barrucand 1999). One notion that has emerged in a study of Alcoholics Anonymous members who have been in recovery for variable durations of time is that coffee drinking may assist abstinent alcoholics remain sober from alcohol (Reich, Dietrich, Finlayson et al. 2008).

Until recently, the terms *coffee* and *caffeine* were used almost interchangeably. There was considerable controversy about whether caffeine was an addictive psychoactive agent like recognized drugs of abuse (e.g., alcohol, nicotine, opioids, stimulants, etc.) or had some unique characteristics that made it somehow different. In a genetic epidemiologic study of caffeine intake among women in the Virginia Twin Registry, Kendler and Prescott (1999) reported:

> "Caffeine is an addictive psychoactive substance. Similar to previous findings with other licit and illicit psychoactive drugs, individual differences in caffeine use, intoxication, tolerance, and withdrawal are substantially influenced by genetic factors."

In contrast, in an extensive review of neuroscience research related to caffeine dependence, tolerance, reinforcement and withdrawal, Nehlig (1999) concluded:

> "…it appears that although caffeine fulfils some of the criteria for drug dependence and shares with amphetamines and cocaine a certain specificity of action on the cerebral dopaminergic system, the methylxanthine does not act on the dopaminergic structures related to reward, motivation and addiction."

Swanson, Lee and Hopp (1994) reported:

> "A review of 86 studies of nicotine withdrawal, caffeine withdrawal, and caffeine toxicity suggests that the symptoms are similar enough to be confused, and that reported nicotine withdrawal symptoms may be a mixture of nicotine withdrawal and caffeine toxicity."

Therefore, whether or not coffee drinking *per se* is addictive or harmful, it is so closely linked in the behavioral repertoire with use of other addictive agents, namely smoking cigarettes (nicotine) and drinking alcohol, which each have very harmful effects on health, that it has been far too easy to blame coffee along with its "co-travelers."

Two research directions eventually settled these unresolved issues about the putative detrimental effects of coffee on health. First, research into the chemistry of coffee has progressed beyond the study of caffeine. Many other compounds have been identified in relatively high concentrations within this complex plant, each with independent bioactivity (Farah, de Paulis, Moreira et al. 2006). Of particular relevance to the field of addiction, has been determination that chlorogenic acids in coffee specifically bind to the mu-opioid receptor (Boublik, Quinn, Clements et al. 1983) and can reverse the antinociceptive actions of morphine *in vivo* (de Paulis, Schmidt, Bruchey et al. 2002). Modifying activation of this receptor has become a major pharmacological strategy to treat alcoholism (Altshuler, Phillips and Feinhandler 1980; Sinclair 1990) and opioid use disorder (Dole and Nyswander 1965; Jasinski, Pevnick and Griffith 1978) and supports the benefits of coffee in recovering alcoholics mentioned above (Reich, Dietrich, Finlayson et al. 2008).

The second research direction has consisted of re-examining the presumed negative effects of coffee consumption identified in the mid-20th century using imperfect epidemiologic approaches. By parsing out the effects of concurrent smoking, drinking and other harmful lifestyle factors in consumers of coffee, it has become possible, not only to reverse earlier conclusions of harmful effects of coffee (MacMahon, Yen, Trichopoulos et al. 1981; Gordis 1990), but also to identify real health benefits. Demonstration of reduced rates of cirrhosis, especially in alcoholics, specifically associated with increasing coffee consumption has furthered the notion that coffee drinking has protective effects against a major complication of alcoholism (Klatsky and Armstrong 1992). Another relevant factor concerning the role of coffee in addiction has been studying the chronological initiation of alcohol drinking, cigarette smoking and coffee drinking. Among recovering alcoholics, coffee drinking was the last initiated of these concurrently used psychoactive drugs, starting in the late teens, which is inconsistent with coffee being a gateway drug as proposed above for coffee inebriety (Reich, Dietrich and Martin 2011).

Coffee is now considered a healthy component of the diet and consumption has been demonstrated to be significantly associated with reduced *all-cause mortality* (Freedman, Park, Abnet et al. 2012). Additionally, many beneficial health effects of coffee have been documented in the medical literature in the last three decades using advanced statistical techniques that have allowed parsing out of the effects of the co-travelers, showing a significant inverse relationship between daily coffee consumption and rates of many specific disorders; of note, most of these beneficial effects are still present in those consuming decaffeinated coffee.

Conditions for which protective effects of coffee consumption have most consistently been demonstrated include Type 2 diabetes mellitus and obesity, suicide, cirrhosis, various types of cancer, cardiovascular mortality and neurodegenerative disorders (Farah 2019). Of note, there are clinically meaningful potential connections of a number of these with beneficial outcomes in addiction which remain to be as well investigated as the protective effect of coffee consumption on alcoholic cirrhosis. For example, reduced rates of suicide associated with coffee consumption is quite relevant to addiction because of the high rates of suicide in this patient population. However, it might be difficult to explain how coffee might reduce suicide risk via any antidepressant/anxiolytic effects of caffeine alone – caffeine is highly anxiogenic due to antagonism of adenosine receptors. Discovery that chlorogenic acids in coffee inhibit reuptake of adenosine (de Paulis, Commers, Farah et al. 2004) provides a feasible mechanism whereby coffee drinking may enhance mood and anxiety (Marangos and Boulenger 1985). Finally, obesity can be conceptualized as an addictive process characterized by over-eating (Martin, Weinberg and Bealer 2007). The protective effects of coffee consumption with respect to obesity and type 2 diabetes mellitus may have tremendous implications, as the highest projected increases in obesity and diabetes are in those parts of the world that have traditionally not been drinkers of coffee (Seidell 2000).

Competence

According to the current electronic version of the Oxford English Dictionary (OED), the noun *competence* is derived from the French *compétence*, first defined by the English lexicographer Randle Cotgrave (died *c.* 1634) as "competencie, conueniencie, sufficiencie, aptnesse, fitnesse, agreeablenesse; also, concurrencie, compettitorship" in *A Dictionarie of the French and English Tongues* (Cotgrave, Hollyband and Sherwood 1632). The French word originated from the post-classic Latin *competentia* ("meeting together, agreement, symmetry, planetary conjunction"), *competent-* being the present participle of the verb *competĕre*. The verb *competĕre* is a combination of *com-* ("together") and the verb *petĕre* ("to fall upon, assail, aim at, make for, try to reach, strive after, sue for, solicit, ask, seek."). There are two original meanings of *competĕre*: 1) "in its earlier neuter sense, 'to fall together, coincide, come together, be convenient or fitting, be due'"; and 2) "in its post-classical active sense, 'to strive after (something) in company or together'." These senses are intermixed in the derivatives that follow, but *competence*, and its derivatives belong in the main to the earlier sense.

The first use in the English language of *competence* ("Rivalry in dignity or relative position, vying") as documented in OED is from the sense of the verb *to compete* ("To strive with another, for the attainment of a thing, in doing something"). An example appeared in a translation by Richard Carew (1555–1620), a Cornish translator and antiquary, of *the examination of mens wits* (Huarte and Carew 1616): "Man… seeing that the Angels, with whom he had competence, were immortall [cf. 'Made a little lower than the angels']." This is recognized as the volume in which the Spanish physician and psychologist Juan Huarte de San Juan (1529–1588) attempted for the first time to link psychology to physiology. The second use of *competence* ("An adequate supply, a sufficiency *of*"), now obsolete, is from the other sense of the verb *to compete* ("To be suitable, applicable, or 'competent'"). This is the meaning employed by William Shakespeare (1564–1616), the English playwright, in his *Henry the Fourth* (Shakespeare 1600): "For competence of life, I wil allow you, That lacke of meanes enforce you not to euills."

The general meaning of *competence* ("Sufficiency of qualification; capacity to deal adequately with a subject") acquired a distinctly legal sense ("The quality or position of being legally competent; legal capacity or admissibility"). Accordingly, the conceptualization of competence gained importance in psychiatry, especially in *forensic psychiatry* ("Pertaining to, connected with, or used in courts of law; suitable or analogous to pleadings in court"). Additionally, understanding competence as it pertains to *addiction* presents unique challenges among psychiatric disorders. An example of the legal meaning as first used in the English language is found in *Dictionarium Anglo-Britannicum* edited by John Kersey the younger (*c.* 1660-1721), an English philologist, and lexicographer (Kersey 1708): "Competence, or Competency in Law, the Power of a Judge, for the taking Cognisance of a Matter."

The term *competence* has been examined specifically with respect to addiction and its ethical treatment (Charland 2020). Understanding that addiction belongs squarely within psychiatry, a medical/scientific discipline, the competence to accept or refuse recommended treatment of an individual suffering from an addictive disorder may be conceptualized as having at least the following three elements:

1) An *understanding of the meaning of addiction*, which is defined in OED as: "Immoderate or compulsive consumption of a drug or other substance; specifically, a condition characterized by regular or poorly controlled use of a psychoactive substance despite adverse physical, psychological, or social consequences, often with the development of physiological tolerance and withdrawal symptoms..." This definition should rightly be expanded to include behavioral addictions. Accordingly, a more contemporary definition of addiction is self-destructive and out-of-control *behavior* with or without involvement of psychoactive substances (Martin, Weinberg and Bealer 2007).

2) The presence of *informed consent*, defined in OED as: "… consent to a medical or surgical procedure given after all relevant information (especially regarding potential risks and benefits) has been disclosed to the patient or the patient's guardian; an instance of such consent."

3) Possessing *decision-making capacity*, namely the ability to be informed and then to consent, which is understood to require both *mental capacity* and *mental competence*. In OED, mental capacity is defined essentially in psychometric terms that can be operationally measured ("Power or ability…[specifically] mental…") and mental competence, as noted above, is considered a legal matter adjudicated within a court of law.

Decision-making capacity seems at the heart of the competence to accept or refuse treatment for addiction, however, each of the three factors mentioned above are nonetheless important.

Possibly more for addiction than for many other medical/psychiatric conditions, there are additional issues that should be considered with respect to competence to accept or refuse treatment. Understanding what addiction is and having both mental capacity and mental competence to provide informed consent for treatment are no assurance that an individual can recognize the disorder in themself and either seek or accept treatment when it is offered. It may be difficult to engage a patient in addiction treatment unless the twin characteristics of *insight* and *motivation* are also present or can be developed (see Motivation). In OED, *insight* is defined as: "In studies of behaviour and learning, the sudden perception of the solution to a problem or difficulty... perception of one's mental condition." The definition of *motivation* is: "The [conscious or unconscious] stimulus for action towards a desired goal, especially, as resulting from psychological or social factors; the factors giving purpose or direction to human or animal behaviour… the reason a person has for acting in a particular way, a motive."

Helping an individual recognize that they do, in fact, have a significant problem with addiction that they are willing to tackle are essential for treatment of these disorders. Only with insight and motivation is it possible for the patient to face the challenges required for recovery from addiction - understanding their own role in the development and perpetuation of the disorder and accepting the pharmacopsychosocial treatment that will help them mend a disrupted life (see Recovery). Because of the very real distinction between the treatment of addiction and many other disorders, insight and motivation must factor into a discussion of competence. For example, in common conditions such as appendicitis or pneumonia, the treatment is essentially conducted by the physician with the patient being an interested "bystander." Even for the most severe psychiatric disorders, the focus of the treatment process (electroconvulsive treatment and antipsychotic, antidepressant or mood stabilizing medications) is administered under the supervision of a psychiatrist.

On the other hand, addiction treatment has long relied primarily upon the individual who has the disorder (Wilson 1855) with variable contributions from a treatment team and/or peers. Accordingly, achieving *insight* and *motivation to change* one's behavior have become the essence of the management of addictive disorders today (Miller 1983; Prochaska and DiClemente 1983). Despite the recent emphasis on pharmacological agents in treatment of addiction, the major role of the physician is to help the patient seize the opportunities offered within the context of a multi-disciplinary treatment program, an integrated blend of pharmacopsychosocial components, in which the patient occupies the central role (Martin, Weinberg and Bealer 2007).

The essential responsibility of the person who is suffering from the disorder in its treatment represents a true paradox for both the patient and for the prevalent viewpoint held within society — if the patient must do much of the work of recovery, is addiction truly a medical disorder? While there is well-accepted scientific evidence that addiction is a disease of the brain and thus a *bone fide* psychiatric condition (Leshner 1997), accepting that one truly has the disorder can be very difficult as many of the behaviors involved *seem* to be under the individual's control. The cavalier attitude of society (and paradoxically, expressed wisdom) about the difficulty associated with discontinuing drugs of abuse is exemplified by a quote attributed to the American writer, humorist and lecturer Samuel Langhorne Clemens (1835–1910), known by his pen name Mark Twain: "Giving up smoking is the easiest thing in the world. I know because I've done it thousands of times."

The notion that the fundamental problem in addiction is *loss of control* over a pathological behavior is actually very difficult for the patient to understand and acknowledge. Even if the patient can overcome significant denial about having a pathological behavior, it may still be painful to deal with the guilt that typically is a consequence of addiction and the associated stigma (Volkow 2020). Therefore, despite the very real risk of morbidity and mortality associated with addiction, the individual suffering from these disorders may be reluctant to enter treatment.

Physicians who regularly treat patients with addictive disorders have likened addiction to other chronic diseases like type 2 diabetes mellitus (McLellan, Lewis, O'Brien and Kleber 2000). This viewpoint helps patients (and physicians) understand that medical guidance can be an extremely important component of the treatment of addiction. This is because discontinuing such pathological behaviors is not voluntary and can be made even more difficult when the patient is self-medicating a treatable co-occurring other psychiatric disorder (see Self-Medication). Healing addiction requires learning alternate responses to the environment and strategies to manage the emotions that may be the primary reason for engaging in pathological behaviors (Martin, Weinberg and Bealer 2007).

Additionally, the perspective that one is suffering from a medical disorder can assuage guilt an individual is experiencing by falsely blaming the problem on one's own "faults" and "weaknesses." Despite all we have come to know about the pathophysiology and treatment of addiction, consensus is still lacking about attitudes concerning "responsibility" for either the causation or the treatment of addictive disorders, especially whether those who have these problems should be managed within the medical or legal system — should these individuals be considered patients or criminals (Erickson 1992; McLellan, Lewis, O'Brien and Kleber 2000)?

If a patient is unwilling to seek or accept treatment despite serious risk to their health and wellbeing it is far too easy to conclude that this decision is their choice alone to make. On the other hand, if addiction is understood to be a disease of the mind, a psychiatric disorder characterized by loss of control over a pathological behavior, rather than simply a moral failing or depravity, diminished competence to accept or refuse recommended treatment can be recognized as a consequence of the disease process (Kermani and Castaneda 1996; Hall and Appelbaum 2002).

From the legal perspective, the tenet of diminished competence due to addiction can only be accepted if one acknowledges that the pathological behavior associated with addiction ceases to be a *voluntary act* as it is for the non-addicted (Taylor and Hartshorne 1856). Accordingly, the states of *intoxication* (see Intoxication, Blackout) and *withdrawal* (see Withdrawal, Delirium tremens) which result in psychopathology and possible harm to self and others derives from the impairment of choice, namely the inability to choose to stop using. (Note that the concomitants of *neuroadaptation* undergirded by learning also occur with *behavioral addictions* although they were first conceived as fundamental to substance use disorders.) As a result, actions taken by an addicted person while "under the influence," can only be averted by committal of the individual for appropriate treatment, much as would be deemed essential for individuals at risk for suicide or violence towards others.

This is not a new concept as suggested by the minutes of an annual meeting of the American Association for the Insane wherein physician members agreed that for those "deprived of volition," involuntary institutional care was a necessary intervention, declaring that inebriates should be restrained on grounds of moral depravity, detained as diseased requiring treatment, or committed as *non-compos mentis* (Shrady 1860). Although commitment for addiction treatment is still practiced widely (Grahn 2021), mandating treatment that the patient claims they do not want should not occur according to the World Health Organization (2020). In any event, the legal sphere remains uncertain and, in many ways, resistant to the idea that addiction is a disease — because *volition* in the act of substance consumption which renders the altered mental state resulting from intoxication is a predicted *precursor* and hence renders the user *responsible* for the consequences (Gendel 2004; Lewy 2012; Israelsson, Nordlöf and Gerdner 2015).

Competence to accept or refuse recommended treatment is a legal construct (Buchanan 2004) contrary to efforts to understand the patient's perspective (Benaroyo and Widdershoven 2004). The ability to make such decisions is assumed to always be present unless a clinician can gather the requisite data to allow *adjudication of incompetence* in a court of law (Appelbaum and Grisso 1988). Only if a physician recognizes that addiction is a harmful illness that can benefit from treatment rather than simply a variant of normal behavior under the patient's control will they seek to restrict the individual's right to refuse recommended treatment via legal proceedings. Charland (2020) contends that for indicated treatment to proceed, the patient as well must understand the implications of addiction and have an appreciation of the risks and benefits associated with treatment. This necessitates the physician being able to convey such information to their patient in a reliable and compelling manner. Accordingly, determination of the competence to accept or refuse treatment must take into consideration the patient's perspective of the current understanding of the pathogenesis and complications of addiction, its reliable diagnosis, accepted treatment approaches and the likelihood that intervention can improve their clinical outcome.

As suggested above, the determination of competence in a patient with addictive disorders is greatly influenced by the fact that psychopathology in addiction may wax and wane through the clinical course of the disorder. Significant impairment during intoxication or withdrawal combined with an essentially normal mental state during periods of sobriety (Eckardt and Martin 1986) means that the competence to refuse treatment may be absent when the patient is first seen in the emergency department, only to return by the next morning when the patient wishes to leave the hospital. This can represent an almost insurmountable challenge to the physician as limitations in decision-making that may satisfy the criteria for legal commitment to treatment can be fleeting in these disorders. Physicians may find this especially confusing because this is less of an issue with many other chronic mental illnesses (Christopher, Anderson and Stein 2020), in which the predictability of the course and duration of clinical dysfunction are more consistent with the scope and timeline of legal proceedings. One might certainly argue that if an addicted individual is sober and competent to refuse treatment they are still at high likelihood of re-intoxication. Accordingly, entry into treatment should equally be facilitated rather than allowing them to engage in repeated cycles of being "under the influence" with diminished competence and potential for harm to self and others which characterize recidivism.

The major question considering the important role played by the patient in treatment of addiction is whether commitment to treatment against the patient's wishes is effective and alters the clinical course of addiction. Physicians who regularly treat patients suffering from addiction believe that commitment to treatment is worthwhile (Jain, Christopher, Fisher et al. 2021) and once the patient is committed it is only a matter of time before both insight about their disorder and the motivation to change their behavior can be developed through the treatment process so that they can begin their journey to recovery (Miller and Flaherty 2000). An alternative perspective is that much more research is required to determine the effectiveness of compulsory/legally mandated treatment for addictive disorders process (Klag, O'Callaghan and Creed 2005; Jain, Christopher and Appelbaum 2018). Nevertheless, if the patient at least has the *opportunity* to alter their self-destructive and out-of-control behavior (see Recovery) in treatment, it may beneficially change the course of their addictive disorder, which otherwise is very likely to progress over time and can harm not only the patient but also those in their orbit.

Conditioning

As noted in the current electronic version of Oxford English Dictionary (OED), the noun *conditioning* is a combination of the verb *condition* and the suffix *ing*, whose function is to render the verb into a noun of action. The word *condition* has been in use since the 14th century as either a noun or verb; as a noun, the word originates from Middle English and Old French *condicion* derived from the Latin *condiciōn-em* (in later times, commonly spelt *conditiōn-em*) which means "a compact, stipulation, agreement upon terms". As a verb, it originates from the Old French *condicionne-r*, corresponding to medieval Latin *conditiōnāre*, meaning "to impose a condition on, to limit with conditions." The meaning that is the subject of the current discussion is most appropriately linked to the verb, "To teach or accustom (a person or animal) to adopt certain habits, attitudes, standards, etc.; to establish a conditioned reflex or response in." Thus, *conditioning* is defined in OED as: "The training or accustoming of a person or animal to give conditioned responses." Ban (2008) described *conditioning* as: "referring to the learning of some particular response. The conditional stimulus is one that was originally ineffective but that, after being paired with an unconditional stimulus, evokes the conditional response."

First mention in the English language with the relevant meaning of the verb *condition*, according to OED, is attributed to reports (Yerkes and Morgulis 1909) of methods in animal psychology involving the canine salivary response operationalized by the Russian physiologist Ivan Petrovich Pavlov (1849–1936) and his collaborators during the period of 1899-1909: "Pawlow's Method... Separate components of a complex sound which conditions a 'fundamental' reflex, will produce reflexes (the so-called partial reflexes) at a certain relative intensity." This methodology from Pavlov's laboratory consisted of eliciting the canine salivary reflex in response to diverse sensory stimuli (that typically would not produce salivation) by repeatedly pairing the stimulus in question with one that naturally serves to activate the salivary reflex. This is referred to as *Pavlovian, classical or respondent conditioning*. The verb *condition* has subsequently become part of common parlance, widely used in popular psychology, philosophy and literature (Ewing 1944): "During its first twelve months the child acquires many habits and may be conditioned in various ways, for instance in regard to cleanliness. But unless this conditioning is brought into relation with the dynamic structure of focused impulse which develops in the second year, it will wear out or break down."

The noun *conditioning* was first use in the English language, according to OED, in the context of conditioned emotional reactions in infancy (Watson and Rayner 1920): "Steps taken to condition emotional responses... The infant...was tested with his blocks immediately afterwards to see if they shared in the process of conditioning." The authors proposed linkage of emotional reaction patterns to stimuli within the child's environment as the mechanism whereby the much wider range and complexity of adult emotions develop through the process of conditioning—an example of developmental transformation via conditioning of the Lockean *tabula rasa* of earliest childhood. The noun conditioning has subsequently become widely accepted in literature (Huxley 1932): "All conditioning aims at that: making people like their unescapable social destiny."

Skinner (1937) introduced the term *operant* as a descriptor of conditioning: "There is also a kind of response which occurs spontaneously in the absence of any stimulation with which it may be specifically correlated... I shall call such a unit an operant and the behavior in general, operant behavior." Additionally, Kimble and Hilgard (1940) used the term *instrumental* to denote operant conditioning: "When the occurrence of the reinforcement is contingent upon the organism's behavior the procedure may be termed instrumental conditioning." In *operant/instrumental conditioning*, behaviors are shaped by the presentation of reward *after* a desired behavior occurs spontaneously, and the learning is strengthened with each subsequent associated presentation of the *reward* (in OED defined as: "A recompense given after a particular response which reinforces learning or behaviour; the giving of such a recompense, as a method of behavioural control") with spontaneous occurrences of the desired behavior.

Extinction (defined in OED as: "The quenching, putting out [of fire, light, anything burning or shining; figurative hopes, passions, life, etc.]; the fact of being quenched; the process of becoming, or the condition of being, extinct") of a conditioned response, regardless of whether it is classical or operant, occurs when it is no longer rewarded or punished. As a result, diminution, or fading of the non-reinforced conditioned response is observed over time.

As learning forms the mechanistic underpinnings ("the currency") of addiction (Kalant, LeBlanc and Gibbins 1971; Stolerman 1992; Martin, Lovinger and Breese 1995), conditioning provides a heuristic framework for understanding and experimentally modelling components of the disorder (Wikler 1973). Operant conditioning seems most relevant in pathogenesis of primary drug use disorders, wherein initially *rewarding* effects of the drug of abuse precede progression to out-of-control use despite negative consequences (White 1989, Volkow and Morales 2015). On the other hand, in drug use disorder *secondary* to underlying other psychopathology, the notion of *reinforcement* of classical conditioning seems more appropriate (White 1989). For example, in psychiatric disorders in which contextual (situational) conditioned fear responses underpin psychopathologic manifestations (Sotres-Bayon, Bush and LeDoux 2004; Tamminga 2006), self-administration of drugs of abuse can modify neurotransmission in relevant regions of the amygdala/hippocampus/prefrontal cortex so as to diminish the intensity of disturbing psychic symptoms. Repetition of drug self-administration in order to cope with painful psychological symptoms (see Self-medication), may result in the individual eventually developing out-of-control drug use, or addiction.

Treatment of addiction can be understood as *extinction of conditioned response(s)* that contribute to pathological use of alcohol/drugs resulting in diminution/cessation of use through various pharmacopsychosocial interventions (Martin, Weinberg and Bealer 2007). Analysis of self-destructive, out-of-control self-administration of drugs of abuse that characterizes addiction reveals multiple component behaviors, each of which are potentially subject to the principles of conditioning and extinction, e.g., *drug-seeking behavior*, effects of *intoxication* and *withdrawal* (Tatum, Seevers and Collins 1929; Wikler 1973, O'Brien 1975) and, in particular, various elements of *tolerance* (Kalant, LeBlanc and Gibbins 1971). Neuroadaptation to repeated drug use is now recognized to involve *allostatic change* (Koob 2017) in addition to classical constructs of tolerance and dependence (Kalant, LeBlanc and Gibbins 1971), which do not allow the organism to return to its original behavioral state (prior to first drug use) with respect to response(s) to the drug of abuse, and therefore, are not strictly amenable to the principles of extinction. In fact, clinical observation suggests that the earlier in life alcohol/drug use begins and the longer the associated conditioning has persisted within the behavioral repertoire, the more severe and difficult to treat is the disorder (Fleming and Tillotson 1939): "anyone — normal, neurotic or psychopathic, manic depressive or schizoid — can become an alcoholic addict if he drinks long enough and heavily enough (on the average about a decade), and that the younger he is when he starts his drinking, the less likelihood there is for his successful treatment in a mental hospital."

Applying the principles of classical conditioning to treatment of alcohol use disorder was first described in Russia and pursued subsequently in the United States (Thimann 1943). Voegtlin (1940) implemented a method whereby: "the nauseant drugs, emetine and apomorphine, were used to elicit the unconditioned reflex of nausea and vomiting, and the sight, smell, and taste of alcoholic beverages served as the conditioned stimulus." Thereafter, an analogous strategy of linking alcohol use with a distressing state via pharmacotherapy was employed in patients with alcohol use disorder (Hald and Jacobsen 1948): "The organism is sensitised to alcohol after intake of tetraethylthiuramdisulphide… (disulfiram, or Antabuse). Alcohol given to persons previously treated with this otherwise innocuous substance produces dilatation of the facial vessels, increased pulmonary ventilation, raised pulse-rate, and general uneasiness. The symptoms appear to be the result of an increased formation of acetaldehyde from alcohol." So as not to re-experience these very unpleasant symptoms of the alcohol/disulfiram reaction, the patient elects not to drink, ideally progressing in time to extinction of drinking behavior (Martensen-Larsen 1948).

Behavioral pharmacology provides a strategy based on *learning theory* to determine the capacity of drugs of abuse to modify behavior in a test organism (e.g., behaving rodents among others, nonhuman primates, or even humans) using the paradigm of self-administration (Schuster and Thompson 1969) and substitution to suppress withdrawal and determine cross-tolerance or cross-dependence (Kalant, LeBlanc and Gibbins 1971). In the self-administration paradigm, the fundamental task is to quantify the effort that an experimental animal will expend to receive the drug in question via various routes of administration and determine interventions that might modify the rewarding value of drugs. By comparisons of behavioral responses elicited by the test drug with those of other agents that have well-defined pharmacological actions, the test drug's relative ability to reinforce self-administration and the neuropharmacological mechanisms underpinning these responses may be elucidated (Schuster and Thompson 1969). This paradigm may equivalently be employed to determine the capacity of a well-characterized drug to substitute for or treat withdrawal from the test agent. In addition, one can determine if a drug being tested for treatment of addiction to the drug in question may favorably alter the pattern or degree of its self-administration.

Attempts to better understand the fundamental neurobiology of conditioning has led to experiments in much less complex organisms to unravel phenomena involved in learning (Castellucci et al. 1970) with, as yet, unclear reductionistic implications for conditioning as a model of addiction. In addition, other constructs than classical or operant conditioning have been invoked in expanding the role of drives in behaviors that are not readily understandable in terms of survival of the species, which may gain more relevance as one tries to understand what addictive behaviors have wrought in our society (Knoll 2003).

Craving

According to the current electronic version of Oxford English Dictionary (OED), *craving* is the noun of the action *crave*, which is derived from the Old English *crafian* with traces in Old Germanic and akin to the Old Norse, Swedish, Danish forms meaning "to demand, require, exact." These initial meanings of the word *crave* date to *c*1000 and are now mostly obsolete. It is the transferred meaning of *crave* that is the most appropriate with respect to addiction: "Urgent desire; longing, yearning." This transferred meaning of *crave* first appeared in the English language in about 1400-50 (Skeat 1878): "Ʒe couett & craue castels & rewmes." It subsequently took on a more recognizable form with respect to its current meaning in addiction (Heresbach and Googe 1577): "Who so ploweth his Olyue Garden, craueth fruite." As suggested in the work of the English novelist and historian Sir Walter Besant (1836-1901), the meaning continued to evolve and became more compatible with current notions (Besant 1890): "The thing…that feeds the disease and that the disease constantly craves." In these later quotations, one senses the origins of the modern conceptualization of craving into a dichotomy of "liking and wanting" an object (Berridge and Robinson 2016). Likewise, the noun *craving* followed the same evolution as *crave* (L'Estrange 1692): "A Regular Vicissitude, and Succession of Cravings and Satiety." Eventually, the noun came to be used in parallel fashion to the verb (Besant 1890): "A man liable to attacks of craving for strong drink."

Craving for psychoactive agents is different from hunger for food, but sufficiently overlapping that the notion of "drug hunger" is intuitively understood and *hunger* has been a neurobiologically useful construct for understanding *craving* and *vice versa* (Kassel and Shiffman 1992). The definition of *hunger* in OED is instructive: "The uneasy or painful sensation caused by want of food; craving appetite." Intuited parallels between hunger for food and craving for alcohol have provided the impetus for ongoing research using our understanding of the neurobiology of food intake to explore alcohol use disorder (Marfaing-Jallat, Larue and Le Magnen 1970): "Contrary to the classically observed over-responsiveness toward oro-sensory aversive stimuli of hyperphagic hypothalamic rats, a majority of rats in these various experimental conditions increased their intake of the ethanol solution." This notion, reminiscent of the primary thesis that alcohol consumption has nutrient value and thus, is related to the fundamental drive of hunger (Richter 1953), has been extended to elucidation of the mechanistic underpinnings of drug/alcohol use disorders and their pharmacologic treatments (Thiele, Navarro, Sparta et al. 2003; Farokhnia, Grodin, Lee et al. 2018).

In a similar vein, *thirst* has a long historical association with addiction, especially drinking alcoholic beverages, but also other drugs of abuse (Mello 1975; Ramsden 2015), as intimated by its OED definition: "The uneasy or painful sensation caused by want of drink; also, the physical condition resulting from this want." The use of excessive water drinking (Falk 1961) to train laboratory animals to self-administer solutions of alcohol or other psychoactive agents that they might otherwise avoid, has been employed to study the behavioral and neurochemical underpinnings of addiction.

Whether craving for drugs of abuse and thirst are coterminous in the brain is far from certain. For example, in a functional magnetic resonance imaging (fMRI) study of thirsty heroin addicts (Xiao, Lee, Zhang et al. 2006), when brain responses triggered by neutral and drug-related pictures were compared, increased brain activations in frontal, occipital and cerebellar regions were demonstrated for the drug condition. By contrast, water-related pictures compared to neutral cues did not increase brain activation in any of those regions, but triggered activity in the anterior cingulate. The researchers concluded: "Our results show an important role of prefrontal cortex in heroin craving and suggest that heroin craving may involve different neural substrates than do desire from basic physiological drives".

It also seems sensible to convolve *craving* for drugs of abuse with the neurobiological *urge to fulfil drives* required for survival of the species, e.g., sexual activity and exploration, much as just discussed for hunger and thirst (Martin, Weinberg and Bealer 2007). However, on careful examination, while descriptors of *hunger, thirst and drives* are semantically analogous to *craving* for drugs of abuse, they are not identical in terms of the underpinning neural pathways, although some elements may overlap. The emergence of primacy of self-administration of a highly rewarding drug of abuse (e.g., cocaine) compared to fulfilling natural drives as hunger is a well-documented characteristic of the "hijacked brain" in addiction (Leshner 1997), suggesting that the precise brain mechanisms that subserve these states (addictions *vs.* natural drives) may not be entirely superimposable.

Craving as understood in addiction, characterized by intense interest in a free-choice situation, associated approach behaviors and self-administration (Stolerman 1992), is not restricted to psychoactive agents with abuse liability (Richter, Holt and Barelare 1937). While these behaviors are considered distinct from hunger or thirst, they nevertheless, are manifested as "excessive appetite or craving for special food stuffs…." Curt Paul Richter (1894-1988), an American psychobiologist and geneticist, studied appetitive behaviors in experimental animals by depriving them of substances essential to survival, demonstrating pre-programmed, genetic-based forms of behavior (Schulkin, Rozin and Stellar 1994). He recognized that cravings for foods "have their origin in deficiencies…or by altered metabolism" but craving for vitamin B_1 is powerful in rats regardless of whether they are deficient in this essential nutrient. Richter, Holt and Barelare (1937) concluded: "It is of general biological interest that such powerful craving should be associated with a food stuff of the great nutritive importance of vitamin B_1." Of particular and intersecting interest, vitamin B_1 was demonstrated to play a significant role in self-administration of alcohol, an unusual psychoactive agent in that it possesses both abuse liability and role as a foodstuff (Mardones, Segovia and Onfray 1946).

Craving is inexorably intertwined with *addiction* which denotes "out-of-control and self-destructive behavior" involving self-administration of a psychoactive agent to which the individual is drawn at many levels (see Addiction), currently dichotomized as "wanting and liking" (Anselme and Robinson 2016). In this context, the term is also readily applicable to addictive disorders *not* involving self-administration of drugs, the so-called behavioral addictions, such as gambling, problematic hypersexuality, etc. Craving is unquestionably related to the phenomenology of *withdrawal* from every drug of abuse (see Withdrawal), such that the characteristic withdrawal syndromes can include intense craving for the specific drug to which the individual is addicted; accordingly, more often than not, the craving is acted upon and the active addiction continues.

This does not mean that craving ceases once withdrawal has abated. Craving represents a significant component of learning-related and enduring brain changes that occur with repeated use of psychoactive substances with abuse liability. These cravings are triggered even after acute withdrawal has abated by relevant memories, experiences, affective states, and situations previously associated with drug use which, using modern neuroimaging tools, can be identified to have left traces within brain circuits (Grant, London, Newlin et al. 1996; Childress, Mozley, McElgin et al. 1999). All the same, it is uncertain whether an "urgent desire; longing, yearning" to use a drug that has been discontinued for extended periods is intended to relieve the distress associated with protracted withdrawal phenomena, and hence, is a form of *self-medication* (see Self-medication). In fact, the experience of craving experienced and acted on much beyond when the acute withdrawal state has subsided is what makes addiction a *life-long condition* as intimated by Wikler (1961):

> "physicians, lawmakers and the general public every-where are concerned above
> all with one aspect of the problem, namely, the persistent tendency to repeated
> relapse after successful withdrawal of the drug in question."

Investigations of recovery from addiction consequently have focused on mechanistic understanding of craving. Craving seems to be best evaluated in the context of learning and memory and these brain functions are tightly bound to the underlying processes which can be understood and perhaps, even modified, in terms of conditioning (see Conditioning; Wolpe 1964).

Delirium Tremens

According to the current electronic edition of the Oxford English Dictionary (OED), *delirium tremens* is directly taken from medical Latin and means "trembling or quaking delirium." The complete OED definition is: "A species of delirium induced by excessive indulgence in alcoholic liquors, and characterized by tremblings and various delusions of the senses." The first use of the term *delirium tremens* was by the English physician Thomas Sutton (1767-1835) in his *Tracts on Delirium Tremens, on Peritonitis, and on Some other Internal Inflammatory Affections, and on the Gout* (Sutton 1813), in which he presented several case reports with careful clinical descriptions linking the syndrome to over indulgence in alcohol and described the important diagnostic features that differentiated delirium tremens from *phrenitis*, the then-prevailing term for delirium due to inflammation of the brain or from mania. Sutton prominently cited the work of the Scottish physician William Saunders (1743-1817), whom Sutton credited with first describing the syndrome he would call delirium tremens. The French physician Pierre Francois Olive Rayer (1793-1867) acknowledged both Sutton and Saunders on the very first page of his treatise *Mémoire sur le delirium tremens* (1819). Eventually, the eponym for delirium tremens became the Saunders-Sutton syndrome (Cutshall 1965).

To appreciate the essence of delirium tremens and its history requires understanding of the meaning of its root, as well as the conditions from which it primarily needed to be differentiated in clinical practice. According to OED, the noun *delirium* is derived from the Latin *dēlīrium* attributed to the 2nd century Greek physician/philosopher Celsus (Celsus and Spencer 1935), meaning "madness, derangement" and was derived from *dēlīrāre*, meaning, "To be deranged" in distinction to the verb *delire* meaning, "To go astray, go wrong, err," signifying that this condition was indeed involuntary. The primary definition of *delirium* in OED is: "A disordered state of the mental faculties resulting from disturbance of the functions of the brain, and characterized by incoherent speech, hallucinations, restlessness, and frenzied or maniacal excitement." According to OED, the first documented use of the word was theological, echoing the experience of a descent into hell, *Master Broughton's letters, especially his last pamphlet to and against the Lord Archbishop of Canterbury, about Sheol and Hades, for the descent into Hell, answered in their kind* (Anonymous 1599): "It is but the franticke delirium of one, whose pride hath made him φρεναπατᾶν [frenzied]." The first documented use in medical context was by the 17th century English physician John Smith (1630-1679) in his volume *A compleat practice of physick* (Smith 1656): "The signs are a weak Pulse…delirium." The historical noun *phrenitis* is defined in OED as: "Delirium, especially when associated with or attributed to inflammation of the brain; inflammation of the brain or of the meninges, encephalitis or meningitis." Phrenitis is also borrowed from classical Latin *phrenītis* ("delirium" from 2nd Century AD) and derived from the ancient Greek φρενῖτις < φρεν- , φρήν ("mind"), according to OED. Its meaning is succinctly stated in the first apparent use in English (Barrough 1583): "Phrenitis in Greeke and in Latin is a disease, wherin the mind is hurte." Of note is use of the word *phrenitis* in description of *melancholia* by Robert Burton (1577–1640) the English writer and fellow of Oxford University in his encyclopedic book *The Anatomy of Melancholy* (Burton 1621): "Phrenitis, …is a Disease of the Minde, with a continuall Madnesse or Dotage, …or els an inflammation of the Braine." Burton's mention of melancholia in association with phrenitis rather than delirium is insightful as we now know that hyperthymic mood disorders and alcoholism frequently co-occur and may represent a difficult differential diagnostic challenge (Rich and Martin 2014).

Understanding the pathogenesis of *delirium tremens* has reflected the evolution of medical science over the two centuries since the syndrome was first described, especially advances in the neurosciences and elucidation of the pharmacological actions of alcohol. American physician John Ware (1795–1864) who, with Dr. Walter Channing, was editor of the New England Journal of Medicine and Surgery from 1824 to 1827, wrote (Ware 1832): "Morbid anatomy has thrown no light upon the nature of that affection of the brain and nervous system, which gives rise to the peculiar symptoms of delirium tremens. Indeed, its history would rather lead us to expect that these symptoms do not depend on any organic changes discoverable by dissection, but merely on a disturbance in their functions." Robley Dunglison (1798–1869), an English physician who moved to America to join the first faculty of the University of Virginia, the personal physician to Thomas Jefferson and considered the "Father of American Physiology," proposed (Dunglison 1860): "that the irregularity of nervous action is usually induced by the withdrawal of an accustomed stimulus, and that the recuperative powers are generally entirely sufficient to bring about the necessary equalization — we have treated the mass of the cases which have fallen under our care without either excitants proper, or opiates."

By mid-19th century it was clear that delirium tremens was characterized by confusion, motoric activation, sensory hyperarousal and autonomic hyperactivity in individuals who had consumed significant quantities of alcohol. Additionally, it was demonstrated that the disorder did not benefit from the then-accepted medical practice of bloodletting (Renton 1829). State-of-the-art treatment of delirium tremens was sedation with opium as described in the *New Sydenham Society Lexicon* (Mayne et al. 1881). Identification of more effective and specific treatment approaches became the key to understanding the mechanistic underpinnings of delirium tremens. For example, the English physician Dr. J. Corbet Fletcher wrote in the *The British Medical Journal* of the benefits of chloral hydrate in delirium tremens (Fletcher 1870): "…to try hydrate of chloral as a tentative remedy in delirium tremens… being unwilling to give opium except as a dernier ressort, I gave half-drachm doses of hydrate of chloral every two hours until sleep was secured." He concluded: "Truly, the effects of chloral in this case were almost miraculous." Chloral hydrate, then used as a sedative-hypnotic, had been synthesized by chlorination of ethanol by the German chemist Freiherr von Liebig (1803–1873) who is considered one of the founders of organic chemistry (Liebig 1832). Accordingly, chloral hydrate would be anticipated to possess very similar, though more potent, pharmacologic actions as ethanol. Hence, the beneficial effect on delirium tremens is not unexpected if the condition were the consequence of discontinuing to drink alcohol, a novel conjecture at the time of Fletcher's observation.

How alcohol consumption was mechanistically related to development of delirium tremens came into sharp focus with an important observation: "The proof of the pudding is in the eating, and the proof that delirium tremens is due to the sudden deprivation of alcohol is shown by the fact that the attack of delirium can be cut short in an early stage by administration of the normal quantity of alcohol (Anonymous 1917)." A fundamental experiment was conducted at the Addiction Research Center in Lexington, Kentucky, involving former morphine addicts that formally tested the association between drinking and delirium tremens (Isbell, Fraser, Wikler et al. 1955). (It should be underscored that such an experiment, despite its importance, would never be conducted in the present day due to ethical concerns.) Under experimental conditions, subjects consumed alcohol continuously for many weeks and when alcohol consumption was discontinued, alcohol withdrawal symptoms emerged in all, while some developed delirium tremens with the "intensity of symptoms roughly correlated with length of intoxication and amount of alcohol consumed." This work unequivocally demonstrated that delirium tremens is caused by precipitously stopping heavy drinking and the major determinant of severity is the quantity of alcohol consumed while the individual was actively drinking. However, this experiment left unresolved why alcohol can "cut short" delirium tremens, but only "in an early stage" of the disorder (Anonymous 1917). This observation suggests that physiologic stress responses (Selye 1937) to discontinuing alcohol consumption are distinct from the simple absence of alcohol and the notion of providing alcohol to a patient in delirium tremens hardly seems a wise or practical approach to treatment (Piker 1937), especially as the course of the condition progresses.

By the mid-20th century there was consensus that treatment of delirium tremens could be accomplished using any of the available central nervous system depressants given in a timely fashion in combination with proper hydration, nutrition and replacement of vitamins and electrolytes (Smith 1953). Further elucidation of the pathophysiology of *alcohol withdrawal* and *delirium tremens* have led to rational pathogenesis-based treatment strategies (Sellers and Kalant 1976) and most recently, "evidence-based treatment" (Mayo-Smith, Beecher, Fischer et al. 2004). These treatment approaches fall into two broad categories: 1) use of pharmacological agents that are cross-tolerant to and cross-dependent with alcohol and are more slowly eliminated from the body to replace alcohol (substitution); and 2) use of agents that minimize the neuronal hyperexcitability and the associated autonomic hyperarousal that ensue from acute disturbance of neuroadaptive alterations due to chronic alcohol consumption (stress response). Substitution is the most straightforward approach and after chloral hydrate (mentioned above) there followed a series of trials of any number of central nervous system depressants as each was introduced into clinical use, including barbiturates (Essig, Jones and Lam 1969), the sedative-hypnotic chlormethiazole (Giacobini and Salum 1961) and benzodiazepines (Frommel, Fleury, Schmidt-Ginzkey and Beguin 1960). Determining whether one pharmacological class or individual members of a given class were superior in head-to-head comparisons then became the focus. Additionally, as various non-barbiturate hypnosedatives were introduced into the pharmacopeia and were joined by more specific anxiolytic benzodiazepines, it became very clear that the delirium tremens-like syndrome was characteristic not only of the discontinuation of alcohol but of all but the most slowly eliminated central nervous system depressants (Ewart and Priest 1967; Martin, Bhushan, Kapur et al. 1979).

The second approach to treatment of delirium tremens requires additional understanding of the consequences of chronic alcohol consumption and the pathophysiologic underpinnings of each sign and symptom of the syndrome. The first such consequence of alcohol consumption was thought to be depletion of B-vitamins (Mainzer and Krause 1939): "Formerly these disturbances were thought to be due to the toxic effects of alcohol, but it has now been demonstrated that they are for the most part signs of a nutritional deficiency (avitaminosis)." Whether depletion of thiamine plays a specific role in the pathophysiology of delirium tremens *per se* or is involved indirectly via a possible role in modulating alcohol consumption (Mardones, Segovia and Onfray 1946) or its well-recognized nutritional influence on alcohol-induced neurotoxicity (Victor, Adams and Collins 1971) were likely reasons for synthesis of a sedative-hypnotic, chlormethiazole, which is structurally related to thiamine (Osterman, Bellander-Lofvenberg and Lassenius 1959). All the same, standard of care now involves replacement of thiamine immediately upon entry to care and there is little evidence of the superiority of chlormethiazole (Sychla, Gründer and Lammertz 2017). Depletion during chronic alcohol consumption of specific electrolytes was also recognized to be associated with the severity of delirium tremens (Flink, Stutzman, Anderson et al. 1954; Wadstein and Skude 1978); these electrolytes are now implicated in neuronal depolarization and thus their depletion may explain the hyperexcitability of the nervous system well-document in alcohol withdrawal. As the focus in biological psychiatry turned to biogenic amines in the pathogenesis of brain dysfunction in psychiatric disorders it was suggested that (Giacobini, Izikowitz and Wegmann 1960): "The high excretion of urinary catecholamines [in delirium tremens] may reflect the sympathetic hyperactivity observed clinically. This is probably a result of central stimulation." This important observation was further investigated and substantiated over ensuing years, clearly supporting that ethanol withdrawal was a state of *autonomic hyperarousal* which if severe enough could lead to alteration of the sensorium (Linnoila, Mefford, Nutt and Adinoff 1987). Consequently, various sympatholytic agents were investigated in treatment of alcohol withdrawal (Björkqvist 1975; Sellers and Kalant 1976). Additionally, post-mortem comparisons between Addison's disease and delirium tremens led to attempts to augment overwhelmed stress responses in delirium tremens using steroids, particularly components of the adrenal cortical system (Dowden and Bradbury 1952).

Various other pathophysiological abnormalities were identified that explained the proclivity among certain drinkers to develop delirium tremens and hence, provided strategies for its treatment, including abnormalities in endogenously produced alcohol (Ostrovsky 1986), levels of body and brain hydration (Smith, Chick, Kean et al. 1985; Bezzegh, Nyuli and Kovács 1991), abnormalities in cerebral blood flow (Hemmingsen, Vorstrup, Clemmesen et al. 1988) and cortical atrophy (Maes, Vandoolaeghe, Degroote et al. 2000) among others. Auditory evoked potentials were employed to understand the disturbed sensorium so characteristic of delirium tremens with the conclusion that (Gross, Tobin, Kissin et al. 1964): "…acute disturbances of acoustic response may be present in delirium tremens and when present may have a significant relationship to the formation of auditory hallucinations." Based on a literature that electroconvulsive treatments may be effective in treatment of various delirious states, Dudley and Williams (1972) conducted a retrospective controlled study of ECT in delirium tremens and found that: "A prompt response to ECT was observed in all cases." This finding seems difficult to explain based on what we now know about the pathophysiology of the alcohol discontinuation syndrome (see above) but may act through resetting of excitatory/inhibitory neurotransmission or immune-inflammatory responses resulting from induced convulsions. A recent case report (Kranaster,

Aksay, Bumb et al. 2017) provides guarded support for this approach: "It has to be emphasized that we do not want to encourage… uncritical usage of ECT for alcohol withdrawal delirium, but we hope that the reported case might contribute to an alternative approach in very severe and prolonged alcohol withdrawal delirium." Electrochemical disturbances from repeated episodes of heavy alcohol consumption and withdrawal resulting in changes in synaptic efficacy during a lifetime formed the basis of the "kindling" hypothesis of Ballenger and Post (1978) and the shared elements of tolerance with learning and memory (Kalant, LeBlanc and Gibbins 1971). Genetic approaches to gain insights into interindividual differences in susceptibility to severe alcohol withdrawal and development of syndrome components of delirium tremens are currently of considerable research interest (Kosobud and Crabbe 1986; Sander, Harms, Rommelspache et al. 1998; Gorwood, Limosin, Batel et al. 2003).

Due to the clinical presentation of delirium tremens and the association of alcoholism with other psychiatric disorders (Rich and Martin 2014), it remained controversial whether this condition was not a psychotic disorder in its own right (Soyka 1990). Krystal (1959) studied 700 patients with delirium tremens and concluded that this condition, "was found to be a combination of a physiological disturbance and an emotional stress in an individual whose relation to reality is, at best, tenuous." Therefore, it seemed reasonable to determine whether delirium could be effectively managed with phenothiazines. In a formal comparison of promazine and paraldehyde, Thomas and Freedman (1964) addressed this controversy and conclusively demonstrated that paraldehyde was superior. In contrast to findings that might be expected in patients with schizophrenia and related psychoses, they concluded: "Our experience in this trial suggests that promazine might be regarded as a dangerous drug when given to severely ill delirium tremens patients." Nevertheless, neuroleptics continue to be studied and used in treatment of alcohol withdrawal delirium without regard to the underlying pathophysiology of diminished inhibitory (Nestoros 1980) and accentuated excitatory (Lovinger, White and Weight 1989) neurotransmission predicted from the pharmacologic actions of alcohol and the pharmacologic propensity of neuroleptics to lower the seizure threshold. This unfortunate choice of pharmacotherapy is likely due to partially overlapping phenomenology of delirium tremens with psychotic disorders and common co-occurrence of alcoholism with almost any other psychiatric disorder.

Empathy

According to the current electronic version of the Oxford English Dictionary (OED), the noun *empathy* was formed within English by derivation and combination of the prefix *em-* ("Transitive verbs [often found only in verbal noun, past participle, or participial adjective]") with *-pathy* ("Forming nouns denoting kinds of feeling or ways of being affected."). The combining form *-pathy* is a borrowing from ancient Greek -πάθεια. The sense of *-pathy* employed here is according to OED "…attested from the late 16ᵗʰ century" similarly to other nouns such as *sympathy* and *antipathy*."

The conceptual underpinnings of the word *empathy* were formulated in the German language at the turn of the 20ᵗʰ century. The first sense of the word was after the German *Empathie* as used in the psychological theory of Kurd Lasswitz (1848–1910), a German author, scientist and philosopher who has been called "the father of German science fiction." This now obsolete meaning of *empathy* is defined in OED as: "In the psychological theory of K. Lasswitz: a physical property of the nervous system analogous to electrical capacitance, believed to be correlated with feeling." The second sense of *empathy* was as used by Theodor Lipps (1851–1914). Lipps was a German philosopher who was known for his theory regarding aesthetics and laying the foundation for a new branch of interdisciplinary research between psychology and philosophy using the concept of *Einfühlung* (empathy) that he defined as "projecting oneself onto the object of perception." This now rarely used meaning of the word is defined in OED as: "The quality or power of projecting one's personality into or mentally identifying oneself with an object of contemplation, and so fully understanding or appreciating it."

The first use of the word *empathy* in the English language was pertaining to Psychology and Philosophy and was published in *Philosophical Review* in a translation of *Ueber psychophysische Energie und ihre Factoren* (Lasswitz 1895): "For the capacity factor of psychophysical energy the name 'empathy' is proposed. Empathy is then a physical quantity, a physiological brain-function, and is defined as the relation of the whole energy at any change of the central organ to the intensity." This perspective based in Physics presages and draws upon the then emerging understanding of the nervous system in terms of its electrophysiologic properties, contemporaneously studied by the English neurophysiologist Sir Charles Scott Sherington (1857–1952) who received the Nobel Prize in Physiology or Medicine together with Edgar Douglas Adrian (1889–1977) in 1932 for their discoveries regarding the functions of neurons.

An early example in the English language of the second sense of the word *empathy* relating to Psychology and Aesthetics is found in a quote from Edward Bradford Titchener (1867–1927) in his *Lectures on the experimental psychology of the thought-processes* (1909): "Not only do I see gravity and modesty and pride… but I feel or act them in the mind's muscles. This is, I suppose, a simple case of empathy, if we may coin that term as a rendering of *Einfühlung*." Titchener, an English experimental psychologist, is best known for creating his version of Psychology describing the structure of the mind (Structuralism). In the same volume, Titchener also wrote: "All such 'feelings'… normally take the form, in my experience, of motor empathy." These quotes attempt to portray *empathy* as a tangible and measurable expression of brain functioning, namely motoric activity, thereby presaging subsequent recognition of the mirror neuron system (di Pellegrino, Fadiga, Fogassi et al. 1992). However, this reification of empathy as muscular activity abjures the subtlety and ephemeral qualities of thoughts and feelings as suggested in a recent analysis (Ganczarek, Hünefeldt and Olivetti Belardinelli 2018) of the thinking of the German philosopher Robert Vischer (1847–1933) who is credited with inventing the term *Einfühlung* as a predominantly aesthetic formulation (Vischer 1873).

While having less palpable manifestations than motoric activity, thoughts and feelings are essential for the second definition of *empathy* that has come to be used in Psychology and in everyday parlance: "The ability to understand and appreciate another person's feelings, experience, etc." An early example in the English language of this use of *empathy* appeared in an article describing a form of psychotherapy in *the dynamics of non-directive psychotherapy* (Meister and Miller 1946): "A 'man-to-man' regard for the client, characterized (ideally) by the understanding of empathy without the erratic quality of identification or the supportiveness of sympathy." Perhaps a less technical and more easily understood example is found in a quotation of Sir Cecil Beaton (1904–1980), the British fashion, portrait and war photographer noted for his depictions of the British Royal Family (Beaton and Buckle 1979): "It is her [sc. the Queen Mother's] empathy and her understanding of human nature that endears her to everyone she talks to." This last perspective of empathy is now recognized as fundamental to the practice of medicine, especially to psychiatry and the field of addiction.

Empathy must be distinguished from the commonly used word *sympathy*. While these words are often confused in common vernacular, their different etymologies reveal that they are conceptually distinct. Sympathy is derived from late Latin *sympathia,* which, in turn, originated from the Greek συμπάθεια, comprised of συμπαθής ("having a fellow feeling"), a combining of the prefix σύν (Latinized sym, meaning "having the same or a like form") and παθ-, which is the root of πάθος ("suffering, feeling") from πάσχειν ("to suffer"). The original meaning of *sympathy* is: "A (real or supposed) affinity between certain things, by virtue of which they are similarly or correspondingly affected by the same influence, affect or influence one another (especially in some occult way), or attract or tend towards each other." An example of the first use of this meaning in the English language can be found in *The arte and science of preseruing bodie and soule*, a volume written by the Welsh physician John Jones (1644 or 1645—1709) on the care of infants and small children that he dedicated to Queen Elizabeth I (1579): "Plato also testifieth suche a Sympathia to be betweene the bodye and the soule, that if either exceede the meane, the one suffereth with the other." Accordingly, the appearance of sympathy in the English language predates empathy by more than three centuries, suggesting that the conceptual basis of empathy was relatively late in the development of European languages and that sympathy may embody a more primal emotion. All the same, there are overlapping elements in the emotions these words represent (and in their neurobiological underpinnings discussed below) as suggested by a quote from Robert L. Katz (1933–2010), an American social and organizational psychologist who created the concept of managerial skills (1963): "It is true that in both sympathy and empathy we permit our feelings for others to become involved."

Humans are highly social and tend to live in groups that rely on each other for survival throughout life. Collaborative human interactions require experimentally distinguishable emotional and cognitive brain functions that have become neurobiologically intertwined through evolution (Preston and de Waal 2002; Chen 2018; Heyes 2018). Shared goals and behavioral responses to environmental challenges necessitate that individuals in a group draw upon cohesive responses, based on complex behavioral phenomena, to the feelings, cognitions and expressed behavior of other members of one's "tribe" (Batson 2011). The capacity to be able to experience the world through another's perceptions and motivations appears to be a survival mechanism with primal roots (de Waal and Preston 2017).

Probably the first manifestation of this interconnectedness in humans is the mother-child bond (Bowlby 1966). The capacity to understand and appreciate another person's emotions and motivations further develops through collaborative relationships with family members. Continued involvement of the individual with their social group allows full maturation of empathy to the mutual benefit of the individual and the other members.

While it is controversial whether the foundations of *empathy* are inherited or learned (Heyes 2018), there is an expanding body of research on the neurobiological mechanisms involved (Engen and Singer 2013; Chen 2018; Lamm, Rütgen and Wagner 2019; Oscar-Berman, Ruiz, Marinkovic et al. 2021).

A mechanistic linkage to addiction research has recently emerged from findings of opioid modulation of human social learning, bonding and empathy in relation to affiliative and protective tendencies (Meier, van Honk, Bos and Terburg 2021). This *mu-opioid feedback model of social behavior* extends the role of the endogenous mu-opioid system beyond the hedonic value of pain and pleasure to have implications for stress, anxiety, depression and attachment behaviors.

Currently accepted neurobiologically-based models of empathy include the *perception-action model* and *mirror-neuron theories* (de Waal and Preston 2017). Emotional states of others may be understood by personal, embodied representations that progress to empathy based on the observer's past experiences. *Affect mirroring* in offspring and *emotional contagion* in adults are related phenomena that have been observed in many mammalian species. Mirror neurons that respond similarly to performed and observed actions were first identified in macaque monkeys, providing evidence for brain activation based on perception–action encoding in the brain (di Pellegrino, Fadiga, Fogassi et al. 1992). This finding was extended to humans using positron emission tomography by demonstrating that premotor cortex brain activation occurs on observing pictures of tools (e.g., hammers) or silently naming the use of the tool (Grafton, Fading, Arbib and Rizzolatti 1997).

The foundations of empathy in the brain were further supported by the finding that somatosensory damage resulted in impaired decoding of facial expressions of emotion (Adolphs, Damasio, Tranel et al. 2000). Overlapping neural circuits for experiencing and observing affective states, including happiness, anger, fear, disgust, sadness and pain have been delineated using neuroimaging techniques (de Waal and Preston 2017). While learning and conditioning (see Conditioning) are mechanistically important in the neurobiology of empathy, there is also evidence supporting the role of genetic determinants of attachment based on allelic variation of the oxytocin receptor gene (Insel and Young 2001; Smith, Porges, Norman et al. 2014).

Various interacting biopsychosocial risk and resilience factors have been associated with the likelihood that an individual develops addiction and the tempo at which the disorder progresses (Martin, Weinberg and Bealer 2007). While many of these determinants can be observed well before addiction is clinically manifested, others emerge subsequently as complications of the disorder *per se*. Cognitive and emotional processing that contribute to empathy can be considered as developmental precursors of executive functions, externalizing personality traits and related biopsychosocial determinants of addictive disorders (Le Berre 2019; Cristofani, Sesso, Cristofani et al. 2020; Rabin, Parvaz, Alia-Klein and Goldstein 2021). For example, empathy has been conceptualized as the converse of aggression

(Blair 2018; see Aggression) which has been found to be related to callous and unemotional behaviors (Waller and Hyde 2018) as well as the inability to verbalize one's own emotions (Psederska, Savov, Atanassov and Vassileva 2019). Thereby, empathy may be understood as inversely associated with antisocial traits, psychopathy and alexithymia which have all been implicated in etiopathogenesis of addiction (see Resilience). These ideas are supported by the suggested role of empathy in the capacity of adolescents to resist peer pressure for binge drinking (Laghi, Bianchi, Pompili et al. 2019). Of note, an analogous role for empathy may pertain to development of behavioral addictions such as out-of-control and self-destructive internet use (Jiao, Wang, Peng and Cui 2017).

The multifaceted biopsychosocial trait of *empathy* can have an even wider role in development and course of addiction. As an individual progresses in addiction, neuroadaptive brain changes accumulate so that the salience of alcohol/drugs and related behaviors overwhelms the behavioral repertoire, diminishing the capacity of the individual to stem their engagement in the self-destructive behaviors with which they struggle (see Salience). Additionally, the capacity of the addicted individual for empathy is progressively diminished with less ability to consider complex behavioral phenomena as the feelings, cognitions and expressed behavior of other members of their social group. Such diminution of empathy has been associated in neuroimaging studies with disturbed neural circuit connectivities among relevant brain regions (Wei, Wu, Bi and Baeken 2021; Baez, Fittipaldi, de la Fuente et al. 2021). Accordingly, human relationships of the addicted individual suffer to a considerable extent as obtaining, using and recovering from the effects of the drug take precedence over everything else in the behavioral repertoire.

Re-acquiring empathy via interactions with a social network seems to be an important component of recovery from addictive disorders (Preller, Hulka, Vonmoos et al. 2014; Rupp, Junker, Kemmler et al. 2021; see Recovery). Among those in whom this trait is primarily lacking, acquiring empathy may be a part of recovery from addiction as suggested by the finding that socio-cognitive deficits and cluster B personality traits of chronic cocaine users correlated with cocaine use as reflected by concentrations of cocaine in hair (Vonmoos, Eisenegger, Bosch et al. 2019). Hence, abstinence orientation and training of social cognition and interaction might improve social functioning and should be considered an important therapeutic element in treatment of addictive disorders. This focus on social functioning and empathy for others who are also on the road to recovery from addiction is clearly demonstrated by the processes involved in participation in mutual support self-help programs (Galanter 2014; Preller, Hulka, Vonmoos et al. 2014). Those who suffer from addictive disorders may also experience empathy that can promote recovery through nurturing and healing relationships with their physicians and other healthcare providers (Miller and Moyers 2015). Reduced empathy as focus for treatment is not limited to drug use disorders but extends to behavioral addictions as gambling (Tomei, Besson and Grivel 2017).

In summary, *empathy* is essentially a biopsychosocial *resilience* factor in development and progression of drug use disorders and behavioral addictive disorders. Due to the increasing salience of out-of-control and self-destructive behaviors that are incompatible with and supplant empathy, addiction is a disorder characterized by disruption of collaborative human interactions. This capacity to be meaningfully engaged in human relationships with other individuals in one's "tribe" must be acquired or restored if recovery is to be achieved.

Exercise

According to the current electronic version of the Oxford English Dictionary (OED), the noun *exercise* is from Middle English, derived from the Old French *exercice* and the Provençal *exercici, exercise*. These originate from the Latin noun *exercitium*, transformed from the verb *exercēre*, which means "to keep at work, busy, employ, practise, train." The etymology of *exercēre*, according to OED, "is obscure… often regarded as having meant primarily 'to drive forth (tillage beasts),' and hence 'to employ, set to work.'" The verb *exercēre* is a combination of the Latin prefix *ex-* and the verb *arcēre* which means "to shut up, restrain." An example of the first use of *exercise* in the English language is from *c.* 1340 in the *Psalter* of Richard Rolle (*c.* 1300–1349), an English hermit, mystic and religious writer, also known as Richard Rolle of Hampole or de Hampole (Everett 1922): "I rase fra ded til lyf, fra ydelnes til excercise in godis seruys." The definition of *exercise* in this quotation is: "The action of employing in its appropriate activity (an organ, a faculty, or power), of giving practical effect to (a right), of exerting (influence or authority); the state or condition of being in active operation."

Of the many definitions of *exercise*, the one that seems most relevant to addiction is: "Exertion of the muscles, limbs, and bodily powers, regarded with reference to its effect on the subject; especially such exertion undertaken with a view to the maintenance or improvement of health." This sense of the word was first used *c.* 1386 in *Nun's Priest's Tale* a part of *Canterbury Tales* by Geoffrey Chaucer, the English poet and author widely considered the greatest English poet of the Middle Ages (Chaucer 2013): "Attempre dyete was al hir phisik, And exercise and hertes suffisaunce." Later quotations support the role of exercise in health and a balanced life. Francis Bacon (1561–1626), the English philosopher and statesman who served as Attorney General and as Lord Chancellor of England and was highly influential in the scientific revolution, expressed in his *Sylva sylvarum* (Bacon and Rawley 1626): "Use not Exercise and a Spare Diet..if much Exercise, then a Plentifull Diet." This quote accurately expresses the fundamental principle of nutrition, specifically, calories must be consumed via food to sustain exercise. John Dryden (1631–1700), the English poet, literary critic, translator and playwright who was appointed England's first Poet Laureate in 1668 and dominated the literary life of Restoration England, wrote in his *Fables Ancient and Modern* (Dryden 1774): "The Wise, for Cure, on Exercise depend." Dryden herein referred to the role of exercise in prevention and healing of disease. Samuel Johnson (1709–1784), an English writer who made lasting contributions to English literature as a poet, playwright, essayist, moralist, literary critic, biographer, editor and lexicographer in 1779, wrote in *The letters of Samuel Johnson*

(1992): "Exercise is labour used only while it produces pleasure." Johnson's quotation points to a paradoxical aspect of exercise – even though it can cause the physical exhaustion of labor, nevertheless, it may be rewarding to some.

Exercise has been considered desirable throughout history, as physical exertion, despite exhaustion, can lead to a balanced and healthy life and can also provide joy. Hence, physicians deemed it appropriate to prescribe exercise for various medical indications. Sir Arthur Brooke Faulkner (1769–1845), an English physician who served with the army in Spain, Holland, Sicily and Malta and was knighted in 1815 for his service, recommended exercise for dyspepsia and attributed beneficial effects to consequences on the integument of the body (1806):

> "…I have been enabled, by experiments repeatedly and cautiously instituted, to ascertain that a few minutes only of exercise, conducted so as to induce perspiration, have enabled a dyspeptic person to digest a quantity of food which a whole day of his accustomed sluggish exercise was inefficient for. It was necessary, however, to employ the exercise just before eating. I hold it, therefore, as a circumstance of indispensable consequence in the treatment of dyspepsia that exercise be employed to the extent of promoting a free and copious perspiration; and I conceive that the less violent the exertions are for this purpose, the effects will be the more happy and permanent. It should be an object of the first consequence, in the treatment of this disease, to derive to the skin in these cases where dryness of the cuticle opposes this derivation. In such cases, those means which have been termed indirect are the only ones upon which any perfect confidence can be placed. The exhibition of medicines, and the regulations of diet, in such cases, ought to be regarded only as auxiliary and co-operative.

> "It has long been observed, that there subsists a very remarkable sympathy between the stomach and surface of the body. There is scarcely an aphorism in medicine more hackneyed. It seems, therefore, extraordinary that it should not be more attended to in the treatment of the disease I have been considering. Since it is our great object to effect a change in the functions of depraved digestion, when the cure of dyspepsia is undertaken, one obvious method of effecting this, according to the principle I have alluded to, is to produce a change in the surface.

But this does not seem to be accomplished by exercise, except by inducing its perspiring condition."

To truly appreciate the wisdom of Faulkner's recommendation, it should be emphasized that, in his time, *dyspepsia* signified a great many disorders, a number of which are now viewed as having significant psychosomatic underpinnings. Moreover, many conditions that result in dyspepsia, in common parlance termed *indigestion*, are actually due to *overindulgance* in food and drink, evocative of what today are considered addictive disorders. Robert Kinglake (1765–1842), an English physician known as a medical writer, emphasized the broad clinical swath of this diagnosis and that such conditions are particularly difficult to treat (1802):

"The experienced medical practitioner will admit that a large majority of chronic diseases, and not a small proportion of those of an acute description, owe their origin to indigestion; nor will it be denied by the most intelligent of the profession, that the difficulties in the way of restoring the stomach to a due performance of its digestive function, are such as often to baffle the most approved modes of treatment."

These early 19th century quotations describe the beneficial effect of regular, perspiration-inducing exercise in medical management of a range of chronic conditions, understood as dyspepsia, but also including mental disorders and over-indulgence in food and drink.

Very much research was needed before the *intuitive* prescription of exercise for the very wide range of disorders implied by "dyspepsia" could be *scientifically* supported. Exercise was reported to activate the cardiopulmonary system along with intense muscle contractions (Smith 1859). That substantial energy expenditures occurred without detectable increase of body temperature was first recognized by the English physician known for his invention of the clinical thermometer, Sir Thomas Clifford Allbutt (1836–1925), upon carefully monitoring his own body temperature during a strenuous ascent of Mont Blanc. The lack of a significant elevation of body temperature despite energy combustion from exercise, has been shown to be due to hypothalamic activation of heat dissipation mechanisms, among them perspiration, to maintain body temperature in the optimal range (Lomax and Schönbaum 1979). That combustion of foodstuffs is required for muscular contractions and elements of the body are catabolized in the process was suggested by the accompanying increase in urinary nitrogen output as reported by Austin Flint II (1836–1915), an American physician who carried out extensive experimental investigations in human physiology, including establishing the glycogenic function of the liver (Flint 1877). If exercise is sufficiently strenuous, it activates the sympathetic-adrenal system, much as the physiological response to threat, termed in 1920 as "fight or flight" by Walter Cannon (1871–1945), a leading American physiologist of the first part of the 20th century. Controlled and limited episodes as occur during exercise are likely not sufficient to activate the pathological stress response, initially described by Hans Selye (1907–1982), the pioneering Hungarian-Canadian endocrinologist (Selye 1937). Additionally, exercise can trigger a complex series of molecular changes in acute inflammatory markers (e.g., interleukin 6) and metabolic pathways (e.g., glycolysis and fatty acid oxidation). All in all, it is well accepted that exercise remains a pillar of cardiovascular, immune and cognitive health (Contrepois, Wu, Moneghetti et al. 2020).

Obesity has become an ever-mounting clinical challenge in recent decades. Large proportions of the population are affected (Ogden, Carroll, Curtin et al. 2006) and obesity-associated comorbidities reduce the life expectancy of severely obese persons by an estimated 5–20 years (Fontaine, Redden, Wang et al. 2003), mirroring another devastating disorder in which lifestyle interventions were the predominant treatment strategy – addiction. Clinical descriptions of over-eating in obesity share many of the characteristics of addictive disorders (Martin, Weinberg and Bealer 2007) and the neurobiology of brain reward circuitry that are activated by drugs of abuse overlay those that mediate food motivated behaviors (Volkow and Wise 2005). Exercise has, accordingly, been prescribed for the treatment of obesity with the goal of increased catabolism over food intake (Chlouverakis 1975). Pharmacologic strategies to reduce appetite, predominantly involving stimulants, have been implemented to circumvent the need for exercise and diet changes for weight reduction. However, use of stimulants have significant abuse liability and addiction potential (Craddock 1976) and such anorexigens have shown no significant advantages over behavioral approaches which include exercise (Öst and Götestam 1976).

The paradigm shift of viewing obesity as over-eating and its conceptualization as a *behavioral addiction* (Holden 2001), opened the door to treatment of drug use disorders with exercise interventions. Accumulating research has demonstrated that exercise is a potentially useful adjunct to treatment of drug or behavioral addiction. Aerobic exercise produces a host of positive psychological effects, including increased self-esteem and well-being, enhanced mood and stress reduction (Norris, Carroll and Cochrane 1990). Human and animal studies have reported that exercise produces interoceptive changes that can resemble those produced by addictive drugs, including subjective ratings of joy, pleasure and euphoria that are attributable to activation of the endogenous opioid system (Janal, Colt,

Clark and Glusman 1984) as well as increased central dopamine concentrations (Heyes, Garnett and Coates 1988). Given that many addictive drugs produce their reinforcing effects by increasing dopamine neurotransmission in mesolimbic and mesocortical pathways, chronic exercise may produce functional changes in these pathways, leaving an organism less susceptible to drug reward (Goeders and Smith 1983).

Chronic exposure to drugs of abuse as occurs in addiction causes specific regions of the brain to become responsive to drug cues, especially when a person is attempting to discontinue addictive drug use (see Salience). For example, during nicotine abstinence (see Nicotine), the presence of cigarette images has been shown by functional magnetic resonance (fMRI) to increase activation in both the mesolimbic (nucleus accumbens, amygdala and hippocampus) and the mesocortical (prefrontal cortex, orbitofrontal cortex (OFC) and anterior cingulate) dopamine circuits, in anticipation of both the reinforcing effects and the incentive salience of the drug (Due, Huettel, Hall and Rubin 2002). Specifically, the value of the drug and drug-related stimuli is enhanced at the expense of other reinforcers in the environment. The changes in brain dopamine function are likely to result in decreased sensitivity to natural reinforcers since dopamine also mediates the reinforcing effects of natural reinforcers and on disruption of frontal cortical functions, such as inhibitory control and salience attribution (Volkow, Fowler and Wang 2003). It seems reasonable that exercise, due to its own rewarding effects, can serve to compete with salience of drugs of abuse.

The most compelling evidence that exercise could refocus brain activation and reduce drug cravings has come from research on nicotine addiction (Ussher, Taylor and Faulkner 2008). When cigarettes are withheld, smokers show increased activation of the OFC when presented with cigarette-related cues, along with increased cravings. Following exercise and exposure to the same cues, the previously activated areas of the frontal cortex become less activated. This suggests that following exercise, individuals find cigarette stimuli less salient and demonstrate less cravings and activation of OFC, supported by behavioral data that exercise reduces subjective desire to smoke and that cue-elicited cravings are attenuated (see Craving). Taken together, these results demonstrate that exercise can reduce the motivational drive (via OFC activation) towards smoking even in the presence of smoking stimuli although other neurobiological mechanisms may be relevant, such as stress reduction, altered mood and enhanced well-being and motivation for health. An exercise intervention was also associated with diminished salience and craving for cannabis cues and reduced use in individuals who previously expressed no intention to stop using cannabis (Buchowski, Meade, Charboneau et al. 2011; Charboneau,

Dietrich, Park et al. 2013). Additionally, benefits of exercise programs may extend to neuropsychiatric benefits and cognitive outcomes for subjects with co-occurring psychiatric diagnoses and drug use disorders (Ashdown-Franks, Firth, Carney et al. 2020)

Epidemiological studies report that participation in activities that promote physical fitness is associated with a lower incidence of tobacco and substance use among adolescents (Field, Diego and Sanders 2001). These findings support the use of exercise in both prevention and treatment of addiction (see Prevention). Interestingly, over-eating has become the major cause of steatohepatitis, a disorder that was in the past a signal of alcohol use disorder (James and Day 1999), and exercise is a cornerstone of its treatment (Linden, Sheldon, Meers et al. 2016). Additionally, bariatric surgery, the most efficient means of treating severe obesity has been found to have a post-surgical risk of development of new-onset alcoholism, possibly "trading" addictions (Hsu, Benotti, Dwyer et al. 1998; Hagedorn, Encarnacion, Brat and Morton 2007). The multiple inverse relationships between exercise and behavioral/alcohol/drug addictions suggest a potential evolutionary role of physical activity in maintenance of physical and emotional health that has been dislocated by our affluent society. More important, these observations point to the importance of exercise to help recreate the level of activity that is required to maintain health and vitality (Warburton, Nicol and Bredin 2006) we appear to have lost in the "developed" world.

Gambling

The noun *gambling*, according to the current electronic version of the Oxford English Dictionary (OED), is a derivative or variant of either the verb or noun *game* in combination with the suffix *-ing*. The verb *game* itself was formed in English by conversion of the noun *game*, inherited from Germanic, as in "Middle Dutch (rare) *game* prank, mockery, Old Saxon *gaman* jollity, entertainment, amusement, Old High German *gaman* pleasure, amusement, something that causes laughter, joy, delight… Middle High German *gamen* fun, play." The verb *game* has many meanings in OED, including the first listed meaning in the English language of this word, which was in Old English: "*intransitive*. To amuse oneself; to play, sport, jest; [occasionally] to indulge in amorous or flirtatious play". The meaning of the verb *game* that is most relevant to addiction is defined in OED as: "To take part in an indoor game, of a kind on which stakes or wagers may be placed; especially to play games of chance for such stakes or wagers; to gamble."

The definition of the noun *game* pertinent to addiction is: "An activity played for entertainment, according to rules, and related uses… An activity or diversion of the nature of or having the form of a contest or competition, governed by rules of play, according to which victory or success may be achieved through skill, strength, or good luck… in early use also chiefly restricted to indoor amusements, especially, those involving cards, dice, or playing-pieces, and to pastimes of a more or less light-hearted character." Accordingly, the noun *gambling* is defined in OED as: "The action, practice, or pastime of playing games for stakes, as cards, dice, etc., or betting money on the outcome of particular events, e.g., the result of a race or other sporting contest; (also occasionally) an instance or example of this. Also more generally: the taking of risks in the hope of gaining some advantage, benefit, or success."

The first meaning listed in OED of the verb *game* appeared in a quotation in the *Old English Hexateuch* (Dodwell and Clemoes 1974): "Þa wæs him geðuht swylce he gamenigende spræce." Although such texts are difficult to date, an approximation derives from the fact that this was a collaborative translation project during the late Anglo-Saxon period of the six books of the *Hexateuch* into Old English, presumably under the editorship of Ælfric of Eynsham (*c.* 950–1010), a Benedictine abbot of Eynsham and a scholar. An example of the first use of the verb *game* in the English language as it pertains to addiction is found in *the privy purse expenses of King Henry the Eighth* by Sir Nicholas Harris Nicolas (1799–1848), an English antiquary (Nicolas 1827): "Item delivered to the kinges grace owne handes for to game therew[t] now at this tyme of Cristemas, C *li*." An example of the first use of the noun *game* as relevant to addiction is found in *Old English glosses* (Meritt 1945): "[*Turmas*] *ludi* [*participes et laboris consortes superans*]: ga[menes]." First use of the noun *gambling* in the English language is as found in the translation of *the history of the renown'd Don Quixote de la Mancha* by Peter Antoine Motteux (1663–1718), a French-born English author, playwright and translator (Cervantes Saavedra 1700): "The Room where it stood was an old gambling Cock-loft [Spanish *un camaranchón*]."

Many quotations in OED reflect the stigma associated with *gambling*, especially as it relates to addiction, wantonness and crime: "The three glorious purposes of gluttony, drunkenness and gambling (Anonymous 1778)"; "She had an in-bred abhorrence of gambling" (Roberts 1792); and "Robberies are a natural consequence of universal gambling" (Darwin, Fitzroy and King 1839). Additionally, there are expressed concerns about the harmful *consequences of gambling* for those who partake, but also gambling as a societal responsibility (Westcott 1897): "The State… must deal in some way with gambling." In fact, government legislation can pertain to gambling much as it does to other criminal activities or to drugs of abuse (Gover 1964): "The Senator gave the green light go-ahead for the recent crack down on gambling and prostitution." The role of government regulation appears needed because engagement in gambling affects even those who do not have resources to waste and can be devastating to all social strata (Vaughan 1906): "This passion for gambling is not, I am sorry to say, confined to the Smart Set." Various of these quotations about gambling intimate shared features with addiction, a theme destined to appear as future studies elucidate the mechanistic underpinnings of these disorders (Potenza 2008).

A quotation by Richard Whately (1787–1863), an English academic, logician, economist and theologian, in his *Introductory Lessons on Morals* reflected on the role of gambling (chance-taking) in human behavior. He sensibly observed that gambling can be practiced without the exchange of valued objects or currency (Whately 1857):

> "People may, and often do, play at games of chance without any stake at all. And again, at billiards, which is altogether a game of skill, much gambling often takes place."

Therefore, behaviors characteristic of gambling (chance-taking) should not *per se* be pathologized as there are many who engage in these activities for entertainment without negative consequences, much as those who drink alcohol in moderation.

Seeking, engaging in and observing others in exciting activities can be thrilling and joyful even if the anticipation does not produce the hoped-for outcomes because they are due more or less to chance. Such activities are present in the behavioral repertoire as play from an early stage of life (Hutt and Bhavnani 1972). They comprise the underpinnings of exploration, observation, experiencing and seeking to understand one's world, which may underpin being a spectator at a sports event or betting on the outcome; playing hide-and-seek, cards or the stock market; and scientific discovery. Risk/chance-taking is a normative aspect of personality and behavior (Chiu and Storm 2010) — it is the degree to which gambling is practiced and its consequences that can disrupt a normally balanced life that render it pathological.

Gambling was first considered to belong in the realm of anthropological studies of human interactions and their expression in forms of play (Roberts, Arth and Bush 1959). Henry Lesieur, author of a classical description of the psychological and sociological aspects of compulsive gambling, *The Chase: Career of the Compulsive Gambler* (1977) wrote (Lesieur 1985):

> "Archaeologists have found evidence of sheep ankle bones (called astragals) being used to cast lots, and anthropological field work with primitive cultures shows they cast lots to decide which way to hunt and whether a person was guilty of violating the rules of society. The movement from casting lots to complex gambling games is a simple one. Many tribal peoples (including American Indians) were avid gamblers. Excavations of Egyptian, Chinese, and Indian sites have uncovered artifacts of gambling games as well as writings attempting to explain the origins of gambling and describing gods playing gambling games. Historians have uncovered evidence that whether legal or not, gambling has persisted and so have problems associated with it. Slaves, kingdoms, and fortunes have been won and lost using dice, cards, chariot races, horse races, and numerous other gambling events."

Subsequently, analyses of the mathematical properties of the games and how a person performed became a subject of scientific inquiry (Dale 1958):

> "It is well known that subjective ideas of probability differ from predictions made using statistical laws.

> "It is also well known that persons in general like to gamble. If they have the choice of a number of different courses of action which, on the average, will yield the same benefit, they will prefer to risk some loss in order to chance some

gain, rather than to choose a course which has a certain outcome. This preference has been shown in laboratory studies.

"Did the more intelligent subjects have sophisticated ideas about subjective probability, or did they have the usual ideas but prefer to use the alternative, systematic, approach? In order to throw light on this question the results of my subjective probability study were re-examined from the point of view of intelligence. This showed that intelligence and subjective probability were not related. It would seem, then, that intelligence determined not the hunches the man had, but whether he chose to be guided by them."

Descriptive studies of the phenomenology of games humans play and *gambling behaviors* eventually led to formulations of mathematical theories of probabilities of given outcomes as well as brain functions involved in decision-making, which, in turn, revolutionized many disciplines, including economics, psychology, neurology and psychiatry (Von Neumann and Morgenstern 1947; Bechara, Damasio, Tranel and Damasio 1997; Sanfey, Rilling, Aronson et al. 2003). Moreover, new ways of considering decision-making in pathological gamblers has led to identification of similar dysfunctions in neuropsychological, psychophysiological, neuroimaging, neurochemical and genetic studies as those with alcohol and other drug use disorders (Goudriaan, Oosterlaan, de Beurs and Van den Brink 2004; Potenza 2008; Lawrence, Luty, Bogdan et al. 2009). Consequently, even though gambling-related activities can be considered part of the normal behavioral repertoire, out-of-control and self-destructive gambling came to be considered a significant mental health concern (Martin, Weinberg and Bealer 2007):

"Partly as a consequence of [the] greatly expanded venues for gambling, it is estimated that 80 to 90 percent of adults gamble to some extent. Gambling, then, affects a substantially greater proportion of the population than alcohol and drugs do. In general, as the availability of gambling opportunities expands, so does the proportion of the population that develops problems associated with gambling. Therefore, as gambling has spread, compulsive gambling has been on the rise. It is now estimated that 1 to 2 percent of the adult population of the United States are compulsive or pathological gamblers..."

Only relatively recently has *gambling* found acceptance in the realm of medicine, as a psychopathological construct and a psychiatric disorder in its own right (American Psychiatric

Association 1980). A distinct syndrome, the pathological expression of chance-taking activities that comprise gambling and its consequences, are now included in the Diagnostic and Statistical Manual of the American Psychiatric Association (DSM-5) as an *addictive disorder* termed *gambling disorder* (2013). *Gambling disorder* includes features which strongly resemble alcohol and drug use disorders: preoccupation with and the persistent urge to gamble with dysphoria when unable to gamble or trying to stop (withdrawal); loss-of-control over gambling and forgoing other activities that comprise a balanced life; the need to progressively increase the money that is put at risk (tolerance); denial about the extent of gambling and losses; using gambling to ease depressed mood or tension and anxiety (self-medication); and loss of relationships, job or a significant career opportunity. In addition, there are rather specific aspects of gambling disorder, namely, repeatedly attempting to win back gambling losses and relying on others for money to deal with financial problems caused by gambling (American Psychiatric Association 2013). Gambling means the willingness to risk something of value in the hope of getting something of even greater value with little objective likelihood of success. Therefore, *gambling disorder* is rightfully considered an addictive disorder, the uncontrollable urge to keep gambling (loss-of control) despite the toll it takes on one's life (self-destructive).

The epistemological *evolution* of our understanding of the pathophysiology of gambling disorder prior to its acceptance as a *bone fide* mental disorder has resembled the course but not the more measured progression of alcoholism or other drug use disorders (see Alcoholism). The centuries required for emergence of alcoholism as a psychiatric disorder have seemingly been telescoped to about a half century of human history for recognition of *gambling*. The devastation of gambling behaviors has been part of our literary heritage (Dostoevsky 1964) and has been considered in psychoanalytic thinking as expression of a neurotic form of development (Lindner 1950). However, the veritable leap of gambling into public awareness as a disease is perhaps most related to accelerating development of communication media (McLuhan 1964) which have provided the ideal venues for expression of pathological gambling behaviors and their consequences (Fauth-Bühler and Mann 2017). The following are considered the important milestones in the evolution in our understanding of gambling disorders (Lesieur 1985): 1) the emergence of the *disease concept* of pathological gambling; 2) founding of Gamblers Anonymous in Los Angeles in 1957 by Jim Willis (Jim W.), an alcoholic who applied his experience in Alcoholics Anonymous in the new self-help mutual support (12-step) program; and 3) implementation of pioneering treatment in the medical milieu by Dr. Robert L. Custer (1927-1990) at Brecksville, Ohio Veterans Administration Hospital. However, the first scientific journal devoted to pathological gambling (*Journal of Gambling Behavior*) was not founded until 1985, consistent with the relatively late arrival of gambling in the realm of biomedicine.

It is of both historical and nosological significance that when the pathological complement of gambling behaviors was first recognized as a psychiatric disorder by the American Psychiatric Association in DSM-III (1980), it was classified as a disorder of *impulse control* rather than an *addiction* (Lesieur and Rosenthal 1991; Clark 2014). Internet gaming disorder, a recent arrival to psychopathologic and nosologic debates, was considered a "condition for further study" in DSM-5, although current evidence suggests that internet gaming disorder shares very similar neurobiological substrates with gambling disorder (Fauth-Bühler and Mann 2017). Both disorders have as their neurobiological underpinnings impulsivity, compulsivity and sensitivity to reward and punishment. As discussed above, the phenomenology of gambling disorder has much in common with that of addiction and neurobiological research continues to support this nosological decision by the American Psychiatric Association (Reuter, Raedler, Rose et al. 2005; Potenza 2008). All the same, the debate about whether inclusion of gambling disorder as a mental disorder is justified has continued (Martin and Petry 2005).

The issue of nosology is at the heart of diagnosis and treatment. However, inclusion of gambling disorder as an addictive disorder becomes a moot point unless it can also be demonstrated that the neurobiological findings are consistent with those of addiction. Potenza (2008) reviewed data on the neurobiology of pathological gambling and considered its conceptualization as a behavioral addiction. He found impulsivity as an underlying construct for both drug and behavioral addictions and presented brain imaging findings investigating the neural correlates of craving states in pathological gambling which compared to those for cocaine use disorder. Blanco, Hanania, Petry et al. (2015) employed a statistical model, originally developed for contributory factors in major depression, to model the development of pathological gambling. After statistically adjusting for recognized risk factors, nicotine dependence and independent stressful life events predicted life-time pathological gambling. Additionally, despite the large proportion of variance accounted for by life-time history of pathological gambling, past-year nicotine dependence and personality disorders were also associated significantly with 12-month pathological gambling. This supports parallels between gambling and drug use disorders and especially, the abuse of drugs with psychostimulant effects. The relevance of disturbances in frontoparietal, salience and default mode neural circuits have recently been demonstrated for individuals with both cocaine use disorders (Yip, Scheinost, Potenza and Carroll 2019) and those with internet gaming disorder (Liu, Potenza, Lacadie et al. 2020). Finally, treatment of gambling and internet use disorders have many parallel strategies to those employed for alcohol/drug use disorders and continue to be equally challenging and important to pursue due to their prevalence and significant negative consequences for mental health (Petry 2003; Koo, Wati, Lee and Oh 2011; King, Wölfling and Potenza 2020).

Intoxication

According to the current electronic version of Oxford English Dictionary (OED), *intoxication* is the noun of the action *intoxicate*, which is the participial stem of the medieval Latin verb *intoxicāre*. Specifically, *intoxicate* is a merging of the prefix *in-* with *toxicāre*, meaning "to smear with poison"; in Latin, poison is *toxicum*, derived from the Greek *τοξικόν*. Understandably, *intoxicate* was initially defined as "to poison" but more recently has come to mean: "To stupefy, render unconscious or delirious, to madden or deprive of the ordinary use of the senses or reason, with a drug or alcoholic liquor; to inebriate, make drunk" or "To stupefy or excite as with a drug or alcoholic liquor; to render unsteady or delirious in mind or feelings; to excite or exhilarate beyond self-control." This historical progression of meanings encapsulates a paradox that persists to this day: whether the intoxication process *per se* should be understood as toxic, harmful, and akin to self-poisoning, or rather, as rewarding, a positive experience, likely to be repeated, and thereby represents the underpinnings of addiction, which may eventually be complicated by organ pathology (see Addiction). In the former view, it is the drug that poisons and is the culprit, whereas in the later it is the out-of-control use of an agent (that may be harmful only if consumed in sufficient quantity) that eventually overwhelms the behavioral repertoire.

A version of the word *intoxicate* was first used in the English language (despite the French title of the book) in 1530 by John Palsgrave (*c.* 1485-1554), a priest and tutor in the royal court of Henry VIII of England, in his *L'esclarcissement de la langue francoyse* (1972): "I intoxycat, I poyson with venyme." This quotation refers to a meaning of *intoxicate*, the act of poisoning, now considered obsolete usage according to OED, even though medical science has repeatedly demonstrated that repeated administration of most drugs of abuse is associated with toxicity independent of psychoactive effects (Abbott 1896). The use of *intoxicate* that more closely corresponds with the current meaning was expressed (1885) by the Elizabethan geographer Richard Hakluyt (*c.* 1552-1616): "It..goeth downe very pleasantly, intoxicating weake braines." The word *intoxication* seems to have acquired the meaning it now has in the field of addiction by the second half of the 17th century, suggested by a quotation from Sir Thomas Browne (1605- 1682), the English polymath and physician (1672): "The prevalent intoxication is from the spirits of drink dispersed into the veynes and arteries." Historically, the term *intoxication* was most used with respect to overindulgence in alcohol. However, the word reflects a generic phenomenon, the subjective and objective effects on the nervous system and other organs of the body of self-administration of any psychoactive agent. These consist of a wide range of consequences on physical and mental functioning governed by the characteristic pharmacological actions of the particular agent in the individual within their psychosocial context, often including altered mood, sensorium, consciousness and reaction to the environment and impaired insight and judgement (Mitford, L'Estrange and Harness 1870): "He [Coleridge] had for some time relinquished his English mode of intoxication by brandy and water for the Turkish fashion of intoxication of opium." Recognition of *intoxication* as a temporary state of compromised mental and bodily functions necessitated formal consideration of the term in social mores and the legal system. For example, Jeremy Bentham (1748-1832), the English philosopher, jurist and social reformer and founder of modern utilitarianism viewed the state of intoxication as non-contributory in adjudication of criminal activity (1789): "The English law does not admit intoxication as a ground of excuse." On the other hand, in ancient Greece, not being of sound mind due to intoxication was considered a crime *per se* (Plato and Jowett 1875): "In Sparta…anyone found in a state of intoxication is severely punished."

The fundamental determinants of the state of *intoxication* are based on the pharmacological actions of the agent, the dose and time course of self-administration, as well as previous experience with the drug (Martin et al. 1995). We have known, probably even before the time of Seneca (c. 4 BC-AD 65), the Roman Stoic philosopher, statesman and dramatist, that "every vice is loosened and comes forth" upon intoxication with alcohol (Motto and Clark 1990). Also, that "When wine's fierce power has taken effect on a man, and its heat has disseminated and spread into his veins, his limbs grow heavy, the wobbling man's legs are impeded, his tongue falters, his mind is soused, his eyes swim: shouting gasping, quarreling ensue." More recently Benjamin Rush (1746 – 1813), a physician and signer of the United States Declaration of Independence described alcohol intoxication as:

> "…unusual garrulity…unusual silence…a disposition to quarrel…uncommon good humor and an insipid simpering or laugh…disclosure of their own or other people's secrets…a rude disposition to tell those persons in company whom they know, their faults…certain extravagant acts which indicate a temporary fit of madness."

The now well recognized clinical characteristics of intoxication with alcohol or other central nervous system depressants include anxiolysis, disinhibition, somnolence, impaired attention and memory, slurred speech, incoordination, unsteady gait and nystagmus, possibly progressing to stupor or coma (Martin, Lovinger and Breese 1995); when memory is disproportionately affected, the so-called *blackout* may occur (see Blackout). Understanding that this complement of findings constitutes a clinical syndrome that might be quantified not simply described, dates to more recent times. The beginning of this approach to a classificatory system of intoxication is exemplified in *Phenomena of the More Advanced Stages of Intoxication, with Cases and Dissections* by Francis Ogston (1803–1887), a professor of medical jurisprudence in Aberdeen (Ogston 1833):

> "The present attempt to illustrate, from personal observation, the phenomena usually presented by the more advanced stages of intoxication from spirituous liquors, it is hoped will not be deemed supererogatory… The facts which follow have been chiefly derived from the notes of cases treated at the Police Office of this city for some years back, and the histories having been drawn up either on the spot, or very soon after they were observed, their accuracy may be relied on."

In Ogston's examination, the so-called "Phenomena of the more Advanced Stages of Intoxication" included examination of the pupils, pulse, sensorium, extremities, face and breathing and based on these findings:

> "two or three natural groups have been formed, of which, while the members are found to differ considerably from each other, yet the cases in each, when considered as a separate class, present a corresponding degree of mutual resemblance. Thus, if we take the cases which agree in having a contracted pupil, they coincide as much, it will be seen, as regards the state of the circulation, respiration, and animal temperature, as they differ in these respects from the remainder. The cases with dilated pupil have fewer symptoms in common, but their disagreement will be considerably lessened if this class be subdivided into two sets, the one with dilated pupil and imperceptible pulse, and the other with a like condition of the eye, but with less prostration of the circulation. In the remarks which follow, this arrangement, though liable to some objections, will be adopted."

The next advance in understanding intoxication parallels the emergence of pharmacology as a new scientific discipline in the mid-19th century, with the founding at the University of Dorpat in Estonia of the first pharmacological institute by Rudolf Buchheim (1820-1879), whose student Oswald Schmiedeberg (1838-1921) was generally recognized as the founder of modern pharmacology. From the pharmacologic perspective, it became apparent that the clinical observations regarding intoxication could be related to the dose and the agent that was self-administered. Furthermore, with advances in chemical analysis it was clear that estimates of how much of the agent was consumed and the level of resulting impairment could be predicted from measurement of concentrations of the inciting agent in body fluids (Carter 1927). A challenge when elucidating dose-response relationships of a drug of abuse is specificity of the intoxication syndrome with respect to changes of brain functioning due to various other causes (Engel, Webb and Ferris 1945). Additionally, when the patient has self-administered more than one drug of abuse simultaneously, the dose-response relationship may be disturbed.

As mentioned above, the syndrome of intoxication is determined by the pharmacological actions of the self-administered agent (Martin, Lovinger and Breese 1995). For example, intoxication with stimulants is characterised by mental stimulation (euphoria, hypervigilance, anxiety, tension, anger, impaired judgement), psychomotor agitation (stereotyped behaviors, dyskinesias, dystonias), energy (decreased need for sleep), anorexia, autonomic arousal (tachycardia, hypertension, pupillary dilation, perspiration, chills), cardiac arrythmias, respiratory depression, confusion and seizures. Intoxication with opioids is quite different but with some overlapping features: activation or "rush" and sedation/apathy or "nod"; euphoria or dysphoria, facial flushing or warmth; impaired judgment, attention or memory; analgesia, constipation, pupillary constriction and drowsiness; respiratory depression, areflexia, hypotension, tachycardia; and in the most severe cases, apnea, cyanosis and coma. It can probably be predicted that these different classes of drugs which have distinctly different pharmacological effects can be combined by either the physician to therapeutically modify intoxication (Hargrove and Ford 1952) or by patients to augment or modify their experience of intoxication (Jasinski and Preston 1986). Moreover, it is apparent that physicians who see patients who have been experimenting with combinations of drugs of abuse, may have considerable difficulty distinguishing the cause of intoxication based on the characteristics of the manifested clinical presentation alone and might require the assistance of toxicology laboratory for clarification (Martin, Lovinger and Breese 1995).

It is also challenging for many physicians to distinguish *intoxication* from *withdrawal* as these manifestations are closely related in most clinical situations. Whereas the clinical findings of intoxication are an expression of the specific pharmacological actions of the drug of abuse, withdrawal is typically the opposite progression of events enhanced by the accompanying stress response (see Withdrawal). It is meaningful to dichotomize these phenomena only if one recognizes that they represent stages of a *longitudinal* process, namely the interaction between an individual and a self-administered psychoactive agent — intoxication always progresses to a withdrawal syndrome, which for central nervous system depressants can be as minor as a hangover to as severe as *delirium*, the severity being a function of dose and duration of exposure of the drug of abuse and previous experience with the drug. The likelihood of confusing intoxication and withdrawal is illustrated in the following characterization of intoxication as a "brain fever" (Armstrong 1813):

> "There is an interesting disorder of the brain, the effect of intoxication, and which deserves infinitely more attention from the faculty in general than, as far as I know, it has hitherto received… This disease, which I shall continue to designate brain-fever, is preceded by restlessness, defective recollection, paleness of the face, and slight tremors of the limbs; by anxiety, and irregularity of thought. At first the patient's slumbers are short, and interrupted by frightful dreams; but he soon becomes watchful, and passes days and nights without sleep; he dislikes to be alone, and if his friends have him in private, he is clamorous till they return, or goes about the house in search of them. His appetite is considerably diminished, and he frequently loaths the very sight of animal food. He is more especially sick at the stomach towards the morning; he often vomits his breakfast; and the slightest exercise, or agitation of mind, produces perspiration. As the complaint advances, the skin becomes hot and dry, the tongue parched, and the pulse weak and rapid. The surface of the body, however, soon grows cooler, and is covered with sweat, and the tongue puts on a cleaner appearance; but the irregularity of mind increases; the patient imagines that his friends are all conspiring against him, or that they have suffered some great misfortune, in which he is himself deeply implicated: — at other times he supposes that his chamber is haunted by spectres, and furiously calls for assistance to drive them away; or supposes that he is in a prison, and that his friends have all deserted him; sometimes, however, he is in high spirits, laughing and talking by turns incessantly. Occasionally, too, he converses with the medical attendant about his ordinary business, with apparent precision; tells him that he has been continually engaged and walked or rode to several places in the neighbourhood, since he last saw him, when, in reality, he had never left his own room: — at the next visit he mistakes the physician for some other person and loads him with abuse. If anyone happen to contradict him, he most pertinaciously adheres to his opinion, and becomes highly indignant. If he be soothingly dealt with, he will sometimes answer questions readily and distinctly; but if many

interrogations be put to him in succession, he grows confused, and relapses into delirium.

"The symptoms already described continue more or less urgent for four, five or six, and seldom longer than 10 days. If the patient falls into a sound and tranquil sleep he generally wakens refreshed and collected, and from that time recovers rapidly: but short disturbed slumbers, accompanied with *subsultus tendinum*, from which the patient starts with affright, and then falls into a low muttering delirium, are amongst the most dangerous indications. I have seen one case accompanied by convulsions from the very beginning of the disease; but they were speedily subdued by a large dose of aether, and the patient recovered very well."

It is apparent to the modern reader that this comprehensive clinical description is of the phenomena *associated* with intoxication and that it incorporates the entirety of the longitudinal course from intoxication to withdrawal from alcohol. This description would certainly be more confusing in modern times when the challenge becomes unpacking intoxication and withdrawal in patients who may have been intoxicated with more than one drug of abuse simultaneously, say alcohol, methamphetamine and opioids; for example, as mentioned above, intoxication with methamphetamines shares characteristics of alcohol withdrawal.

Junkie

According to the current electronic version of the Oxford English Dictionary (OED), the noun and adjective *junkie* and its other versions *junky* and *junkey* were derived from the noun and adjective *junk* which was originally and chiefly a nautical term ("An old or inferior cable or rope; [sometimes] specifically, one used as a fender") in combination with the suffix *y* ("Used to form pet names and familiar diminutives. The forms *-y* and *-ie* are now almost equally common in proper names as such, but in a few instances one or other spelling is preferred, as Annie, Betty, Sally"). The first use of *junk*, now obsolete, dates to 1410 as documented by Sir Nicholas Harris Nicolas (1799–1848), British antiquary and author, in *A history of the royal navy from the earliest times to the wars of the French Revolution* (Nicolas 1847): "La hulk...ove lapparaill..v. ankres dont un de eux est unstokked, un junk, [etc.]."

The word *junk* has subsequently had very many quite unrelated meanings: "Old or discarded items or materials that may be reused or recycled, such as used clothing, bottles, scrap metal, worn-out machinery…"; colloquially, "Any objects, possessions, etc., which are considered to be of little or no use or value, or which make a place cluttered…"; in criminal slang, "Jewellery made from inexpensive materials or artificial gemstones…"; "Worthless or absurd ideas, talk, writing... nonsense…"; in baseball, "Pitches that rely on unpredictable movement rather than speed, such as breaking balls and knuckleballs…"; "Food that appeals to popular taste but has little nutritional value, typically having a high sugar and fat content, and often sold pre-prepared for convenience"; in slang, "The male genitals."; and in computing, "Unsolicited or unwanted email, typically in the form of advertising or promotional material sent to a large number of recipients." In addition to these meanings, there is one sense of *junk* that is widely used in slang and has acquired relevance in the field of addiction, "Any of various intoxicating or narcotic drugs, especially heroin; such drugs collectively." This meaning of *junk* was first used in the English language according to OED in the October 21, 1921, edition of *Variety* magazine: "We found out later that he was a pipe fiend... He would get a skin full of junk and tell everybody he met to drop him quick."

The slang expression *junkie* was formed from the last sense of *junk*, meaning, "A person who is addicted to drugs, especially heroin; a habitual user of drugs. Also occasionally: a drug dealer." This expression was first used in the English language in *the hobo: the sociology of the homeless man* by Nels Anderson (1889–1986), an early American sociologist who studied hobos, urban culture, and work culture (Anderson 1923): "One type of dope fiend is the Junkie. He uses a 'gun' or needle to inject morphine or heroin." The meaning of the word became firmly established in popular culture and literature with publication of the novel *Junkie* by William Seward Burroughs II (1914–1997), an American writer, visual artist and a primary figure of the Beat Generation (Burroughs 1953): "Lupita got her start with one gram of junk and built up from there to a monopoly of the junk business in Mexico City." This was Burroughs' first published work, a semi-autobiographical novel depicting his life as a drug user and dealer that came to be considered a seminal text on the lifestyle of heroin addicts in the early 1950s.

Junkie is a highly stigmatizing word which emphasizes membership of the person in the drug using culture in the periphery of society rather than recognizing them as an individual who is suffering from a medical disorder. There are many other examples of such stigmatizing language still in use that portray a similar lack of respect for the patient that are inconsistent with a humane model of addiction and its treatment as a medical condition (Saitz et al. 2021). These terms minimize the medical nature of the out-of-control and self-destructive behaviors that comprise addiction, which are pathological, can be treated and belong in the realm of psychiatry rather than the legal system as criminal activity. Much has been written about how the stigma represented by such language can adversely affect the medical care and physician's ability to alleviate the suffering of individuals who deserve better (Kelly and Westerhoff 2010, Volkow 2020).

Kindling

According to the current electronic version of the Oxford English Dictionary (OED), the noun *kindling* was formed within English from a combination of the verb *kindle* and the suffix *-ing* (used to form a noun of action). Since there were originally two distinct meanings of the verb *kindle*, the nouns that were subsequently formed have corresponding senses.

The first version of *kindle* ("With reference to a fire, flame, or flammable substance") is probably a borrowing from early Scandinavian combined with an English element used as follows: "To start or light (a fire); to set fire to, ignite (something flammable)"; "To begin to burn; to catch fire; to burst into flame"; or "To arouse, give rise to, or inflame (a feeling, emotion, etc.)". In early use of this meaning of *kindle*, it was still difficult to distinguish it from the other sense ("Of a female animal [especially a hare or rabbit]: to bring forth or give birth to [young])."

The meaning of the word *kindling* formed from the first version of *kindle* ("The action of kindle…" or "Flammable material [typically small pieces of wood or paper] used in lighting a fire") is the focus of discussion. This meaning eventually developed a very specific and intuitive sense in Medicine ("In experimental models of epilepsy: the process of producing seizures by repeated electrical stimulation of an area of the brain, or by repeated administration of chemical agents; the development of seizures following such treatment."), which evolved to include not only seizures but also facilitation of various behaviors and emotional states. It is this last meaning that pertains to the neuroscience of addiction.

The first use of *kindling* in the English language is from Middle English dated to 1324 as collected in a compendium *Reliquiae antiquae scraps from ancient manuscripts, illustrating chiefly early English literature and the English language* (Wright and Halliwell-Phillipps 1845): "Iche Edward Kynge Have yeoven of my forest the keping… To Randolph Peperking ant to his kyndlyng." This is an example of the word *kindling* referring to "a brood or litter." The first use of the meaning of *kindling* under discussion here was around 1400 in the poem *Cursor mundi* also in Middle English (Morris 1874): "His gode werkes ai to þaim ware Bot soru and kindling of care." By the 17th century, the current meaning of *kindling* is easily recognizable (Sandys 1605): "After the kindling of many precursory lights of knowledge."

The British-born neuroscientist Graham Goddard (1938—1987) was the first to recognize that lasting changes within the brain could be generated by repeated electrical stimulation of the same locus, a phenomenon for which he would coin the term *kindling* (Goddard 1967; Goddard, McIntyre and Leech 1969). Goddard emigrated to Canada where he received his doctorate in psychology under Donald Olding Hebb (1904—1985) at McGill University. Hebb has been considered the "father of neuropsychology" because of the way he was able to merge the worlds of psychology and neuroscience, a road that Goddard actively pursued through his own research. Goddard (1967) published his initial observations of the phenomenon of *kindling* in *Nature*:

> "The experiments to be reported show that daily electrical stimulation of certain sub-cortical areas of the rat brain will eventually cause convulsions even though the intensity of stimulation is relatively low and initially has no such effect.

> "The primary observation is that not one animal [of the 77 rats included in the experiment] had a convulsion on the first day [of stimulation]. …The number of days of stimulation required before the first convulsion varied considerably, the range being between 4 and 136 days.

> "[O]nce convulsions have been elicited in a given animal, subsequent convulsions occur reliably in response to stimulation. A check on the permanence of this change was made on some animals after a resting interval of several weeks… At the end of this rest interval each rat was stimulated for a maximum of 15 sec at threshold intensity. On the first day convulsions were observed in eight of the eighteen animals… Whatever the neural change responsible for the development of convulsions, it is relatively permanent.

> "All the details involved here require a great deal of further study, but one thing is quite clear; there are some areas of the rat brain in which a progressive sensitization, leading to convulsions, will result from daily stimulation for 1 min each day. It is not clear why some areas of the brain are more disposed to this sensitization than other areas. In fact, it is not known whether the phenomenon is due to local changes in the area, or to the establishment of connections with other parts of the brain. Histological examination of the site of stimulation reveals no gross peculiarities …it can be argued that the phenomenon described in the present note is analogous to learning. At the very least it is a relatively permanent change

in behaviour that depends on repeated experience… It is an appealing notion and deserves the attention of physiologists and psychologists alike."

In his subsequent publication, Goddard, McIntyre and Leech (1969) concluded that the "kindling effect":

"…was due to neuronal activation by the electrical stimulus. This conclusion receives further support from experiments showing that repeated chemical activation of the rat amygdala, with low doses of locally injected carbachol, will also mimic the kindling effect and increase the likelihood of seizure development. If it is accepted that the necessary condition for kindling is electrical activation, it is then appropriate to consider which regions of the brain can be altered in this fashion, what types of change are involved, and what types of activation are necessary… it was seen that the effect was produced mainly from the limbic system and closely associated structures... Differences in the rate of kindling were observed between different structures within the limbic system, with amygdala being the most responsive. The majority of the neocortex, thalamus and brain stem were refractory to the kindling procedures."

Goddard strongly believed that his discovery of the kindling phenomenon was mechanistically closely related to an earlier observation (Morrell 1961) made by the American neurologist Frank Morrell (1926—1996): "the development of an independent focal discharge (now called a 'mirror focus') in the hemisphere contralateral to a dominant epileptic focus." Therefore, it was in the Stanford laboratory of Morrell that Goddard decided to spend a sabbatical year. At Stanford, Goddard began to explore the relationship between *kindling* and *learning* (Goddard and Douglas 1975; Morrell 1987). Ultimately, much as Goddard had predicted, mechanistic understanding of the *kindling effect* and its similarities with learning, such as its relative permanence, positive and negative transfer effect, and involvement of the limbic system, became a fertile area of investigation (Gaito 1974).

Interestingly, Frank Morrell had also trained at the Montreal Neurological Institute (MNI). During his time in Montreal with the eminent epileptologist Herbert Jasper (1906–1999), Morrell had an opportunity to become involved in some of the first electrophysiological approaches to understanding the neuronal substrates of conditioning, brain plasticity and mechanisms of learning.

One area of early interest for Morrell was the relationship of epileptic neural activity and conditioning (Engel 2001).

Jasper was an important collaborator of Wilder Penfield (1891–1976), the American-Canadian neurosurgeon who established the MNI at McGill University with Rockefeller Foundation philanthropy. Under Penfield, the MNI became a mecca for pioneering intraoperative neural stimulation studies in patients undergoing surgical ablation of seizure foci (Hebb and Penfield 1940; Penfield, Erickson, Jasper and Harrower 1941). This work led to neuroanatomic localization of brain functions, including the cortical homunculus and a variety of mental processes such as hallucinations, illusions and *déjà* and *jamais vu*. Studying some of these neurosurgical patients, Brenda Milner (1918—), who also received her doctorate under Hebb, began to elucidate the specific role of the temporal lobes in conjunction with the limbic system in learning and memory (Scoville and Milner 1957; Penfield and Milner 1958).

Both the American neuroscientist James Olds (1922–1976) and his collaborator Peter Milner (1919–2018), a British electrical engineer who immigrated to Canada, had advanced training under Hebb. Analogous to human neurostimulation studies conducted by Penfield and colleagues at the MNI and those at other centers in awake animals (MacLean and Delgado 1953), Olds and Milner (1954) devised experiments which allowed laboratory animals to signal by their behavior which brain regions they found reinforcing on stimulation:

"A preliminary study was made of rewarding effects produced by electrical stimulation of certain areas of the brain... needle electrodes were permanently implanted at various points in the brain. Animals were tested in Skinner boxes where they could stimulate themselves by pressing a lever. They received no other reward than the electrical stimulus in the course of the experiments. The primary findings may be listed as follows: (a) There are numerous places in the lower centers of the brain where electrical stimulation is rewarding in the sense that the experimental animal will stimulate itself in these places frequently and regularly for long periods of time if permitted to do so. (b) It is possible to obtain these results from as far back as the tegmentum, and as far forward as the septal area; from as far down as the subthalamus, and as far up as the cingulate gyrus of the cortex, (c) There are also sites in the lower centers where the effect is just the opposite: animals do everything possible to avoid stimulation. And there are neutral sites: animals do nothing to obtain or to avoid stimulation. (d) The reward results are obtained more dependably with electrode placements in some areas than others, the septal area being the most dependable to date. (e) In septal area preparations, the control exercised over the animal's behavior by means of this reward is extreme, possibly exceeding that exercised by any other reward previously used in animal experimentation."

Through these experiments, Olds and Milner determined in the rat brain that the *medial forebrain bundle* (the mesolimbic pathway, a collection of dopaminergic neurons that projects from the *ventral tegmental area* to the *nucleus accumbens*) was characterized by a unique capacity to sustain self-stimulation. These brain regions became known as "reward pathways" and have become a focus in elucidation of the pathophysiologic underpinnings of addiction (Olds 1958; Kornetsky and Esposito 1981; Wise 1996; Kalivas and Volkow 2005). Moreover, these brain regions that support *self-stimulation* in animal models are also highly susceptible to the *kindling effect*.

This convergence of cellular properties supports the roles of learning, conditioning and brain plasticity in mechanistic understanding of addiction (Kalant, LeBlanc and Gibbins 1971; O'Brien 1975) and provide insight into the neuroanatomic locations at which the molecular machinery involved in its pathogenesis should be investigated (Hyman, Malenka and Nestler 2006).

The underlying physiological mechanism of the kindling effect began to be elucidated within a decade after its first description. Specifically, what are the lasting changes that occur either locally within the stimulated neuron or through neural inputs to the neuron through formation of connections with other parts of the brain? The Norwegian physiologist Terje Lømo (1935—) and the British neuroscientist Timothy Bliss (1940—) reported (Bliss and Lømo 1973; Lømo 2003) evidence for long-lasting enhancement of signal transmission between repeatedly stimulated neurons which they called *long-term potentiation* (LTP). Interestingly, Bliss received his undergraduate (1963) and doctoral (1967) education at McGill University where he likely was influenced by Hebb's theory of synaptic changes with learning.

Hebb hypothesized in *The Organization of Behavior: A Neuropsychological Theory* (1949) that permanent memory traces could be laid down by the sustained activation of reverberatory circuits, or neural networks that would echo and in effect hold the information after the event itself had passed. A permanent change in the reverberatory circuit would occur if activated to sufficient levels, thereby allowing the information to be more easily retrieved or remembered. *Enhanced synaptic efficacy* in LTP discovered by Bliss and Lømo was essentially as first proposed by Hebb.

Electrical stimulation of the pre-synaptic cell makes the synapse more responsive to future stimulation by enhancing efficacy of *signal transduction* between cells through both pre- and post-synaptic changes (Nicoll 2017). The enhanced efficacy of the synapse by LTP results from a cascade of molecular signals within relevant neurons, most importantly resulting in increased permeability of the N-Methyl-D-aspartate (NMDA) receptor channel complex and the entry of the Ca^{2+} ion into the cell (Bliss and Collingridge 1993). Associated changes occur in the expression of genes in neurons within the brain network that mediates drug reward (Hyman, Malenka and Nestler 2006; Galaj and Ranaldi 2021).

LTP is the most extensively studied model of memory at the cellular level in hippocampus (Morris, Anderson, Lynch and Baudry 1986) and has become the paradigm within which kindling-related phenomena, especially those underpinning addiction, are specifically studied at the molecular level in neurons of the reward pathway (Estill, Ribeiro, Francoeur et al. 2021).

As conduction in the nervous system is neurochemical, it is hardly surprising that the kindling effect can also be elicited by brain stimulation using proconvulsant pharmacologic agents (Baxter 1967; Goddard and Douglas 1975). So-called *chemical kindling* is exemplified by progressive decreases in seizure threshold of neurons with repeated administration of the proconvulsant psychostimulant cocaine (Stripling and Ellinwood 1977). Post and Kopanda (1975) proposed that chemical kindling effects may contribute to development of cocaine use disorder as learning-related cumulative changes in reward circuits are caused by repeated self-administration of initially subconvulsant doses of cocaine (see Cocaine).

Of note, the stimulant cocaine is not only reinforcing by enhancing dopamine neurotransmission in the reward pathways but is also proconvulsant by effects on sodium channels and excitatory neurotransmission (Martin and Patel 2017). It has been demonstrated that even a single dose of cocaine induces LTP in dopamine cells in the ventral tegmental area (Ungless, Whistler, Malenka and Bonci 2001).

Post and colleagues (Post, Uhde, Putnam et al. 1982; Post, Weiss, Smith et al. 1997) have suggested that kindling mechanisms, so called *behavioral sensitization*, may also apply to increasing behavioral responses with repetition of the same stimulus over time during a lifetime. This model may have important implications for the progressive development of psychopathology in a variety of neuropsychiatric syndromes as for example in bipolar disorder and posttraumatic stress disorder (Adamec 1990), disorders that often co-occur with drug use disorders (Martin, Weinberg and Bealer 2007).

Carbamazepine, an effective anticonvulsant for treatment of temporal lobe and limbic seizures, also inhibits the kindling effect and has been demonstrated useful as a treatment of affective illness and PTSD (Post 1982; Post, Weiss, Smith et al. 1997), also cocaine use disorder (Halikas, Crosby, Pearson and Graves 1997).

The chemical kindling effect may also provide as a heuristic explanation for progression of alcoholism throughout the course of a lifetime of drinking (Ballenger and Post 1978). Since alcohol is a central nervous system depressant, its pharmacological actions do not *per se* facilitate chemical kindling as do proconvulsant stimulants. Rather, repeated episodes of intoxication with alcohol are followed by widespread neuronal excitation during the withdrawal syndrome. Accordingly, withdrawal from central nervous system depressants can be conceptualized as resembling the kindling effect and thereby may contribute to neuroadaptive changes associated with progression of the disorder (Martin and Patel 2017).

Interestingly, chemical kindling has also been proposed to contribute to the addictive effects of cannabinoids (Karler, Calder, Sangdee and Turkanis 1984) and opioids (Tanaka, Takeshita, Kawahara and Hazama 1989), although the role of this mechanism in the respective use disorders are not as fully developed. Kindling effects with all drugs of abuse whether they are proconvulsant *per idem* may operate via learning associated mechanisms of behavioral sensitization or the increasing behavioral responses with repetition of the same stimulus (Robinson and Berridge 1993).

Mindfulness

According to the current electronic version of the Oxford English Dictionary (OED), the noun *mindfulness* was formed within English by derivation of the adjective *mindful* (common current usage, "A mental state or attitude in which one focuses one's awareness on the present moment while also being conscious of, and attentive to, this awareness. Also: the cultivation and practice of this, especially as a therapeutic technique.") and its combination with the suffix *-ness* ("Forming abstract nouns from adjectives, participles, adjectival phrases, and [more rarely] nouns, pronouns, verbs, and adverbs.").

The adjective *mindful* was, in turn, formed within English by combination of the noun *mind* ("Mental and psychic faculty. The seat of awareness, thought, volition, feeling, and memory; cognitive and emotional phenomena and powers considered as constituting a presiding influence; the mental faculty of a human being [especially as regarded as being separate from the physical]; [occasionally] this whole system as constituting a person's character or individuality") and the suffix *-ful* ("Forming adjectives with the sense 'full of, or [more generally] having or characterized by [what is expressed by the first element]'.").

Historically, the first meaning of *mindfulness*, now obsolete, is defined in OED as: "The quality or state of being conscious or aware of something; attention." The first use of the word in the English language is exemplified by a quotation of John Palsgrave (*c.* 1485–1554), a priest and tutor in the royal household of Henry VIII of England, in his instructional textbook for Englishmen learning the French language *L'esclarcissement de la langue francoyse* (Palsgrave 1972): "Myndfulnesse, pencee."

The currently used meaning of *mindfulness* is defined in OED as: "A mental state or attitude in which one focuses one's awareness on the present moment while also being conscious of, and attentive to, this awareness." Thus, the sense of the word evolved significantly from its first use, simply noticing something or being aware, to denoting a highly active process that focuses the effort of attention. This adaptation of meaning was needed, presumably, to describe some of the emerging influences from Asia on Western philosophy.

An early example appeared in the following quotation by Sir Monier Monier-Williams (1819–1899), the Boden Professor of Sanskrit at Oxford University (Monier-Williams 1889): "Extinction of lust, craving, and desire, and cessation of suffering are accomplished by perseverance in the noble eightfold path.., viz. right belief or views.., right mindfulness (sati..), [etc.]." These are highly insightful observations about the role of learning in the etiology, consequences and treatment of drug use disorders and other addictive behaviors. *Buddhism*, the book in which this quotation appeared, was intended by Monier-Williams to enhance Western understanding of the history of a spiritual tradition distinct from Christianity, practiced for centuries in distant parts of what was then the British Empire. It was from Buddhist philosophy that *spirituality* ("The fact or condition of being spiritual…, especially in nature, outlook, or behaviour; attachment to or concern for spiritual [as opposed to worldly or material] matters or pursuits; spiritual quality or character.") as distinct from Western concepts of *religion* ("A particular system of faith and worship") was popularized in Europe and America in the second half of the 20th century through *mindfulness techniques.*

Accordingly, *mindfulness* refers also to the training necessary to be able to achieve such a state of consciousness, as described in OED: "the cultivation and practice of this, especially as a therapeutic technique…[or] ….as mindfulness meditation, etc." This suggests that the state induced during mindfulness may have therapeutic benefits for lessening suffering associated with many human medical and psychiatric conditions. The etymology of the word invokes the spiritual realm and the role that mindfulness techniques have played in Eastern philosophies of living: "Frequently and originally with reference to Yoga philosophy and Buddhism…"

In the sense of a mental state or attitude, the etymologic discussion proceeds: "after Pali *sati* (as one of the steps of the Eightfold Path in fuller form *sammā-sati* right mindfulness); compare [this with the] Buddhist Sanskrit *smṛtyupasthāna*…but from the late 20th century [the technique was] increasingly taught and practised outside these contexts as a formal discipline, often involving meditation with a focus on, or acknowledgement of, one's emotions, thoughts, and bodily sensations." Coping with life's stresses by acknowledging and addressing one's "emotions, thoughts and bodily sensations" is preferable to dismissing them using problematic out-of-control and self-destructive behaviors that constitute drug use and other addictive disorders (see Self-medication). Therefore, practicing mindfulness techniques to manage the range of stimuli that have become associated with *self-medication* and related addictive behaviors are useful skills in self-management and achieving *recovery*. It is probably for this reason that the idea of *spirituality* has become foundational in the traditions and practice of 12-step mutual support programs (see (see Recovery and Self-help) for management of addiction (Miller 1990).

Behavioral management (in contradistinction to religious healing) of a wide range of physical diseases began to emerge in Western medicine, likely reflecting the evolving curiosity concerning Eastern philosophies. Scientifically, these approaches were the direct consequence of conceptualizing distressing emotions as responses to internal and environmental stimuli that can be intensely stressful for the organism (Cannon 1920; Pavlov and Gantt 1928; Selye 1937). The reasoning was that some maladaptive emotions may be perceived as stress-inducing based on previous experiences and thus, they become the source of pathologic bodily and mental changes (see Trauma). Control of these stress-inducing responses is not readily accessible to the affected individual as it is predominantly mediated by the autonomic nervous system. However, as discussed in the next paragraph, they were shown to be modifiable using conditioning, as well as related mindfulness techniques that can be taught and learned (see Conditioning). (Note that in the construct of psychodynamics the lack of access to maladaptive responses are due to their being *subconscious*, and hence, requiring another approach to treatment, namely psychotherapy.)

The therapeutic value of mindfulness techniques was first deduced from demonstration that experimental tachycardia could be conditioned in dogs (Dykman and Gantt 1956) and that behavioral training could effectively control arterial blood pressure in non-human primates (Benson, Herd, Morse and Kelleher 1969). These seminal findings were soon extended to the clinic by showing that treatment of hypertension was feasible using meditation techniques by reducing autonomic nervous system activation (Benson, Shapiro, Tursky and Schwartz 1971; Benson, Marzetta, Rosner and Klemchuk 1974). The discipline of "mind-body medicine" continues to evolve to this day (Dossett, Fricchione and Benson 2020) and it has been demonstrated that the "relaxation response" as elicited by *mindfulness techniques* may be therapeutically useful within diverse domains of medicine and psychiatry. There are now randomized, controlled trials that suggest improved outcomes and quality of life in many health conditions that are related to or are exacerbated by stress, including chronic pain, anxiety, depression, insomnia, post-traumatic stress disorder, weight control and obesity, cancer-related fatigue, inflammatory bowel disease, and cardiovascular disease (Zhang, Lee, Mak et al. 2021).

After first reporting the benefits of meditation for hypertension control, Benson (1969) suggested that similar approaches should be explored for "alleviation of drug abuse." Benson's proposal to those in the addiction field was initially met with skepticism, as indeed was the mind-medicine approach generally. This uncertainty was described by Marlatt (2002), an innovator in the field of psychological treatment approaches to addiction, in recollections of how in 1970 he first became interested in the clinical applications of meditation.

After developing borderline hypertension "as an assistant professor faced with the publish-or-perish stress of academic life," his physician recommended he engage in transcendental meditation (TD) as a desirable treatment approach, which Marlatt initially almost rejected. He indicated that this was "in sharp conflict with my training as a budding behavioral psychologist, in which overt behavior was considered more scientifically objective than anything to do with subjective mental states, much less the 'mind'." Marlatt and Gordon (1985) eventually came to realize that mindfulness techniques have important clinical applications in treatment of addictive behavioral issues and became an advocate for these techniques.

Mindfulness is now appreciated as a protective trait on the risk/resilience spectrum (see Resilience) for development of addictive disorders (Lau, Bishop, Segal et al. 2006) as well as a clinically measurable psychological attribute that is likely enhanced during addiction treatment and related to outcome (Leigh, Bowen and Marlatt 2005). There are many other primary psychopathological symptoms, such as mood and anxiety, that are triggered by stressful experiences which may also predispose an individual to addiction and are improved by mindfulness interventions.

Hofman, Sawyer, Witt and Oh (2010) conducted a meta-anlaysis of anxiety and mood symptoms in various clinical samples, including cancer, generalized anxiety disorder, depression and other psychiatric or medical conditions and found that mindfulness-based treatments were moderately effective in improving anxiety and mood symptoms. One of the first longitudinal studies to document the effects of mindfulness on drug use and heavy drinking was reported by Bowen, Witkiewitz, Clifasefi et al. (2014). There are now many studies of variable quality, some randomized and nonrandomized control trials, of the treatment of drug use disorders with mindfulness-based interventions (Cavicchioli, Movalli and Maffei 2018).

In the first meta-analysis of mindfulness treatment for substance misuse, it is reported that mindfulness treatment is a positive intervention for substance use disorders, with a small effect on use, medium effect on craving and large effect on reducing the stress associated with these disorders (Li, Howard, Garland et al. 2017). Recent studies have shown that mindfulness training has a promising potential for smoking cessation treatment (Oikonomou, Arvanitis and Sokolove 2017) and significantly improves levels of pain, physical and emotional limitations, depression and anxiety compared to treatment as usual of opioid use disorder patients in methadone maintenance treatment (Cooperman, Hanley, Kline and Garland 2021). A systematic review supported the efficacies of mindfulness-based interventions in both substance and behavioral addictions (Sancho, De Gracia, Rodríguez et al. 2018). Therefore, mindfulness-based techniques rationally belong in comprehensive pharmacopsychosocial treatments of drug use disorders and behavioral addictions, predominantly augmenting the individual's capacity for coping with stress (Martin, Weinberg and Bealer 2007).

The implementation of mindfulness-related techniques in medicine seems to have been motivated by fundamental studies of their physiological consequences. Particularly influential was the systematic investigation of meditation by Wallace (1970) concluding that:

> "There were significant changes between the control period and the meditation period in all measurements. During meditation, oxygen consumption and heart rate decreased, skin resistance increased, and the electroencephalogram showed specific changes in certain frequencies. These results seem to distinguish the state produced by transcendental meditation from commonly encountered states of consciousness and suggest that it may have practical applications."

As the benefits of mindfulness techniques were increasingly employed in medicine and psychiatry, emerging research focused on associated neurobiological changes (Dossett, Fricchione and Benson 2020; Zhang, Lee, Mak et al. 2021). Mindfulness meditation is thought to exert its effects by enhanced self-regulation, including attention control, emotion regulation and self-awareness as deduced from neuroimaging studies (Tang, Hölzel and Posner 2015).

The anterior cingulate cortex (ACC) is particularly involved in attention and is also the region in which changes in brain structure and/or neural activity have most consistently been reported in association with mindfulness meditation. The ACC is part of a network implicated in self-regulation whose connectivity changes dramatically in development in late adolescence, thus increasing ACC activity and improving self-regulation. Practicing mindfulness techniques also improves emotional regulation and reduces stress by engaging fronto-limbic networks involved in these processes. Tang and colleagues (2007) reported that students given mindfulness-related training showed greater improvement in attention, lower anxiety, depression, anger, and fatigue, and higher vigor, a significant decrease in stress-related cortisol, and an increase in immunoreactivity.

Lazar, Kerr, Wasserman et al. (2005) found that brain regions associated with attention, enteroception and sensory processing were of relatively greater volume in those who practiced meditation than in matched controls. These differences in brain regions included the prefrontal cortex and right anterior insula and the between-group differences in prefrontal cortical thickness were most pronounced in older participants, possibly offsetting age-related cortical thinning and the thickness of two of these brain regions correlated significantly with meditation experience. Brewer, Worhunsky, Gray et al. (2011) found that meditation practice has the potential to affect self-referential processing and improve present-moment awareness by altering activation of default mode networks as the midline prefrontal cortex and posterior cingulate cortex, which support self-awareness. Tang, Lu, Geng et al. (2010) reported that integrative body–mind training increases fractional anisotropy, an index indicating the integrity and efficiency of white matter, in the corona radiata, an important white-matter tract connecting the ACC to other structures.

Mindfulness techniques are a family of mental practices that encompass a wide array of exercises employing distinctive mental strategies. Fox, Dixon, Nijeboer et al. (2016) systematically reviewed the functional neuroanatomy of various mindfulness practices in a meta-analysis of 78 functional neuroimaging (fMRI and PET) studies and found reliably dissociable patterns of brain activation and deactivation for four common styles of meditation (focused attention, mantra recitation, open monitoring and compassion/loving-kindness) and suggestive differences for three others (visualization, sense-withdrawal and non-dual awareness practices) and dissociable activation patterns congruent with the psychological and behavioral aims of each practice. The insula, pre/supplementary motor cortices, dorsal ACC and frontopolar cortex were recruited consistently across multiple techniques with effects noted for both activations and deactivations, suggesting shared brain functions involved in a range of mindfulness techniques.

The wide range of benefits for health that have been documented in association with practicing mindfulness techniques lends support to the term *mind-body medicine* (Dossett, Fricchione and Benson 2020) and is greatly reminiscent of the work of Franz Alexander (1891-1964), the Hungarian-born American physician and psychoanalyst who proposed that emotional tension can generate physical illness, coining the term *psychosomatic disease* (Alexander 1950). Not only are brain neural connections associated with attention and self-awareness strengthened by practicing mindfulness techniques, but an emerging literature points to mindfulness techniques reducing systemic effects of exposure to stress during a lifetime.

Epel, Blackburn, Lin et al. (2004) reported that accelerated telomere shortening provided a cellular measure of the cumulative effects of stress on the organism during a lifetime. The enzyme telomerase, through its influence on telomere length, is associated with health and mortality. In a meta-analysis, Schutte and Malouff (2014) reported a moderate effect size for the beneficial effects of mindfulness meditation on telomerase activity in peripheral blood mononuclear cells. A more recent meta-analytic study provided tentative support for a dose-dependent effect of meditation-based practices on telomere length (Schutte, Malouff and Keng 2020).

Mindfulness interventions that included yoga postures were associated in a meta-analysis with improved regulation of the sympathetic nervous system and hypothalamic-pituitary-adrenal system in various populations, including reduced evening cortisol, waking cortisol, ambulatory systolic blood pressure, resting heart rate, high frequency heart rate variability, fasting blood glucose, cholesterol and low-density lipoprotein, compared to active controls (Pascoe, Thompson and Ski 2017). Possibly the extensive therapeutic consequences of practicing mindfulness techniques are mediated by changes in gene expression networks with general benefits to cellular health (Epel, Puterman, Lin et al. 2016) with implications for brain fitness and lowered susceptibility to diseases due to stress which is highly relevant to prevention and management of addictive disorders.

Motivation

The noun *motivation*, according to the current electronic version of Oxford English Dictionary (OED), was formed within English by derivation modelled on a German lexical item, *Motivierung* (a noun meaning motivation or motive). Thus, *motivation* is a combination of the verb *motive* ("To motivate [an action, etc.; occasionally a person]; to provide with a motive or inciting cause; to give or supply a motive to; to be the motive of. Also, in passive: to be prompted by something as a motive") and the suffix -*ation* ("the particular form of the compound suffix which forms nouns of action from Latin participles"). The verb *motive* was formed within English, by conversion of the noun *motive*; the noun has multiple origins, as it is partly borrowed from French (*motif*), Latin (*motivum*) and Anglo-Norman (*motif, motive*).

The noun *motive* first appeared in the English language *c.* 1390 with a currently obsolete meaning ("An impression or apprehension that prompts a person to action; a counsel; a prompting or suggestion; specifically, a divine or angelic prompting.") as in Chaucer (*c.* 1340s–1400), the English poet and author of the Middle Ages best known for *The Canterbury Tales* (Chaucer, Coghill and Tolkien 1904): "This gentil kyng hath caught a gret motyf Of this witnesse." Clearly this original meaning is a prompt or demand to action from an objectifiable outside entity, whereas in the current usage, an intrapsychic call to act, is more due to interoceptive cues or an internalized perception of the environment. The OED definition that seems most relevant to the field of addiction is: "A circumstance or external factor inducing a person to act in a certain way; a desire, emotion, reason, argument, etc., influencing or tending to influence a person's volition. Also, a contemplated end the desire for which influences or tends to influence a person's actions." This meaning was used *c.* 1439 by John Lydgate (*c.* 1370–1449), the English monk and poet, known for his prodigious poetic output (Lydgate and Bergen 1923): "In this purpos, he... Ches for to deie... And to preferre... The comoun proffit: this was his motiff." A contemporary meaning of *motive* compatible with use in addiction is more evident in a quotation of John Locke (1632–1704), the English philosopher and physician, widely regarded as one of the most influential of Enlightenment thinkers in *An Essay concerning Humane Understanding* (Locke 1694): "The motive to change, is always some uneasiness... This is the great motive that works on the Mind to put it upon Action..."

The definition in OED of *motivation* most compatible with use in addiction is: "The (conscious or unconscious) stimulus for action towards a desired goal, especially, as resulting from psychological or social factors; the factors giving purpose or direction to human or animal behaviour… the reason a person has for acting in a particular way, a motive." An example of this meaning of *motivation* can be found in the first issue of the *Princeton Review* (Cocker 1879): "Even psychological determinism is displaced by rigid mechanical necessity, and objective motivation is always real physical impulsation." The underlying hypothetical construct that the organism is propelled toward use of psychoactive agents or engagement in other self-destructive and out-of-control behaviors via a multi-factorial process termed *motivation* has continued to this day. As mechanistic explanations of relevant contributing factors to *motivation* are actively sought through current models of behavior merged with neuroscience, it has become evident that its modification is essential if such propulsive forces toward active addiction are to be diminished, diverted or stopped (Marlatt, Baer, Donovan and Kivlahan 1988; Heilig, Epstein, Nader and Shaham 2016; Lepack, Werner, Stewart et al. 2020).

The concept of *motivation* has its origins in philosophical thought, namely the study of metaphysical questions such as the processes and causations underlying the relationship between mind and body. By the 20th century, studies of motivation emerged as a founding principle of the relatively new discipline of psychology, in which the term came to encapsulate "all determinants of behavior" (Young 1936). Since addiction is fundamentally expressed through behavior (see Addiction), motivational psychology (Madsen 1973) and its underpinnings in neuroscience (Kalivas and Volkow 2005) have become the foundation upon which our understanding of the disorder has been built. The scientific revolution launched by Charles Darwin (1809–1882), the English naturalist, biologist and geologist best known for contributions to the scientific discipline of evolution (1859), introduced a perspective that allowed the behavior of humans to be examined by comparison to those of other species from which they evolved. This has led to enrichment of the study of human motivation to include explanatory terms derived from studies of behavior in animals, such as *drive, need, instinct, force, incentive, valence, salience,* among many others. Madsen (1973) described how modern *motivational psychology* emerged and evolved from Darwinian thinking. Three seminal contributions to this new motivational perspective of human behavior originated from the works of the following innovators: William McDougall (1871–1938), a British-American psychologist whose "instinct" theories buttressed *social psychology* (1908); Edward Thorndike (1874 –1949), the American educational psychologist whose learning theories developed from studies in *experimental psychology* (1905); and Sigmund Freud (1856 – 1939), the Austrian neurologist and founder of psychoanalysis whose studies led to an appreciation of personality theories and *drives* underpinning behaviors (2001).

Learning forms the mechanistic underpinnings of addiction and conditioning has emerged as a heuristically useful behavioral technique for understanding and experimentally modelling components of the disorder and its treatment (see Conditioning). Elucidating the linkages between *learning* and *motivation* has become an essential element in comprehensive understanding of addiction as a pharmacopsychosocial disorder (Solomon 1980; Marlatt, Baer, Donovan and Kivlahan 1988; Venniro, Zhang, Caprioli et al. 2018). Perhaps the most valuable consequence of incorporating motivation into our understanding of addiction is the identification of experiential elements of the disorder that may be modifiable and incorporated into *treatment* (Miller 1983; Prochaska and DiClemente 1983). To motivation we attribute *why* individuals act as they do. Therefore, only by better understanding the psychic forces that contribute to approach and avoidance behaviors of individuals within their environment (Martin, Weinberg and Bealer 2007), might we hope to modify the out-of-control and self-destructive behaviors that constitute addiction. Stated otherwise and incorporating the motivating notion of *craving* (see Craving) in conceptualizing what is the active component of treatment: "The treatment forces and motivation together must be stronger than the craving if there is to be any chance of success (Bejerot 1972)."

The treatment approaches that are currently most well-supported by experimental evidence have as their focus *enhancement* of the motivation to achieve *recovery* from addiction either through mutual support groups or individual psychotherapeutic approaches (see Recovery). A heuristic behavioral model that has become widely promulgated throughout medicine and has demonstrated efficacy in treatment of addiction was proposed by Prochaska and DiClemente (1983). In this model, they describe how therapeutic modification of addictive behaviors involves progression of the patient through five stages of change, in essence, stages of *motivation to change*: precontemplation, contemplation, preparation, action, and maintenance. Through the course of treatment, individuals typically recycle through these stages several times before recovery of extended duration is accomplished. To facilitate individuals through these stages of change, Miller (1983) implemented a psychotherapeutic approach he coined *motivational interviewing*, based upon principles of experimental social psychology, applying processes such as attribution, cognitive dissonance, and self-efficacy in which motivation is conceptualized not as a personality trait but as an interpersonal process.

Whether pharmacologic interventions can actually enhance progression through the stages of *motivation to change* in order to achieve *recovery* has not been formally investigated. Suffice it to say, this is a somewhat different question from the significant research that is now available on reduction of alcohol/drug use with pharmacotherapy resulting in *harm reduction* (see Recovery). However, the goal of significant restructuring of motivation and behavior to enhance progression to true recovery can be achieved by judicious parallel use of pharmacological and psychosocial strategies (Martin, Weinberg and Bealer 2007). For example, treatment of opioid use disorder with the partial *mu*-opioid agonist buprenorphine allows the patient who suffers from severe opioid use disorder to awake each morning without the thought of having to look for the next "fix," thus allowing enhanced self-efficacy and the motivation to face and modify life challenges which are the antecedents of true recovery. Similarly, a patient suffering from bipolar disorder and accompanying poor judgement, resulting in addiction, may become more motivated to engage in behavioral changes needed for recovery if his/her psychopathology can be regulated by pharmacotherapy with lithium. Although there are ample examples from behavioral pharmacology of altering motivational systems that contribute to drug self-administration (Bardo, Neisewander and Kelly 2013; Berridge and Robinson 2016; Bohus 1979; Lepack, Werner, Stewart et al. 2020; Volkow, Wise and Baler 2017), the major challenge in motivational research is how to augment psychological enhancements with pharmacotherapeutic approaches and *vice versa*. It remains to be determined whether these two foundational constituents of behaviors that comprise addiction are, at this time, structurally compatible so as to be combined with the appropriate stoichiometry to reliably enhance therapeutic change in motivation and ultimately, the behavioral repertoire.

Nicotine

According to the current electronic version of OED, the noun *nicotine* was formed within English by derivation from the nouns *nicotian* and *nicotiana* and the suffix *-in*. The noun *nicotian*, now only rarely used, is a borrowing from French *nicotiane* defined in OED as: "The tobacco plant, *Nicotiana tabacum*; any plant of the genus *Nicotiana*. Also: tobacco." Of note, the tobacco plant is named after Jean Nicot de Villemain (1530–1600), French ambassador in Lisbon and lexicographer, who introduced tobacco into France in 1560. Some experts at that time proposed smoking for health and possibly protection from the plague. The name *Nicot* was thus combined with the suffix *-ian*, meaning "of or belonging to," representing a Latin suffix *-iānus*, i.e., an original or connecting vowel *-i-*, with suffix *-ānus*. The noun *nicotiana* is a borrowing from Latin, a version of which has spread to Italian and Spanish, which is employed to designate the genus and related species of tobacco. The noun *nicotine* is defined in OED as: "A toxic, colourless or yellowish, oily liquid alkaloid which is the chief active constituent of tobacco, acting as a stimulant in small doses, but in larger amounts blocking the actions of autonomic nerve and skeletal muscle cells; 3-(1-methyl-2-pyrrolidinyl) pyridine, C10H14N2."

The noun *nicotian* was the first used in the English language in the translation of *The Three Books* (Monardes 1577): "This Hearbe is called Nicotiane, of the name of hym that gaue the firste intelligence thereof into this Realme." An example of the first use of the noun *nicotiana* in English appears in *Maison Rustique; or, The Countrie Farme* translated by Richard Surflet (*c.* 1560–1606), a British physician, surgeon and translator (Estienne, Liebault and Surflet 1600): "This herbe is called Nicotiana of the name of an ambassadour which brought the first knowledge of it into this realme." It was not until much later that the noun *nicotine* was first used in technical English. An example is found in the text of *A System of Chemistry* (1817), written by the Scottish chemist and mineralogist, Thomas Thomson (1773–1852), whose writings contributed to the early spread of <u>Dalton's</u> atomic theory: "Of nicotin. This substance exists in the leaves of the *nicotiana latifolia*, or *tobacco*, and gives that plant its peculiar properties." The noun is also found in literature as in the novel *Of Human Bondage* by William Somerset Maugham (1874–1965), an English playwright and novelist, who qualified as a physican but gave up medicine due to his literary success (1915): "She had long, beautiful hands, with fingers deeply stained by nicotine."

The importance of *nicotine* with respect to addiction is that it is the major psychoactive substituent in *tobacco*. The noun *tobacco* is altered from Spanish *tabaco*, according to OED, "the name in the Carib of Haiti of the Y-shaped tube or pipe through which the Indians inhaled the smoke; but [others claim it is] applied to a roll of dried leaves which was kindled at the end and used by the Indians like a rude cigar… the name had been taken by the Spaniards as that of the herb or its leaf, in which sense it passed from Spanish into the other European languages…The original forms *tabaco*, *tabacco*, were retained in English to the 18th century, but gradually driven out by *tobacco*."

The OED definition of the noun *tobacco* is: "The leaves of the tobacco-plant (Any one of various species of *Nicotiana* (N.O. [natural order of plants] Solanaceæ), especially *N. Tabacum*, a native of tropical America…) dried and variously prepared, forming a narcotic and sedative substance widely used for smoking, also for chewing, or in the form of *snuff* and to a slight extent in medicine." An example of its first use in the English language is in *The Description of England* by William Harrison (1535–1593), an English historian and topographer (Harrison 1877): "In these daies [1573] the taking-in of the smoke of the Indian herbe called Tabaco, by an instrument formed like a litle ladell, wherby it passeth from the mouth into the hed & stomach, is gretlie taken-vp & vsed in England." The noun *snuff* is probably derived, according to OED, from "Dutch and Flemish *snuf* or *snuif* (West Frisian *snuf*) in the same sense, apparently an abbreviation of *snuiftabak*" and is defined as: "A preparation of powdered tobacco for inhaling through the nostrils (in the southern United States, usually taken orally)." An example of its first use in English is from *The London Gazette* (Anonymous 1683): "James Norcock, Snuffmaker and Perfumer, …sells all sorts of Snuffs, Spanish and Italian."

The uncertain role of tobacco in the medicine of the day is described in an editorial entitled "Remarks on the History and Use of Tobacco" (Medicus 1810):

> "The powers and the properties of the vegetable narcotics, either to destroy or to save, have been enough distinguished, to make those who wish for the improvement of medical science, lament that our knowledge of them is still so indeterminate, that it may be said to approximate to ignorance. Some of the properties of some of these substances, may have been tolerably explained; but of others, so little is ascertained, that they still remain, as to their influence upon the animal functions, in a state of great obscurity…

> "It has been the fate of the NICOTIANA TABACUM to have credulous and hyperbolical friends; enemies prejudiced, malignant, and unjust. With the one party it was the great *Panacea* (Everard 1587), the curer of every evil, the soother of every care. –With the other, it was a debaser of the human mind, enervated the body, and

was fit only to be used by diabolical spirits in Pandaemonium. Both its friends and enemies were found in every rank of society, from the King to the peasant. Poets, priests, physicians, and moralists, were, by turns, its panegyrists and its defamers.

"A writer of the period when Tobacco was at the acme of its influence, has brought together, into one paragraph, all its virtues and its vices, in a manner peculiar to himself. "*Tobacco*, divine, rare, superexcelient Tobacco, which goes far beyond all their panaceas, potable gold, and philosopher's stones, a sovereign remedy to all diseases. A good vomit, I confesse, a virtuous herb, if it be well qualified, opportunely taken, and medicinally used; but, as it is commonly abused by most men, which take it as tinkers do ale, it is a plague, a mischief, a violent purger of goods, lands, health; hellish, devilish and damned Tobacco, the ruine and overthrowe of body and soul." With this curious summary of honest Burtons, I must conclude these miscellaneous Remarks on a Plant, whose dominion over mankind has been, for a period, most extensive."

Based on this quotation, the notion of abuse/addiction in much the same vein as occurs with alcohol ("as tinkers do ale") seems to have been accepted for at least two centuries. While tobacco was considered to play a role in medicine at one point, recognition of diverse toxicities began to accumulate as discussed in the editorial, "Pathogeneses of Tobacco and Nicotine. —Neuroses Produced by Tobacco" (Anonymous 1873). Eventually, the negatives associated with tobacco outweighed the positives. Horatio Curtis Wood, Jr. (1841–1920), an American physician and biologist, stated in his influential text *A Treatise on Therapeutics: Comprising Materia Medica and Toxicology* (1874): "Tobacco ...has almost passed out of sight as a therapeutic agent."

The major psychoactive agent of tobacco continued to be of tremendous scientific interest. Nicotine was originally isolated from the tobacco plant (Posselt and Reimann 1828) by two German scientists, a physician Wilhelm Heinrich Posselt (1806–1877) and a chemist Karl Ludwig Reimann (1804–1872); the empirical chemical formula was described (Melsens1843) by a Belgian physicist and chemist, Louis-Henri-Frédéric Melsens (1814–1886); the structure of nicotine was discovered (Pinner 1893) by a German chemist, Adolf Pinner (1842–1909); and nicotine was first synthesized (Pictet and Rotschy 1904) by a Swiss chemist, Amé Pictet (1857–1937).

The early era of studies on the pharmacology of nicotine and its role in cholinergic neurotransmission (Dixon and Hoyle 1929) are summarized in a lecture (1935) delivered to the Royal Society of Medicine entitled "Pharmacology of Nerve Endings" by Sir Henry Dale (1875–1968). Dale was an eminent English pharmacologist and physiologist who, for his study of acetylcholine as agent in chemical neurotransmission, shared the 1936 Nobel Prize in Physiology or Medicine.

Over the years, it was demonstrated that nicotine acts as an agonist at nicotinic acetylcholine receptors (NAChRs) that are linked to ion channels and are found predominantly in the central and peripheral nervous system and muscle. Most important with respect to addiction, the mechanisms of action of nicotine in the central nervous system are very similar to the stimulant amphetamine which has high proclivity for self-administration and abuse liability (Izquierdo and Izquierdo 1971):

> "Both these drugs have several well-known central effects in common: (a) cortical and hippocampal EEG alerting; (b) increased performance and retention of conditioned responses; (c) central catecholamine depletion or increased turnover; (d) increased hippocampal RNA concentration, probably secondary to the EEG effect. Effects (a), (b), and (c) are shared, in general, by a number of amphetamine analogs... Amphetamine and nicotine increase self-stimulation rates. The former is less effective when electrodes are in the posterior hypothalamus than when they are in the septum, anteromedial hypothalamus, or midbrain tegmentum."

Nicotine facilitates acquisition of a variety of learned tasks due to central not peripheral actions of the drug and these facilitating effects of nicotine on learning are based on adrenergic mechanisms (McGaugh 1973). Additionally, nicotine acts on reward circuits of the brain by activating NAChRs in the ventral tegmental area to cause dopamine release in neurons that project to the nucleus accumbens which may contribute to nicotine use disorder and also the high prevalence of co-occurrence of other alcohol/drug use disorders with smoking cigarettes (Hyman, Malenka and Nestler 2006). Finally, nicotine affects the set point around which body weight is regulated and nicotine suppresses hunger and cessation of smoking increases appetite and caloric intake (Perkins 1992; Romero, Daniels, Gipson and Sanabria 2018).

It was reasoned that the percentage of nicotine in various kinds of tobacco was probably relevant to smoking behavior if nicotine was the key ingredient in tobacco (Anonymous 1909):

"[I]t would appear to be true as a general proposition that the more nicotine there is in a cigar or any other form in which tobacco is smoked, the more the smoker is likely to take into the system. It is, therefore, of some importance to know the relative amounts of nicotine contained in different kinds of tobaccos. Further, if the results of such an inquiry show that the percentage of nicotine rises and falls *pari passu* with the character of the tobacco as 'strong' or 'mild' when judged by a smoker, collateral evidence will be afforded of the correctness of the view that the effects of smoking are principally due to the nicotine."

Of note, there are those who have proposed that nicotine content is not as important for all with the "cigarette habit" (Finnegan, Larson and Haag 1945). However, nicotine content can now be regulated by industrial processes (Connolly, Alpert, Wayne and Koh 2007), thus complicating estimates of the level of use in the population and simultaneously estimating nicotine use disorder based only on cigarettes smoked.

Tobacco use can result in nicotine use disorder which, in turn, is frequently associated with co-occurring alcohol and drug use disorders as well as mood, anxiety and personality disorders (Grant, Hasin, Chou et al. 2004; Martin, Weinberg and Bealer 2007). Tobacco use also has enormous healthcare costs in the United States, recently estimated at almost $200 billion per year (Ekpu and Brown 2015). Tobacco use is the leading cause of preventable morbidity and mortality among adults worldwide, e.g., tobacco use is associate with 1 in 5 deaths per year in the United States (United States Surgeon General 2014). The major health consequences associated with tobacco use, substantively due to pyrolysis products formed on smoking of tobacco products, include coronary heart disease; stroke; chronic obstructive pulmonary disease; lung and other cancers; and increased risk of pre-term delivery and low birth weight, among many other conditions. Despite the availability of many delivery platforms, like cigars, snuff, or dipping/chewing tobacco, the major instrument for self-administering nicotine remains cigarette smoking. An electronic form of nicotine delivery, called "vaping" in the vernacular, was initially considered safer than cigarettes. Accordingly, vaping began to be used for smoking cessation and its prevalence rapidly increased, especially in the young who often initiated nicotine use with vaping instead of cigarettes. Now it promises to have its own set of even more severe medical complications (Lerner, Sundar, Yao et al. 2015; Palazzolo 2013).

The most recently available rates of smoking reflect the distinction between nicotine use as typically quantified (numbers of cigarettes, cigars, snuffing, etc.) and whether a consumer actually meets diagnostic criteria (DSM-IV) for nicotine use disorder (Fagerström 1978; Grant, Shmulewitz and Compton 2020). Representative U.S. data on 12-month prevalence of nicotine use, nicotine dependence and nicotine dependence among users were determined during the periods 2001-2002 and 2012-2013. Recent declines in nicotine use were found, presumably due to population-level public health interventions. However, there were significant increases in prevalence of severely dependent users during this timeframe. These are the individuals who are less likely to quit, require most healthcare expenditures and may need other than currently available public health prevention efforts (e.g., increased price, elimination of advertising, protections against secondhand smoke) that have demonstrated beneficial effects in less severe users. Instead, these severely dependent individuals may profit from evidence-based addiction treatment interventions based on a pharmacopsychosocial model (Martin, Weinberg and Bealer 2007; Fisher, Pauly, Froeliger and Turner 2021).

As the health consequences of smoking cigarettes became recognized (Larson, Haag and Silvette 1968), scientific interest arose concerning the differences between those who do and those who do not smoke (Heath 1958). Initially, the focus was on descriptive features that may serve as risk factors for developing nicotine use disorder, such as taste perception (Krut, Perrin and Bronte-Stewart 1961), among others. In subsequent decades, research expanded to include genetic and neurobiological characteristics of those at particular risk for nicotine use disorder and its complications. Focus has been on co-occurring psychiatric disorders, especially depression (Moriguchi, Inagaki, Yi et al. 2020) and severe mental disorders (Wei, Wang, Wei et al. 2020) that are demonstrated to be significantly associated with nicotine use disorder (Bierut 2020). The goal has been implementation of precision medicine approaches in treatment of nicotine use disorders employing antidepressants, nicotine replacement approaches and the partial agonist of α4β2NAChR, varenicline (Frank, Cinciripini, Deweese et al. 2020). The goal in treatment of nicotine use disorders should eventually progress to the identification and reversal of plastic changes associated with learning and addiction (Jin, Tucker and Drenan 2020).

Opium

According to the latest electronic version of the Oxford English Dictionary (OED), the noun *opium* originated from the Hellenistic Greek ὅπιον (poppy juice, opium), which in turn, was from the ancient Greek ὀπός (vegetable juice) in combination with the diminutive suffix *-ιον*.   Ancient Greek writings from the 9th century B.C. mention what might well be *opium* in Homer's Odyssey (Brownstein 1993): "Presently she [Helen] cast a drug into the wine of which they drank to lull all pain and anger and bring forgetfulness of every sorrow."

The first documented use of the word *opium* was a description by Caius Plinius Secundus (AD 23/24 –79), or Pliny the Elder, the Roman author, naturalist and natural philosopher, in his *Naturalis Historia* (Plinius Secundus 1866). Subsequently the noun *opium* has related forms in French (*opium* in 13th century in Old French; *opion* in 15th century in Middle French), Italian (*oppio also opio* in 14th century) and Spanish (*opio*, 1555). The primary definition in OED is: "A reddish-brown strongly scented addictive drug prepared from the thickened dried latex of the unripe capsules of the opium poppy, *Papaver somniferum*, used illicitly as a narcotic, and occasionally medicinally as a sedative and analgesic."

As the opium poppy extracts began to be formulated into medicinal preparations, a related term, the noun/adjective *opiate* began to be used, originally defined as: "any medicinal preparation containing opium, used chiefly to induce sleep or relieve pain." This definition was later modified: "specifically any drug derived from opium, especially morphine and codeine; any of a group of narcotic drugs structurally related to morphine or having physiological effects similar to those of morphine." Finally, the noun/adjective *opioid* came into use as pharmacognosy progressed and allowed the synthesis of molecules with similar actions to those extracted from the poppy, defined as: "any synthetic narcotic drug derived from or having properties similar to those of morphine." Eventually, the terms *opioid* and *opiate* came to be used almost interchangeably.

The first use of the word *opium* in the English language according to OED was in about 1398 by the Cornish scholar John Trevisa (*fl.* 1342–1402) who translated the *Bartholomaeus Anglicus* (Bartholomew the Englishman) compilation of the encyclopedia *De proprietatibus rerum* (On the properties of things), the most widely circulated medieval encyclopedia (Bartholomaeus 2010): "Popy hatte papauer…Ther of comeþ Ius þat phisicians clepeþ opium oþer opion." The first use in English of the term *opiate* was in translation of *Chirugia Magna* (de Chauliac 1659) of the French physician and surgeon Guy de Chauliac (*c.* 1300–1368): "Solaced or conforted with croco or mirra storacus, as castorio, as in philoneo & in opiatez [L. *filonio et opiatis*] & suppositoriez." The term *opioid* was introduced in the 1950s (Gross and Schiffrin 1955): "Acheson has suggested that the morphinans and other synthetic morphine substitutes should be called opioids."

The earliest quotes suggested the significant role of extracts from the opium poppy in the physician's armamentarium. A mention of the uses of opium and opiates for analgesia in surgery is found in the translation of the book *Noble Experyence Vertuous Handy Warke of Surgeri* (Brunschwig 1539) written by the German surgeon, alchemist and botanist Hieronymus von Brunschwig (*c.*1450–*c.*1512): "Whan the payne is grete, then it is nedefull to put therto a lytell Opium." Also, medical uses for various complaints are noted in the first illustrated herbal produced from woodcuts by the English printer Peter Treveris (*fl.* 1525–32) *Grete Herball* (Treveris 1529): "Agaynst payne of the heed called mygreyne or cephale gyve some hote opiate.").

Laudatory quotations from eminent physicians have continued through history, including one widely attributed to Sir Thomas Sydenham (1624–1689) who has been referred to as the *English Hippocrates*: "Among the remedies which it has pleased almighty God to give to man to relieve his sufferings, none is so universal and so efficacious as opium." Sir William Osler (1849–1919), the esteemed Canadian physician of the Victorian era, analogously proclaimed that opium was, "God's own medicine."

While the role of opium in medicine was being explored, it soon became apparent that problems were associated with repeated use of poppy extracts and not all about opiates was positive, especially recognition of potential toxicity and addiction. For example, the writer and traveler George Sandys (1578–1644) alluded to out-of-control use of opium (Sandys 1615): "The Turkes are also incredible takers of Opium"; the English satirist Edward Ward (1667–1731), referred to a potential for loss of temper and possibility of violence related to taking opium (Ward 1699): "Offer violence to your most pretious Lives, by taking…Opium"; and the disturbing consequences of discontinuing chronic opioid use were commented upon by Horace Walpole (1717–1797), the author, politician and arts patron (Walpole, Wright and Dover 1846): "Lady Stafford used to say to her sister, 'Well, child, I have come without my wit to-day;' that is, she had not taken her opium."

The physician Robert Godfrey wrote in his treatise *Various Injuries and abuses in chymical and galenical Physick committed by Physicians and Apothecaries* (1674): "Instances… of such who with Opiates slept to Death." This quotation presaged by three centuries the current notion that physician prescribing was the basis for overdose deaths in the "opioid epidemic" of our day (Baumblatt, Wiedeman, Dunn et al. 2014). Horatio Curtis Wood (1841–1920), the American physician, succinctly wrote (Wood 1874): "Death occurs from opium, in the great majority of cases, by failure of the respiration." Wood's observation resonates with present-day reports of declining life expectancy fueled by opioid overdose deaths (Hedegaard, Miniño and Warner 2018); such an unexpected decline has not been documented in the U.S. in the past century since a four-year period which simultaneously included World War I and the Spanish Flu Pandemic of 1918.

Opium has been used by mankind for thousands of years (Rudgley 1999). Its use in prehistoric times preceded even that of alcohol with which it was subsequently combined, predominantly to relieve pain (see above) as well as to enhance religious rituals and spiritual enlightenment by altered sensory experiences. The opioid poppy has been domesticated by farmers in the northeastern part of the Mediterranean since 6000 B.C. Cultivation of the poppy spread westward during the Neolithic period with records of the seed found in Switzerland, Germany and then extending northward to the British Isles and Poland. Sumerians, in what today is Iraq, started using opium extracts derived from the seed capsules of the poppy at the end of the 3rd century B.C. Arab traders brought opium to India and China between the 10th and 13th centuries and subsequently opium made its way from Asia Minor to all parts of Europe.

Friedrich Sertürner (1783–1841), a German pharmacist, is credited with isolating the active ingredient from opium extracts at the beginning of the 19th century (Serturner 1806). Sertürner called the isolate *morphium* after Morpheus, the Greek God of Dreams, as in his experimentation the compound highly effectively induced sleep. The French chemist J.L. Gay-Lussac (1778–1850) is known for popularizing Sertürner's discovery and eventually changing the name to *morphine* (Brook, Bennett and Desai 2017).

Morphine was first listed in the *London Pharmacopeia* in 1836, but it was the creation of the hypodermic needle (Rynd 1845) which fueled the meteoric rise in use of morphine (Brook, Bennett and Desai 2017). The combination of high potency and the ability to inject the solution directly into the bloodstream to provide rapid pain relief on the battlefield led to morphine supplanting opium except in patent medicines. Toxicity, especially addiction to opiates, became more apparent as potency rose. Consequently, a great deal of energy was spent trying to develop a safer, more efficacious, opiate that did not cause addiction.

Diacetylmorphine, or morphine diacetate, was first synthesized in 1874 by C. R. Alder Wright (1844–1894), an English chemist, but became popular only after it was independently re-synthesized 23 years later by another chemist, Felix Hoffmann (1868–1946), working at Bayer Pharmaceutical. Bayer's management reputedly coined the drug's name, "heroin" based on the German *heroisch*, which means "heroic, strong" and pronounced the drug to be more potent than morphine and free from abuse liability. This was the first of several such claims for novel opiates throughout the 20th century that have continued until the present with the introduction of the blockbuster painkiller Oxycontin (Van Zee 2009; Keefe 2021).

Another strategy to contain opiate addiction has been legislation to diminish supply, e.g., the International Opium Convention signed in 1912 by the United States and many other countries. The Harrison Narcotics Tax Act became United States federal law on December 17, 1914, for regulation and taxation of the production, importation, and distribution of opiates and coca products; this law is considered an important first step in the eventual criminalization of opioid users (Anonymous 1915).

The British organic chemist Sir Robert Robinson (1886–1975) discovered the molecular structure of morphine (Gulland and Robinson 1923) for which he was awarded the Nobel Prize in Chemistry in 1947 (Bentley 1987). In 1939, meperidine, the first drug with a structure altogether different from that of morphine but with very similar pharmacological properties was discovered by serendipity. Meperidine has found use predominantly as an analgesic. In 1946, methadone, another structurally unrelated compound with similar pharmacological profile to morphine was synthesized. Methadone is widely used in the treatment of opioid use disorder due to its pharmacokinetic characteristic of a very slow elimination from the body and reduction of both craving ("narcotic hunger") and the withdrawal syndrome experienced from other opioids with higher abuse liability like morphine or heroin (Dole and Nyswander 1965). Both compounds are considered *opioids*, a point succinctly made (Martin 1967): "We have adopted the term *opioid*, which was proposed by Professor George H. Acheson, to designate those analgesics whose pattern of pharmacological and agonistic effects is similar to that of morphine and… have called this pattern of effects the *opioid syndrome*."

The final chapter in understanding the compelling history of the opium poppy and man is the discovery of the *site of action* of the opioid molecule within the central nervous system at stereospecific binding sites (Pert and Snyder 1973) and the discovery that these physiologically active receptors bind endogenously produced molecules (Goldstein, Lowney and Pal 1971; Hughes, Smith, Kosterlitz et al. 1975). These last discoveries followed logically from the derivation of opiates from the opium poppy, progressed to synthesis of related compounds by chemically modifying opiates to alter their effects and finally synthesis *de novo* of various opioids in the pharmaceutical laboratory. However, discovery of physiologically active *opioid receptors* would not ultimately have been possible without the synthesis of nalorphine (N-allylnormorphine) (Weijlard and Erikson 1942), the first *opiate antagonist* (Unna 1943), which could reverse many actions of opioids, including the respiratory depression produced by morphine or methadone (Fraser, Wikler, Eisenman and Isbell 1952). Interestingly, nalorphine had analgesic properties but also caused anxiety and dysphoria because it was a mixed agonist-antagonist. Nevertheless, synthesis of nalorphine eventually led to the first discovered pure antagonist devoid of agonistic activity and that was a competitive antagonist at several opioid receptors (Martin 1967).

It should not escape the reader, that the word *opium* has extended meanings beyond physiology and medicine. These definitions of the word have significant social and historical implications as defined in OED: "Something which soothes or dulls the senses; a stupefying agent; or something regarded as inducing a false sense of contentment amongst the general populace, especially whilst diverting attention from more important matters or pursuits (originally and especially with reference to religion)." This meaning appeared in English quickly after the original sense of the word as in a quote from Bishop Thomas Morton (1564–1659) a churchman and polemical writer against Roman Catholic views in the times of James I (Morton1608): "Stupified with that Opium of implicit faith and blinde deuotion." Karl Marx (1818–1883) the German philosopher and socialist revolutionary known for his classic contributions *The Communist Manifesto* and *Das Kapital* gave the word *opium* a very special meaning in 20th century political philosophy (Marx and Stenning 1926): "Religion is the moan of the oppressed creature, the sentiment of a heartless world, as it is the spirit of spiritless conditions. It is the opium of the people.").

Finally, the tremendous role in medical practice, the economy and the geopolitics of opium *per se* and subsequently, synthetic opioids should not be forgotten. First, there is a strong belief that the opioid epidemic of the early 21st century in the United States (and possibly globally) has been substantially influenced by the opioid prescribing of physicians manipulated by sophisticated marketing by the pharmaceutical industry with the tacit acquiescence of regulating government agencies (Keefe 2021). Additionally, there is little doubt that the western world literally destroyed China's sovereignty, society and its economy in the mid-19th century via the opium trade (Bradley 2015). As the American journalist William Atherton DuPuy (1876-1941) wrote (DuPuy 1916): "The smuggling of opium and of Chinamen was known to go hand in hand." Prior to the Opioid Wars, China had ranked first in the world for many centuries in gross domestic product (GDP) before it tumbled precipitously during the 20th century (Maddison 2013). China now seems to be returning the favor as the United States must struggle with its own Opioid Crisis fueled in part by synthetic opioids first manufactured in China and distributed illicitly (Wee and Hernández 2017).

Pain

According to the current electronic version of the Oxford English Dictionary (OED) the noun *pain* is a borrowing from the French *peine* which was derived from Anglo-Norman and French variants meaning "physical or bodily suffering" (from the second half of the 10th century); "trouble taken in accomplishing something, effort" (from *c.* 1050); "mental suffering" (from *c.* 1100)' "difficulty" (from early 12th century); "punishment or suffering thought to be endured by souls in hell" (from early 12th century); and "legal punishment" (from *c.* 1165). The noun *pain* also has origins in the classical Latin noun *poena* meaning "penalty, punishment."

The noun *pain* was first used in the English language according to OED *c.* 1300, extolling the life of Saint Thomas Becket (1119 or 1120–1170), Archbishop of Canterbury until his murder by followers of Henry II (Horstmann 1887): "Ich hote ov euerechone þat ȝe beon..at Clarindone…For-to confermi þis lawes; ope peyne þat i schal ou sette, Ich hote þat ȝe beon þare." The meaning of *pain* in this quotation ("Punishment; penalty; suffering or loss inflicted for a crime or offence") is somewhat different from another entry in the same volume, lauding the life of Saint Mary Magdalen ("The punishment or suffering thought to be endured by souls in hell, purgatory, etc."): "God us schilde fram peyne and to heouene us bringue!" Both quotations refer to *pain* as a consequence of a misstep, either a legal offence or a religious transgression, the punishment of which is in this life or the afterlife, respectively.

There are two meanings of *pain*, from among multiple definitions in OED, which seem appropriate in the context of addiction. These refer to the word's original meanings, namely the *experience* of either physical or emotional distress, feelings that may seem most amenable to *self-medication* and eventual progression to a drug use disorder (see Self-medication). Later uses of the word, which relate to *punishment* for one's actions or thoughts, seem derivatives from the original meanings of *pain* as they cause suffering not directly from one's own body or mind, but rather via an external decree or law, which is likely not responsive to self-medication. The first of the relevant definitions is: "Physical or bodily suffering; a continuous, strongly unpleasant or agonizing sensation in the body (usually in a particular part), such as arises from illness, injury, harmful physical contact, etc." This was first used *c.* 1330 in the Middle English poem *Of Arthour and of Merlin* (Macrae-Gibson 1973): "What for sorwe & eke for paine, Sche les winde." A very relevant quotation for understanding addiction can be found in the novel *The American* written by Henry James (1843-1916), the American author considered a key transitional figure between literary realism and literary modernism (James 1877): "He had a fit of his great pain, and he asked her for his medicine." The other meaning for *pain* that is also compatible with addiction refers to: "Mental distress or suffering; anguish, grief; an instance of this." This use first appeared in the English language *c.* 1330 in *Sir Tristrem*, a Middle English Romance based on the legend of Tristan and Iseult (MacNeill 1886): "Tristrem..sikeþ..Wiþ sorwe and michel pain." A modern use, reflecting emotional pain is found in a semi-autobiographical, precursor of the psychoanalytical novel *Way of Flesh* (1903) by the English author, Samuel Butler (1835-1902): "He still felt deeply the pain his disgrace had inflicted upon his father and mother."

It is evident to clinicians who deal with addiction that a significant proportion of their patients report that they suffer from "pain," whether it be physical or emotional in nature (Martin, Weinberg and Bealer 2007). Patients often recount that their pain, which frequently has a *combination* of physical and emotional elements that may be difficult to disentangle, antedated their regular use of drugs or alcohol. Patients explain that part of the reason they continued to use these psychoactive agents was because they initially reduced the pain. However, many patients continue drugs or alcohol, even after the cause for beginning drug use subsides. Alternatively, patients in whom pain persists may notice that their pain eventually becomes more severe and disabling as sporadic drug use progresses to full-blown addiction (Ho and Dole 1979; Zale, Maisto and Ditre 2015; Witkiewitz and Vowles 2018).

As a direct consequence of the *opioid epidemic* that began in the 2010s and still persists, it has become evident that initiation of pain relieving medications all-to-often begins with a physician's prescription (Shah, Hayes and Martin 2017). This is explained by the unfortunate fact that many pain medications are so very effective at first, but quickly result in neuroadaptation and have abuse liability. Additionally, it is important to recognize the frustration physicians who desire to alleviate their patient's suffering feel, when eliciting pain as a symptom without being able to objectively determine that it is present. Indeed, the answer to the question — What then is pain? — has challenged practitioners throughout medical history. A quotation of Edward Henry Sieveking (1816-1904), a German-trained English physician who was fascinated by pain and in 1858 invented the aesthesiometer, a device for measuring tactile sensitivity of the skin, exemplifies this conundrum (Sieveking 1867):

> "Few inquiries in physiology and pathology would be fraught with more general interest and with more practical results, if conducted to a satisfactory conclusion, than a comprehensive investigation of pain in all its relations. Strange to say, although pain is man's melancholy birthright, he scarcely knows what it is: attempts

to define it end in vague assertions or tautological phrases; and, as no means of measuring it are known, we cannot in any way render it tangible, tabulate its variations, or train our students to a proper estimate of its relative importance. When Unzer [Johann August Unzer (1727-1799) was a German physician whose work with the central nervous system, reflexes and consciousness influenced modern physiological studies] says, "A very strong disagreeable impression is pain (Unzer 1851)," he does not, in reality, get much further than Polonius, who, in attempting to define madness, avers: "To define true madness, What is it else than to be mad?""

Sieveking's explanation of pain via the trope of madness in his quotation may be more tautologic than he intended, as pain is very frequently associated in those suffering from physical and emotional disorders (Shulman 1977).

Mechanistic understanding of pain has been a focus of traditional Chinese medicine (Chen 2011):

"The term for pain appeared for the first time in the ancient medical book *Huang Di Nei Jing* more than 3000 years ago, which was translated into English as *The Yellow Emperor's Classic of Internal Medicine* (Veith 1966) …and *The Medical Classic of the Yellow Emperor* (Zhu 2001) …pain was believed to be a result of imbalance between *yin* and *yang*. Predominance of *yin* results in 'han' (cold), causing damage to the 'xing' (form of a substance) which is now known as tissue injury or damage, and leads to swelling, while predominance of *yang* results in 're' (hyperthermia or heat) which causes damage to the 'qi,' namely pneuma (previously referred to as 'chi,' the concept of energy circulating in the hypothetical 12 channels) and leads to pain. That was probably the first description of the symptoms and signs of nociceptive and inflammatory pain in the medical literature. Based upon this principle, …treatment of pain, regardless of pharmacological or non-pharmacological approaches, has focused on restoration of the balance between *yin* and *yang*, including the use of acupuncture analgesia."

The reported effectiveness of acupuncture for treatment for opioid withdrawal using traditional Chinese medicine offers support for a mechanistic relationship between pain and addiction (Chen 1977).

In ancient Greece, pain was first described in the epics of Homer (*c.* 8th century BCE), the *Iliad* and the *Odyssey* (Chen 2011). In Western philosophy and medicine, physical and emotional aspects of pain have long been confounded, as documented historically (Dallenbach 1939) and supported by the range of descriptors of pain employed by patients (Melzack and Torgerson 1971). Perl (2007) suggested that this has contributed to most of the uncertainties encountered in elucidating the underpinning mechanisms of pain:

> "…since Aristotle (384–322 BC) considered the heart to be the seat of feelings. Taking cognizance of pain's usual importance for disposition, he argued it to be an emotion… Galen (130–201), a leading physician-surgeon of Alexandria, used experimental studies along with earlier observations to disagree [with the Aristotelian perspective]. Galen recognized the brain as the organ of feeling and placed pain into the sphere of sensation. Avicenna (980–1037), a renowned Muslim philosopher and physician, noted that, in disease, pain can dissociate from touch or temperature recognition, and proposed pain to be an independent sensation… [New ideas] in the eighteenth century [were] due in part to changing insight into the physical world and proposals by Newton (1642–1727) and Hartley (1705–1757) that neuronal messages were vibrations of substance in nerves. Despite much work and thought… fundamental issues about pain remain unresolved…"

Nevertheless, since the American dentist William T. G. Morton (1819-1868) publicly demonstrated the use of inhaled ether as a surgical anaesthetic in 1846 (Thoma 1946), significant advances have been achieved in managing often intolerable pain during surgery. The importance of this discovery to mankind was poetically honored on 16th October 1896 at the commemoration of the fiftieth anniversary of the first public demonstration of surgical anesthesia, by S. Weir Mitchell (1829-1914), an American physician, considered the father of medical neurology, who discovered causalgia (complex regional pain syndrome) and erythromelalgia and pioneered the rest cure:

> "Though Science patient as the fruitful years,
>
> Still taught our art to close some fount of tears,
>
> Yet who that served this sacred home of pain
>
> Could e'er have dreamed one scarce-imagined gain,
>
> Or hoped a day would bring his fearful art

No need to steel the ever-kindly heart."

It is much more challenging to relieve pain that continuously compromises daily life than is counteracting pain using anesthesia when an individual can essentially be rendered insensate during a finite period of a surgical procedure. In addition, conceptualization of the pathophysiology and treatment of *chronic pain* has been particularly muddled in Western medicine, in part, a legacy of the Cartesian mind-body dualism (Descartes, Haldane and Ross 1912). Parenthetically, the altered states of consciousness repeatedly experienced during addiction-associated intoxication by self-administration of alcohol or other drugs are not dissimilar in character and goals to that achieved in anesthesia (see Intoxication), a notion supported by the adage *to feel no pain*, which is used in the vernacular to mean "to be insensibly drunk." Accordingly, it is not difficult to appreciate why repeated self-intoxication is often used but is destined to fail in management of chronic pain — the major consequences being neuroadaptation, increasing use with diminished pain control and progression to addiction (Andrews 1943).

It was not until the second half of the 20th century that integration of the multiple neuronal inputs that contribute to the character and intensity of pain was proposed by Melzack and Wall (1965) as the *gate theory of pain*:

> "The model suggests that the action system for pain perception and response is triggered after the cutaneous sensory input has been modulated by both sensory feedback mechanisms and the influences of the central nervous system... A 'modality' class such as 'pain,' which is a linguistic label for a rich variety of experiences and responses, represents just such an abstraction from the information that is sequentially re-examined over long periods by the entire somesthetic system."

In fact, the emotional features of pain are supported by the vocabulary patients use to describe the experience (Melzack and Torgerson 1971). This conceptual advance has led to development of *multimodal pain management* rather than simply using opioids that may often lead to addiction. This approach is intended to result in "significant decreases in pain, depression, anxiety, somatization, hostility, and analgesic ingestion (Khatami and Rush 1982)," all recognized concomitants of the chronic pain syndrome that must be addressed to enhance quality of life. In fact, there is considerable overlap of multimodal pain management and broadly based addiction treatment programs (Martin, Weinberg and Bealer 2007).

We owe the tremendous impetus to manage chronic pain (Keefe and Somers 2010) and even to conduct surgical anesthesia without opioids (Devin, Lee, Armaghani et al. 2014) to the greater cognizance by the medical profession and society of the risks of addiction as a result of the opioid epidemic of recent years (see Opium). As reviewed above, very important clinical linkages have long been recognized between the suffering that results from physical and mental pain and addictive disorders. These connections go beyond phenomenology and also include the recognized benefits of antidepressants and anticonvulsants in management of the various presentations of syndromes associated with chronic pain (Martin, Weinberg and Bealer 2007) as well as the particularly impressive antidepressant effects of opioids (Medakovic and Banic 1964; Benningfield, Dietrich, Jones et al. 2012). Not until recent advances in immunology, has it become possible to understand that these associations may mechanistically operate through the pathophysiology of inflammation (McClintick, Xuei, Tischfield et al. 2013; Yuan, Chen, Xia et al. 2019; Mehta, Stevens, Li et al. 2020). Appreciation of these interconnections has arrived relatively late in Western medicine. Nevertheless, this newly recognized interdigitation of mind-body elements through neuroinflammation seems to agree with concepts that have been accepted in treatment of mental and physical disorders for centuries in Asia.

Prevention

The noun *prevention* is partly a borrowing from Latin and from French according to the current electronic version of the Oxford English Dictionary (OED). In post-classical Latin, from late 4th century, the meaning of *praevention-, praeventio* is "action of anticipating and forestalling". The meaning evolved within French from the Middle French *prevention, prevencion* and the French *prevention*: "(planetary) opposition," an astrological meaning from the 13th century in Old French; "action of coming first" from 1374; "legal privilege of an overlord over other courts," from 1461; "action of forestalling someone in a course of action," from 1530; "precaution," from 1580; and "preconception" from 1637. There are multiple modern meanings of the word *prevention* which have been categorized into two broad classes: 1) "Senses related to precluding or hindering something" and 2) "Senses related to preceding or anticipating something." The use most relevant to addiction is derived from the first of these classes.

The noun *prevention* was first used in the English language in 1447 according to OED (Beckington and Williams 1872): "I verrely trow…ye wold…stur al tho to whom sholde longe the preuencion and redresse in that behalue, to do and execute thes same truly." In this quotation, the word *prevention* means: "The action of keeping from happening or making impossible an anticipated event or intended act." The most appropriate of the meanings of *prevention* with respect to use in the field of addiction from the first class of definitions mentioned above is: "A means of preventing something; a safeguard; a hindrance, an obstruction." The following quotation (Calvin, Pagit and Fetherstone 1584) exemplifies its first such use in the English language: "But this is a preuention wherewith hee shieldeth vs against offences [L. *occupatio, qua..praemunit*]."

An apposite use of the word *prevention* with respect to addiction is a quotation from Horace Smith (1779-1849), an English poet and novelist, in his book *The Tin Trumpet*: "Gallows—A cure without being a prevention of crime." This quotation alludes to the unfortunate fact that as policymakers try to prevent addiction and detrimental consequences of a drug in the population through legal and other social interventions, there is little guarantee *a priori* that the desired outcomes will be achieved. A case in point is the legal status of marijuana, which has been debated for more than a half a century, leaving in its wake many young people criminalized and incarcerated for minor nonviolent crimes or because of racial prejudice during the 1960-70's (LeDain 1970; Kandel 1975; Joffe and Yancy 2004).

While access to drugs, in theory, should be based in pharmacology (Eddy and Isbell 1959), Erickson has emphasized (1992) that historically, in most societies, legal control of access to substances of abuse has never been consistent with pharmacological understanding of harmfulness:

"To inquire about the relationship between drugs and the law, one logical question is: What does knowing a drug's legal status tell you about its pharmacological properties or its dangers? If a drug is *prohibited*, it may be a stimulant, depressant, analgesic or hallucinogen (e.g., cocaine, cannabis, heroin, LSD). If a drug is *legally available*, it may also fall into a variety of pharmacological categories (e.g., nicotine, alcohol, codeine). To reverse the question: What does knowing a drug's effects on the health of a population tell you about its legal status? Those drugs whose known long-term effects are harmful to a significant proportion of users are likely to be legal: 'The drugs carrying the greatest health and safety risks are not, in fact, illegal.' If a drug's short-term effects are potentially lethal, it may be medically prescribed (e.g., barbiturates) or illicit (e.g., cocaine, heroin). Since all the examples thus far cited are addictive drugs, in the sense that they can be used compulsively and destructively, the property of addictive potential is no guide to legal status. Thus, no apparently straight-forward relationship between a drug's pharmacological properties and effects, and its position inside or outside the ambit of law, exists.

"Nevertheless, the field of addictions is divided into *licit* and *illicit* drugs. Although we tend to take this as a given, it is a phenomenon that originated only in this century. At different times since 1900, all the drugs that present society with problems today (plus a few newcomers like LSD, amphetamines and steroids) have been variously, and at different times, freely available, medically prescribed, considered a candidate for prohibition, considered a candidate for legalization, banned, re-legalized, aggressively marketed and severely restricted. If there is one feature that epitomizes the interrelationship between the law and drugs, it is ongoing controversy as to how they should be controlled."

It might be argued that odds of success for prevention strategies may be optimized if interventions are based on etiopathogenesis of the disorder rather than the pharmacology of the drug of abuse or, better still, the interaction between these factors. Such mechanistic considerations should be grounded in reliable biopsychosocial phenomena rather than misconceptions attributable to the stigma these conditions often carry. Granville Stanley Hall (1846-1924), a pioneering American psychologist, educator and the first president of the American Psychological Association, whose research focused on childhood development (Thorndike 1925), in *Senescence, the last half of life* rightly emphasized *psychosocial* processes as the most meaningful components of prevention (Hall 1922): "Far more… deaths and preventions and postponements of death than we know are amenable to mind cure because they are mindmade." J.D. Reichard, Medical Director (1939-1946) of the USPHS Hospital in Lexington Kentucky underscores this point (Reichard 1947): "Addiction is in itself an important phenomenon; an understanding of it also involves many of our concepts concerning human behavior and misbehavior in general." These observations clearly apply to addictive disorders but also to co-occurring other psychiatric disorders that can be the precursors or consequences of addiction (see Self-medication).

Prevention strategies for alcohol and drug use disorders can be conceptualized in terms of two broad classes of interventions. *Demand reduction* refers to efforts aimed at reducing the desire for alcohol/drugs among individuals in the population. Such approaches typically include altering the public health or expectations through media or education; addiction treatment and re-integrating those in recovery into the community; and reducing poverty through economic opportunities. In contrast, *supply reduction* policies are intended to reduce availability of these substances to the population by limiting access by taxation; restricting the age for legal access; destruction or substitution of crops from which drugs are derived; limiting availability of precursor chemicals required for illicit synthesis of drugs like methamphetamine; and policing drug trafficking within a country and across national borders. Although such approaches have typically referred to reducing the demand and/or supply of *illegal or illicit* drugs (Tennyson 1953), there is, in fact, a long history of significant societal gains obtained by legislation to contain use of legally available psychoactive substances with abuse liability, such as alcohol (Vingilis and Smart 1981; Waller 2002) or tobacco (DiFranza, Norwood, Garner and Tye 1987). As suggested, one of the greatest difficulties in crafting policies to moderate the harms to society and to the individual from alcohol/drugs is to determine the appropriate balance between these two forms of interventions, succinctly summarized (Ramsey 1986) as follows:

> "While encouraged… to continue efforts directed toward demand reduction
> endeavors, some of the unanswered questions troubling the mind… include:

1. Are there community-wide, supply-reduction, focused drug abuse prevention strategies which through evaluation have been shown to be effective and portable to other communities?
2. Should funding agencies support prevention strategies that include a mixture of demand and supply initiatives?
3. Does evidence exist which suggests that demand reduction strategies should proceed or follow supply strategies?

"The answers to these and other questions can assist us in the search for successful prevention programs. It is useful to consider each of these strategies separately. However, doing so should not imply that a combination of them cannot be forged, as in the case of impaired driving counter-responses, to culminate into one macro-prevention initiative. Nor presently is there available access to any definitive or rigorous scientific studies that compare strategies. Given this, we are left with some knowledge, experience, data and common sense upon which to base decisions for the purpose of allocating scarce resources on an ethical and cost-effective basis… given the evolution and development of new prevention strategies, common sense suggests that future substance abuse counter-responses should not be preferentially limited to one approach, resulting solely from the demand reduction side of the prevention equation."

While the debate over drug policy in the U.S. has focused on choices and combinations of demand and supply reduction, the Dutch have pioneered an alternative strategy of *harm reduction* (Duncan and Nicholson 1997). The philosophy of harm reduction is to encourage alcohol/drug users to progress towards reducing harm from their drug/alcohol use and thereby improve health at a speed which is acceptable and realistic for them. This strategy dovetails very nicely with motivational treatment approaches but less well with abstinence-focused philosophy which has been predominant in North America (see Recovery). The aim of harm reduction is to keep alcohol/drug users alive, well and as productive as possible until they are able or willing to attain recovery and can be reintegrated into society (Ritter and Cameron 2006). Harm reduction involves multiple strategies including drug substitution programs (methadone, buprenorphine and medically supervised self-administered heroin); outreach programs and peer education typically in the addicts' own environment rather than in the clinic; and needle and syringe exchange programs to reduce spreading of infectious diseases (HIV/AIDS, Hepatitis

B and Hepatitis C) among intravenous drug users. Harm reduction has recently been recognized to offer an increasingly advantageous perspective on treatment benefits of pharmacotherapy of alcohol use disorder (Witkiewitz, Falk DE, Litten et al. 2019).

The prevention strategies discussed, to this point, have some value for moderating the toll of addiction in the population, but are not easily applicable to treatment of individuals. For a physician who encounters a youngster with unique clinical characteristics that might put him/her at risk for addiction, it is not readily apparent how results from prevention studies conducted in populations can be extrapolated to the clinical situation. Nevertheless, there are increasingly recognized opportunities to apply lessons learned from the population to the clinic and *vice versa*. This is ideally accomplished in controlled *prospective* prevention studies in moderate size samples, such as school classrooms that allow careful evaluation and longitudinal follow-up. Kellam, Ensminger and Simon (1980) were able to identify predictive factors for development of drug use disorder among a sample of elementary school students — higher IQ, male sex and aggressiveness. Subsequently, these investigators demonstrated significant improvements in behavior through middle school, among the males who were more aggressive in first grade, in a prospective two-year classroom-based randomized preventive intervention (Kellam, Rebok, Ialongo and Mayer 1994). The ultimate test of prospectively altering such predictive factors is to modify these characteristics and demonstrate they significantly influence development of drug use many years later (Wang, Storr, Green et al. 2012). Once ascertained, such cohorts can be valuable to translate epidemiological observations to the clinic and to retrospectively investigate modifying factors in the efficacy of the intervention, such as genetic characteristics (Musci, Fairman, Masyn et al. 2018), so as to provide insight into genetic-environmental interactions in addiction prevention.

Recovery

According to the current electronic version of Oxford English Dictionary (OED), the noun *recovery* is derived from Anglo-Norman *recoverie*, referring to the "action of regaining as a result of a legal process or judgement, legal remedy" and Middle French *recouvré* "making good a loss, help," also *recovree* "remedy, making good, action of regaining or recovering." The primary meaning of the noun *recovery* according to OED is: "Senses relating to gaining or regaining possession, especially of something lost or taken away (primarily immaterial things)." This is essentially a legal concept: "A fine, charge, etc., recovered at law." The term has been used thus since 1422 as noted (Smith and Smith 1870): "[To pay fines, etc.] recovered in the seide Maires Court, vnto the seide Maire and to such persone3 as the seide recovrees belongeth to of right." Nevertheless, some of the definitions of *recovery* in OED are compatible with current usage in addiction psychiatry. However, the breadth of meanings, which swings as a pendulum between medical and psychosocial/spiritual/philosophical, does suggest a lack of certainty about the term.

The first OED definition of *recovery* that fits in the context of addiction is: "The restoration of a person (or more rarely, a thing) to a healthy or normal condition, or to consciousness." This meaning was first used in the English language in a 1517 translation by an English churchman Bishop Richard Fox (*c.* 1448–1528) of *The Rule of Saint Benedict*, a book of precepts originally written in 516 by Benedict of Nursia (*c.* 480-550). The following appears in the section of the book addressing the care of the sick, the old and the young: "Eatynge of fleshe, may be graunted all way, to suche as be seeke and feble, for their more spedy recouery" (Collett 2016). Another example of this meaning of *recovery* is: "The greatest and most important Strokes for the Recovery of the Patient, must be made at the time of the Invasion, or first State of this Disease" (Arbuthnot 1732). In these quotes, *recovery* signifies useful and specific instructions to healthcare providers about how to best help an ill patient to attain wholeness of body and spirit.

The second definition in OED is: "The regaining or restoration of one's health or a mental state." This meaning indicates what an individual must do to regain vigor and health: "It is wyckednes, to ieste uppon holye thinges, …euen as a man shulde sprinkle durte in a medicine, adorned for recouerie of helthe" (Vives, Morison R, Paynell et al. 1550). This use represents the challenge the sufferer faces to accomplish the task of *self*-healing, as clearly exemplified in the following: "I made the recovery of my health my chief care" (Nugent 1771).

The third of the compatible definitions in OED refers to the bipartite task of addiction treatment, namely the balance between self-help and having one's illness healed by an outside agent: "Restoration or return to a higher or better (especially, spiritual) state." This third meaning of *recovery* conveys the concept that treatment of addiction often requires medical intervention to complement the *self-help* process, including a spiritual element (see Self-help). This use first dates to 1542 (Erasmus and Udall 1877): "A manne wylfully beeyng as a bonde seruaunt to pleasures of the bodye... In suche persons..there was nomaner hope of recouerie." This quotation exemplifies the essential element of the addiction syndrome, namely *out-of-control* use and/or pathological behaviors, which need to be overcome as the major goal of *recovery*. This theme continues to encompass the uncertainty of the recovery process and the need to accept a (higher) power beyond oneself to facilitate the process (Wilson 1939), e.g., "It shall be lawfull sometime to determine, whether he that falleth, fall desperately, or whether there be any place for recouery" (Bedford 1621).

The fourth definition of *recovery* in OED that is compatible with our understanding of addiction also seems consistent with the view that a drug use disorder is, in fact, a medical disorder: "Restoration or return to health from illness, an injury, etc.; an instance of this. Also used with respect to an injury: restoration to a healthy state." The first example of this meaning dates to 1513 when the German scholar Ulrich von Hutten (1488-1523) wrote of symptoms he experienced suffering from syphilis of which he died: "My body semed to droppe awaye in fylthy matter, to my great peyne and sorowe, and no hope at all of recouerye (Hutten and Turner 1730)." This quotation succinctly describes the antithesis of *recovery*, namely, the experience of hopelessness and powerlessness when one realizes that suffering will continue and there is no possibility of return to health. (Oftentimes, description of the opposite may be the best way to define a concept like *recovery*.) The feelings described in Hutten's quotation share characteristics of the beginnings of a new life of recovery from addiction, which can well be a terminal disease if the individual does not purposefully engage in an alternate pathway (Wilson 1939). Another quotation sheds light on this last definition: "Recovery is generally rapid under suitable treatment" (Bristowe 1878). This quotation suggests that recovery viewed from the medical perspective may tend to simplify a complex and ephemeral concept, as recovery from addiction is thought to be. Viewing addiction as "simply" a medical illness excludes some characteristics of recovery: "We are much more likely to be able to look beyond the mere disappearance of symptoms and signs for indication of true recovery…in those illnesses that easily become 'latent'" (Malan, Bacal, Heath and Balfour 1968). Hence, reconciliation of a possibly simplified pathophysiological view and that of the more intricate biopsychosocial perspective (Engel 1977) is not easy because *recovery* is so much more than disappearance of the symptoms, signs and laboratory findings of the illness and resolution of complications.

So, one must merge these two perspectives — disappearance of signs and symptoms *versus* restoration of health and fullness of life — in explaining the meaning of *recovery* within the context of addiction. Adding to the difficulty of defining the elements of *recovery* is, in part, the challenge of specifying what addiction *per se* really is (see Addiction). Surely, addiction is not simply the medical complications that ensue with continued use but also comprises what occurred before *out-of-control* substance use first manifested in the vulnerable person in a biopsychosocial conceptualization. Stated otherwise, "Is an alcoholic on a desert island without available alcohol still an alcoholic?" Is the goal of recovery stopping use or making the person whole, or both? Is the *sine quoi non* of recovery the cessation of out-of-control use, or is reduction of use a meaningful alternative? Does *recovery* require treatment, or can it happen spontaneously? These are useful questions to try to answer and each provides a perspective that is part of the explanation.

To address the first issue, much effort has been expended to identify genetic and other interacting risk factors for developing alcohol and drug use disorders (Kendler, Ohlsson, Sundquist and Sundquist 2019). Prior to the era of massive genome wide screening studies, many of the investigated hypotheses concerning pathogenesis were derived from identification of phenotypes through clinical observation of chronic alcoholics or those with other drug use disorders. Eventually, as understanding of pathophysiology evolved, candidate genes were identified and statistical associations between diagnosis, phenotypes, or genes could be examined. An example of this process was carried out using electrophysiological studies in chronic alcoholics in whom auditory evoked brain potential findings were outside the normal range, presumably a complication of their alcohol use. Similar findings in sons of alcoholics before they ever started drinking was quite unexpected and suggested that this indicator of brain dysfunction may play a role in pathogenesis of alcoholism and may be a useful phenotype for studying risk for developing alcohol use disorder (Begleiter, Porjesz, Bihari and Kissin 1984; Chen, Manz, Tang et al. 2010). Analogously, it was well accepted that brain injury in alcoholism was in part caused by insufficient brain concentrations of the water-soluble vitamin thiamine in those who drank heavily (Mardones, Segovia and Onfray 1946; Victor, Adams and Collins 1971). The observation that the enzyme transketolase had reduced affinity for its cofactor thiamine in young sons of alcoholics prior to any drinking was of considerable interest, suggesting a risk for development of thiamine insufficiency compared to those without this transketolase variant (Mukherjee, Svoronos, Ghazanfari et al. 1987).

Another approach to the question of risk for substance use disorders has been to determine if brain impairments attributed to chronic alcohol/drug use improve with abstinence. Longitudinal studies of individuals after stopping use of alcohol or other drugs suggest that some, but not all measures of brain impairment attributed to neurotoxicity do improve during prolonged abstinence (Volkow, Chang, Wang et al. 2001; Parks, Dawant, Riddle et al. 2002). Interestingly, certain of the brain dysfunctions that do not recover may have subserved behavioral characteristics of these individuals prior to any drug abuse (Tarter, Hegedus, Goldstein et al. 1984). Therefore, *recovery* in addiction must include adaptation to premorbid brain dysfunctions that may have played a role in why the individual started to abuse alcohol or drugs in the first place, not simply stopping out-of-control use and allowing neurotoxicity and allostatic changes to reverse.

This notion of acquiring the ability to cope with one's limitations does not readily concur with the definitions of *recovery* discussed above but is understood by those in the field — recovery requires personal growth, not simply returning to a previous state before pathological use began. When a person develops addiction due to self-medication of a primary psychiatric disorder this point is more easily understood (see Self-medication). Even if the person may be able to stop using drugs/alcohol, the primary disorder *per se* must be addressed as it is associated with impairments that likely will not recover fully with abstinence alone. Hence, the recovering person must *learn* to deal with these premorbid impairments in a more constructive manner than self-medication, likely involving a range of plastic brain changes, or learned coping mechanisms. These may allow the person to participate in life without (or substantially diminished) drug use, overcoming impairments that might have contributed to pathological use in the first place, neurotoxic and allostatic consequences of drug use, as well as impairments due to psychosocial stressors from a variety of causes including secondary psychiatric diagnoses (Starzer, Nordentoft and Hjorthøj 2017).

A straightforward and perhaps simplified view of substance use disorder is that the cause of the problem is out-of-control use. Accordingly, recovery is equated with discontinuing use and allowing the plastic brain changes just described to progress with alacrity. Another perspective, *harm reduction*, has gained increasing proponents, especially as addiction is becoming accepted as a chronic medical illness (McLellan, Lewis, O'Brien and Kleber 2000) that plays a significant role in spread and progression of co-occurring disorders that are exhausting societal healthcare resources (Drummond, Edwards, Glanz et al. 1987).

The history of harm reduction in treatment of alcoholism has had a checkered past. While behaviorists proposed that controlled drinking was a viable approach for recovery, others claimed it was irresponsible because the fundamental problem of alcoholism was loss of control and abstinence was essential (Pendery, Maltzman and West 1982; Sobell and Sobell 1984). Advances in pharmacological treatment for alcoholism beyond the abstinence-focused medication disulfiram (see Alcoholism) have led to a renaissance of the goal to *diminish* drinking rather than to strive for abstinence (Falk, O'Malley, Witkiewitz et al. 2019). Medication-assisted treatment (MAT), an approach that is quite consistent with treatment strategies employed for other chronic diseases such as hypertension, diabetes, HIV, kidney transplantation, among others, that are never "cured" but must be managed throughout a lifetime, has become the preferred response to the "opioid epidemic" in the United States (see Opium). The goal of treatment has become reduction of morbidity and mortality by enhanced compliance with physician recommendations. Accordingly, quality of life has become an important consideration (Kelly, Greene and Bergman 2018), with recognition that relapse even after treatment is very common (Hunt, Barnett and Branch 1971). As addiction treatment becomes integrated into the rest of medicine, harm reduction with improved quality of life becomes a compelling way to view treatment outcomes. In fact, the addiction community recognizes this notion by designating individuals with addiction who are improving their quality of life by attaining repeated periods of sobriety as being *in recovery*, indicating that recovery is an active journey rather than the destination.

The last question posed above is whether treatment is necessary to achieve recovery? Although a significant number of people can achieve remission spontaneously, without the use of clinical treatment or recovery services, those who undergo addiction treatment combined with mutual support groups had approximately twice the chance of discontinuing alcohol/drug use compared to those who did not receive formal treatment (Dawson, Grant, Stinson and Chou 2006; Lopez-Quintero, Hasin, de los Cobos et al. 2011).

Nevertheless, it is well accepted that relapse is a common characteristic of addiction to all substances of abuse (Hunt, Barnett and Branch 1971). Therefore, if addiction is viewed analogously to other chronic illnesses such as diabetes and hypertension, the goal becomes helping the patient approach the best feasible control of physiological parameters with regular visits to the healthcare provider and ongoing compliance with provider recommendations rather than an intensive episode of treatment without further medical oversight (McLellan, Lewis, O'Brien and Kleber 2000). Of course, this is where the medical approach to management of chronic diseases can learn a great deal from addiction treatment in which the focus is self-help through mutual support groups and being in recovery becomes a way of living and thinking differently than heretofore. Although relapse seems to be unavoidable for many individuals, it can be modified resulting in reduced consumption, likely beneficial to health, including less time devoted to out-of-control behaviors, accompanied by enhanced self-esteem and higher quality of life for both the addict and those he loves. The active nature of the process is exemplified by the goal of being *in recovery*. This term suggests that recovery is not an absolute or passive term but potentially an exciting and engaging journey on the road to improvement of one's life.

Resilience

According to the current electronic version of Oxford English Dictionary (OED), the noun *resilience* is probably a borrowing from the post-classical Latin *resilientia* ("the action of rebounding") and classical Latin *resilient-*, *resiliēns*, present participle of the verb, *resilīre* ("To draw back, withdraw, or distance oneself from an undertaking, declaration, course of action, opinion, etc.") and the suffix, *-ia*.

The first use of the word *resilience* in the English language was with a now obsolete meaning ("The action or an act of rebounding or springing back; rebound, recoil."), as exemplified by a quotation of Francis Bacon (1561-1626), the English philosopher and statesman who is credited with developing the scientific method and has been called the father of empiricism in *Sylva sylvarum; or, A naturall historie. In ten centuries* ... (Bacon and Rawley 1626): "Whether there be any such Resilience in Eccho's." Subsequently, the meaning of *resilience* was used in physics to describe elasticity of matter ("…the power of resuming an original shape or position after compression, bending, etc."). This meaning appeared in a lecture by Thomas Young (1773-1829), a British physician and natural philosopher, with notable and extensive contributions to the fields of vision, light, solid mechanics, energy, physiology, language, musical harmony and Egyptology (Young 1807): "The resilience is jointly proportional to its strength and its toughness and is measured by the product of the mass and the square of the velocity of a body capable of breaking it."

The word was then applied to the study of mechanics ("The energy per unit volume absorbed by a material when it is subjected to strain; the value of this at the elastic limit."). This meaning is found in a quotation from William John Macquorn Rankine (1820-1872), a Scottish mechanical engineer who made significant contributions to civil engineering, physics, mathematics and the science of thermodynamics in *A Manual of Applied Mechanics* (Rankine 1858): "The Resilience or Spring of a Beam is the work performed in bending it to the proof deflection."

At about this same time, the word *resilience* spread to the biological sciences and found a particular meaning in the emerging field of psychology and in medicine ("The quality or fact of being able to recover quickly or easily from, or resist being affected by, a misfortune, shock, illness, etc.; robustness; adaptability."). A quotation from John Cassell's *Illustrated History of England* provides an example: "In their struggles with the ponderous power of England [the Scotch] discovered an invincible vigour, not only of resistance, but of resilience" (Smith and Howitt 1856). This quotation does well to underline that fundamental attribute some possess, which only emerges with adversity, to which instead of succumbing as many do, a characteristic robustness or adaptability allows the individual to survive and even thrive.

The meaning of *resilience* used in the field of addiction is that from medicine and psychology. The word has found an important role in conceptualization of individual predisposition to alcohol/drug use disorder—*resilience* diminishes, while *risk* increases, the likelihood of developing addiction by virtue of genetic and/or by environmental factors (Enoch 2006). Additionally, *resilience* may contribute to success of addiction treatment and achieving recovery (Yi, Vitaliano, Smith et al. 2008; see Recovery). It is generally agreed that alcohol/drug use disorders tend to run in families but which of the many factors that tend to be passed from generation to generation are most relevant remains to be established.

A plethora of characteristics have been statistically linked with individual *resilience/risk* to addiction in family and other studies. Conceptually, susceptibility may operate through interactions among features of the individual, the drug of abuse and the environment: (1) the acute psychopharmacological effects of the drug; (2) the pharmacokinetics of the drug; (3) neuroadaptive brain changes with chronic use; (4) psychopathological characteristics of the user; and (5) vulnerability of the user to medical and psychiatric complications (Omenn and Motulsky 1972; Martin 1981; Enoch 2006).

The relative importance of environmental and hereditary factors in etiopathogenesis continued to be a subject of heated debate throughout most of the last century. Essentially the same evidence has been marshalled to reach diametrically opposite conclusions in the *nature-nurture controversy*, as these disorders occur in roughly equal numbers among individuals with and without a positive family history (inherited *vs.* sporadic cases). Only relatively recently, through advances in molecular and epidemiologic genetics, has the complexity of this pivotal debate become appreciated in its entirety (Cloninger 1987; Cadet 2016).

We now know that both arms of the machinery of heredity have important roles in transmission of biological information to the next generation through interaction of genes and the environment. Lasker (1969) anticipated an enhanced role for adaptation of the human population via environmental pressure compared to what was understood in classical genetics: "This implies an evolutionary tendency to shift human adaptability from genetic selection to ontogenetic plasticity to reversible adaptability." In fact, the nature-nurture controversy has been reconciled to some degree through recognition of molecular alterations of gene expression by environmental events: "epigenetics allows the peaceful co-existence of Darwinian and Lamarckian evolution" (Handel and Ramagopalan 2010). (Darwinian and Lamarckian evolution are meant as evolutionary selection via genetic inheritance or acquired characteristics, respectively.)

The sometimes-vociferous debate about relative contributions of genes and the environment to development of addiction has been further complicated by inexact descriptions of the relevant *phenotypes*. For example, consensus about the definition of addiction was relatively late in coming, most definitions served to identify with confidence only the most severe cases and there was tremendous biologic heterogeneity in these disorders, even in clinically similar patient populations (Martin 1981; Kwako, Schwandt, Ramchandani et al. 2019). Also, many of the clinical characteristics of individuals, defined as having alcohol/drug use disorder, may actually represent complications of self-medication of co-occurring psychiatric disorders, rather than predisposing factors to harmful use of these psychoactive agents (see Self-medication). Nevertheless, since abuse of alcohol/drugs is the *sine qua non* of the disorder, there exists a unique opportunity to study genetically high-risk individuals *prior to exposure* to the etiologic agent. Additionally, it is possible to examine acute response to known amounts of the substance of abuse or the complications of prolonged use in individuals at variable degrees of risk (genetic and/or environmental). From such studies, it is possible to identify factors that either increase or diminish the likelihood of development of addiction.

The concept of *resilience* has acquired an increasingly important meaning in understanding the pathogenesis of addiction and as an attribute of individuals who possess certain characteristics that seem to protect them from the disorder. Much like apportioning elements of the *risk* for development of addiction, *resilience* can be partitioned as being within the realm(s) of the biological, psychological or social (Engel 1977). Nevertheless, biologically based *resilience* factors, predominantly the capacity to successfully cope with various forms of stress (Selye 1937), are actually represented by brain functions which can incorporate and orchestrate all elements of the behavioral repertoire, so that psychosocial and biological elements are inexorably intertwined, as articulated by Sinha (2001):

> "This conceptualization permits separate consideration of (1) events that cause stress (stressors or stressful life events); (2) cognitive and affective processes evaluating the event and available coping resources (appraisal); (3) biological responses and adaptation needed to cope with the stressor; and (4) behavioral and cognitive response to the stressful event (coping)."

Hence, the tripartite elements comprising *resilience* modulate and can counteract to some degree determinants that enhance the likelihood of developing addiction; similarly, *resilience* can augment the prospect of recovery. This hopeful perspective of *resilience* has widespread acceptance as expressed by Jerome Kagan (1929—), an American psychologist and one of the pioneers of developmental psychology (1976): "Young mammals seem to retain a capacity for recovery from early experiences that retard normal development if they are fortunate enough to be moved to a more benign context." Thus, the challenge is to understand the contributing factors of *resilience* through the life cycle so that they can be modified to help overcome experience of stress and either prevent or change the clinical course of addiction.

Various models of observed and experimentally induced psychosocial stress have been implemented to study *risk versus resilience*. Attachment theory emerged from the observations of John Bowlby (1907—1990), a British psychiatrist and psychoanalyst, notable for his interest in child development (Bowlby 1966). Harry Harlow (1905—1981), an American psychologist known for his experiments on rhesus monkeys elucidating the roles of maternal separation, dependency needs and social isolation (Seay, Hansen and Harlow 1962). These studies demonstrated the fundamental role of caregiving and companionship to social and cognitive development and identified the implications of disturbed attachment in various forms of psychopathology. The relevance of separation-related stress in pathogenesis of addiction was only inferred until it was formally demonstrated in a nonhuman primate model of alcohol abuse by the intellectual progeny of Harlow (Higley, Hasert, Suomi and Linnoila 1991).

Michael Rutter (1933—), a British child psychiatrist whose clinical research examined the implications of attachment for general child psychopathology, commented (Rutter 1985): "although an appreciation that a variety of stressors may play a role in the genesis of psychiatric disorder has a long history, the systematic study of such effects is much more recent."

Investigation of intrapsychic responses to adversity and stress, representing more or less effective coping mechanisms that might moderate the expression of psychopathology throughout development, have been incorporated into psychoanalytic thinking. For example, Vaillant (1985) examined the "utility of the model of ego mechanisms of defense to explain psychological resilience in 307 middle aged men with socially disadvantaged childhoods" who were prospectively studied for 40 years. He proposed that the "maturity of defenses" served as a means of coping with developmental stress. Steinglass, Weiner and Mendelson (1971) suggested that rigidity of interactions within the family played a role in pathogenesis of alcoholism—clearly a means whereby genetic and environmental factors can interact at a psychological level.

Somewhat consonant with stress experienced from disturbed family interactions, is the experimental paradigm of "learned helplessness" wherein self-protective escape by rats from electric shock is prevented, resulting in lifelong neurobiological consequences (Garber, Fencil-Morse, Rosellini and Seligman 1979). Impaired family coping of individuals can spread to communities via psychosocial phenomena related to "behavioral mimicry and contagion" (Chartrand and Lakin 2013). The consequences of such and related psychobiological forms of stress and coping can be assessed using functional magnetic resonance imaging (fMRI) and adaptations of brain functions associated with recovery and resilience in addiction and its neurobiological correlates may be identified and studied (Burt, Whelan, Conrod et al. 2016; Charlet, Rosenthal, Lohoff et al. 2018).

Elucidation of the biological mechanisms underpinning the effects of stress on the central nervous system offers a complementary perspective to clinical observations that stressful events often presage psychopathology and that the *experience* of stress itself, not only is associated with addiction, but is also exacerbated by alcohol/drug abuse (Meerloo 1954; McEwen 2007; Cadet 2016). Covington, Maze, Sun et al. (2011) investigated how "substance abuse increases an individual's vulnerability to stress-related illnesses, which is presumably mediated by drug-induced neural adaptations that alter subsequent responses to stress." They identified "repressive histone methylation in nucleus accumbens, an important brain reward region, as a key mechanism linking cocaine exposure to increased stress vulnerability." Moreover, the investigators demonstrated that specific epigenetic modification of gene expression protected mice from the consequences of subsequent increases in stress susceptibility associated with social stress and repeated cocaine exposure.

Of note, using a "food addiction mouse model," Domingo-Rodriguez, Ruiz de Azua, Dominguez et al. (2020) demonstrated that "the development of food addiction-like behavior… is enhanced… associated with synaptic excitatory transmission in the medial prefrontal cortex (mPFC) and in the nucleus accumbens (NAc)… In contrast, chemogenetic inhibition of neuronal activity in the mPFC-NAc pathway induces compulsive food seeking." These findings are important because they support similar neurobiological underpinning of resilience and risk in behavioral addictions as those that have been identified for out-of-control self-administration of alcohol and drugs. Enhancement of resilience with respect to drug-seeking behavior has also been demonstrated using cognitive training in mice (Boivin, Piscopo and Wilbrecht 2015) underlining that resilience is both pharmacologically and behaviorally modifiable as might be expected in a biopsychosocial disorder.

Risk and resilience to the *experience* of stress is a characteristic that can be transmitted from one generation to the next based on epigenetic mechanisms, identified in animals in which maternal rearing practices were experimentally modified (Meaney 2001). Translation of this idea to humans is found in the work of Yehuda, Schmeidler, Wainberg et al. (1998) who examined the progeny of mothers who survived the inordinate stress of the Holocaust prior to the birth of their children. They found "an increased vulnerability to posttraumatic stress disorder and other psychiatric disorders among offspring of Holocaust survivors, thus identifying adult offspring as a possible high-risk group within which to explore the individual differences that constitute risk factors for PTSD." Subsequently, the means of this intergenerational transmission of psychiatric vulnerability, resilience, and symptoms of PTSD in Holocaust survivors' offspring, was found to be associated with epigenetic changes in expression of a protein regulator of glucocorticoid receptor responsivity (Bierer, Bader, Daskalakis et al. 2020).

A specific linkage of PTSD to alcohol/drug use disorders was demonstrated by Reed, Anthony and Breslau (2007), who prospectively followed incidence of drug use disorders in a sample of youngster who experienced traumatic events with and without developing PTSD. They concluded that: "Posttraumatic stress disorder might be a causal determinant of drug use disorders, possibly representing complications such as attempts to self-medicate troubling trauma-associated memories, nightmares, or painful hyperarousal symptoms." Enoch (2006) placed these various determinants of *intergenerational transmission* of alcohol/drug use in perspective:

> "Severe childhood stressors have been associated with increased vulnerability to addiction, however, not all stress-exposed children go on to develop alcoholism… Genetic vulnerability is likely to be conferred by multiple genes of small to modest effects, possibly only apparent in gene-environment interactions… It is likely that a complex mix of gene(s)-environment(s) interactions underlie addiction vulnerability and development. Risk-resilience factors can best be determined in longitudinal studies, preferably starting during pregnancy."

This quotation suggests that, at this point in history, *resilience* is a characteristic which, in a practical sense, is only to be retrospectively inferred in humans. Nevertheless, aspects of *resilience* can be recognized and possibly serve to allow those at *risk*, to choose positive aspects of their environment to mitigate development of addiction.

In conclusion, *resilience* is a more optimistic way to view the development of addictive disorders than is *risk*. It allows focus on biopsychosocial factors that potentially can be modified to help either prevent or change the clinical course of addiction. Most importantly, for those who are at risk for the disorder by virtue of their family and social circumstances, wherein addiction seems ubiquitous, this perspective provides pharmacopsychosocial options, which if chosen, increase the likelihood that s/he are *not predestined* to suffer from addiction and its complications (Martin, Weinberg and Bealer 2007).

Salience

The noun *salience,* according to the current electronic version of the Oxford English Dictionary (OED), is a combination of the adjective/noun *salient* and the suffix *-ence.* The word *salient* is derived from Latin *salientem,* the present participle of *salīre,* meaning "to leap," frequently assimilated wholly or partly to the French *saillant.* The suffix *-ence* is from the French via the Latin *-entia,* forming abstract nouns, usually of quality, rarely of action, on participial stems in *-ent-* (e.g., *audient-em* hearing, *audient-ia* the process of hearing, audience). An example of the first use of the noun *salience* in the English language, according to OED, was by James Henry Leigh Hunt (1784-1859), an English poet, journalist and literary critic, in his work *The Seer; or, Common-Places Refreshed* (1840): "The suddenness and salience of all that is lively, sprouting, and new." This is a rarely used meaning of *salience:* "The quality of leaping or springing up."

A more recent and commonly used meaning of the word ("A salient or projecting feature, part, or object.") can be found in *Self-formation; or, The history of an individual mind; intended as a guide for the intellect through difficulties to success* by Capel Lofft (1806-1873), an English classical scholar, poet, and writer (Lofft 1837): "To people who would merely lounge along, side by side, these saliences are sorely annoying, they are abominable things." The most current meaning of *salience* is: "The fact, quality, or condition of being salient or projecting beyond the general outline or surface. Also, of immaterial things." This use is found in the following quotation of Sir George Gilbert Scott (1811-1878), a prolific English Gothic revival architect chiefly associated with the design, building and renovation of churches and cathedrals: "These subsidiary shafts may be …subordinated one to another, both in size and salience."

The rather concrete meaning of *salience* as used in architecture was transformed into a more abstract sense as the word lept to a distant field, social psychology, from whence it evolved to become pivotal in the field of addiction: "The quality or fact of being more prominent in a person's awareness or in his memory of past experience." An example of this use of the word in psychology is found in the English translation of *General Psychology from the Personalistic Standpoint* by William Stern (1871-1938), a German psychologist and philosopher, known for the development of personality psychology which emphasizes the individual by examining measurable personality traits as well as the interaction of those traits to create the self (Stern 1938): "The different proportions of salience and embedding give the process and content of every experience its special character." Contemporaneously, Gordon Willard Allport (1897-1967), an American psychologist often referred to as one of the founding figures of personality psychology, employed a very similar meaning in *Personality: A Psychological Interpretation* (Allport 1938):

> "At other times... consciousness is embedded ...more deeply; there is less clearness, less salience. Salience represents an act of pointing, a directedness of the person toward something that at the moment has special significance for him."

This last quotation accurately portrays the heightened role occupied by the pharmacologic actions of a drug of abuse or an aspect of the behavioral repertoire in the experiential framework of an individual who is suffering from an addictive disorder (see Addiction).

Salience is the basis of *preference* and *choice*, a guiding feature of a behaving organism, free to engage with the world to seek fulfillment. Attribution of salience can involve perceptual experiences in one or multiple sensory modalities, as exemplified by olfactory stimuli (Moskowitz and Gerbers 1974). Salience and other elements of a sensory experience may be encoded in structurally disparate brain regions. For example, the functional separation of sensory and affective aspects of pain perception (see Pain) appears to extend to the memory of pain as well, such that distinct brain regions process sensory discriminative and affective components of pain (Albanese, Duerden, Rainville and Duncan 2007).

However, declaring that there is an emotional phenomenon termed "salience" that equates with *positive biasing or attributions* concerning experiential elements of the world that can guide behavior at a fundamental level is not fully satisfactory unless it can be measured. Psychometric methods were initially all that were available to empirically evaluate topics of high, moderate or low importance (salience) in an individual's life situation (Jackson, Manaugh, Wiens and Matarazzo 1971) – of course, declaration of the relative importance of an issue by a person has its own biases and sources of error but, nevertheless, can yield useful data. Progressing from the psychometric approaches with only face validity, measures of the subjective bias of attention and other relevant brain functions can be more objectively measured using newer neuroimaging techniques, including positron emission tomography (PET), functional magnetic resonance imaging (fMRI) and event-related fMRI, which allows cognitive neuroscientists to examine brain processes related to salience using measures of neural activity (Driver and Frackowiak 2001). For example, brain activation characteristics of the response to a sensory stimulus may be determined in terms of its magnitude and anatomic location. As demonstrated by event-related fMRI, the emotional salience of a logical reasoning task can alter the region of the prefrontal cortex that was engaged in the cognitive process (Goel and Dolan 2003). Event-related fMRI was employed to demonstrate that both *valence* which means how positive or negative an emotion feels (Olds and Milner 1954) and *salience* each partially accounts for nucleus accumbens (NAcc) activation during incentive processing (Cooper and Knutson 2008). This is a vital observation because of the pivotal role the NAcc in the reward pathways that are implicated in addiction (Wise 1987).

Addiction constitutes a *narrowing* of the behavioral repertoire, limiting preference and choice because only a focused element of the world remains salient. The behavioral changes accompanying addiction may occur, in part, because salience is an important modulator of learning (Beach and Shoenberger 1965), the fundamental brain mechanism underpinning addiction (see Conditioning). The salience inherent in a specific experience can change depending on the stage of development of the addiction process in the individual. For example, the salience of each cigarette smoked becomes significantly more powerful as one attempts to diminish smoking (Berecz 1984) and the salience of smoking-relevant cues in the environment can influence the magnitude of the desire to smoke (Payne, Schare, Levis and Colletti 1991). The basis of the enhanced salience to smoking-related cues during smoking abstinence involves significant potentiation of neural responses in brain regions subserving visual sensory processing, attention and action planning in dorsomedial prefrontal cortex (McClernon, Kozink, Lutz and Rose 2009). Drug and drug-associated stimuli may also activate memory circuits including the amygdala, hippocampus and dorsal striatum, all of which have dopamine-innervation and thus dopamine may influence motivational salience of the drug and associated stimuli (Volkow, Fowler, Wang and Goldstein 2002). Accordingly, withdrawal after repeated ethanol exposure produced several alterations in the physiological properties of ventral tegmental area (VTA) dopamine neurons, which could ultimately increase the ability of VTA neurons to produce burst firing and thus might contribute to reinitiating addiction-related behaviors (Hopf, Martin, Chen et al. 2007). Another way that salience and attentional biases towards cigarettes in addiction (see Nicotine) may be modified is through physiological states such as acute exercise (see Exercise) which can reduce desire to smoke (Van Rensburg, Taylor and Hodgson 2009).

The role of salience in shaping addictive behavior is demonstrated by the psychometric factors that may explain why one begins to use marijuana and continues its use, each potentially very different from the other (Lucas 1978). This underlines that addiction is a *process* that changes the affected person – what is considered important to the individual (salient) is predictably transformed as a function of the time and quantity of drug use (Martin, Lovinger and Breese 1995). Similarly, salience of food cues has been found to be associated with eating behaviors, expressed somewhat differently under circumstances of trying and not trying to lose weight, compatible with the notion that the phenomenon of salience is basic to addictive behaviors of all kinds, not simply drug use disorders (Collins 1978). Importantly, corticosterone has been demonstrated to enhance the salience of saccharin, a non-caloric surrogate for motivated food intake (Bhatnagar, Bell, Liang et al. 2000). As hypercortisolism from stress experienced during withdrawal occurs during each and every epoch of addiction to drugs or food, this accentuates the vicious cycle of repeated self-administration and perpetuates the likelihood of re-initiating use (Martin, Weinberg and Bealer 2007). Moreover, it has been argued that *allostatic* changes alter salience making it less likely to self-administer enough of the drug to which an individual is addicted, thereby enhancing the pace of progression of the disorder (Koob and Le Moal 2006).

Robinson and Berridge (1993) have interwoven *salience* into their *Incentive-Sensitization Theory of Addiction*, which has become pivotal for subsequent research in neurobiological underpinnings of addiction. The theory posits:

> "…that addictive behavior is due largely to progressive and persistent neuroadaptations caused by repeated drug use. It is, if you will, a 'neuroadaptationist model'. It is proposed that these drug-induced changes in the nervous system are manifest both neurochemically and behaviorally by the phenomenon of 'sensitization', which refers to a progressive increase in a drug effect with repeated treatment… it is proposed here that *the defining characteristics of addiction (craving and relapse) are due directly to drug-induced changes in those functions normally subserved by a neural system that undergoes sensitization-related neuroadaptations.*

> "The neural system that is rendered hypersensitive ('sensitized') to activating stimuli is hypothesized to mediate a specific psychological function involved in the process of incentive motivation: namely the *attribution of incentive salience* to the perception and mental representation of stimuli and actions. This makes stimuli and their representations highly salient, attractive and 'wanted.' It is the activation of this neural system that results in the experience of 'wanting,' and transforms ordinary stimuli into incentive stimuli.

> "Sensitization of this neural system by drugs results in a pathological enhancement in the incentive salience that the nervous system attributes to the act of drug taking. The co-activation of associative learning directs the focus of this neurobehavioral

system to specific targets that are associated with drugs and leads to an increasing pathological focus of incentive salience on drug-related stimuli. Thus, with repeated drug use the act of drug taking and drug-associated stimuli, gradually become more and more attractive. Drug-associated stimuli become more and more able to control behavior, because the neural system that mediates 'wanting' becomes progressively sensitized. 'Wanting' evolves into obsessive craving and this is manifest behaviorally as compulsive drug seeking and drug taking. Therefore, by this view, drug craving and addictive behavior are due specifically to sensitization of incentive salience.

"But 'wanting' is not 'liking.' The neural system responsible for 'wanting' incentives is proposed to be separable from those responsible for 'liking' incentives (i.e., for mediating pleasure) and repeated drug use only sensitizes the neural system responsible for 'wanting.' Because of this, addictive behavior is fundamentally a problem of sensitization-induced excessive 'wanting' alone. This is in contrast to 'pleasure-seeking' theories of addiction, which explicitly assume that the incentive motivational properties of drugs are due directly to their subjective pleasurable effects; i.e., their ability to produce positive affective states…The Incentive-Sensitization Theory is unique, however, because we propose the progressive increase in drug 'wanting' that characterizes addiction is not accompanied by an increase in the pleasure derived from drugs. Repeated drug use does not sensitize neural systems responsible for the subjective pleasurable effects of drugs, only those responsible for incentive salience – transforming 'wanting' into craving."

They conclude that "…the neuroadaptations underlying behavioral sensitization are long-lasting and in some cases, they may be permanent…" and propose the hypothesis "that the neural substrate for incentive-sensitization (that is the neural system[s] that normally attributes salience to incentive stimuli and becomes sensitized by addictive drugs) is the mesotelencephalic dopamine system."

This theory has provided an important framework for evolution of the understanding of addiction, including the relevance of salience. From a purely behaviorist construct of drug self-administration based primarily on conditioning (see Conditioning), the theory makes place for emotional modulation of addictive behaviors. In a sense, this is the first attempt to examine addiction, not simply as a function of the pharmacologic actions of a drug, but how these actions interact with *individual characteristics and desires* of the user. This theory has led the way to elucidating the underpinning neural circuits (Zhang and Volkow 2019) and intracellular events within these circuits (Kalivas and Volkow 2005) that subserve the self-destructive and out-of-control behaviors that are characteristic of addiction. Finally, Everitt and Robbins (2005) reconcile the interactions of conditioning with individual emotional attributions and weave in underpinning neuroplastic brain circuits that involve dopaminergic neurotransmission and thereby, explicate the *process* of addiction:

> "…as the endpoint of a series of transitions from initial drug use – when a drug is voluntarily taken because it has reinforcing, often hedonic, effects – through loss of control over this behavior, such that it becomes habitual and ultimately compulsive… these transitions depend on interactions between pavlovian and instrumental learning processes… the change from voluntary drug use to more habitual and compulsive drug use represents a transition at the neural level from prefrontal cortical to striatal control over drug seeking and drug taking behavior as well as a progression from ventral to more dorsal domains of the striatum, involving its dopaminergic innervation. These neural transitions may themselves depend on the neuroplasticity in both cortical and striatal structures that is induced by chronic self-administration of drugs."

The role of salience in the longitudinal process of acquiring out-of-control and self-destructive behaviors that characterize addiction should not be forgotten, as it is always there, even though it transforms and is transformed by the face of addiction at each stage of its development and progression.

Screening

According to the current electronic version of the Oxford English Dictionary (OED), the noun *screening* was formed within English by derivation and combination of the verb *screen* and the suffix *-ing*. The verb *screen* itself was formed in English by conversion of the noun *screen*, a variant or alteration of the French *escrein*, which evolved to *écran*, meaning "fire screen (13th century), protective shield (mid-13th century), dividing screen, partition (1538)" and most recently defined in OED as "A movable panel, and related senses." The verb *screen* has very many meanings in OED, including its first listed meaning in the English language, which is now obsolete ("To protect, conceal, or divide, and related senses. As an *intransitive*: To interpose oneself between (also betwixt) a person and something harmful or unpleasant, as a protective shield.")

It was not until the 20th century that the verb *screen* acquired a meaning now used in medicine and is relevant to the field of addiction: "To examine (a person, especially as one of a large group) for the presence of disease or abnormality, especially as part of a survey rather than as a response to a request for treatment." The first use of the noun *screening* in the English language ("The action of sheltering, protecting, or concealing someone or something with or as with a screen. Also *figurative*: the action of hiding or keeping something from knowledge.") is not relevant to this discussion. However, the contemporary meaning of *screening* that is applicable to addiction is defined in OED as: "Medical examination of a person or group to detect disease or abnormality, especially as part of a broad survey rather than as a response to a request for treatment."

As just indicated, the meaning of *screen/screening* has evolved over the centuries — initially, these words referred to an impermeable, protective barrier, then the barrier became permeable, letting some of everything through and eventually, the barrier became selectively permeable and could ideally exclude all but entities that met decided-upon criteria. The first meaning of the verb *screen* in the English language was employed in the play *Hamlet* by William Shakespeare (1564–1616), the English playwright, poet and actor, widely regarded as the greatest writer in the English language (Shakespeare 1604): "Tell him… your grace hath screend and stood betweene Much heate and him." An example of the meaning of *screen*, relevant to addiction, appeared in an article in the *Journal of the Royal Statistical Society* (Jones 1938): "A coefficient of correlation… provides a measure of the *general* association of an index with clinical assessment, whereas practical interest is directed on the particular boys whom it is desired to screen." The noun *screening* was first used in the English language as follows (Watson 1651): "If these

Flames warme by degrees at a distance (and some danger drawes on of being scorch'd without screening) their dutie should prompt them to withdraw in due season." The first use of *screening* as relevant to addiction was in an article in *Archives of Diseases in Childhood* (Anonymous 1920): "The working party persist in using the term screening as a synonym for the detection of abnormality while claiming to be scientific in their approach for surveillance."

This last quotation refers to *screening* as, putatively, the first step in identifying with some certainty, an affected person from amongst many who likely do not have a particular condition. In medicine, screening typically is followed by the process of *diagnosis* to establish, with greater certainty still, the presence of the condition in question. Thus, the role of *screening* is to select the persons who should undertake the full effort required to establish the diagnosis of a disorder and simultaneously, to exclude those who have only a small, but finite likelihood of having the condition, as all screening tests have some level of uncertainty. An individual can present without previous screening for evaluation and diagnostic testing should they believe there is a health concern; this can be called *self-screening*. Screening is an important issue in all branches of medicine, especially in the diagnosis of disorders that may be occult, but nonetheless harmful to health — classic examples are screening for cancer, an infection or a genetic abnormality which may increase risk for developing a disorder. The goal is identifying a condition that neither the physician nor the patient may know is present, in order to choose an appropriate treatment or, equally important, to provide reassurance that the patient is *not* affected. Diagnosis has been fundamental to medicine throughout history (Ritchie 1820):

> "As there is nothing which can more immediately affect the accuracy or success of a physician's practice than the truth or fallacy of the diagnosis which he is accustomed to form; so there is nothing which ought so powerfully to excite his attention as the peculiarities which different diseases assume. This is a subject of inquiry so essential in our profession indeed, and one which is so apt either to be neglected, or conducted on improper principles, that it cannot be too frequently recurred to, or too strongly insisted on. The experience of the medical practitioner is constantly presenting him with pathological facts to which he is a stranger, and with combinations of disease which he has never anticipated; while the precepts of his art, the most general in their application, are often fettered with exceptions, and the best established of the principles which direct him are subject to changes. A physician, in the exercise of his professional duties, is thus like a mariner in an

unknown sea. The leading features of the scene may be familiar in both cases to the imagination, and their probable dangers estimated pretty correctly from analogy, but those of a minuter character cannot be so well judged of, and must consequently require an incessant examination.

"In attempting the solution of a case in medicine, we will be often deceived, and almost always perplexed in our conclusions; for, as we have little save analogy to guide us, and are ever in danger of being misled in the application even of this, it cannot be expected that medicine will have either the precision or the constancy of a regular science. But methinks the very disadvantages under which medicine labours, as a science, should operate on properly tempered minds, as so many additional inducements to cultivate an acquaintance with it."

A distinctly different challenge is to determine whether a patient is suffering from addiction, a diagnosis that the physician may only suspect and might feel uncomfortable to address for several reasons (Mendelson, Wexler, Kubzansky et al. 1964). Also, the patient may not easily divulge this problem to the physician for significant shame they experience from the associated stigma or, additionally, may not actually believe they have the disorder and completely deny the issue (Morey and Martin 1989). So, even if the physician desires to help, they and the patient may be at cross-purposes. Hence, there are two tasks of screening under these circumstances: first, to support the accuracy of the physician's suspicions and second, to help the patient accept the problems associated with addiction and understand the challenges they face to achieve a more fulfilling and healthful life. There certainly are other situations in medicine, aside from addiction, that similarly challenge the physician's diagnostic and therapeutic acumen, but not many.

An example of an analogous clinical trial faced by physicians over the centuries is described in the following editorial, "On the Diagnosis of Syphilis" (Anonymous 1806):

"It has been justly lamented, by accurate and eminent practitioners, that no criterion could be formed, at least by appearance, of the difference between, the true and spurious venereal sore; this, I confess, in numerous cases, is a difficult and almost impossible thing, and whoever solely trusts to the appearance of either a primary or secondary affection, without being guided by the history of the case, will be subject to perpetual error."

This quotation suggests that an accurate diagnosis requires understanding of as much of the historical foundations of the clinical situation as can be obtained with the caveat that the patient may not feel free to discuss this. If there are missing elements of the historical underpinnings due to denial of the problem by the patient, the physician is at a distinct disadvantage. Accordingly, the physician must rely on clinical acumen or intuition and any and all the tools in the armamentarium.

For syphilis, laboratory testing has telescoped screening into diagnosis with a high level of confidence (Browne and Coffey 1958). In contrast, skillful clinical evaluation has remained the standard for recognition of alcoholism, as discussed by O'Hollaren and Wellman (1958) in their article *Hidden Alcoholic*:

> "In light of data on the prevalence of alcoholism and the recent indications of drastic change in the general description of the typical alcoholic, it seems logical to point out the following factors:
>
> 1. Alcoholism is a major medical problem.
>
> 2. Approximately 6 per cent of the total alcoholic population is receiving treatment of some type. It is certain that the vast majority of alcoholics have physiological symptoms as a result of their alcoholism. Many of them must be under medical care for these symptoms but have not yet been discovered to be alcoholics. Physicians are treating alcoholics in many cases without the benefit of realizing they are alcoholics.
>
> 3. Because of the 'hidden' alcoholic's compulsive need to keep his addiction hidden, he will usually not report to a physician the full extent of his drinking or the effect that alcohol has on his general health. In such cases, the importance of obtaining an accurate history of the patient's characteristic response to alcohol cannot be overemphasized. Where hidden alcoholism is suspected, the physician should carefully check the history of the patient with the spouse or some other member of the immediate family. If a positive history of hidden alcoholism is obtained, the patient should be confronted with the diagnosis and advised to face the problem and the need for treatment.

4. Because of the popular misconception of the 'typical' alcoholic, physicians are failing in many cases to recognize alcoholism as the underlying cause of physical symptoms."

It is, of course, important to understand that the term "hidden" equally applies to other drug use disorders and behavioral addictions and an analogous explanation can be advanced for why diagnosis is so difficult (Martin Weinberg and Bealer 2007).

Screening for addiction can be accomplished by a range of approaches, from a few clinical questions related to consequences of alcohol/drug use elicited in the clinical exam or through a paper and pencil task (Manson 1949; Mayfield, Mcleod and Hall 1974; Ewing 1984; Morey and Martin 1989), validated comprehensive questionnaires that are now often computerized for self-completion (McLellan, Luborsky, Woody and O'Brien 1980) and laboratory or toxicological tests which identify abnormalities resulting from alcohol or drug use or the presence/quantification of the substance(s) in body fluids (Magliozzi, Kanter, Csernansky and Hollister 1983; Skinner, Holt, Schuller et al. 1984; Eckardt, Rawlings and Martin 1986; Mueller, Fleming, LeMahieu et al. 1988; Schwartz 1988; Neumann, Beck, Helander and Böttcher 2020; Trana, Mannocchi, Pirani et al. 2020). The results of these measures typically have undergone validation research studies to be able to yield probabilistic statements about the likelihood that the tested individual has the condition in question (Griner, Mayewski, Mushlin and Greenland 1981; Sox 1986). For example, an approach using a simple screening test comprised of four questions which can seamlessly be incorporated into a clinical examination has striking sensitivity and specificity (Bush, Shaw, Cleary et al. 1987).

A clinically useful strategy is simply to ask whether there is a family history of alcohol use disorder, which can support the presence of alcohol and drug use disorder in a patient in which this disorder may be suspected based on the clinical presentation (Miller, Gold, Belkin and Klahr 1989). Multiple testing approaches using laboratory tests have been implemented over the years, but none are strikingly superior to skillfully asking the patient the questions identified in the simplest screening tests (Bernadt, Taylor, Mumford et al. 1982). An inclusive screening/assessment/diagnostic approach is provided by the Addiction Severity Index (McLellan, Luborsky, Woody and O'Brien 1980). This instrument provides a comprehensive assessment of the disorder and its complications via a problem severity profile across six domains: substance (drug and alcohol) abuse, medical, psychological, legal, family and social and employment/support and can also be utilized for developing a treatment plan.

Finally, single, or combined laboratory findings can be used to provide enhanced mathematical modelling of the presence of a drug use disorder (Ryback, Eckardt, Rawlings and Rosenthal 1982).

Screening tests can serve to anchor the physician's understanding of the clinical situation and allow them to approach the patient more confidently with the perceived problem. Perhaps more important, the results of screening can provide an entrée to a therapeutic interchange with the often-reluctant patient. The goal of this clinical discussion is to help the patient begin to appreciate that a problem *does* exist. Therefore, screening can serve as a useful starting point for initiating progression of the patient through the *stages of change* using *motivational interviewing*, a heuristically useful behavioral approach with demonstrated efficacy in treatment of addiction (Miller 1983; Prochaska and DiClemente 1983; see Motivation). Nevertheless, every one of these validated tests must be combined with clinical skills and judgement as there is no single test which alone renders the positive results into a diagnosis with certitude. For addictive disorders, making the diagnosis does not mean that the physician can treat and "cure" the patient as has become possible for the previously discussed sexually transmitted disease, syphilis, for which diagnosis and treatment are now both widely available (Ropper 2019). Rather, clinical identification of addiction is a call to action for the patient (and perhaps also the physician), a challenge which they may choose, or not, to transform a harmful disease into the process of recovery (see Recovery).

Sedative

The title of this entry was selected because according to the Oxford English Dictionary (OED), the word *sedative* was the first one used in the English language (*c.* 1425) of the many others that have very closely related meanings. Almost all of these are relevant to addiction as they are often used for self-medication of various distressing symptoms and are prescribed by physicians for their patients with recalcitrant medical and psychiatric conditions (see Self-medication). Each will be discussed in the sequence and context they appeared in the English language. These closely related words are all nouns, and some are also adjectives: *hypnotic* (1625)*, soporific* (1690) *sedative-hypnotic* (mentioned in OED in relation to pentobarbital, 1931)*, hypnosedative* (not mentioned in OED)*, ataractic/ataraxic* (1941), *minor tranquillizer* (1960) – although *tranquillizer* alone appeared much earlier (1800) – and *anxiolytic* (1962).

According to the current electronic version of OED, the noun *sedative* is derived from the French *sédatif* and from the medieval Latin *sēdātīvus* and Latin *sēdāre*. The noun *sedative* is defined as: "That has the property of allaying, assuaging, or soothing. A sedative medicine." An example of its first use in the English language appears in *Treatises of Fistula in Ano* by John of Arderne (1307–1392), an English surgeon considered one of the fathers of surgery, who in his writings set out not only his operative procedures but also his code of conduct for the ideal medical practitioner (Arderne 1400): "Oile roset complete is resolutiue, confortatyue, and conueniently cedatyue of akyng." He also recommended opium, so that the patient "shal sleep so that he shal feel no cutting" (Anonymous 1965). In *A System of Medicine* edited by Sir Thomas Clifford Allbutt (1836–1925), an English physician who was commissioner for lunacy in England and Wales 1889-1892, also states that sedation is not a unique consequence of only one medicine, but many medicines can have this pharmacological action (Allbutt 1899): "Sedatives such as bromides and valerian… must be administered."

The noun *hypnotic* is derived from the French *hypnotique* and from the Latin *hypnōticus* and the Greek ὑπνωτικός meaning "inclined to sleep, sleepy; also, putting to sleep, narcotic" and ὑπνοῦν meaning "to put to sleep." The noun *hypnotic* is defined in OED as: "An agent that produces sleep; a sedative or soporific drug." An example of the first appearance of this word in the English language was in the book *The Anatomie of Vrines* (Hart 1625): "Not neglecting hypnoticke, cordiall, and deoppilatiue medicines." Thomas Willis (1621–1675), an English physician, a founding member of the Royal Society and a pioneer in research into the anatomy of the brain, nervous system and muscles, provides an example of the noun (Willis 1681): "Hypnoticks are oft necessary in this Disease." Willis thus recognized that sedation can be a helpful component of treatment of certain conditions, not only to cause sleep and allow surgery in healthy individuals.

The noun *soporific* is derived from the Latin *sopōrificus* which is a combination of *sopor*, meaning "sleep" and the suffix *-fic*, forming adjectives from nouns, with the sense "making, causing, producing." The noun *soporific* is defined in OED as: "A substance, especially a medicament, which induces sleep." An example of its first use in the English language is in *An Essay Concerning Humane Understanding* by John Locke (1632–1704), the British philosopher who contributed to modern empiricism (1690): "The Colour and Taste of Opium… as well as its soporifick or anodyn Virtues." The philosopher and historian David Hume (1711–1776) raised the notion that medicines may not work in an identical manner in every patient, much before personalized (precision) medicine emerged as pivotal concept in modern medicine (Hume 1777): "Nor has rhubarb always proved a purge, or opium a soporific." Although the word *soporific* is not commonly used today, it was widely employed in the 19th century, as suggested by Sir Thomas Clifford Allbutt (1899): "The use of soporifics is limited by the extent of their other pharmacological effects." This phrase alludes to the fundamental concept that sedation can be produced by various, pharmacologically distinct agents and that understanding the characteristic action mechanisms is essential for rational pharmacotherapy.

As noted above, the word *hypnosedative* is not mentioned in OED and *sedative-hypnotic* is only mentioned in relation to pentobarbital, which is defined as: "A synthetic sedative-hypnotic and anticonvulsant barbituric drug." Neither the word *sedative-hypnotic* nor *hypnosedative* significantly refine the meaning of either word by their combination as each element means much the same thing — that the agent is a *sedative* drug.

The adjective *ataractic/ataraxic* is derived from Greek ἀτάρακτος, meaning "not disturbed, calm," combined with the suffix *-ic* which is used to form adjectives, many of which can also be nouns. The adjective is closely related to the noun *ataraxy* ("Freedom from disturbance of mind or passion; stoical indifference"). The OED definition of *ataractic/ataraxic* is: "Calm, serene." An example of the word's first use in the English language is in the novel *Colossus of Maroussi,* by the American writer Henry Miller (1891–1980) describing his time in Greece (Miller 1941): "Mycenae… reared in anthropophagous luxury, reptilian, ataraxic, stunning and stunned." This word does seem reasonably closely related to *sedative*. However, as the word evolved, it acquired another meaning. The medical definition of *ataractic/ataraxic* is: "Of drugs: inducing calmness, tranquillizing."

The first use of *ataractic* was by Howard Fabing (1907-1970), an American neurologist who was "a pioneer in the field of psychotherapeutic drugs, being the first to use LSD to produce a mock psychosis as a means of searching for a preventative for true psychosis" (Mayfield, Schwemlein and Hawkins 1971). He stated (Fabing 1955):

> "The Epicureans were especially fond of the term 'ataraxia' which meant *freedom from confusion, peace of mind*... It is proposed, therefore, that drugs of this type be designated *ataraxics*, and that the adjectival form, *ataractic*, be used to describe this therapeutic property in drugs."

Fabing then proceeded to apply this term to an entire class of drugs with seemingly little similarity to the psychopharmacologic actions of *sedatives*:

> "Proposal is made to adopt the generic term, *ataraxics*, for pharmacological agents such as chlorpromazine, rauwolfia compounds, Frenquel, and others, which bring about *ataraxy*, or freedom from confusion."

The noun *tranquillizer* is related to the verb *tranquillize* which is a combination of the adjective *tranquil* and the suffix *-ize* ("with the transitive sense of 'make or conform to, or treat in the way of, the thing expressed by the derivation'"). *Tranquil* is defined: "Free from agitation or disturbance; calm, serene, placid, quiet, peaceful" and is derived from the Latin *tranquillus*, meaning "quiet" and related to the French *tranquille*. The definition of *tranquillizer* in OED is: "that which tranquillizes; specifically*,* any of a large class of drugs in widespread use since the 1950s for the reduction of tension or anxiety and the treatment of psychotic states."

The word *tranquillizer* was used in *the journals and letters of Fanny Burney (Madame D'Arblay)* by Frances Burney (1752–1840), an English satirical novelist, diarist and playwright (Burney and Hemlow 1972): "I find, however, *useful* employment the best tranquiliser, &… I have less of the violent emotions which have hitherto torn me." In this quotation, the word is not used to refer to effect of a medicine, but rather, to a circumstance that can lessen the intensity of emotions, easing tension and anxiety. Such is a very important observation as comparable beneficial effects have been demonstrated for psychotherapeutic and psychopharmacologic treatments in management of mild to moderate anxiety/depressive symptoms (Holland, Morrow, Schmale et al. 1991). An example of the contemporary meaning of the word appears in a quotation of Thomas De Quincey (1785–1859), an English essayist best known for his *Confessions of an English Opium-Eater* (De Quincy 1856):

"A tranquilliser of nervous and anomalous sensations." A tranquillizer is intended to allow a person to carry on in a seemingly normal state without objective signs of the effects of the medication, lessening tension, anxiety or related distressing symptoms; this differs from sedation and calming so as to facilitate sleep; of note, however, as the dose of a tranquillizer is increased, objective evidence of sedation can occur. This is explained by Hollister (1958):

> "The distinguishing features of tranquilizing drugs in contrast to conventional sedatives is that they calm without producing sleep and that their site of action in the central nervous system [CNS] is predominantly subcortical. The principal sites of action are important regulating centers of the brain: thalamus, hypothalamus, reticular activating system and portions of the limbic system."

Of note, the nouns *tranquillizer* and *ataractic/ataraxic* seem interchangeable, but the latter is not now commonly used.

It makes little sense to modify the word *tranquillizer* with the adjective *minor*, borrowed from French and Latin, meaning "smaller, lesser, younger" because the differences are not simply of degree. A *minor tranquillizer* was intended to be distinctly different from the *tranquillizers*. Instead, they were considered to be among the least sedating members of the *sedative* group of drugs, the *anxiolytics* (see below). Accordingly, the noun *minor tranquillizer* is defined in OED as: "any of a group of sedative drugs, including especially the benzodiazepines, used to treat anxiety states (as opposed to psychoses)." An example of its first use in the English language (Hinsie and Campbell 1960) is: "Four classes of tranquilizing drugs are generally recognised: ... Classes (3) and (4) [*sc.* substituted propanediols and diphenylmethane derivatives] are sometimes called *minor tranquilizers*...; their principal effect is on the psyche to reduce anxiety." This latter classification (Hollister 1958) may seem confusing today because it was conceived prior to the introduction of the benzodiazepine *anxiolytics*, which have become synonymous with *minor tranquillizers*. It should be noted, however, that medications primarily intended as *anxiolytic sedatives* had been introduced a decade before the benzodiazepines (Berger 1954). A quotation from William Styron (1925–2006), an American novelist who wrote about depression in his novel *Darkness Visible: A Memoir of Madness*, exemplifies the lack of precision in the vernacular concerning the word *tranquillizer* (Styron 1991): "Aided by the minor tranquilizer Halcion [triazolam], I had managed to defeat my insomnia and get a few hours' sleep." A particularly appropriate quote to explain the connection between *tranquillizers, minor tranquillizers* and the *anxiolytics* is found in the *British National Formulary* (1996): "Anxiolytics, particularly the benzodiazepines, have been termed 'minor tranquillisers. This term is misleading because not only do they differ markedly from the antipsychotic drugs ('major tranquillisers') but their use is by no means minor."

The noun *anxiolytic* was formed within English, after the French *anxiolytique* by compounding the noun *anxiety* ("Worry over the future or about something with an uncertain outcome; uneasy concern about a person, situation, etc.; a troubled state of mind arising from such worry or concern") and the connective term *-o-* and *lytic* ("ending of adjectives corresponding to nouns that end in *-lysis*). The definition in OED is: "A drug or substance that reduces anxiety; specifically, any of a class of drugs that reduce anxiety without producing significant sedation." An example of the first use of the word *anxiolytic* is in the proceedings of a scientific meeting on electroencephalography and clinical neurophysiology in Paris (1962): "Librium, or Ro 5-0690, is essentially an anxiolytic drug without hypnotic effect which has been recently introduced into psychiatry." This quotation depicts chlordiazepoxide (Librium) as a *sedative* having greater specificity, namely able to reduce the distress of tension/anxiety while allowing wakefulness and (near) normal performance of daily activities.

While *anxiolytics* seem an ideal solution to the familiar concerns faced in the modern world, a wise word of caution is raised in the *British National Formulary* (1986): "Anxiolytic treatment should be limited to short periods." This is a prescient warning of the serious risk of addiction to these presumably "very safe" drugs, initially publicized as being without abuse liability (Martin, Weinberg and Bealer 2007). If treatment continues beyond "short periods," increasing doses of the medication tend to be self-administered due to neuroadaptation, brain functioning can become subtly compromised over time and if use is precipitously discontinued, a withdrawal syndrome ensues (Martin, Bhushan, Kapur et al. 1979; Busto, Sellers, Naranjo et al. 1986). Insightful comparisons of anxiolytics to other drugs of abuse are plentiful in the lay press, for example, "Liquor is western man's oldest anxiolytic (Anonymous 1975)"; "Benzodiazepines have replaced barbiturates as the most common type of 'anxiolytics' or 'anxiety dissolving' drugs" (Anonymous 1988); and "Valium is simply alcohol in tablet form" (Martin, Weinberg and Bealer 2007). Moreover, the benzodiazepine anxiolytics may carry significant risks if taken over extended periods of time even when taken according to the prescribed dose without evidence of abuse (Finlayson, Macoubrie, Huff et al. 2022).

It is instructive to review how Robert Kinglake (1765–1842), an English physician and medical writer, understood the role of sedatives in the medicine of his day (1802):

"No question in Physiology has been less satisfactorily agitated than that which divides the medical world on the operation of sedative substances… It is familiarly imagined, that certain substances act on the animal economy as direct sedatives, that is, that they repress the action of motive power; but those who entertain this opinion do not feel equal facility, in assigning a reason for this extraordinary effect.

"Sedative influence may obtain in two different ways, either by universally exciting and invigorating the system, or by withholding or prohibiting excessive stimulation; in the former order of efficiency may be ranked whatever may be capable of subduing, by congenial excitement, morbid debility and its consequent quickened action; in the latter may be included a suitably reduced temperature, abstinence, increased evacuations, shaded light, and mental depression.

"The mode in which these positive and negative powers operate, is formally opposite but efficiently familar; the one retards hurried action by the superseding influence of accessorial vigour, while the other obviates undue exhaustion by withholding noxious excitement. These different species of sedative power are applicable to opposite states of disease; the positive influence is adapted to restrain and control the quickened action of debility, while the negative is suitable to diminishing immoderate excitement.

"How such opposite effects can arise from the same power, on different parts of the animal body, does not appear, nor does any principle of philosophising, applicable to the animal economy, warrant such a contradictory inference; it has therefore been unscientifically assumed to subserve the delusion of a pre-conceived erroneous opinion."

That a sedative can cause both psychic inhibition and disinhibition and can heal and cause pathological states, especially addiction, remains an enigma to this day (Stein and Berger 1969; Vashchinkina, Panhelainen, Aitta-aho and Korpi 2014).

The word *sedative* refers to shared pharmacologic action(s) of all CNS depressants, rather than that of a single agent. Therefore, despite the different names for *sedatives* throughout history, all these medications are characterized by the fact that they very effectively calm and soothe and allow rest and sleep. Stressful circumstances can cause tension and anxiety; relief from these distressing symptoms can rapidly be obtained through *self-medication* with sedatives. All sedatives depress the CNS by activating inhibitory GABAergic neurotransmission (Tallman, Thomad and Gallager 1978; Paul, Marangos and Skolnick 1981), and inhibiting excitatory glutamatergic neurotransmission (Moreau, Pieri and Prud'hon 1989).

The basis of the activation/inhibition enigma, mentioned above, resides in the complexity of neural circuits within the brain on which sedatives act, such that intoxication is typically biphasic, stimulation followed by inhibition; stimulation likely results from inhibition of inhibitory neurons, leading to disinhibition, resembling relative stimulation (Martin and Patel 2017). Recent hypotheses have proposed that predisposition to addiction to CNS depressants (alcohol and sedatives) are related to their stimulatory properties (Quinn and Fromme 2016), rather than the inhibitory effects, which have been the primary focus of ongoing research on the risk for developing alcoholism (Paulus, Schuckit, Tapert et al. 2012).

With repeated use of any sedative, neuroadaptive changes occur, including the need for increasing doses and the emergence of a characteristic withdrawal syndrome on discontinuing use. Each of the drugs discussed above, including tranquillizers/ataractics, have, at one time or other, been deployed to treat severe CNS depressant withdrawal, however tranquillizers/ataractics are not as effective and may even precipitate withdrawal seizures (see Delirium Tremens).

An important characteristic that sets the tranquillizers/ataractics apart from the CNS depressant sedatives is their limited abuse liability. Deneau, Yanagita and Seevers (1969) demonstrated that non-human primates self-administer all CNS depressants but not tranquillizers/ataractics. For this reason, treatment of anxiety symptoms can be accomplished with low doses of tranquillizers/ataractics (Denber 1982) and are actually preferred in individuals who are addicted to CNS depressants and are struggling to remain abstinent (Martin, Weinberg and Bealer 2007). Ultimately, the major question that remains is the origin of anxiety. There are those who would consider anxiety as a psychiatric disorder, whereas others recognize its promiscuous occurrence throughout medicine — from hyperthyroidism, myocardial infarctions, pneumonia, schizophrenia and depression among many other conditions. The parsimonious explanation is that anxiety is a signal to the organism that all is not well, whether that contention is based in reality — addressing the cause seems to make more sense than suppressing the symptom or calling it a disorder in its own right.

Self-help

According to the current electronic version of Oxford English Dictionary (OED), the noun *self-help* is a combination of the prefix *self* and the noun *help* ("The action of helping; the supplementing of action or resources by what makes them more efficient; aid, assistance, succour") with the prefix in objective relationship to the noun. The word *self* was inherited from the Germanic and *help* is from Old English. The definition of the term *self-help* is: "The action or faculty of using one's own efforts and resources to achieve something, or provide for oneself, with little or no assistance from others; (in later use) specifically, the action of managing or overcoming personal or emotional problems in this way."

The notion of *self-help* first appeared in the English language translation of *Eclogues* by the ancient Roman poet Virgil (70–19 BC) of the Augustan period (Gent 1628): "All Selfe-helpe, and hope, both faild." However, the use of *self-help* with respect to treatment of addiction is a more recent and evolving concept. As indicated in OED, the word *self-help* has commonly taken the form of an attributive construct as in terms such as *self-help book*, *self-help group*, etc. The long tradition of self-improvement guides in book form (not necessarily in a medical sense) dates to a volume appropriately titled *Self-Help*, the first page of which began with the following aphorism (Smiles 1859):

> "'Heaven helps those who help themselves' is a well-tried maxim, embodying in a small compass the results of vast human experience. The spirit of self-help is the root of all genuine growth in the individual; and, exhibited in the lives of many, it constitutes the true source of national vigor and strength. Help from without is often enfeebling in its effects, but help from within invariable invigorates."

The author, the Scotsman Samuel Smiles (1812-1904), endorsed the notions of hard work, thrift and sobriety as the road to success for both elite and the masses. Although the tradition of the self-help book has continued in its various forms to this day, its ultimate expression with respect to what is considered a serious medical illness is embodied in the generally known *Big Book* (*Alcoholics Anonymous*), first published in New York City (Wilson 1939). Of note, the noun *Alcoholics Anonymous* is defined in the latest electronic version of OED as originating in the United States where it is a proprietary term: "an association for the mutual support and rehabilitation of alcoholics; abbreviated *A.A.* The organization was founded at Akron, Ohio, in 1935." It is perhaps not a coincidence that the formation of A.A. was so close in time to the end of Prohibition in the United States, a nationwide constitutional ban on the production, importation, transportation and sale of alcoholic beverages from 1920 to 1933.

In the Foreword to the First Edition of the *Big Book* it is quite clearly stated that A.A. is not simply *self-help*, but rather *mutual support* (Wilson 1939):

> "We, of Alcoholics Anonymous, are more than one hundred men and women who have recovered from a seemingly hopeless state of mind and body. To show other alcoholics *precisely how we have recovered* is the main purpose of this book. For them, we hope these pages will prove so convincing that no further authentication will be necessary. We think this account of our experiences will help everyone to better understand the alcoholic. Many do not comprehend that the alcoholic is a very sick person. And besides, we are sure that our way of living has its advantages for all."

Therefore, social connection and shared beliefs between those in the fellowship are perceived as fundamental to the process of A.A., allowing social learning and modelling (Bandura and Walters 1963) as a means for a person suffering from alcoholism to achieve recovery. Moreover, alcoholism is considered a *medical* illness in A.A., a notion for which there was almost a century of precedent by the time A.A. was established (Huss 1849). A.A. was not the first mutual support organization for those suffering from alcoholism as early temperance societies (e.g., Washingtonians, Oxford Group) were first founded in America in the nineteenth century (Tyrrell 1979). However, A.A. has become influential worldwide and has served as a model for healing and recovery through human connectedness with others sharing similar misfortunes from various chronic psychiatric, medical and social disorders/problems, not always related to alcohol/drug use disorders (Trice and Staudenmeier 1989).

As a result of A.A. and related programs, a vocabulary has emerged, which while idiosyncratic, is understood in psychiatry and other specialties of medicine. For example, the noun *Al-Anon* is defined in OED as: "A mutual support organization for the families and friends of alcoholics, especially those of a member of Alcoholics Anonymous." The noun *Alateen* is: "A division of the Al-Anon mutual support organization, dedicated to helping (especially teenage) children who are affected by the alcoholism of a family member (especially a parent) or friend." The noun *twelve step* was first used in the *Big Book* (Wilson 1939): "He has read this volume and says he is prepared to go through with the twelve steps of The Program of Recovery." In OED *twelve step* is defined as: "The twelve stages of a programme designed by Alcoholics Anonymous to help people recover from alcoholism; (hence) twelve stages comprising any similar programme designed to help people recover from addiction or compulsive behaviour." The term connotes sequential passage through individual tasks and challenges of recovery via *twelve steps*. In OED the noun *step* is defined as: "An act of bodily motion consisting in raising the foot from the ground and bringing it down again in a fresh position; usually, an act of this kind as constituting by repetition the progressive motion of a human being or animal in walking, running, or climbing." In the vernacular of A.A., the noun is even used as a verb *(twelve stepping)* the ultimate indication of a widely accepted and understood concept (Clark and Clark 1979).

The *AA Big Book* contends that for those who live according to its principles, "we hope these pages will prove so convincing that no further authentication will be necessary." In addition, the chapter entitled "How it works" begins:

> "Rarely have we seen a person fail who has thoroughly followed our path. Those who do not recover are people who cannot or will not completely give themselves to this simple program, usually men and women who constitutionally incapable of being honest with themselves."

Although this may seem circular thinking and hardly follows the scientific method, there are clearly those who are successful with Alcoholics Anonymous and the challenge is to understand why. Alcoholics Anonymous has received scientific recognition by a Lasker Award in 1951 (laskerfoundation.org/awards):

> "…in recognition of its unique and highly successful approach to that age-old public health and social problem, alcoholism…
>
> Alcoholics Anonymous works upon the novel principle that a recovered alcoholic can reach and treat a fellow sufferer as no one else can. In so doing, the recovered alcoholic maintains his own sobriety; the man he treats soon becomes a physician to the next new applicant, thus creating an ever-expanding chain reaction of liberation, with patients welded together by bonds of common suffering, common understanding and stimulating action in a great cause.
>
> This is not a reform movement, nor is it operated by professionals who are concerned with the problem. It is financed by voluntary contributions of its members, all of whom remain anonymous. There are no dues, no paid therapists, no paid professional workers.
>
> Historians may one day point to Alcoholics Anonymous as a society which did far more than achieve a considerable measure of success with alcoholism and

its stigma; they may recognize Alcoholics Anonymous to have been a great venture in social pioneering which forged a new instrument for social action; a new therapy based on the kinship of common suffering; one having a vast potential for the myriad other ills of mankind."

Psychiatrists who worked with alcoholics in the 1950s referred patients to A.A., "Yet they believed only 10 per cent of the persons who join A.A. remain sober for over two years. This, against the claim of A.A. that 60 per cent or more of their fellowship are recovered emphasized the pessimism of the psychiatrists questioned (Hayman 1955)." Of course, one of the methodological issues in research conducted on A.A. has been that "A self-help group such as A.A. is also self-selecting, and the person who cannot identify with the image is self-excluding" (Edwards, Hensman, Hawker and Williamson 1966). Additionally, the "treatment" employed is not fully standardized nor subject to experimental modification by virtue of the organization, and hence, all research is descriptive by its very nature (Bebbington 1976). All the same, A.A. is so widely used that a panel of experts of the Institute of Medicine (1990) commented: "Given its great importance in U.S. treatment programs, it is unfortunate that A.A. has not been the subject of more empirical research… the enduring success of this organization in attracting alcoholics to recovery is itself worthy of study. There is, therefore, a pressing need for high-quality research on the impact and mechanisms of AA."

Psychological research has demonstrated that participation in A.A. is of demonstrable benefit and highly cost-effective compared to other approaches that are available, however, the mechanisms involved are unclear (Project MATCH Research Group 1998; Kelly 2017). Foster Kennedy (1884-1952), who was professor of neurology at Cornell University and former president of the American Neurological Association, stated in the Appendix to the "Big Book" (Wilson 1939): "This organization of Alcoholics Anonymous call on two of the greatest reservoirs of power known to man, religion and that instinct for association with one's fellows…the 'herd instinct'." So, the scientific challenge is perhaps no longer to determine whether and in whom A.A. is helpful but to better understand the social forces that are fundamental to the fellowship. There has been a long history of research related to the fundamental human link, namely the maternal-child bond in humans (Bowlby 1969) and in non-human primates (Harlow and Zimmermann 1959). This research has evolved to be reflected in our understanding of neurobiology and to motivate questions related to other human connections and social emotions (Insel and Young 2001), all of which seem highly relevant to understanding how *mutual support groups* might help in healing addiction. The self-absorption and anhedonia of continuous drinking and drug addiction can, in fact, yield to the awakening of altruism and the joy of recovery when aided by mutual support.

Finally, the notion of stigma that is associated with addiction must not be forgotten and the self-loathing and social isolation that those who have lost control over their lives feel by virtue of addiction. There is a tendency to blame oneself rather than understanding that one is suffering from an illness; acceptance by others is vital in eventually finding self-worth. Self-help has its origins in finding the answer to one's problems rather than benefitting from a professional to help to do so. On one hand, it represents independence and know-how that are considered attributes, but on the other, it is unrealistic, especially if one recognizes that the problem is as serious and potentially life-threatening as is addiction and therefore require professional skills to heal. Recognizing and accepting this is, in fact, part of the problem in recovery as outlined previously (Martin, Weinberg and Bealer 2007).

The notion of self-help and why Alcoholics Anonymous was implemented derives from the still highly prevalent belief that addiction is not really an illness, and hence, does not "merit" medical assistance (not to mention that physicians were at best ambivalent about whether addicts were "worthy" patients). Another perspective is that addiction is much more complex than a simple medical illness and requires more than medical intervention, namely, the person in his/her entirety must be remade through illumination or a mystical experience. Man's search for meaning in life is a *spiritual* phenomenon. This searching for *meaning* may begin with, but is impossible to achieve, with the limbic anesthesia of continuous intoxication. Alcohol and drugs may initially remove anxiety, pain, and emotional suffering, all human emotions that must be reckoned with in health. However, intoxication becomes effective for shorter and shorter periods and leaves the individual feeling lost for extended periods of their life. So, the notion of self-help is not that at all. Self-help is shorthand for *mutual support* engaged with others who are on the same journey of recovery and enlightenment and the formation of social connections that aid recovery in a scientifically explicable process. However, mutual support likely works best if it also uses all that medicine can offer, including pharmacopsychosocial treatments because it is a *bone fide* illness, not simply a failing.

Self-medication

The term *self-medication* was formed in English, as noted in the electronic version of the Oxford English Dictionary (OED), by a combination of the noun *medication*, meaning "The action of treating medically; treatment with a medicinal substance," and the prefix *self-*, which is in objective relation to the second element.

The word *medication* is a borrowing from the classical Latin *medicātiōn-*, *medicātiō* where *medicāt-* is the past participial stem of *medicāre*, *medicārī* (to medicate) and is combined with the suffix *-iō -ion* which is used to form nouns of action from verbs. Initially the noun *medication* according to OED was "used only in the sense 'treatment of food or wine with a preservative, flavouring, or similar'…[whereas] the sense 'treatment, curing' is attested from the second half of the 5th century in post-classical Latin, and from the 10th century in British sources; the sense 'medicament, drug' is attested from the late 13th century in British sources." The word *medication* was first used in the English language in translation of *Chirugia Magna* (de Chauliac 1659), the work of the French physician and surgeon Guy de Chauliac (*c.* 1300–1368): "For to binde forsoþ vlcerate particlez bifalleþ not wele any man bot if he take medicacioun of þe plasmacion of þe particle." The current sense of the word is exemplified by its use by Sir Thomas Clifford Allbutt (1836–1925) in his medical treatise, *A System of Medicine* (Allbutt 1897): "It is better to assist the external measures by internal medication."

In the OED, *self-medication* is defined as: "Administration of a drug or other remedy to oneself without advice from a medical practitioner; (also) use of narcotics, alcohol, etc., in an attempt to alleviate depression, anxiety, or another condition." The term initially denoted *compliance* with self-administration of medications that a treating physician recommended the patient take strictly according to prescription but could not directly oversee, e.g., antibiotics that must not be skipped so as to avoid emergence of highly resistant infections as in tuberculosis and more recently human immunodeficiency virus (Anonymous 1958). However, the meaning of the term that is most relevant to addiction, namely the ingestion of psychoactive agents at will and without medical guidance to relieve distressing mental symptoms, is the topic for discussion here.

According to the OED, the first use of *self-medication* in the English language with the relevant meaning of alleviating mental suffering by administration of a psychoactive substance like alcohol appeared in an editorial in *The British Medical Journal* (Anonymous 1886). The initial precept underpinning *self-medication* was noted as recognition by an individual of "being 'below par'." Self-medication becomes the choice if one does not fully appreciate or accept that:

> "…the proper treatment is, undoubtedly, not to stifle the feeling by injudicious blending of the effects of alcohol, tobacco, and excitement, but to afford an opportunity for the recuperative powers of the system to assert themselves, and so restore the mental tone which is wanting."

In modern psychiatry, this has come to mean that it is preferable to enhance functioning through various forms of lifestyle improvements including diet, exercise, sleep or mindfulness techniques such as yoga, meditation and relaxation techniques (see Exercise, Mindfulness and Sleep) as well as formal psychotherapy from an expert practitioner than to self-medicate (Martin, Weinberg and Bealer 2007). The editorial discussion (Anonymous 1886) proceeds as follows:

> "In the excellent little work on *Digestion*, recently published by Sir William Roberts, he suggests, with great plausibility, that, although the effect of habitual alcoholic indulgence is, beyond question, injurious to the average constitution, yet it may, under circumstances of intense and passing worry, save the individual whose mental equilibrium is menaced from positive mental aberration, by rendering him simply insusceptible of the violent emotions which unhinge and deprave the intellect. The idea is, doubtless, correct in a limited number of cases, but, from its nature, it is very undesirable that it should be generally accepted."

The editorial concludes:

> "People are very partial to self-medication as it is, and rush to alcohol as a panacea for the ills to which flesh is heir."

The notion that a self-administered psychoactive agent can alleviate emotional suffering over the long term is hardly realistic — most agree that such "self-treatment" will not resolve the problem and, more often than not, can lead to a pattern of out-of-control and self-destructive use characteristic of a drug use disorder as a result of rewarding effects of the drug (see Addiction). This conceptualization of *self-medication* has become the cornerstone for both behavioral pharmacologic (Tatum, Seevers and Collins 1929; Schuster and Thompson 1969) and psychodynamic (Radó 1957; Khantzian, Mack and Schatzberg 1974) understanding of the pathogenesis of drug use disorders or addiction. There is, however, an alternate argument, namely, that drugs of abuse themselves actually *produce* specific psychiatric disorders over time in individuals who use these agents based on their preference for specific classes of pharmacologic agents (McLellan, Woody and O'Brien 1979) or that neurotoxicity of drugs of abuse lead to psychopathological syndromes of impairment (Martin, Adinoff, Weingartner et al. 1986). Therefore, despite the fact that drug use disorders are epidemiologically associated with specific other psychiatric disorders, as persuasively documented in the National Institute of Mental Health Epidemiologic Catchment Area Program (Regier, Farmer, Rae et al. 1990), the direction of the path that undeniably links drugs of abuse with psychopathologic conditions remains controversial.

Although a syndrome of self-destructive and out-of-control use of neuropsychopharmacologic agents has been accepted among psychiatric disorders for the better part of a century (Nathan, Conrad and Skinstad 2016), it is still widely held that drug use disorders are actually complications of underlying other psychiatric disorders, developing predominantly due to self-medication to alleviate emotional suffering. Stated otherwise, anxiety, depression, mania or schizophrenia were considered the *primary* causes of addiction. It seems completely justified and understandable why humans self-administer drugs because (Grahame-Smith 1975):

> "one of the intrinsic evils of man's neurobiological make up is that a prime motive of the brain seems to be to bring comfort, security and pleasure for itself. Therefore, it is not surprising that drugs—notably the barbiturates and more recently the benzodiazepines (tranquillizers)—have been prescribed to give to the brain that peace of mind that it seeks".

Along the way between evolution of behavioral pharmacologic and psychodynamic constructs of the pathogenic role of *self-medication* in addiction, the polemic of "self-medication as a fundamental right" of an individual rather than a medical problem emerged (Szasz 1971). It was not until elucidation of *reward mechanisms* in the brain that could shape behavior did it became feasible to conceptualize addiction as a psychiatric disorder in its own right (Olds 1958). All the same, it is far too easy to invoke primary symptoms of anxiety, depression, pain, insomnia, desire for cognitive enhancement as primary motivating factors via conditioning (see Conditioning) for problematic use of neuropharmacological agents (Wikler 1948). However, the ultimate question may well be why stimulation of brain reward centers by self-administration of drugs of abuse leads to development of neuroadaptation and addiction in some but not all individuals (see Resilience)

Sexual Addiction

The term *sexual addiction* cannot be found in the current electronic version of the Oxford English Dictionary (OED), possibly because these words convey a controversial and evolving concept that is not appreciated or fully accepted in psychiatry. However, understanding the histories of each word component of the term, *sexual* and *addiction*, allows a rather good sense of the evolution of the concept that conveys when the words are joined together. Additionally, it can be instructive to understand the origins of several other terms that have been employed historically to portray essentially the same meaning as *sexual addiction*, namely the *loss of control* over harmful sexual activity.

According to OED the noun and adjective *sexual* is a borrowing from post-classical Latin *sexualis* ("of a woman…, of, relating to, or arising from the fact or condition of being either male or female"), which, in turn, is derived from compounding of the classical Latin *sexus* and a suffix *-ālis* ("Forming adjectives with the sense 'of or relating to that which is denoted by the first element'"). The Latin *sexus* is the *u*-stem of noun *sex* meaning, "Either of the two main categories (male and female) into which humans and many other living things are divided on the basis of their reproductive functions; (hence) the members of these categories viewed as a group; the males or females of a particular species, especially the human race, considered collectively."

The first use of the word *sexual* in the English language (in a meaning that is now obsolete) was as an adjective by Thomas Adams (1583–1652), an English clergyman who was called "The Shakespeare of the Puritans" (Adams 1622): "That blessed Queene… who, as by her Sexuall graces shee deserued to bee the Queene of women, so by her masculine vertues to bee the Queen of men." The word has continued to evolve, and the following of some subtly different meanings seem relevant to addiction: "Relating to, tending towards, or involving sexual intercourse, or other forms of intimate physical contact"; "Of or relating to sexuality as a social or cultural phenomenon; regarding sexual conduct"; and "Characterized by sexual instincts or feelings, or the capacity for these; possessing or displaying sexuality." This sense of the word was first used in the English language in *an essay on celibacy* (Anonymous 1753): "Sexual commerce is natural, and, when it is the consequence of marriage, virtuous." William Wordsworth (1770–1850), the English Romantic poet, who with Samuel Taylor Coleridge helped launch the Romantic Age in English literature with their joint publication *Lyrical Ballads*, described sexuality therein as an *appetite* (Wordsworth and Coleridge 1800): "From this principle the direction of the sexual appetite, and all the passions connected with it take their origin."

This last meaning of *sexual* naturally fits with and, therefore, can readily be understood when combined with the term *addiction*, to obtain the concept of interest here. This union of words is reasonable because *addiction* is now accepted as appropriate not only for drug use disorders but also can be applied to out-of-control and self-destructive *behaviors* (Martin and Petry 2005). These two forms of addiction are defined in OED from the perspective of a *drug use disorder* ("Immoderate or compulsive consumption of a drug or other substance; specifically, a condition characterized by regular or poorly controlled use of a psychoactive substance despite adverse physical, psychological, or social consequences, often with the development of physiological tolerance and withdrawal symptoms…") or of a *behavioral addiction* ("The state or condition of being dedicated or devoted to a thing, especially an activity or occupation; adherence or attachment, especially of an immoderate or compulsive kind"). The distinction between categories of addiction is also now accepted in psychiatric nosology as enunciated in the *Diagnostic and Statistical Manual* (DSM) of the American Psychiatric Association (American Psychiatric Association 2013). However, whereas the concept of a *behavioral addiction* in the current APA nosology includes *gambling disorder*, out-of-control and self-destructive sexual behavior remains to be recognized as such. This decision of not including sexual addiction as a behavioral addiction in DSM has been highly contentious (Carnes 1992; Goodman 1998; Kraus, Voon and Potenza 2016). It has been argued that one can readily develop descriptors of pathological sexual behaviors and substitute them for criteria that are currently employed to define substance use or gambling disorders in DSM (American Psychiatric Association 2013). The criteria so conceived accurately describe the syndrome of sexual addiction as well as drug use and gambling disorders, and thus, the concept of sexual addiction does have face validity and its exclusion seems somewhat arbitrary.

Examining the origins of several other terms that have been employed historically to represent essentially the same meaning as *sexual addiction* can be instructive. The following are among many such terms that have been employed in this manner: *sexual dependence, problematic hypersexuality, hypersexual disorder, compulsive sexual behavior, hypersexuality (nymphomania and satyriasis), erotomania, Don Juanism,* and *paraphilia-related disorders.*

The notion of *hypersexuality* has been discussed within the construct of *dependence* (Orford 1978), the precursor in DSM of the current terminology. Although the word *dependence* (defined in OED as, "The relation of having existence hanging upon, or conditioned by, the existence of something else; the fact of depending upon something else") is still appropriate in the context of the *dependence syndrome*

(Edwards and Gross 1976), the term has been superseded in DSM by *drug use disorder* and *non-drug addictive disorder*, or behavioral addiction (American Psychiatric Association 2013).

Use of such qualifiers as *problematic* ("Of the nature of a problem; constituting or presenting a problem or difficulty; difficult to resolve; doubtful, uncertain, questionable"), *compulsive* ("Acting from, related to, or typical or suggestive of a compulsion [An insistent impulse to behave in a certain way, contrary to one's conscious intentions or standards]") as well as *-hyper* ("…the prefix [which] has the prepositional force of 'over, beyond, or above'…) are clearly consistent with the notion of behavior that is sufficiently salient (Sinke, Engel, Veit et al. 2020) within the behavioral repertoire that there is little room for anything else, namely the sexual behavior can be considered out-of-control, and hence likely self-destructive. Importantly, there is little consensus about pathogenic mechanisms that underpin the syndrome, which have been considered as obsessive-compulsive, impulsive, addictive, posttraumatic or combinations of these (Ragan and Martin 2000; Kafka 2010; Kraus, Voon and Potenza 2016).

Another element to be considered in addition to the time devoted to sexual behavior relative to other aspects of the behavioral repertoire is that of the "normalcy" of the *object* of sexual activity. The disorder here termed *sexual addiction* has been described in conventional psychiatric thinking (although not strictly in DSM) as a syndrome of *paraphilic* ("Sexual desires regarded as perverted or irregular; specifically attraction to unusual or abnormal sexual objects or practices…") or *nonparaphilic* (so-called "normal" object of sexual desire) sexual disorders with an emphasis conceptually on a *loss of control* over sexual activities and a persistent engagement in sexual behaviors despite adverse social, psychological and biological consequences (Ragan and Martin 2000).

The concept conveyed by *sexual addiction* has a very long history. The plethora of terms that have been used to describe problematic hypersexuality suggests not only that the condition was well recognized, but also reveals historical iterations toward eventually understanding this well-known collection of symptoms as a *clinical* syndrome. These iterations also demonstrate that that there has been significant ambivalence about pathologizing behavior like sexual activity that humankind has considered rewarding, even lyrical, an expression of love and procreation but nevertheless, so subjective, but all the same, governed by mores. It may well be that extremes in sexual behavior have been more difficult to resolve in human consciousness than those of drink and drugs, although there are striking similarities among all of these that are only now becoming recognized.

Literary descriptions much preceded attempts to view the syndrome of problematic hypersexuality from a psychiatric perspective. For example, the figure Don Juan was predominantly characterized in literature by his intense preoccupation with sexual conquests, romanticized to be sure, but also with the effect of bringing such proclivities to the awareness of society. According to OED, "the name of Don Juan, a legendary Spanish nobleman whose dissolute life was dramatized by Gabriel Tellez in his *Convivado de Piedra (Stone Guest)*; the name was adopted in various popular imitations of this play and by Byron in his well-known poem." Tellez (1583–1648), better known as Tirso de Molina, was a Spanish Baroque dramatist, poet and Roman Catholic monk who wrote the play in which Don Juan was the protagonist (Molina 1986). The name of Don Juan has subsequently acquired the meaning, according to OED, of "A rake, libertine, roué" and the name is used attributively, namely *Don Juanism* as an expression to depict an extreme of human heterosexual behavior. An example of this meaning as first used in the English language by the novelist William Makepeace Thackeray (1811–1863) can be found in *Vanity Fair* (Thackeray 1848): "Don't trifle with her affections, you Don Juan!"

An important example of terms related to problematic hypersexuality is the noun *satyriasis*, which is partly a borrowing from Latin ("permanent erection of penis…, form of leprosy or elephantiasis…") and the Greek σατυρίασι ("permanent erection of the penis, form of leprosy or elephantiasis… already in ancient Greek denoting swelling of the glands about the ear"). As exemplified in the writings of Guy de Chauliac (*c.* 1300–1368), the French physician and surgeon who wrote the influential treatise on surgery in Latin translated into many other languages (including Middle English) *Chirurgia Magna* (de Chauliac 1659), *satyriasis* was portrayed as the equivalent of an anatomical deformity *priapism* and hence, as a surgical condition ("Prolonged or painful erection of the penis, especially when associated with sexual stimulation; [in later use also] obsessive desire for erection… similar to *priapism* [now historical and rarely used]"): "The priapasme is vnwilfull stondynge of þe ȝerde, and it dyuerseth fro satiriasis…in þat þat þerynne is wille and desire of þat dede."

A later, and now historical, sense of *satyriasis* focused predominantly on excessive sex drive ("Great or inordinate appetite for sex, especially in the male; specifically a medical condition occurring in men or male animals, characterized by sexual desire or activity judged to be excessive") was from the English poet Francis Quarles (1592–1644) in his *Argalus and Parthenia* (Quarles 1629): "Now... euery eare Hath got the Saturyasis to heare This tragicke sceane." A more succinct statement, while still not fully acknowledging the very problematic nature of the behavior and its breadth of consequences for the individual, was from the English herald painter Randle Holme (1627–1700): "Satyriasis,..is an immoderate desire of venery, which upon Coition vanishes."

The corresponding condition in women is *nymphomania* ("Uncontrollable or excessive sexual desire, specifically in a woman"). This noun is a borrowing from Latin, a combination of the noun *nympha* ("in classical Latin *nympha* semi-divine spirit, young woman, maiden, larva of an insect, in post-classical Latin also labia minora… ancient Greek νύμφη young bride, maiden, semi-divine spirit, larva of an insect, a type of mollusc, in Hellenistic Greek also clitoris, (in poetic use) water…") and the combination form *-mania* ("Forming nouns referring to kinds of mental illness, desires, and passions marked by wild excess or delusion, enthusiastic [and often fashionable] participation in certain activities, or enthusiastic admiration for certain things or persons"). The word was first employed in English by the professional lexicographer John Kersey the Younger (born c. 1660) in the *Dictionarium Anglo-Britannicum: or a general English dictionary* (Kersey 1708): "*Nymphomania*, the same that *Furor Uterinus*." Subsequently, the potential association of hypersexuality (not necessarily satyriasis or nymphomania) with other psychopathology such as depression was noted by the University of Edinburgh medical professor William Cullen (1710–1790), who was a central figure in the Scottish Enlightenment and translator of *Synopsis of methodical nosology* (Cullen 1830): "Melancholia…(c) With vehement love, without satyriasis or nymphomania." Sir David Ferrier (1843–1928), a Scottish neurologist and psychologist, expressed the notion that hypersexuality may be an expression of brain damage (Ferrier 1876): "The girl… in whom the cerebellum was absent suffered from nymphomania."

Others have viewed hypersexuality as something that was easily overcome and a rather trivial element of human development (Whitehead, Hoff and Stoll 1928): "It is said that maidens suffering from peculiar nervous diseases, such as nymphomania… and some forms of hysteria, should marry, as a cure usually follows." Importantly for both satyriasis and nymphomania, Alfred Charles Kinsey (1894–1956) the American sexologist considered such hypersexual disorders on a range of distribution of normal sexual appetites rather than a sexual disorder as expressed in his *Sexual Behavior in the Human Male* (Kinsey 1948): "The attempts to recognize such states as nymphomania and satyriasis as discrete entities, can, in any objective analysis, refer to nothing more than a position on a curve which is continuous."

Benjamin Rush (1746–1813), a Founding Father of the United States who signed the United States Declaration of Independence and was also a physician who became a professor of chemistry, medical theory and clinical practice at the University of Pennsylvania carefully examined this topic in a chapter entitled, "Of the Morbid State of the Sexual Appetite," in his classic *Medical Inquires and Observations Upon the Disease of the Mind* (Rush 1812). Rush described the case of a man who:

> "…imputes his indisposition to his excessive devotedness to Venus, which he thinks has been induced by a morbid state of his body. He has been married three years, had no connection with sex before he married, and, although he feels disgusted with his strong venereal propensities, he cannot resist them. I advised him to separate himself from his wife by travelling [sic], which he did, but without experiencing any relief from his disease. He has earnestly requested me to render him impotent, if I could not give him command of himself in any other way."

At the end of the 19th century, Richard Freiherr von Krafft-Ebing (1840–1902), a German psychiatrist and author of the foundational *Psychopathia Sexualis*, devoted his academic career to a thorough study of the paraphilias and other sexual disorders, illustrated with almost 200 case histories (Krafft-Ebing 1892). He described a case of abnormally increased sexual appetite:

> "…to such an extent that permeates all his thoughts and feelings, allowing no other aims in life, tumultuously, and in a rut-like fashion demanding gratification and resolving itself into an impulsive, insatiable succession of sexual enjoyments. This pathological sexuality is a dreadful scourge for its victim, for he is in constant danger of violating the laws of the state and of morality, of losing his honor, his freedom, and even his life."

Problematic hypersexuality still remains a "foster child of sorts" within psychiatric nosology. Because the pathogenesis of the syndrome is uncertain and problematic sexual behavior is not widely appreciated as a psychiatric disorder, the syndrome has not gained acceptance in psychiatric nosology, despite the fact that it really does seem to fit into the conceptual understanding of behavioral addictions which has recently gained acceptance within the DSM (American Psychiatric Association 2013). Emphasis has been on dysfunction of the motivations underpinning the behavior, not the behavior itself, a distinctly different perspective from that for drug use disorders and non-drug addictive disorders. Not only has problematic hypersexuality been documented in clinical work, but elements of the syndrome can also be identified as a complication of a range of psychopathologic conditions, including bipolar disorder, personality disorders, traumatic and neurocognitive deficits among others and the side effects of various psychopharmacologic agents (Finlayson, Sealy and Martin 2001). These can result from disturbances in the physiology of sexual activity which involve: the autonomic nervous system; the hypothalamic/pituitary complex; and the limbic system, which include inhibitory connections derived from the frontal cortex and enhancement of the sexual drive by activation of the reward circuits of the brain (Ragan and Martin 2000; Kühn and Gallinat 2016).

Lack of acceptance in psychiatric nosology has not deterred attempts to study the underpinnings of problematic hypersexuality using the latest approaches in neuroscience. These have of necessity required the development of clinical criteria elicited using a reliable psychometric diagnostic instrument (Bőthe, Bartók, Tóth-Király et al. 2018). Neuroimaging methods have been used to identify abnormalities of brain functioning, including brain activation by sexual stimuli (Antons, Brand and Potenza 2020), impulse regulation (Gola and Draps 2018), decision making, sexual templates and personality characteristics (Bőthe, Tóth-Király, Potenza et al. 2019), among other mechanisms.

The microstructure of white matter in anatomic substrates of the relevant neural pathways have been demonstrated as atypical in patients with problematic hypersexuality (Draps, Kowalczyk-Grębska, Marchewka et al. 2021). It is of tremendous importance that most of these neuroimaging studies have shown strong parallels with gambling disorder, which in turn, resembles drug use disorders (Gola and Draps 2018). Dysregulation of the hypothalamic/pituitary axis, foundational in stress responses, have been demonstrated in problematic hypersexuality (Chatzittofis, Boström, Ciuculete et al. 2021), as well as impairment of regulation of the bonding hormone oxytocin (Flanagan, Chatzittofis, Boström et al. 2022). An indication that hypersexuality is a disease entity that has tremendous adverse consequences to both the person who is affected as well as those with whom they are close, is that there is increasing interest in pharmacotherapy of the condition, always drawing on parallels with drug use disorders and behavioral addictions (Chamberlain and Grant 2019; Malandain, Blanc, Ferreri et al. 2020; Savard, Öberg, Chatzittofis et al. 2020).

Sleep

According to the current electronic version of Oxford English Dictionary (OED), the noun *sleep*, corresponding to the verb *sleep*, comes from the Old English *slǽp* (*sláp*), *slép*, Old Frisian *slêp*, Middle Dutch *slaep*, Old Saxon *sláp*, Old High German *sláf*, *sclâf*, *sclâph*, Gothic *slēps*. The relevant definition in OED with respect to addiction is: "The unconscious state or condition regularly and naturally assumed by man and animals, during which the activity of the nervous system is almost or entirely suspended, and recuperation of its powers takes place; slumber, repose." In addition to the main definition, OED adds the following: "Also, a similar state artificially induced, as hypnotic (or magnetic) sleep."

The word *sleep* was first used in the English language *c.* 825 in *The Vespasian Psalter* (Kuhn 1965), an Anglo-Saxon illuminated psalter produced in the second or third quarter of the 8th century, containing the oldest extant English translation of any portion of the Bible: "Ðonne seleð scyldum his slep." The meaning of the word is easily recognizable to modern readers from the *c.* 1369 quotation of the great English literary figure, Geoffrey Chaucer (*c.* 1340s –1400), in *The booke of the Duchesse* (1954): "Goo..to Morpheus, Thou knowist hym well, the god of slepe." This was an invocation to the Greek God of Sleep and Dreams, whose name was to become synonymous with the highly addictive substance, *morphine*. John Lydgate (*c.* 1370–1449), the English monk and poet, in *c.* 1430–40 referred to the ability of milk to enhance the quality of sleep (Lydgate 1923): "She gaue him milke, ye slepe fell in his hede." This description, so reminiscent of the soothing nature of the primal nutrient, mother's milk, was considered scientifically grounded even to the modern era (Brezinová and Oswald 1972), presumably due to absorption of the amino acid precursor of the sleep hormone *melatonin*.

Throughout history, mankind has sought sleep as a pleasant and restful state after an active day (Goldsmith 1774): "Sleep is,..to some, a very agreeable period of their existence." In addition, sleep has been considered a period for healing and recovery of health (Allestree 1658): "Sleep comes as a Medicine to..weariness, as a repairer of..decay." The German physician Franz Anton Mesmer (1734−1815), who was interested in astronomy and the transfer of natural energy between animate and inanimate objects ("animal magnetism"), viewed the associated phenomena, resembling sleep, as a means of healing. He induced such states, known as *mesmerism* or *hypnosis*, by having patients ingest "healing metals" and placing magnets on different parts of the subject's body; later on, he used movements with his bare hands to transfer "fluidum" from one person to another (Mesmer 1785).

Physicians have always been fascinated by sleep and how this state differs from time awake (Stancliffe 1810):

> "That state in which our perceptions are distinct, and in which we direct the muscles of voluntary action according to the will, is that in which we are awake; that in which we are neither sensible (of external objects) nor capable of producing motion by the will is called sleep."

Recent research in sleep physiology and chronobiology has established that sleep plays a vitally important integrating role in the *circadian cycle* of animals and humans and hence, influences all aspects of health (Karatsoreos, Bhagat, Bloss et al. 2011; Poggiogalle, Jamshed and Peterson 2018). Such research findings are inconsistent with the OED definition of *sleep* that indicates (see above), "the activity of the nervous system is almost or entirely suspended."

Formal scientific examination of sleep seems to have begun with identification by Loomis, Harvey and Hobart (1935) of changes in the electroencephalogram between when a person was awake and sleeping:

> "During sleep trains of waves appear which cannot be correlated with any detectable external stimulus, but which may be connected with internal disturbances of unknown origin. The cause of these very regular bursts is now under investigation."

It was still uncertain whether hypnosis was another state of consciousness underneath a person's awake self or a variant of sleep until it was formally demonstrated by electroencephalography that any resemblance to sleep was only superficial (Dynes 1947). Sleep research quickened with the discovery of rapid eye movement (REM) sleep by Aserinsky and Kleitman (1953). Rechtschaffen and Kales (1968) operationalized sleep parameters based on conventional visual sleep scoring, leading to normative data that could be used to distinguish normal from pathologic sleep; thus, it could be demonstrated that many neuropsychiatric disorders were characterized sleep abnormalities.

Alcoholic beverages have a very long history of use by man for the purpose of inducing sleep in those who were unable to do so of their own accord. In fact, this role has given rise to a specific noun, *sleep-drink*, derived from the Dutch *slaapdrank* and German *schlaftrunk*, which is defined in OED as "a portion of liquor taken just before bed-time." This term is found in the novel *The four Georges sketches of manners, morals, court and town life* by William Makepeace Thackeray (1811–1863), the British novelist, author and illustrator (Thackeray 1861): "Every evening they shall have their beer, and at night their sleep-drink." Thomas Sydenham (1624–1689), "The English Hippocrates", in his …*medical observations concerning the history and cure of acute and chronic diseases*… (Sydenham and Pechey 1722), recommended a tincture of opium in alcohol, or *laudanum*, for insomnia and many other ailments.   Certain electroencephalographic similarities were eventually identified between opioid-induced and natural sleep (Wikler 1952). Other agents have been employed in medicine to help patients sleep (MacDonald 1887):

> "Those [new hypnotics] I propose shortly discussing are: hyoscyamine, paraldehyde, urethane, and the hydrobromate and hydriodate of hyoscine… With the question of hypnotics is closely associated the great question of sleep, the physiology and pathology of which we yet know so little. One day the necessary and natural element of health, the next by its absence a symptom of disease."

The search for sleep-inducing pharmaceutical agents, or *hypnotics*, has continued through the 20th century, even to the present day (see Sedatives), starting with the barbiturates (Fischer and von Mering 1903; Willcox, Pickworth and Young 1927), non-barbiturate hypnosedatives (Berger 1954; Gruber, Kohlstaedt, Moore and Peck 1954), benzodiazepines (Sternbach Fryer, Keller et al. 1963; Greenblatt and Shader 1971) and most recently, the non-benzodiazepine hypnosedatives, or so-called "Z-drugs" (Dundar, Boland, Strobl et al. 2004). Additionally, agents such as the cannabinoids that can be sedating (Kubena and Barry 1970) but are not typically used clinically as a hypnotic because of legal reasons and concerns about their abuse liability. The goal in pharmaceutical development of hypnotics has always been to improve natural sleep without toxicity, such as hangover, overdose or abuse liability. Relative improvements in toxicity were achieved at each stage of medication development, but changes in addictive potential were ephemeral (Martin, Bhushan, Kapur et al. 1979).

Although sleep is considered pleasant and healing by many, there are those for whom this state seems but a distraction from other activities deemed of greater priority due to the press of work, seeking pleasure or thrills or various forms of psychopathology. This conundrum of a need for alternatives to restful sleep and associated dangers have been understood for some time (Hart 1892):

> "That all men and women feel the weariness of life is testified by the fact that the people of all nations and climes have the universal habit of daily seeking a restorative and stimulant in one of the vegetable products which contain a

substance or alkaloid capable of exercising a definite effect on the nervous and cardiac systems. Thus, the Chinese and Japanese sip their tea, and the English, following their example, brew the five o'clock cup of the fragrant herb to sustain them in the day's work; the Arab and Turk seek, like the French and Germans, restorative powers in the aromatic coffee berry; the Cingalese chew the betel nut; and the natives of Peru on the slopes of the Andes find in coca leaves a principle which sustains the body in fatigue and comforts the mind in hopelessness. Von Bibra says of coca: 'It satisfies the hungry, lends new strength to the weary and fatigued, and makes the unhappy forget his grief.' What, then, is this strange substance which seems to conceal a fairy's wand? We shall find, however, that, resembling other fairies' wands for the cure of the plagues of life, it may turn, like the magician's rod, into a viper."

Historically, attempts to frustrate the natural need for sleep started with the use of plant-derived stimulants (see Stimulants). Subsequently, chemists purified the active substances from plants, progressed to synthesis of chemical modifications of the nature-derived substances and eventually succeeded in synthesis of novel compounds, modeled on nature, possessing even more powerful pharmacological effects. The typical course begins as exemplified by the work of Ko Kuei Chen (1898–1988), a Chinese-American scientist known for bringing the natural sympathomimetic ephedrine to the western world (Chen 1927): "MA HUANG has been identified as *Ephedra vulgaris*, var. *helvetica*. It is a low, dioecious, practically leafless shrub, 60 to 90 cm. high. The stem, which is green, ribbed, and channeled, is the part sold in Chinese drug stores. It is usually cut into pieces, 1 to 1.5 cm. long. Ephedrine, a natural secondary amine, is the physiologically active constituent and can be easily isolated from the plant by immiscible solvents. It was first discovered by Nagai in 1889, and its structural formula has been studied by different observers."

In 1887, only two years after first synthesis of ephedrine, Lazăr Edeleanu (1861–1941), a Rumanian chemist, synthesized amphetamine from ephedrine. In 1929, Gordon A. Alles (1901–1963), an American chemist and pharmacologist first reported the physiological properties of amphetamine as a synthetic analog of ephedrine, and therefore, received credit for this discovery (Fairchild and Alles 1967). Soon after Alles' discovery, pharmaceutical companies developed amphetamine-related medications for treating nasal congestion and asthma, and eventually, also for treatment of depression, obesity, attention deficit disorder, and narcolepsy.

Other uses of these agents were eventually revealed, including as an aphrodisiac, euphoriant and cognitive or physical enhancer. Scientific enquiry has demonstrated that over the long run, these putative enhancement effects were more apparent than real. Rather, such beneficial effects obey the Yerkes–Dodson law, an empirical relationship between arousal and performance, indicating that performance increases with physiological or mental arousal, but only up to a point; when levels of arousal become too high, performance decreases (Yerkes and Dodson 1908). As Wood, Sage, Shuman and Anagnostaras (2014) state in their review of popular stimulants (cocaine, amphetamine, methylphenidate, modafinil, and caffeine):

> "...dose is the critical determining factor [although dose-response relationships may differ among individuals] in cognitive effects of stimulant drugs... One common graphic depiction of the cognitive effects of psychostimulants is an inverted U–shaped dose-effect curve. Moderate arousal is beneficial to cognition, whereas too much activation leads to cognitive impairment. In parallel to this schematic, we propose a continuum of psychostimulant activation that covers the transition from one drug effect to another as stimulant intake is increased. Low doses of stimulants effect increased arousal, attention, and cognitive enhancement; moderate doses can lead to feelings of euphoria and power, as well as addiction and cognitive impairment; and very high doses lead to psychosis and circulatory collapse."

Accumulating research has clearly demonstrated that sleep is an active neurobiological state with multiple physiologic roles, most importantly, body energy and temperature regulation which underpin many physical illnesses (Karatsoreos, Bhagat, Bloss et al. 2011; Poggiogalle, Jamshed and Peterson 2018) and consolidation of memory which allows the individual to accumulate and appreciate life-long experiences in all sensory modalities and thus, greatly affects mental health (Ngo and Born 2019). However, by use of a variety of *hypnotics* and *analeptics*, mankind has acquired the means, almost-at-will, to enter into or postpone the need for sleep, but not with impunity.

A significant consequence of the use and eventual overuse of either hypnotics or analeptics is *disturbed sleep*. In particular, drug-induced toxic effects on sleep are well-recognized for all drugs of abuse and these effects can occur during intoxication, withdrawal, chronic use and well beyond when the person has achieved abstinence (Yules, Freedman and Chandler 1966; Oswald 1968; Brower 2001; Reid-Varley, Ponce and Khurshid 2020). It is not difficult to appreciate how useful hypnotics or analeptics can appear to an individual for self-medication of sleeplessness due to anxiety, stress and pain from various causes, or for lagging mood or energy, as a euphoriant, aphrodisiac and as a cognitive or performance enhancer (see Self-medication). Therefore, *insomnia* may be both a precursor to and consequence of alcohol/drug use disorders. In addition, disturbed sleep *per se* is characteristic of many medical (e.g., pain, impaired respiratory function or neurocognitive disorders) and psychiatric (e.g., anxiety, depression or psychosis) conditions which can result in self-medication to enhance sleep and can progress to addiction. Therefore, it is important to disentangle whether a drug use disorder is primary or secondary to a medical or psychiatric cause for poor sleep and address underlying conditions. In addition, there has been a recent emphasis on using behavioral (Okajima, Akitomi, Kajiyama et al. 2020) and other techniques (Figueiro, Plitnick, Roohan et al. 2019) to treat sleep disorders that are not strictly a result of treatable medical or psychiatric conditions so as to circumvent the slippery slope of the progression of sedative-hypnotic use to addiction.

Sleep disturbance, whether primary or secondary, is very closely intertwined with alcohol/drug use disorders (Martin, Weinberg and Bealer 2007). If the individual begins to use central nervous system depressants to allow sleep when suffering from sleeplessness, the drug use can progress to an out-of-control and self-destructive pattern. Conversely, if an individual desires not to sleep and uses an analeptic to "burn the candle at both ends," going without sleep may eventually have significant health consequences, including the inability to sleep and compounding the situation by self-administration of hypnotics, which can more greatly disrupt circadian rhythms and result in exhaustion. Importantly, all of these medications have abuse liability, and their repeated use alters the central nervous system circadian rhythm and sleep in a way that perpetuates use. The neuroadaptive changes, or *allostasis*, that accompany the progression of addiction have been mechanistically associated with the neurobiology of sleep disturbances in addiction (Koob and Colrain 2020). In addition, the influence of sleep has been incorporated in conceptualization of not only of the risk for development of addiction, but also in identifying those who are most likely to relapse once they have become abstinent (Brower and Perron 2010).

Stimulant

The title of this entry was selected because the noun *stimulant* has a rather explicit meaning in addiction, even though it is a nonspecific term with a range of uses. The word is employed in the context of *stimulant use disorder*, the out-of-control and self-destructive use of drugs with related pharmacological actions. According to the current electronic version of the Oxford English Dictionary (OED), *stimulant* is only one of several words in the English language that convey a similar meaning. Many of these related nouns and/or adjectives appeared in English before *stimulant* (1728): *restorative* (*a*1398)*, refreshing* (1534)*, uplifting* (1548)*, brisk* (*a*1593)*, invigorating* (1694)*, tonic* (1756)*, bracing* (1761)*, revitalizing* (1849)*, intoxicant* (1863) *pick-me-up* (1867) and *upper* (1968).

The noun and adjective *stimulant* are derived from the Latin *stimulantem,* present participle of *stimulāre*, which means to stimulate ("To rouse to action or exertion as by pricking or goading; to spur on; to incite [a person] *to do* something; to impart additional energy to"; "To act as a stimulus to"; or "To administer stimulants to."). Accordingly, the noun *stimulation*, derived from the Latin *stimulātiōnem*, a noun of action was the first of various forms related to the verb *stimulāre* to be used in the English language. The meaning of the noun *stimulation* is defined as: "A pricking, goading, or spurring on to action; incitement; pricking or compunction of conscience." The OED definition of *stimulation* in physiology and medicine is: "The action of a stimulus: (a) excitation to increased activity, quickening of some vital function or process; (b) excitation of an organ or tissue to its specific activity." The verb *stimulāre* is derived from the Latin *stimulus* ("Something that acts as a 'goad' or 'spur' to a languid bodily organ; an agency or influence that stimulates, increases, or quickens organic activity."). The origin of *stimulus* is "perhaps [from the] root *sti-* [as] in *stilus*", which, in turn, had been transformed from the noun *stylus* ("A tracing-point used to produce the written record in a chart recorder, telegraph receiver, or the like."). Of particular relevance to addiction, the noun *psychostimulant* ("A drug that stimulates the activity of the mind or nervous system") was formed within English relatively recently by compounding the noun *stimulant* with the combination form psycho-, which is a borrowing from Greek used for "Forming words with the senses 'of or relating to the soul or spirit', 'of or relating to the mind or psyche', 'of or relating to psychology'."

The first use of any word related to *stimulāre* in the English language is the noun *stimulation* which appeared in a quotation by William Bonde (*d.* 1530), a Bridgettine monk and author (Bonde 1526): "The stimulacions of the flesshe." An example of the noun *stimulation* as it might pertain to addiction is from Robert James Graves (1796–1853), an eminent Irish surgeon after whom Graves' disease was named (Graves 1843): "We should resort to stimulation by wine." An example of the first use of the noun *stimulant* as relevant to addiction is by Ephraim Chambers (?1680–1740) an English encyclopaedist (Chambers 1728): "Stimulants produce Pain, Heat, Redness, &c." A later use is by Henri Milne-Edwards (1800–1885), a French zoologist (Milne-Edwards 1829): "Such… stimulating remedies as do not appear to act… on a particular organ, but the exciting action of which is equally felt throughout the whole economy." This observation presages subsequent understanding that stimulants affect all parts of the body innervated by the autonomic nervous system and the brain. Finally, the first use of the noun *psychostimulant* is found in a textbook *Modern Pharmacology & Therapeutics* (Musser and Bird 1961): "Prior to the development of these newer drugs, called psycho-stimulants or psychic energizers, apathetic and depressed patients were treated with caffeine and the amphetamines." This underlines that initial use of *stimulants* in psychiatry was for treatment of depression.

In the early 19th century, the word *stimulant* did not convey a specific *pharmacologic* action as it does today but was used along the lines of *restorative, invigorating* or *tonic* – hot and cold water were recommended stimulants for the treatment of burns (Philanthropus 1809). This is not surprising, as it was not until 1849 that the German pharmacologist Rudolf Buchheim (1820–1879), now considered the "Father of Pharmacology," started the first department of pharmacology at the University of Dorpat (now Tartu) in Estonia. In the early days, the role of pharmacology was to elucidate how medications then employed in medical practice interacted with as yet incompletely understood physiological functions. Pharmacologists strove to recognize classes of medicines that putatively shared mechanisms of action and therapeutic indications (Snow 1875):

> "It appears to me that the science of therapeutics is at present much impeded by the want of a rational system of classification; and also by the vagueness of the general terms in ordinary use: that when men speak, for example, of a stimulant or narcotic, their ideas of what constitutes a stimulant or narcotic, of the essential feature in the stimulating or narcotising process, are more or less hazy and empirical. Since Dr. George Johnson's discoveries [contributions of the eminent English physician Sir George Johnson (1818–1896) on the physiology and pathology of the circulation (1871)] have directed attention to the contractility of the arterioles, it has become obvious that nearly all our drugs (excluding those prescribed merely for their chemical affinities) produce their effects upon the body – of course, through

the agency of the nervous system – by the alterations they induce in the calibre of these vessels.

"Premising that the arterioles are dilated by the vaso-motor nerves, which belong to the cerebro-spinal system, and contracted by the fibres of Remak (sympathetic), I will first notice the medicines, which are commonly called stimulants, and which agree in producing exhilaration of the mind, a genial feeling of warmth throughout the body, and increased force and frequency of the heart's contractions. The primary and essential feature of this process, I take to be dilatation of the arterioles (*teste* the flushed face), to which the increased energy of the heart is but secondary, following as a necessary sequence.

"Tea, coffee, and guarana seem to be the purest we have; most of the others, as alcohol and opium, are only purely stimulant in small doses. After a larger dose, that is, after a greater dilatation of the arterioles, a train of other symptoms succeeds; and the former stimulant now becomes either a hypnotic or a narcotic."

The above observations were accurate, but the proposed *unifying* mechanism of action based on vascular dilatation for "stimulants" would soon be supplanted by an emphasis on *neural activity*.

Discoveries during the 18th century that led to understanding of the autonomic nervous system were retold by the British physiologist John Newport Langley (1852–1925), whose own contributions to elucidating the anatomy of the autonomic nervous system included his being the first to explicitly propose that specific receptors in tissues bind drugs or transmitter substances onto cells to initiate or inhibit their pharmacologic actions (Langley 1903, 1916; Maehle 2004). As the anatomy and physiology of the autonomic nervous system (Langley 1903; Elliott 1905) and electrochemical conduction between neural cells (Dale 1935) were clarified, understanding of the physiological substrates for pharmacological actions of stimulants became possible (Vincent and Curtis 1927; Von Euler 1946; Ahlquist 1948).

Advances in pharmacology continued along with those in the biochemistry and physiology of body functions, including investigation of the actions of compounds produced endogenously in the body (Oliver and Schäfer 1895). Once identified, these were purified or synthesized *de novo*, and modified by medicinal chemistry to produce novel pharmaceuticals with shared biochemical or physiological effects. Pharmacologists have also identified and utilized for therapeutic purposes relevant molecules naturally occurring in botanicals used for centuries by mankind to alter sensorium, mood and thinking for medicinal, recreational and ritualistic purposes (Runge 1820; Posselt and Reimann 1828; Chen and Schmidt 1924). Many of these molecules have emerged as pharmaceutical agents employed in medicine and surgery (Phelps 1930; Brun 1947). However, some can also be used for self-medication or for their euphoric effects with progression to addiction in those so predisposed (Martin, Weinberg and Bealer 2007).

Stimulant drugs came to the forefront in medicine due to their sympathomimetic effects (Anonymous 1925):

> "Tasted by the Emperor Shen Nung about 5100 years ago… and described by Li Shih Cheng in 1596 A.D. as a diaphoretic, circulatory stimulant, antipyretic, cough sedative, etc., ephedrine emerged from seclusion in 1887, though really its possibilities have been fully revealed only within the last two years. Ephedrine is the active alkaloid of Ma Huang, or *Ephedra vulgaris* varietal helvetica, closely resembling epinephrine in its actions qualitatively, but differing quantitatively and in some other important particulars. Recent studies of the drug, which is an ingredient of many famous Chinese prescriptions, have been made by… Chen and Schmidt of the Peking Union Medical College (1924) … The promising therapeutic usefulness of ephedrine and its advantages over epinephrine merit attention at this time.

> "The crude drug, *Ephedra vulgaris*, yields two alkaloids, namely, ephedrine and pseudo-ephedrine, the latter being isomeric with ephedrine and their physiological actions are identical. Ephedrine was first isolated by Nagai in 1887 [Nagai Nagayoshi (1844–1929) was a Japanese organic chemist and pharmacologist trained at the University of Berlin in Prussia] … The outstanding effect in animals… is circulatory stimulation, characterized by marked cardiac acceleration and a sustained rise of blood pressure lasting 30 minutes and longer. The cardiac acceleration is due to stimulation of the stellate ganglia and the accelerator endings… With moderate doses, the heart volume is increased and the rate slowed as the maximal level of blood pressure is reached, thus resulting in an increased output of blood from the heart. With high doses and concentrations the heart is depressed and finally stops from direct paralysis by the drug, though the stoppage is usually

preceded by fibrillation... Atropine and section of the vagi do not prevent the circulatory effects, and, hence, they are of sympathetic origin.

"The work of Chen and Schmidt proves conclusively that ephedrine, just like epinephrine, is a sympathomimetic drug, and that it has distinct advantages over epinephrine, namely, that its actions are more prolonged, those of epinephrine being fleeting, and that it is effective by mouth, while epinephrine is not.

"The widest range of therapeutic usefulness of ephedrine will be in the treatment of asthma, hypotension and acute circulatory depression, and in certain congestive nasal conditions.

"Thus, it appears that the newer methods of experimentation confirm, extend and rationalize the effects and uses of an ancient drug understood in a general way and used quite intelligently, though empirically, by the Chinese thousands of years ago."

Shortly following these pioneering studies, the role of the sympathetic arm of the autonomic nervous system were described in psychophysiological responses to threat ("fight or flight"), in stress and in reward (Cannon 1920; Selye 1937; Olds and Olds 1958). Accordingly, studies of the effects of stimulants swiftly expanded beyond the cardiovascular and respiratory systems to include mental stimulation (euphoria, hypervigilance, anxiety, tension, anger, impaired judgement); psychomotor agitation (stereotyped behaviors, dyskinesias, dystonia); energy (less need for sleep) and performance enhancement; anorexia; and delirium, psychosis and seizures. Stimulants were, hence, developed for effects on brain functions to treat disorders such as depression, fatigue, obesity, narcolepsy and more recently attention deficit and hyperactivity disorder (ADHD). These agents were preferentially referred to as *psychostimulants*.

A congener of ephedrine, *amphetamine*, was first synthesized *de novo* at the University of Berlin by Romanian chemist Lazăr Edeleanu (1861–1941) who named it *phenylisopropylamine* (Edeleano 1887). Nagai Nagayoshi synthesized *methamphetamine* (N-methylamphetamine) from ephedrine (1893). Gordon Alles (1901–1963) independently resynthesized *amphetamine* and identified its medically useful sympathomimetic properties (Alles 1927; Rasmussen 2008). In 1933, Smith, Kline and French (SKF) began selling amphetamine as an inhaler under the brand name Benzedrine for asthma and as a decongestant. In 1937, the American Medical Association (AMA) first approved advertising of SKF's "Benzedrine Sulfate" racemic amphetamine tablets for narcolepsy, postencephalitic Parkinsonism, low energy and minor depression (AMA Council on Pharmacy and Chemistry 1937). Reference was made to the work of Abraham Myerson (1881–1948), an American neurologist and psychiatrist, who described his experience with Benzedrine Sulfate administration to normal and "neurotic" persons (Myerson 1936):

> "Drugs that affect mood are few. Alcohol produces in many persons euphoria which is followed by depression, although the changes in mood brought about by alcohol are so diverse as to give rise to the famous aphorism *in vino veritas*, meaning that the true underlying mood of the person comes out while he is drunk. Narcotics deaden the personality and thus bring about an escape from an intolerable mood. The anesthesia of mood which is sought and obtained by this means is purchased at an enormous price, so far as personality worth is concerned.
>
> "Caffeine, in the form of tea and coffee, has a place in the daily habits of the human being largely because of the mild toning-up process which takes place.
>
> "Certain effects of benzedrine sulfate on mood and fatigue… may be stated to exist:
>
>> "First, normal nonpsychotic and nonneurotic persons who suffer from the fatigue and slight malaise due to insufficient rest, especially to insufficient sleep, receive immediate benefit and relief of a pleasant type when from 5 to 20 mg. of benzedrine sulfate is taken on arising. When this dose is taken toward the latter part of the day sleep is impaired in a striking manner.
>>
>> "Second, in certain cases of the neuroses associated with depression, fatigue and anhedonia and in certain cases of the minor stages of the psychoses of the same general type, benzedrine sulfate acts as an ameliorative influence. It is not in any sense curative and its effects are not permanent, but it helps to dissipate the morning apathy and depression, and its ameliorative effect is sufficiently important to recommend it during the treatment of the patient by other means and while the process of natural recovery is taking place."

In the late 1930s, based on these and similar observations, amphetamine began to be widely used for minor ("neurotic") depression. Presumably, the actions of amphetamine provided a means of amplifying adrenergic stimulation in the central nervous system, thereby enhancing the blunted natural drives (*anhedonia*) that characterized minor depression. During World War II both amphetamine and methamphetamine found widespread use for their stimulant and performance-enhancing effects among all combatants but not without adverse psychiatric complications (Rasmussen 2008; Defalque and Wright 2011).

Controlled and limited self-administration of psychostimulants can be highly rewarding because of pleasurable and invigorating effects, which powerfully reinforce repeated use (Ritz and Kuhar 1989; Wang, Volkow, Chang et al. 2004). However, increased frequency of self-administration can progress to out-of-control use, resulting in *allostatic* neuroadaptive changes via *sensitization* which alter the experience despite the augmented urge to continue use (Robinson and Berridge 1993). Extended use can result in toxic effects in many organs of the body, including the nervous system, liver, heart, kidney toxicity (rhabdomyolysis) and psychotic features characterized elevated mood and delusions of persecution (Connell 1968; Kalant 1973; Carvalho, Carmo, Costa et al. 2012).

As the abuse potential of stimulants was recognized, they were designated as controlled (schedule II) substances in the United States in the 1970s. Most commonly abused stimulants are various amphetamines and *cocaine*. Naturally occurring stimulants, *cocaine* (see Cocaine), *caffeine* (see Coffee), *nicotine* (see Nicotine) and *Catha edulis [Khat]* are discussed in independent entries. Synthetic amphetamine-related stimulants, *methamphetamine, ephedrine, 3,4-Methylenedioxymethamphetamine (MDMA) or ecstacy, Methylenedioxypyrovalerone (MDPV), mephedrone, methylphenidate, phenylpropanolamine, propylhexedrine, pseudoephedrine* among others are characterized by sympathomimetic effects (Axelrod 1954; Fairchild and Alles 1967) but can also affect dopaminergic and serotonergic neurotransmission. Amphetamine-type stimulants, most commonly methamphetamine, remain widely used illicit drugs (0.5% to 1.0% of the U.S. population), in part, due to widespread diversion of stimulants (lisdexamfetamine, methylphenidate, and amphetamine) prescribed for treatment of ADHD (Arria and DuPont 2010). Prevalence of amphetamine-type stimulant use disorders have been rising in the last decade in the U.S. population (from 0.1% to 0.2%), especially among individuals aged 18-25 years (Courtney and Ray 2014). Methamphetamine, illegally synthesized in domestic clandestine labs from household chemicals, has wreaked havoc due to physical and emotional injuries (Centers for Disease Control and Prevention 2000). Nevertheless, stimulants continue to be used as performance-enhancing or recreational drugs despite potential behavioral toxicities raising unresolved social and ethical problems (Farah, Illes, Cook-Deegan et al. 2004).

Suicide

The noun *suicide,* according to the current electronic version of the Oxford English Dictionary (OED), is derived from the Latin *suīcīdium*, a combination of *suī* and *-cīdium*. The first part of this combination means "of oneself." The second part is derived from the French *-cide* and Latin *-cīdium*, meaning "cutting, killing or slaying, murder." The Latin words employing these combinations passed frequently via French into English, e.g., *homicide* (late Middle English), fratricide (16th century). The meaning of *suicide* relevant to our discussion is: "The or an act of taking one's own life, self-murder." This is an important term to discuss as suicide is highly prevalent among those who suffer from addiction.

An example of the first use of the noun *suicide* in the English language, according to OED, was by Thomas Blount (1618-1679), an English antiquarian and lexicographer, in his work, *Glossographia: A dictionary interpreting all such hard words…as are now used in our refined English tongue* (1656): "Suicide, the slaying or murdering of himself; self-murder." Acceptance of the fact that taking one's own life is not only theoretical, but actually occurs, led to philosophical, religious and legal deliberation concerning causes, implications and consequences of suicide. Walter Charleton (1620-1707), a natural philosopher and physician known for introducing Epicurian ideas into England, wrote in *Ephesian Matron* (1659): "To vindicate ones self from… inevitable Calamity, by Sui-cide is not… a Crime." John Erskine of Carnock (1695-1768), a Scottish jurist and professor of Scottish law at the University of Edinburgh, wrote in *An Institute of the Law of Scotland* (1773): "Suicide, which is a species of murder, ought to be governed by the common rules of murder." William Cowper (1731-1800), one of the most popular poets of his time, wrote in his poem *Truth*, "Charge not... Your wilful suicide on God's decree." These quotations together represent accepted perspectives of suicide over time – the notion that suicide is a reasonable exit strategy if the calamity one faces is sufficiently great, that suicide is a crime, pure and simple and that such actions are wrong, a sin that may not be forgiven.

It is not metaphysics, religion or the law that will be the focus here, but another equally relevant issue: that such an act is most often a consequence of a *mental illness*, a point that was plainly made in *The Anatomy of Suicide* by Lyttelton Stewart Forbes Winslow (1844-1913), the British psychiatrist involved in the Jack the Ripper case during the late Victorian era:

> "If we examine attentively the majority of cases of suicide, we shall find that the
> unfortunate persons have laboured, either for some time previously or at the very

moment, under depression of spirits, anxiety of mind, and other symptoms of cerebral derangement. Very few cases of suicide take place in which you cannot trace the existence of previous mental depression, produced either by physical or moral agents. It may be said that lowness of spirits is not insanity; certainly not, according to the legal definition of the term; but we may always be assured, that if mental anxiety or perturbation be more than commensurate with the exciting cause, it may be presumed that the individual is labouring under the incipient indications of insanity."

In support of this opinion, whether the person is considered mentally ill or not, such an act seems so unfathomable that it is considered a sin by many religions, subject to legal consequences if failed and may disqualify one's family from death benefits.

Accordingly, there is significant motivation *post hoc* to deny that a death was, in fact, caused by suicide. Therefore, ascertainment of *rates of suicide* represents a challenge for epidemiologists and prevalence in populations are of uncertain reliability and can become a subject of polemics. For example, the early British authority on insanity George Man Burrows (1771-1846), a surgeon-apothecary admitted as a Fellow of the Royal College of Physicians late in life, believed that "treatment of insanity had an optimistic future" (Tubbs 1947) and hence, viewed an outcome of suicide as a medical failure. He engaged in an interchange with leaders of French psychiatry by writing *A Reply to Messieurs Esquirol's and Falret's Objections to Dr. Burrows' comparative Proportions of Suicides in Paris and London* (Burrows 1822) to dispel the impression overseas that the British were "the most devoted to suicide":

"Dr. Esquirol, in the 53[d] volume of the 'Dictionnaire des Sciences Médicales,' article *Suicide*, has entered into an examination of the grounds on which, in my 'Inquiry into certain Errors relative to Insanity,' I have decided that self-destruction is more frequent in Paris than in London… As the contrary has been a favourite axiom with foreign, especially French, writers, it was to be expected that any attempt to controvert it would not long remain unnoticed. Accordingly, not only Dr. Esquirol, but his élève Dr. Falret, in a Work entitled 'De l'Hypochondrie et Suicide, 1822,' following his master's example, has attacked both the premises and deductions I have adopted."

Of course, Jean-Étienne Dominique Esquirol (1772-1840) and Jean-Pierre Falret (1794-1870) were fitting adversaries in debate for Burrow. They were both authorities on insanity, known for efforts to medicalize care in this field, initially inspired to do so at the Salpêtrière Hospital in Paris by Philippe Pinel (1745-1826) and his humane psychological approach to care of psychiatric patients. All the same, one wonders whether this exchange was not simply continuation of a cross-channel rivalry that began at the Battle of Hastings in 1066, rather than a true analysis of the relationship between suicide and mental illness in the two countries, the rates of which were probably quite unreliable at that time.

Whenever the prevalence of suicide has formally been examined, alcoholism is closely linked with the associated psychopathology (Whitehead 1972; Miles 1977). This had been suspected since Magnus Huss (1849) declared in his classic on alcoholism:

> "…that the suicidal impulse is a more frequent accompaniment of the melancholia of drunkards than of melancholia from other causes; and further, that among the uneducated classes suicide frequently follows on the disordered emotional tone, which, sooner or later, results from the abuse of alcoholic liquors."

After weighing various potential mechanisms whereby alcohol use might be implicated in suicidality, the author of the editorial *The Relation of Alcoholism to Suicide* concluded (Anonymous 1902):

> "…the chronic intoxication by alcohol, as we observe it clinically, produces generalised disorders of visceral function throughout the economy, whence there results an alteration and disturbance of those organic stimuli which form the groundwork of our personality; those, stimuli whose activity, as Maudsley [Henry Maudsley (1835-1918) was a pioneering English psychiatrist, commemorated in the Maudsley Hospital in London and in the annual Maudsley Lecture of the Royal College of Psychiatrists] puts it, is 'even of more consequence in determining the tone of our feeling or of our disposition and the character of our impulses than that activity which follows impressions received from the external world.' The depressed emotional tone thereby induced prepares the suicidal impulse, which issues in action when a supervening increase of intoxication has still further lowered the level of function in the brain."

The association between alcoholism and suicide has been extensively documented since these early reports, including implicative drinking among persons who commit suicide, documented occurrence of suicidal thoughts and attempted suicide and completed suicide among persons who are alcoholics (Whitehead 1972). Even if an actual suicidal act cannot be identified, alcoholism may be considered a form of *slow suicide* based on destruction of one's health and personality through drinking (Menninger 1938). Associations with suicide are not restricted to alcoholism, but have subsequently been reported for all drugs of abuse, e.g., sedative hypnotics (Allgulander, Ljungberg and Fisher 1987), opioids (Vaillant 1966) and stimulants (Kalant and Kalant 1975), suggesting that suicide may not relate absolutely to the pharmacological actions of the agent as much as clinical characteristics of the user, the motivation for use, response to the drug and its life consequences (Robins, Gassner, Kayes et al. 1959; Miles 1977; Mann, Waternaux, Haas and Malone 1999).

Most studies demonstrate a greater likelihood of death by suicide in those who have alcoholism/drug use disorder co-occurring with other psychiatric disorders, especially depressed mood and hopelessness (Weissman, Slobetz, Prusoff et al. 1976). Also, since in early epidemiologic studies, mood disorders and addictive disorders each accounted for the highest rates of suicidality among all psychiatric diagnoses (Miles 1977), the important question that remains is whether the primary driver of suicide is a mood disorder, an addictive disorder, or their combined effects. In fact, co-occurring mood disorders and alcohol/drug use disorders are very common (Regier, Farmer, Rae et al. 1990) and such individuals may be particularly at risk for suicide. Among the various psychiatric diagnoses associated with suicide, common wisdom has pointed to the significant preponderance of depressive features. However, this viewpoint has evolved to recognizing the important role of *mood instability*, as manifested in patients with bipolar disorders in depressed phase or mixed state and unipolar depression with mixed features, as well as the state precipitated by selective serotonin receptor uptake inhibitors in these individuals (Bunney, Murphy, Goodwin and Borge 1970; Jamison 2000; Akiskal, Benazzi, Perugi and Rihmer 2005). Recent research has suggested that the mood disorders most associated with alcohol/drug use disorders may not be unipolar depressive disorders at all, as was previously thought, but rather hyperthymic mood disorders which may play a mechanistic role in development of addiction (Rich and Martin 2014). Finally, Mann, Waternaux, Haas and Malone (1999) have proposed that a more useful approach to determining risk for suicidal behavior may be the concept of a predisposing *stress diathesis*, which makes room for other psychiatric disorders and traumatic experiences in the formulation.

Investigations of the inheritance of suicidality have proceeded down a similar path as have epidemiologic studies of the associations of suicidal behavior with psychiatric diagnoses – the initial focus was linking suicidal behaviors to the genetics of depression (Roy 1993). Although this approach yielded advances, Chistiakov, Kekelidze and Chekhonin (2012) have described a strategy for linking suicidal behaviors with *endophenotypes*, namely separation of behavioral symptoms into more stable phenotypes with a clear genetic connection (John and Lewis 1966). Proposed endophenotypes have included impulsive/aggressive traits as mediated by low serotonergic function, neurocognitive impairment resulting in disinhibition of impulses and decision making, particularly severe (early onset) major depression, profound stress as manifested by hyperactivity of hypothalamic–pituitary–adrenal axis, functional neuroimaging measures of brain responses as emotions and impulse inhibition, lowered skin conductance, personality disorders characterized by interpersonal hyperreactivity and lithium treatment response. It is important to note that many of these endophenotypes are closely inter-related and the presence of alcohol/drug use disorders alone is a powerful predictor of risk for subsequent suicides in historical attempters (Oquendo, Galfalvy, Russo et al. 2004). So, regardless of whether a psychiatric diagnostic or endophenotypic strategy is selected to identify risk for suicidal behaviors, alcohol/drug use disorders emerge as highly predictive.

This discussion naturally leads to the current "opioid epidemic" in the U.S. Deaths due to overdose from opioids and accompanying other central nervous system depressants have increased substantially over the last decade (Tori, Larochelle and Naimi 2020). This time frame parallels the observation of a decreased life expectancy in the U.S. during this same period, for the first time since World War II (Woolf and Schoomaker 2019). A major contributing factor to this change in life expectancy has been an increase in mortality from specific causes, especially drug overdoses and suicides among young and middle-aged adults of all racial groups. How to distinguish suicide and accidental death from overdose? Menninger (1938) recognized that chronic alcoholism often progresses to death over years of hazardous use and coined the term "slow suicide," even though an actual suicidal act could not be documented with precision. Addiction to drugs that can be deadly due to their pharmacological potencies (especially a consideration with expanding availability of illicit street drugs adulterated with fentanyl-related opioid compounds) may not allow a person to survive intoxication if an impulsively chosen combination results in respiratory arrest and death. The result of this is the same as might have occurred if the drug was taken to voluntarily to end one's life in a suicidal act. Not knowing if one might die from self-administration of drugs to which one is addicted, or not caring, are not at all the same thing.

Tolerance

According to the latest electronic version of the Oxford English Dictionary (OED) the noun *tolerance* originates from the French *tolérance*, first used in the 14th century (Hatzfeld and Darmesteter 1964), which in turn was derived from the Latin verb *tolerāre*, to tolerate ("To allow to exist or to be done or practised without authoritative interference or molestation; also generally to allow, permit") combined with the suffix ("Forming nouns of quality, state, or action"). The OED definition that best corresponds to the medical meaning of *tolerance* ("The power, constitutional or acquired, of enduring large doses of active drugs, or of resisting the action of poison, etc.; hence diminution in the response to a drug after continued use") is not the earliest use of the word, nor is specific reference to diminished response to a drug or resistance to a poison the primary meaning of *tolerance* in the current OED. Evolution of the meaning of the word is of interest in gaining understanding of its meaning in neuropsychopharmacology and with respect to the role this phenomenon plays in addiction.

The earliest recorded reference to the word *tolerance* in the English language, according to OED, was in Middle English in the book by John Lydgate of Bury (*c.* 1370 – *c.* 1451) an English monk and poet in 1412-20 as *tolleraunce* (Lydgate et al. 1906): "Riȝt so convenient Is to þe wyse…with suffraunce, In al his port to haue tolleraunce". The word thus was employed in its original meaning: "The action or practice of enduring or sustaining pain or hardship; the power or capacity of enduring; endurance." This very early reference to the word tolerance refers to elements of emotional life/experience (thoughts or inclinations) rather than the capacity of an individual for intake of an exogenous entity such as a pharmacological agent, especially a psychoactive drug. The currently used medical meaning of the word *tolerance* is attributed to Horatio Curtis Wood (1841-1920), the American physician, educator and editor in his pioneering contribution to medicine and science *A Treatise on Therapeutics, comprising Materia Medica and Toxicology, with especial reference to the application of the physiological action of drugs to clinical medicine* (Wood 1874): "By the aid of opiates and careful dilution a species of tolerance was often obtained for these heroic doses". This mention of tolerance as a mechanism of the pharmacological action of a drug actually precedes establishment of pharmacology as a discipline by Wood's student John Jacob Abel beginning in the 1890's.

The notion of tolerance as presented by Curtis Wood broadens understanding of pharmacology beyond simply pharmacognosy to elucidation of the interaction between a drug and the organism to which the drug is administered. Accordingly, individual attributes, including both constitutional characteristics and neurobiological adaptations upon administration of a given drug over time, not chemical/physiological characteristics of the administered molecule alone, became the purview of pharmacology. While the interaction of drug and host adds considerably to the scope of pharmacology, it is nevertheless incomplete. A further conceptual leap, especially relevant for the sub-discipline neuropsychopharmacology, involves another level of analysis, namely, the influence of the environmental milieu and its accommodation by brain mechanisms of the individual who is administered the pharmacological agent.

While recognizing that tolerance has these tripartite determinants, the term itself has been parsed and qualified in various ways (Martin and Patel 2017). The term can be readily dichotomized into: i) *initial* (also called *innate*) *tolerance* which refers to inter-individual variation in sensitivity to a drug (i.e., variations that are present before the first administration of drug to an individual) typically arising from genetic variation of receptors at which the drug acts or differences among individuals in drug absorption, metabolism, or excretion; and ii) *acquired tolerance* which refers to tolerance as a consequence to repeated drug exposure comprising pharmacokinetic, pharmacodynamic and learning-related components.

The meaning of *initial tolerance* is not well understood and continues as an exciting area of research in elucidation of risk for drug use disorders or addiction. *Acquired tolerance* can occur due to identifiable changes in capacity of the organism to dispose of the drug or due to changes in pharmacological effect of the same amount of drug at its site of action. The former, termed *metabolic* or *pharmacokinetic tolerance* typically is due to induction of the enzyme systems responsible for biotransformation of a drug prior to elimination from the body resulting in shortened duration of presence of the drug at its site of action. The latter, termed *pharmacodynamic tolerance* is typically due to changes in signal transduction at the site of action of the drug. Indeed, persistent adaptations to drug use both modify existing synapses and create new synapses, effectively "rewiring" the brain. Pharmacodynamic tolerance also involves another element of tolerance which has been termed *learned tolerance*. In *behavioral tolerance*, a form of learned tolerance, drug use results in compensatory changes in behavior that are not directly related to the pharmacologic action of the drug but rather to accommodation to drug effects through learning acquired while the person is intoxicated or in the environment in which the intoxication occurred. *Conditioned tolerance* occurs when environmental cues associated with exposure to a drug induce preemptive, reflexive compensatory changes, called a conditioned opponent response. The influence of these adaptive brain mechanisms was addressed, parceled and integrated by Kalant, LeBlanc and Gibbins (1971) when they proposed the term *behaviorally augmented tolerance* as being preferable to dichotomizing tolerance into learned and physiological components. Such long-lasting molecular and cellular adaptations of the brain are likely involved in the cravings and relapses that can occur in individuals with drug use disorders even long after drug use has ceased.

Changes in response to a psychoactive drug resulting from prior exposure(s) of which tolerance is a component, now commonly termed *neuroadaptation* (American Psychiatric Association 1987), have become understood as neurobiologically related to learning and memory formation (Kalant, LeBlanc and Gibbins 1971). Thus, exposure to drugs alters the individual and thereby the individual's experience of the environment in which the drug is administered. The current century's scientific agenda of elucidating epigenetic factors in drug action and learning (Sweatt 2016; Francis, Diorio, Liu and Meaney 1999) is the fruit of an early seed planted by Mendel, watered by Garrod and Galton and reaped by Scriver among others (Scriver and Clow 1980). The term *epigenetics* was originally coined by Waddington in 1942 to describe the examination of "causal mechanisms" whereby "the genes of the genotype bring about phenotypic effects" (Waddington 2012). Epigenetic mechanisms are admirably suited to elucidate our understanding of the multi-faceted responses of the unique organism to different drugs of abuse within a given environment, including development of tolerance (Malvaez, Barrett, Wood and Sanchis-Segura 2009). Conceptualization of tolerance using these three interactive factors makes perfect sense, especially because this neuropharmacological action of drugs can play a fundamental role in drug use disorders. In fact, a tripartite model, historically derived from the epidemiologic perspective (agent/host/environment) of infectious diseases (Snow 1855), seems especially suited for drug use disorders because, contrary to other mental disorders, the causal agent (a drug of abuse) is of necessity defined.

There continues to be a striking inconsistency between the meanings of the word tolerance in medical/scientific and other realms. The original (non-medical) understanding of tolerance is of a positive attribute, the power or capacity to endure pain or suffering, presumably strength of character. However, tolerance in the medical sense, a diminution in the response to a pharmacologic agent after continued use, especially drugs that possess dependence liability, does not necessarily connote a desired characteristic and may be considered to bear stigma if associated with addiction. Although in some cultures the capacity to "drink someone under the table" is viewed as a sign of masculinity and strength, presumably a positive attribute, there is accumulating research indicating that increased innate tolerance to central nervous system depressants, such as alcohol, actually may represent a significant risk factor for development of alcoholism (Schuckit and Rayses 1979). Hence, while the earliest uses of the word tolerance connoted positive attributes strongly linked to mystical or religious contexts and even may have involved psychoactive agents, by the 20th century, the description in medical science of a syndrome of self-destructive and out-of-control self-administration of various neuropsychopharmacologic agents (Nathan, Conrad and Skinstad 2016), of which tolerance is an important mechanistic component, has perhaps shed a new light on the debate about whether tolerance to drugs of abuse is good or bad.

Trauma

According to the current electronic version of the Oxford English Dictionary (OED), the noun *trauma* is derived from the Latin *traumaticus* via the Greek τραυματικός, meaning "of or pertaining to a wound or wounds" and τραῦμα, -ματ-, meaning "wound," appearing in the 16th century French as *traumatique*. In fact, the adjectival form appeared in the English language before the noun *trauma* (Blount 1656): "*Traumatick*, belonging to wounds or to the cure of wounds, vulnerary." The relevant OED definition for *traumatic* is: "Of, pertaining to, or caused by a wound, abrasion, or external injury..." An example of the word *trauma* appeared in the book *A physical dictionary; in which all the terms relating either to anatomy, chirurgery, pharmacy, or chymistry*...written by Steven Blankaart (1650–1704), a Dutch physician, iatrochemist and entomologist, who proved the existence of a capillary system, as had been suggested by Leonardo da Vinci (Blankaart 1684): "*Trauma*,... a Wound from an external Cause." The OED definition of *trauma* as used in this quotation is: "A wound, or external bodily injury in general; also, the condition caused by this; traumatism."

Whereas initial understanding of *trauma* was as an *external* and *physical* injury, the meaning has expanded to include an *internal* and, metaphorically, an *emotional* wound. The definition of *trauma* as used in addiction came from neurology/psychiatry: "A psychic injury, especially one caused by emotional shock the memory of which is repressed and remains unhealed; an internal injury, especially to the brain, which may result in a behavioural disorder of organic origin. Also, the state or condition so caused." An example of this sense of the word, as first used in the English language, is by William James (1842–1910), American philosopher and psychologist, who discussed the article *Ueber den psychischen Mechanismus hysterischer Phanomen* in *Psychological Review* (James 1894). This article appeared the preceding year in a German neurology journal, written by Josef Breuer (1842–1925), a distinguished Viennese physician, and his protégé, Sigmund Freud (1856–1939), then a neurologist; these two colleagues had combined forces to lay the foundation of the discipline of psychoanalysis ("talk cure"). Interestingly enough, in the previous pages of this same issue of *Psychological Review* is James' summary of a series of articles written originally by Pierre Janet (1859–1947), a pioneering French psychologist, physician, philosopher and psychotherapist in the field of dissociation and traumatic memory who studied under Jean-Martin Charcot in the Pitié-Salpêtrière Hospital in Paris — *Etat mental des hysteriques: les stigmates mentaux; Etat mental des hysteriques: Les accidents mentaux; L'amnesie continue* — which are referenced below, as follows:

""Hysteria is a disease of the hypnotic stratum," wrote Mr. F. W. H. Myers [Frederic William Henry Myers (1843–1901) was a poet, classicist and philologist whose ideas about a "subliminal self" were influential in his time, but have not been accepted by the scientific community] many years ago, and this important paper is a comment on his dictum and an independent corroboration of Janet's above [pp. 195-199]. The distinguished Viennese neurologists who sign it stumbled accidentally on cures which enable them not only to give a general formula for the disease, but a general method for its treatment. Hysteria for them starts always from a shock, and is a 'disease of the memory.' Certain reminiscences of the shock fall into the subliminal consciousness, where they can only be discovered in 'hypnoid' states. If left there, they act as permanent 'psychic *traumata*' thorns in the spirit, so to speak. The cure is to draw them out in hypnotism, let them produce all their emotional effects, however violent, and *work themselves off*. They make then (apparently) a new connection with the principal consciousness, whose breach is thus restored, and the sufferer gets well."

The OED definition of *traumatic* is: "Of, pertaining to, or caused by a psychic wound or emotional shock, especially leading to or causing behavioural disturbance." This sense of the word was first used in the 1889 English translation of *Clinical Lectures on Diseases of the Nervous System* by Jean-Martin Charcot (1825–1893), a French neurologist and professor of anatomical pathology, known for his work on hypnosis and hysteria and considered "the founder of modern neurology": "The existence of traumatic psychosis [French *psychose traumatique*] adds still more to the gravity of the prognosis." That leaders in medicine, neurology and psychiatry almost simultaneously conceptualized a role of *emotional trauma* in clinical medicine underlines the breath of presentation of trauma-related conditions. The frequent association of trauma with addiction points to one way in which coping with the associated emotional suffering can occur.

Despite the introduction of psychic underpinnings for disease, the word *trauma* has retained its concrete meaning, namely a *physical* wound. This point is illustrated by a quote from *A Text-book of Psychiatry* (Henderson and Gillespie 1927): "Trauma may produce mental symptoms in one of two ways. Either it causes structural injury to the brain, or it causes emotional disturbances... In the first instance the mental reaction is of the organic type… in the second the result is usually a psychoneurosis." This quotation embodied the broadly-based viewpoint of David Kennedy Henderson (1884–1965), a Scottish physician and psychiatrist who served as president of the Royal College of Physicians of Edinburgh and represented the influential Scottish tradition of organic psychiatry and psychological medicine combined with social psychiatry (Cameron 1965).

Recognition of the effects of trauma on humans, not surprisingly, occurred first in the military where both "structural injury to the brain" and "emotional disturbances" are very possible during active service and must be entertained in the differential diagnosis. The American physician Jacob Mendes Da Costa (1833–1900) described a condition of the circulatory system that now bears his name in 300 cases he examined in the military hospital in Philadelphia during the American Civil War (Da Costa 1871):

"In this paper I propose to consider a form of cardiac malady common among soldiers, but the study of which is equally interesting to the civil practitioner... I noticed cases of a peculiar form of functional disorder of the heart, to which I gave the name of irritable heart...

"The general clinical history of many of the cases was this: -- A man who had been for some months or longer in active service, would be seized with diarrhea, annoying, yet not severe enough to keep him out of the field; or, attacked with diarrhea or fever, he rejoined, after a short stay in hospital, his command, and again underwent the exertions of a soldier's life. He soon noticed that he could not bear them as formerly; he got out of breath, could not keep up with his comrades, his accoutrements oppressed him, and all this though he appeared well and healthy. Seeking advice from the surgeon of the regiment, it was decided that he was unfit for duty, and he was sent to a hospital, where his persistently quick acting heart confirmed his story, though he looked like a man in sound condition. Any digestive disturbances which might have existed gradually passed away, but the irritability of the heart remained, and only very slowly did the excited organ return to its natural condition. Or it failed to do so, notwithstanding the use of remedies which control the circulation: thus, the case might go on for a long time, and the patient, after having been the round of hospitals, would be discharged, or, as unfit for active duty, placed in the Invalid Corps.

"This may be stated to be a general summary of a considerable number of cases. But there were many others originating more suddenly, or without previous digestive disorder, presenting also marked disturbance or irregularity of the circulation, and having also the pain in the cardiac region well developed."

Da Costa described a range of symptoms that seem only tenuously linked to the cardiovascular system and he documents the particular beneficial effects of rest and, additionally, of some pharmacological agents, including digitalis, belladonna, laudanum, opium and cannabis. For opium he writes, "This was rather incidentally tested while prescribing for diarrhoea or some other affection in which it was indicated, than used persistently for the irritable heart; for in the long continuance of the treatment required there would have been great risk of making the patient an opium eater." This last point underlines Da Costa's awareness of the susceptibility of the stressed individual to a drug that, on one hand, relieves suffering, but on the other, is highly addictive. This astute observation foreshadows a major theme — the relationship between the chronic consequences of the *experience of trauma* and the development of *addiction* via *self-medication* (see Addiction and Self-medication).

Attempts to elucidate the pathophysiology of Da Costa's syndrome made some progress when the cardiovascular symptoms were conceptualized in terms of dysfunction of the autonomic nervous system, "neurocirculatory asthenia" or as an "effort syndrome" (Piersol 1925). It was not until Paul Wood (1907–1962), "the greatest British cardiologist of his time," concluded the *Goulstonian Lectures* to the Royal College of Physicians of London that the perspective shifted beyond the cardiovascular system and the clinical manifestations were interpreted as a consequence, rather than the cause of the syndrome (Wood 1941): "The symptoms and signs of Da Costa's syndrome more closely resemble those of emotion, especially fear, than those of effort in the normal subject. The mechanism of the somatic manifestations depends upon central stimulation, not upon hypersensitivity of the peripheral autonomic gear. This central stimulus is emotional and is commonly the result of fear."

Nonetheless, even at the end of the Second World War, Friedman (1945) acknowledged that an etiopathogenic conundrum still existed:

> "…whereas most internists have consistently stressed the psychic factors in this disease, they have not succeeded in integrating the latter in any exact, physiologic manner with the actual emergence of cardiovascular symptoms and signs in the same patient. Likewise, the psychiatrists have not succeeded in elucidating the pathogenesis of cardiovascular manifestations in patients suffering from an obvious anxiety neurosis. There exists, then, a physiologic or neurologic void between the

psychic and cardiovascular phases of neurocirculatory asthenia which has not been probed sufficiently by either the internist or by the psychiatrist. Until this void is explored, however, it will be impossible to understand those processes set loose in a person subject to anxiety, which express themselves in trembling, perspiration, flushing, dyspnea, palpitation, and precordial pain."

Friedman's conclusion (1945) placed the problem, for the first time, in the correct organ system of the body: "Evidence was obtained which suggested that the excitation of the sympathetic nervous system, preceding or associated in a causal fashion with the cardiovascular manifestations of neurocirculatory asthenia, resulted from hypothalamic discharge."

It was not until after the Vietnam War, a time of social changes in codes of behavior related to sexuality and gender roles ("Sexual Revolution") in the 1960s, that the perspective of *trauma* in psychiatry progressed beyond notions of "soldier's heart," "shell shock," "neurocirculatory asthenia" and "combat fatigue and neurosis." The focus shifted to the neurobiology of stress (Cannon 1920; Selye 1937; McEwen 2007) and inter-individual vulnerability (Meaney 2001) to the *experience* of stress and its toxicity to various organs, in particular, the brain and its neuroendocrine offshoots (Sapolsky 1996). The diagnostic entity *posttraumatic stress disorder* (PTSD) emerged in the 1970s and was subsequently included in the American Psychiatric Association's *Diagnostic and Statistical Manual of Mental Disorders*, Third Edition (1980). It soon became apparent that this disorder, characterized by pathological responses to stress, also affected women and occurred in civilian life — as was suggested by Da Costa (1871) but not fully appreciated for a century.

In the National Comorbidity Survey, the lifetime prevalence of PTSD was reported as 7.8% (5% of men and 10.4% of women) and strongly comorbid with other lifetime DSM-III-R disorders, including alcohol and drug use disorders (Kessler, Sonnega, Bromet et al. 1995). Furthermore, PTSD was found to be the primary diagnosis if it was a comorbid condition. In addition to effects of war in soldiers, pathological response syndromes to trauma were described in sexual assault (Burgess and Holmstrom 1974) and many other stressful experiences (Grinker and Spiegel 1945). In particular, adverse childhood experiences were profound predictors of adult psychopathology and have become a focus of investigation (Brown and Harris 1993). Not only do disturbing memories of the traumatic events impair functioning throughout life, but in association with re-experiencing these traumatic memories, ongoing memory dysfunctions for current events can be identified (Yehuda, Keefe, Harvey et al. 1995; Jenkins, Langlais, Delis and Cohen 1998). In particular, the association of adverse childhood experiences and development of an addictive disorder has become firmly established (Dube, Anda, Felitti et al. 2002; Turner and Lloyd 2003).

Stress responses leave enduring emotion-laden memory traces in the brain (Rodrigues, Schafe and LeDoux 2004). Traumatic memories cannot be forgotten and emerge into consciousness and disrupt current functioning. Because re-experience of the stressful events further strengthen these memory traces, they become generalized to elements of the environment (Miller 2004). The desire to suppress re-experiencing painful memories during the day and in nightmares are compelling and individuals recognize that temporary relief can be obtained by alcohol or other drugs of abuse (Martin, Weinberg and Bealer 2007). Repeated use of alcohol/drugs, although initially beneficial, likely fade with time and a use disorder due to self-medication emerges and becomes recalcitrant to treatment (Derefinko, Salgado García, Talley et al. 2019). Conceptually, evidence has emerged that vulnerability to development of PTSD is determined by an interaction between experienced stress and characteristic susceptibilities of the individual, complicated by identifiable risk for development of alcohol and drug use (Ohashi, Anderson, Bolger et al. 2019; Martin 2020). Psychiatrists have striven to identify medications that can temper re-experiencing traumatic memories, demonstrated to be associated with over-activation of the noradrenergic system and other CNS impairments which persist indefinitely after the trauma was initially experienced (Cahill, Prins, Weber and McGaugh 1994; Raskind, Peskind, Kanter et al. 2003; Squire and Davis 1981). Additionally, since the response to stress involves a tremendous outpouring of cortisol (Selye 1937), which is toxic to the brain and especially hippocampal regions vital for memory consolidation and emotional linkages via the amygdala to the prefrontal cortex, there has been a focus on both impairments in memory consolidation and the capacity to forget (Sapolsky 1996; Miller 2004).

The story comes full circle from Da Costa with identification of the brain origins of stress-induced cardiomyopathy, the so-called "broken heart syndrome" (Silva, Magalhães, Arantes et al. 2019). Using fMRI to compare neural connectivity during the resting-state and during stressful stimulation in controls and patients recovered from this syndrome, it was found that patients displayed a reorganization of cortical and subcortical networks, including areas associated with emotional responses and autonomic regulation. This suggests that dysregulation of autonomic control at the central level plays a significant role in stress-induced cardiomyopathy. Via neural connection between brain and heart, psychosocial stressors can be expressed in the heart. More recent work has identified the physiologic basis of a central master driver of psychosocial stress responses in a rat model. Kataoka,

Shima, Nakajima and Nakamura (2020) provide evidence for the prominent role of a ventral part of the medial prefrontal cortex in sympathetic responses to social defeat stress. This brain region sends excitatory projections to the dorsomedial hypothalamus as a central coordinator of the psychosocial stress responses throughout the body. This reifies *emotional trauma* to a degree that, heretofore, could only be imagined.

Wernicke-Korsakoff Syndrome

There is no actual definition of *Wernicke-Korsakoff syndrome* in the current electronic version of the Oxford English Dictionary (OED). Rather, listed separately are the names of two physicians, the German neurologist Karl Wernicke (1848–1905) and the Russian psychiatrist Sergei Sergeievich Korsakoff (1854–1900). These physicians are each considered to have described a distinct neuropsychiatric *syndrome* ("A concurrence of several symptoms in a disease; a set of such concurrent symptoms") often found in patients with chronic alcoholism (see Alcoholism). The eponyms *Wernicke* and *Korsakoff (*also *Korsakow, Korsakov)* are typically used as nouns in the possessive form or attributively, e.g., *Wernicke's encephalopathy* and *Korsakoff psychosis.*

Through clinical descriptions, neuropathological correlations and biochemical studies the etiological basis of the syndromes attributed to Wernicke and Korsakoff were demonstrated to be closely related (Victor, Adams and Collins 1971). In due course, *Wernicke's encephalopathy* and *Korsakoff psychosis* were recognized to be two stages in the clinical course of the same disorder. It was finally proven that the pathogenesis of the disorder involved episode(s) of malnutrition associated with a specific deficiency of *thiamine (vitamin B_1),* often exacerbated by the effects of chronic alcohol consumption and co-occurring disorders that can complicate alcoholism. Therefore, half a century after these protagonists' descriptions, their eponyms became joined forever in the English-speaking world as *Wernicke-Korsakoff syndrome (WKS)* (Anonymous 1970). However, *Wernicke's encephalopathy* is not the eponym employed in French psychiatry. The name of the French ophthalmologist Alphonse-Charles Gayet (1833–1904) was attached to the disorder because of the primacy of his description (Gayet 1875) over Wernicke's (1881). Accordingly, *encéphalopathie de Gayet-Wernicke* is accepted usage, despite the fact that there still is no consensus that Gayet's description referred to exactly the same pathological entity as that of Wernicke (Girard, Garde and Devic 1953; Victor, Adams and Collins 1971).

The noun *Wernicke* is defined in OED as: "An encephalopathy caused by vitamin B_1 deficiency and characterized by mental confusion and uncontrolled movements, especially of the eyes. So, *Wernicke–Korsakoff,* [is] applied to *Wernicke's syndrome* and *Korsakoff's syndrome* when both are present in an individual." Based on contemporary understanding (Caine, Halliday, Kril and Harper 1997), *Wernicke's syndrome* is the acute, life-threatening stage of the avitaminosis. With repletion of thiamine, the neuropsychiatric residua of the acute brain insult can manifest as the chronic phase of the disorder, *Korsakoff's syndrome.* Therefore, with recovery from the acute phase of WKS, the clinico-pathological features of both the acute and chronic phases can be simultaneously appreciated as expression of the natural history of the effects of thiamine deficiency on the nervous system. Accordingly, the eponym *Wernicke* is commonly associated with the noun *encephalopathy*, which in OED is defined simply as: "Disease of the brain in general."

The noun *Korsakoff* is defined in OED as: "…denote[s] a type of psychosis, namely a syndrome, often the result of chronic alcoholism, which is characterized by disorientation, memory loss for recent events [anterograde memory], and consequent confabulation." The verb *to confabulate* ("To fabricate of imaginary experiences as compensation for loss of memory") has been used in reference to *Korsakoff psychosis*, suggesting that many cognitive skills and certain aspects of memory are strikingly preserved despite the specific inability to acquire most new learning (Weingartner, Grafman, Boutelle et al. 1983). *Psychosis* is defined in OED as: "Originally: any kind of disordered mental state or mental illness. Later: specifically, severe mental illness, characterized by loss of contact with reality (in the form of delusions and hallucinations) and deterioration of intellectual and social functioning, occurring as a primary disorder or secondary to other diseases, drug ingestion, etc." The characteristic parsing of *mnemic* ("The capacity which a substance or organism possesses for retaining after-effects of experience or stimulation undergone by itself or its progenitors") functions in WKS has contributed substantially to understanding neuropsychological and brain mechanisms of learning and memory in health and disease (Talland 1965; Butters and Cermak 1980; Squire 1987).

In his *Lehrbuch der Gehirnkrankheiten*, Wernicke (1881) described three patients, of which two men had chronic alcoholism and a woman developed persistent vomiting after self-poisoning by drinking sulphuric acid, who all exhibited a clinical *triad* of acute mental confusion, ataxia ("abnormal gait") and ophthalmoplegia ("Paralysis of one or more of the muscles of the eye"). The patients died and neuropathologic examination showed punctate hemorrhages ("An escape of blood from the blood vessels; … due to rupture of a vessel") of the gray matter around the third and fourth ventricles and aqueduct, which Wernicke called "polioencephalitis haemorrhagica superioris" (Victor, Adams and Collins 1971). Other than a possible association with alcoholism and persistent vomiting, the etiology was unknown. The role of *thiamine deficiency* in etiopathogenesis of *Wernicke's encephalopathy* was not established until experiments of thiamine deprivation were performed in animal models (Prickett 1934) and it was found that specific pathological signs and symptoms of the condition and associated biochemical abnormalities could be rectified in humans by administration and repletion of thiamine (Wortis, Bueding, Stein and Jolliffe 1942). Demonstration of clinico-pathologic findings of WKS in

WWII prisoners-of-war in a Singapore hospital who were thiamine deficient due to dietary deprivation, provided strong evidence that WKS was a disease of malnutrition primarily, not alcoholism (De Wardener and Lennox 1947).

In 1887 Korsakoff first described a syndrome characterized by subacute dysmnesia (disturbed memory) and confabulation in his paper "The disturbance of psychic activity in alcoholic paralysis and its relation to the disturbance of the psychic sphere in multiple neuritides of nonalcoholic origin" (Korsakoff 1955; Victor and Yakovlev 1955). He indicated that disturbed memory and neuropathic findings likely represented different aspects of the same disease process and, accordingly, proposed the name "psychosis polyneuritica." In subsequent articles, Korsakoff expressed his thoughts about presentation and etiopathogenesis. He described subtle anterograde memory deficits and behavioral abnormalities, noting that neuropathic features may or not be present. Behavioral findings included apathy and social indifference, superficial and labile emotions, and lack of goal-oriented spontaneous activity with a surprising sparing of intellectual functions considering the level of incapacity. He described an association with alcoholism but recognized that the disorder may also complicate a wide variety of other medical illnesses, such as puerperal sepsis, typhoid fever, intestinal obstruction with persistent vomiting and hyperemesis gravidarum (Victor, Adams and Collins 1971). Although the correct etiology escaped Korsakoff, he postulated that the cause of the disorder was an unknown toxic substance in the blood and coined the term "cerebropathia psychica toxaemica."

Friedrich Jolly (1844–1904), a German neurologist and psychiatrist, first introduced the eponym *Korsakoff's syndrome* (Jolly 1897). The conceptual linkage between Korsakoff's syndrome and alcoholism was mightily reinforced by the German neurologist and psychiatrist Karl Bonhoeffer (1868-1948), who believed that the phenomenology of Korsakoff's syndrome resembled *delirium tremens* (see Delirium tremens). Accordingly, in his seminal textbook *Acute Psychic Diseases of Habitual Drunkards* he grouped Korsakoff's syndrome with the alcoholic psychoses (Bonhoeffer 1901). Bonhoeffer was also one of the first to note amnesic features in Wernicke's syndrome, indicating its overlapping phenomenology with Korsakoff *psychosis* (Bonhoeffer 1904).

The term Korsakoff *psychosis* is now mostly subsumed under *Wernicke-Korsakoff syndrome*. However, the eponym is still commonly employed when referring to the characteristic *amnestic* ("…loss of memory") features, which are considered the hallmark of the syndrome. It is now evident that Korsakoff's syndrome has very little to do with *psychosis*; however, if *delirium* emerges in a patient undergoing complicated alcohol withdrawal, the mistaken classification proposed by Bonhoeffer becomes understandable. In the Diagnostic and Statistical Manual of Mental Disorders (DSM) of the American Psychiatric Association (APA), the term *Korsakoff psychosis* has been mentioned in passing over the years,while the accepted nomenclature to designate the syndrome has continued to evolve (American Psychiatric Association 1980, 1987, 2013). For example, in the first version of the APA diagnostic criteria (DSM-I), the term used to denote Korsakoff psychosis was *chronic organic brain syndrome.* This term was changed in DSM-III to *chronic organic mental syndrome or disorder*, but the new multi-axial classification system raised the issue of whether this diagnosis was a psychiatric or medical disorder. In DSM-IV, *alcohol-induced persisting amnestic disorder* was introduced so as to be compatible with the International Statistical Classification of Diseases and Related Health Problems (ICD). Finally, in DSM 5, the descriptive *alcohol-induced major neurocognitive disorder, amnestic-confabulatory type* was introduced to represent the chronic phase of WKS. Of note, in DSM 5, the term *alcohol-induced major neurocognitive disorder, nonamnestic-confabulatory type* was also introduced, but whether it represents a distinctly different disorder or simply different phenomenology with related etiopathogenesis is still disputed (Wilkinson and Carlen 1980; Lishman 1981; Martin, Adinoff, Weingartner et al. 1986).

Since first described by Wernicke, the characteristic triad of clinical findings has been considered pathognomonic of the encephalopathic stage of WKS. However, Harper (1983) reported that only 20% of the 131 cases of WKS he diagnosed at autopsy had been recognized to have the syndrome on clinical examination prior to dying. Such low accuracy of the clinical diagnosis of the encephalopathic stage of WKS represents a significant challenge because thiamine administration is typically such an effective treatment (Centerwall and Criqui 1978).

These misdiagnoses could be accounted for by evolution of presentation of the disorder in recent times and/or lack of reliability of the classical diagnostic criteria. Due to the current widespread administration of thiamine to alcoholic patients even if assymptomatic (Thomson, Cook, Touquet and Henry 2002), it has been proposed that fewer *classical* cases of Wernicke's encephalopathy are likely to be encountered. Furthermore, as a result, repeatedly treated subclinical episodes of thiamine deficiency may result in a progressive disorder in which the extent and tempo of recovery is the major determinant of the clinical presentation (Witt and Goldman-Rakic 1983).

For example, Alling and Bostrom (1980) found that the mamillary bodies, which are almost always affected in the neuropathology of WKS (Victor, Adams and Collins 1971), showed loss of myelinated fibers and decreased concentrations of cerebrosides, cholesterol and phospholipids compared to normal controls in male chronic alcoholics who had no previous history of WKS.

Determination of the specificity of the classical diagnostic triad of Wernicke's encephalopathy was conducted by Caine, Halliday, Kril and Harper (1997). Reproducibility and validity of the clinical diagnosis in their sample of WKS patients examined at necropsy were optimized by setting the diagnostic criteria as either having the full classic triad or the presence of two of the following: 1) dietary deficiencies, 2) oculomotor abnormalities, 3) cerebellar dysfunction and 4) either an altered mental state or mild memory impairment. The reliability of the clinical diagnosis of WKS in their sample could be enhanced by adding a nutritional criterion to one or more of the signs of the triad. This actually supports the tremendous importance of nutritional deficiencies in brain injury in alcoholic patients (Martin, Singleton and Hiller-Sturmhöfel 2003).

The frequent co-occurrence of alcoholism with WKS continued to confound understanding of etiopathogenesis well into the 20th century (Joyce 1994). The toxic effect of chronic alcohol consumption on nervous system functions has long been suspected, as suggested by a quotation from Sutton concerning *delirium tremens* (1813) "…as an affection of the brain in which some morbid change might be expected." Courville's influential monograph *Effects of Alcohol on the Nervous System of Man* (1955) is noted for its extensive and systematic neuropathological studies of chronic alcoholics presumed to have little evidence of the findings of WKS:

> "Throughout the past quarter century… [the author] has been impressed by the fact that any noteworthy evidence of atrophy of the cerebral cortex occurring before the age of fifty years has, in the great majority of cases, proven to be the result of chronic alcoholism. In his earlier experience with other postalcoholic residuals, an occasional case of alcoholic pellagra was observed. Beyond these incidental observations, opportunity for the routine study of the central lesions in that complex which has eponymically described as Wernicke's encephalitis was [only] occasionally afforded."

These neuropathological findings suggested that atrophy of the cerebral cortex was the most relevant deficit associated with chronic alcoholism. The focus on cortical damage was supported by early neuroradiologic (Pluvinage 1954), electroencephalographic (Bennett, Dot and Mowrey 1956) and neuropsychological (Moore 1941) studies. Therefore, research on the neurotoxic effects of alcohol consumption in humans and as modelled in laboratory animals gained impetus (Freund 1973).

During this era, the neuropathological substrates underpinning brain dysfunction associated with alcoholism effectively shifted from the midline punctate hemorrhages of ventricular and periaqueductal gray matter and the cerebellar vermis due to thiamine deficiency to the relatively poorly understood and nonspecific pathogenesis of cortical atrophy. Neuropsychological studies of detoxified alcoholics "without clinical evidence of malnutrition" showed impairments in performance of visuospatial problem-solving tasks in 50-70% detoxified alcoholics suggesting frontal lobe deficits (Rankin 1975; Parsons 1977; Eckardt and Martin 1986). In parallel, newly implemented, non-invasive neuroimaging techniques began to be utilized to depict cortical atrophy and partial recovery with abstinence (Carlen, Wortzman, Holgate et al. 1978).

The fundamental mechanism(s) of cortical atrophy were revisited as every new neuroimaging technique, in turn, was applied to this issue that was never fully explicated, despite the fact that meaningful clinical correlates were identified (Berglund and Ingvar 1976; Martin, Rio, Adinoff et al. 1992; Martin, Gibbs, Nimmerrichter et al. 1995; Pfefferbaum, Sullivan, Rosenbloom et al. 1993; Parks, Dawant, Riddle et al. 2002). Several interacting factors associated with alcoholism (in addition to malnutrition) may contribute to the neurocognitive deficits found in a given patient (Martin, Adinoff, Weingartner et al. 1986). For example, liver disease complicating alcoholism may result in brain deficits ranging from subtle neuropsychological abnormalities to fulminant encephalopathy, delirium and coma, often difficult to distinguish from WKS (Schenker, Henderson, Hoyumpa and McCandless 1980; Caine, Halliday, Kril and Harper 1997). Also, repeated head trauma and episodes of hypoxemia due to bronchopulmonary infections, exacerbated by sleep apnea and chronic obstructive pulmonary disease are frequent during intoxication, all with cumulative negative consequences on brain functioning over a lifetime of drinking (Weinstein and Martin 1995). Finally, co-occurring drug use and other psychiatric and neurological disorders may also contribute to neurocognitive deficits observed in chronic alcoholics.

As the pathogenesis of cerebral dysfunction and concomitant cortical atrophy in chronic alcoholism is multifactorial, the effects of malnutrition may be overshadowed if not suspected. This conundrum led to a heuristically useful dichotomization of severe chronic organic brain impairment, which eventually develops in about 10% of alcoholic patients, into amnestic and dementia syndromes — the former due to the effects of thiamine deficiency and the later to the neurotoxicity of alcohol consumption (Wilkinson and Carlen 1980; Lishman 1981; Martin, Adinoff, Weingartner et al. 1986). This hypothesis received considerable support, including distinctions in neuroimaging, neuropsychological functioning, and response to treatment (Martin, Adinoff, Eckardt et al. 1989).

More subtle and clinically difficult to recognize brain dysfunction may develop relatively early in life and is so prevalent among alcoholic patients that it may be considered a precursor to, or a consequence of alcohol consumption (Parsons 1977, Eckardt and Martin 1986). Nevertheless, alcoholism-associated brain disease over a broad range of severities share neurobiological and clinical similarities (Ryback 1971; Alling and Boström 1980). Therefore, clinical observations and pathophysiological constructs derived from investigation of alcoholics with severe neurocognitive disorders have contributed to our understanding of the very large population with lesser degrees of cerebral impairment and *vice versa*.

A question that has perplexed clinicians and scientists is why only some individuals develop the most severe forms of alcoholism-associated brain damage. Blass and Gibson (1977) first proposed that genetic abnormalities in the thiamine-requiring enzyme transketolase may predispose alcoholics to develop WKS during periods of thiamine malnutrition which are so common during extended episodes of alcohol consumption. This hypothesis was supported by findings that a similar abnormality in transketolase was identified in genetically at-risk sons of alcoholics prior to ever consuming alcohol (Mukherjee, Svoronos, Ghazanfari et al. 1987). When McCool, Plonk, Martin and Singleton (1993) demonstrated that there were no differences in the genetic sequence of transketolase in severe alcoholics with and without WKS, the putative role of a transketolase abnormality in predisposing individuals to progressive development of cerebral dysfunction due to repeated subclinical episodes of thiamine deficiency during a lifetime of drinking alcohol to excess had to be expanded. Thiamine deficiency in the etiopathogenesis of alcoholism-associated brain dysfunction may involve various thiamine-related molecular processes and transporters required to make thiamine available to neurons found in WKS-related brain regions (Singleton and Martin 2001; Abdul-Muneer, Alikunju, Schuetz et al. 2018; Bordia and Zahr 2020). Finally, the idea that any alcohol-induced toxicity acts *through* thiamine deficiency seems sensible because thiamine deficiency can be demonstrated in up to 80% of alcoholics even in affluent countries (Martin, Singleton and Hiller-Sturmhöfel 2003).

Withdrawal

According to the current electronic version of the Oxford English Dictionary (OED) the noun *withdrawal* originates from Latin and French roots and is formed by the joining of the verb *withdraw* ("To take back or away [something that has been given, granted, allowed, possessed, enjoyed, or experienced]") with the suffix *-al* ("Forming nouns, especially nouns of action, from verbs"). The modern form of the word supersedes the earlier noun *withdrawment* ("Now rare…in various senses; formerly specifically the withdrawal of divine illumination"), which in turn, took the place of other earlier versions, i.e., the noun *withdraught* ("A privy; a sewer") and the noun *withdraw* ("Withdrawal, removal"). The current medical meaning of *withdrawal* corresponds to one of the definitions of the word found in OED, namely "Cessation of use or provision of a drug; specifically, the interruption of doses of an addictive drug, with resulting craving and physical reactions."

Specific reference to the discontinuation of self-administration of a neuropsychopharmacologic agent is not the primary meaning of *withdrawal* in OED, nor is it the earliest use of the word. The earliest recorded written reference to the word *withdraught* in the English language, according to OED (Middle English Compendium), occurred in 1340 in a text attributed to the Benedictine monk Michael of Northgate (fl. 1340) *Ayenbite of Inwyt* (Don Michel 1866) in which the term was employed in its original meaning ("An act of voluntary abstinence from food, restraint in diet; also, a voluntary withdrawal [from evil thoughts and inclinations]"): "Þe castel of þe wombe þet is þe strengþe of þe ulesse ne may him hyealde aye þane gost þanne he is asterued be uestinges and be wyþdraȝþes." This very early reference to the origins of the word *withdrawal* combines restricting intake of an exogenous entity required for life (food) as well as limiting elements of one's internal emotional life/experience (evil thoughts or inclinations). If one expands the medical construct of addiction to include out-of-control and self-destructive behaviors such as overeating, the notion of restricting food intake can readily be viewed as analogous to discontinuation of a self-administered neuropsychopharmacologic agent (see Addiction). However, the idea of removing oneself from "evil thoughts or inclinations" seems more compatible with the recently accepted nosological construct of addictive disorders in which substances do not factor, namely non-substance related addictive disorders according to the *Diagnostic and Statistical Manual of Mental Disorders, Fifth Edition, DSM-5* (American Psychiatric Association 2013). Therefore, it seems that older constructs of the word *withdrawal* are recapitulated in our current broader nosological perspectives of addiction; stated otherwise, we have come full circle since the first very broad meaning of the word in 1340, despite a minor detour in the last century, which restricted our focus to neuropsychopharmacologic agents alone.

According to OED, the first reference in English literature to *withdrawal* as understood in medicine throughout most of the last century, came from an isolated entry in 1897 by Sir Thomas Clifford Allbutt (1836–1925) in his medical treatise, *A System of Medicine*, the first edition of which was published in London from 1896 to 1899 in eight volumes (1897): "All authors agree that withdrawal [of morphine] is more distressing to the injector than to the eater of the drug." Fifty years after the advent of the hypodermic needle (Rynd 1845), and well before we understood that the mechanism of action of opioids was through activation of opioid receptors in the nervous system (Pert and Snyder 1973), Allbutt inferred, based on clinical observation alone, that the route of administration of an opioid may govern the difficulty the user experienced when stopping self-administration of the drug.

Albutt was not likely aware of the pharmacokinetic principles that would dictate greater bioavailability and pharmacological effect of morphine administered via injection. (The relevant notion of *bioavailability*, defined in OED as "the degree to which a drug or other substance is absorbed or reaches a target site in the body; especially the proportion of a dose of a drug taken orally which reaches the bloodstream," was first used in 1961.) However, Albutt's contention did require recognition of a characteristic *withdrawal syndrome* that emerges in individuals upon discontinuation of morphine use, the signs and symptoms ("distress") of which were clinically identifiable and could be compared among individual users and under different conditions of use. In addition, he was likely familiar with the pharmacological actions of morphine as suggested by a comment from 1850 attributed to the great Scottish female letter writer, Jane Welsh Carlyle (1801–1866) by OED (Carlyle, Carlyle and Froude 1893): "I took morphine last night, and slept some." Therefore, Albutt may have noticed that the greater "distress" associated with stopping repeated morphine injections was accompanied by more intense or prolonged pharmacological effects compared to that observed with oral dosing. The particular severity of opioid withdrawal associated with injection use is now well accepted as a general phenomenon for all drugs of abuse, a function of the greater "time of exposure" and "lifetime dose" (Kalant, LeBlanc and Gibbins 1971).

The emergence of the *acute withdrawal syndrome* results from the need for the drug of abuse (regardless of the route of administration) to be present in the brain to maintain "near-normal" functioning. If the drug is eliminated from the body so that it no longer occupies its site of action, homeostatic adaptations, termed *neuroadaptation* (Rounsaville, Spitzer and Williams 1986), are unmasked and manifested as an acute withdrawal syndrome that lasts until the system re-equilibrates to the absence of drug, typically days in duration. The manifestations of drug withdrawal depend on the pharmacological mechanism of action of the class of drug that was abused and can range from mild dysphoria to serious disturbances of the autonomic nervous system and sensorium to life-threatening seizures. Subsequently, a *protracted withdrawal syndrome* (Martin and Jasinski 1969), characterized by craving for the drug (an intense preoccupation with obtaining the drug) associated with subtle dysregulation of learning, drives/motivations, reward and the potential for relapse (Martin and Patel 2017). The characteristic protracted withdrawal is believed to emerge due to subtle residual abnormalities of brain and neuroendocrine functioning resulting from the abused drug manifested by dysregulation of mood, anxiety, sleep, appetite and impulses and may continue indefinitely, typically for years, if not for a lifetime. Distinguishing protracted withdrawal from *premorbid risk factors* for addiction that do not resolve with abstinence and from brain injury sustained as a result of drug use may not always be possible.

Why an individual chooses to repeatedly be under the influence of a drug is likely relevant to the choice of the route of administration of morphine (and likely of other drugs of abuse). The distress associated with attempting to discontinue use and the ensuing reluctance to stop using are to some degree consequences of the route of administration chosen. The repeated self-administration of morphine via injections might reflect a greater need to escape from one's regular (painful) mental state or situation, a contemporary notion in addiction psychiatry (Khantzian, Mack and Schatzberg 1974). It is not commonly appreciated that the term *self-medication* was already in use in the time of Albutt as suggested by a quotation from the *British Medical Journal* (Anonymous 1886): "People are very partial to self-medication as it is, and rush to alcohol as a panacea for the ills to which flesh is heir." This concept can readily be employed to explain why an individual chooses a more efficient route of administration like injection, leading to greater or more continuous intoxication, thereby initiating a cycle of needing increasingly higher doses of morphine in order to obtain the same effect, termed *tolerance* (see Tolerance).

A compelling reason not to discontinue morphine (or other drug) use and also to escalate doses is the fear of predictable disturbing consequences of *withdrawal symptoms* experienced by most, if not all users, as suggested by a quotation from Samuel Dashiell Hammett (1894–1961) an American author of detective novels in *The Dain Curse* (Hammett 1929): "Tears were one of the symptoms of morphine withdrawal". The suffering of withdrawal was deemed to require treatment in its own right (Wilner and

Kassebaum 1965): "Withdrawal of morphine by substitution and subsequent withdrawal of methadon". Even now, the most commonly employed strategies for alleviating withdrawal from most drugs of abuse are to taper the dose of the drug slowly or to use a long-acting drug that demonstrates cross-tolerance (Kalant, LeBlanc and Gibbins 1971, Martin, Bhushan, Kapur et al. 1979).

For many years the severity of withdrawal was considered the primary driver of the disease of addiction, such that the vulnerable individual became imprisoned by fear of impending withdrawal to maintain a state of almost continuous drug use (Bishop 1913). Accordingly, treatment of the opioid withdrawal syndrome evolved into the ready focus for effective treatment of addiction *per se* by addressing "relief of narcotic hunger" (Dole and Nyswander 1965). This approach has continued to evolve (Jasinski, Pevnick and Griffith 1978; Mello and Mendelson 1980) and remains effective (Johnson, Chutuape, Strain et al. 2000), despite awareness of the important roles of reward learning (Stephens 1933) and elucidation of underlying reward mechanisms in the brain (Olds 1958) that can shape behavior such as out-of-control self-administration of psychoactive agents. The challenge for the future is learning to distinguish premorbid risk factors for addictive disorders and the consequences of repeated self-administration of drugs of abuse or engagement in out-of-control and self-destructive behaviors which tend to transform the person who uses them via brain mechanisms that have yet to be fully elucidated.

References

Abbott AC. The influence of acute alcoholism on the normal vital resistance of rabbits to infection. J Exp Med. 1896; 1(3):447–81.

Abdul-Muneer PM, Alikunju S, Schuetz H, Szlachetka AM, Ma X, Haorah J. Impairment of thiamine transport at the GUT-BBB-AXIS contributes to Wernicke's encephalopathy. Mol Neurobiol. 2018;55(7):5937–50.

Abel EL. Marihuana, the first twelve thousand years. New York: McGraw-Hill; 1982.

Abuhasira R, Shbiro L, Landschaft Y. Medical use of cannabis and cannabinoids containing products – Regulations in Europe and North America. Eur J Intern Med. 2018; 49:2-6.

Adamec RE. Does kindling model anything clinically relevant? Biol Psychiatry 1990;27(3):249–79.

Adams T. Eirenopolis: the citie of peace. London: Printed by Aug. Matthewes for Iohn Grismand; 1622.

Adler A. The neurotic constitution. Outlines of a comparative individualistic psychology and psychotherapy. Authorized English translation by Bernard Glueck and John E. Lind. N.Y. Moffat; 1917.

Adolphs R, Damasio H, Tranel D, Cooper G, Damasio AR. A role for somatosensory cortices in the visual recognition of emotion as revealed by three-dimensional lesion mapping. J Neurosci 2000;20(7):2683–90.

Ahlquist RP. A Study of the adrenotropic receptors. Am J Physiol. 1948;153(3):586–600.

Akiskal HS, Benazzi F, Perugi G, Rihmer Z. Agitated "unipolar" depression re-conceptualized as a depressive mixed state: implications for the antidepressant-suicide controversy. J Affect Disord. 2005; 85(3):245-58.

Albanese M-C, Duerden EG, Rainville P, Duncan GH. Memory Traces of Pain in Human Cortex. J Neurosci. 2007; 27(17):4612.

Albert and Mary Lasker Foundation. 1951—Alcoholics Anonymous. Historical Awards. www.laskerfoundation.org/awards

Alexander F. Psychosomatic Medicine: Its Principles and Applications. Norton; 1950.

Allbutt TC. A System of Medicine. Volumes I-VIII / by many writers; edited by Thomas Clifford Allbutt. London: Macmillan; 1899.

Alles GA. The comparative physiological action of phenylethanolamine. J Pharmacol Exp Ther, 1927;32(2):121.

Allestree R. The practice of Christian graces. London: Maxwell; 1658.

Allgulander C, Ljungberg L, Fisher LD. Long-term prognosis in addiction on sedative and hypnotic drugs analyzed with the Cox regression model. Acta Psychiatr Scand. 1987; 75(5):521-31.

Alling C, Boström K. Demyelination of the mamillary bodies in alcoholism. Acta Neuropathol (Berl). 1980;50(1):77–80.

Allport GW. Personality: a psychological interpretation. London: Constable & Company. 1938.

Altshuler HL, Phillips PE, Feinhandler DA. Alteration of ethanol self-administration by naltrexone. Life Sci. 1980; 26(9):679-88.

AMA Council on Pharmacy and Chemistry. Present Status of Benzedrine Sulfate. J Am Med Assoc, 1937;109(25):2064–9.

American Medical Association. House of Delegates Proceedings, Clinical Session. 1956. Seattle, WA. American Medical Association; 1956.

American Psychiatric Association. American Psychiatric Association: Diagnostic and Statistical Manual of Mental Disorders, Third Edition. Washington, DC. 1980.

American Psychiatric Association. American Psychiatric Association: Diagnostic and Statistical Manual of Mental Disorders, Third Edition, Revised. Washington, DC. 1987.

American Psychiatric Association. American Psychiatric Association: Diagnostic and Statistical Manual of Mental Disorders, Fifth Edition. Washington, DC: American Psychiatric Association. 2013.

Anderson N. The hobo: the sociology of the homeless man. Chicago: University of Chicago Press; 1923.

Andersson SA, Ericson T, Holmgren E, Lindqvist G. Electro-acupuncture. Effect on pain threshold measured with electrical stimulation of teeth. Brain Res. 1973; 63:393–6.

Andreae LC. Cannabis use and schizophrenia: Chicken or egg? Sci Transl Med. 2018;10(460): eaav0342.

Andreasson S, Engstrom A, Allebeck P, Rydberg U. A longitudinal study of Swedish conscripts. The Lancet 1987; 330, 1483-86.

Andrews HL. The effect of opiates on the pain threshold in post-addicts. J Clin Invest. The American Society for Clinical Investigation; 1943; 22(4):511-6.

Anonymous. Master Broughtons letters, especially his last pamphlet to and against the Lord Archbishop of Canterbury, about Sheol and Hades, for the descent into Hell, answered in their kind. London: Imprinted by [F. Kingston for] Iohn Wolfe; 1599.

Anonymous. London Gazette. London; 1683;4.

Anonymous. An essay on celibacy from the Bodleian Library (Oxford). London: printed for M. Cooper; 1753.

Anonymous. London Magazine 1778;(Jan 21):1.

Anonymous. The public advertiser, or political and literary diary. 1793.

Anonymous. Monthly Report of Diseases. Med Phys J. 1801;5(23):97–9.

Anonymous. On the diagnosis of syphilis. Med Phys J. 1806;15(83):22–6.

Anonymous. Cloquet, Sarlandière, Pelletan, Carraro, and Pouillet, on Acupuncture. Edinb Med Surg J. 1827;27(90):190–200.

Anonymous. On the preparations of the Indian hemp, or Gunjah (Cannabis Indica), their effects on the animal system in health, and their utility in the treatment of tetanus and other convulsive diseases. Br Foreign Med Rev. 1840;10(19):225-8.

Anonymous. Pathogeneses of tobacco and nicotine. --Neuroses produced by tobacco. Am J Dent Sci. 1873;6(11):510–5.

Anonymous. British and Colonial Druggist. London; 1886.

Anonymous. Worry versus Health. British Medical Journal. 1886;2(1331):33/2.

Anonymous. Cocaine hallucinations. Science, 1889; ns-14(354):332.

Anonymous. Health Matters: Coffeee Inebriety. Science. 1890; 15(385):374-374.

Anonymous. The Relation of Alcoholism to Suicide. Hospital (Rio J). 1902; 31(807):404-5.

Anonymous. The percentage of nicotine in various kinds of tobacco. Br Med J. 1909;1(2519):911–911.

Anonymous. Mental sequelae of the Harrison Law. N Y Med J 1915; 102:1014.

Anonymous. The treatment of delirium tremens. Hospital (Rio J). 1917; 61:364.

Anonymous. Arch Dis Child. 1920; 65:141/1.

Anonymous. Ephedrine, a promising therapeutic agent. Calif West Med, 1925;23(12):1592–3.

Anonymous. Cocaine addicts. Science, 1925;61(1577): xiv.

Anonymous. Self-medication in tuberculosis. Lancet. 1958;272(7053):946-7.

Anonymous. John Arderne (1306-1380). JAMA. 1965;191(9):756–7.

Anonymous. Theophile Bonet (1620-1689) Physician of Geneva. JAMA. 1969;210(5):899.

Anonymous. Daniel Turner (1667-1740) Dermatologist, Surgeon, Physician. JAMA. 1970;213(5):863–4.

Anonymous. Alcoholics Eponymous. JAMA. 1970;213(1):119–20.

Anonymous. Canadian Magazine. Toronto, Ontario 1975;4(2).

Anonymous. The Times. London; 1988;2.

Appelbaum PS, Grisso T. Assessing patients' capacities to consent to treatment. N Engl J Med 1988;319(25):1635–8.

Anrep von B. Ueber die physiologische Wirkung des Cocain. Pflugers Arch Ges Physiol, 1880;12:38–77.

Anselme P, Robinson MJF. "Wanting," "liking," and their relation to consciousness. J Exp Psychol Anim Learn Cogn. 2016; 42(2):123-40.

Antons S, Brand M, Potenza MN. Neurobiology of cue-reactivity, craving, and inhibitory control in non-substance addictive behaviors. J Neurol Sci 2020; 415:116952.

Arbuthnot J. Practical rules of diet in the various constitutions and diseases of human bodies. London: Printed for J. Tonson; 1732.

Arderne J, British Library. John Arderne on Fistula. [Place of publication not identified]: [publisher not identified]; 1400.

Armstrong J. On the Brain-Fever Produced by Intoxication. Edinburgh Med Surg J. 1813; 9(33):58–61.

Arria AM, DuPont RL. Nonmedical prescription stimulant use among college students: why we need to do something and what we need to do. J Addict Dis, 2010;29(4):417–26.

Arwaker E. Truth in fiction: or, Morality in masquerade. A collection of two hundred twenty five select fables of Æsop, and other authors. London: J. Churchill; 1708.

Åsberg M, Träskman L, Thorén P. 5-HIAA in the cerebrospinal fluid: a biochemical suicide predictor? Arch Gen Psychiatry, 1976;33(10):1193–7.

Aserinsky E, Kleitman N. Regularly occurring periods of eye motility, and concomitant phenomena, during sleep. Science. 1953; 118(3062):273.

Ashdown-Franks G, Firth J, Carney R, Carvalho AF, Hallgren M, Koyanagi A, Rosenbaum S, Schuch FB, Smith L, Solmi M, Vancampfort D, Stubbs B. Exercise as medicine for mental and substance use disorders: a meta-review of the benefits for neuropsychiatric and cognitive outcomes. Sports Med. 2020; 50(1):151–70.

Aubin H-J, Laureaux C, Tilikete S, Barrucand D. Changes in cigarette smoking and coffee drinking after alcohol detoxification in alcoholics. Addiction. 1999; 94(3):411-6.

Axelrod J. Studies on sympathetic amines. II. The biotransformation and physiological disposition of D-amphetamine, D-p-hydroxyamphetamine and D-methamphetamine. J Pharmacol Exp Ther, 1954;110(3):315.

Babalonis S, Haney M, Malcolm RJ, Lofwall MR, Votaw VR, Sparenborg S, Walsh SL. Oral cannabidiol does not produce a signal for abuse liability in frequent marijuana smokers. Drug Alcohol Depend. 2017; 172:9-13.

Bach-Y-Rita G, Lion JR, Ervin FR. Pathological intoxication: clinical and electroencephalographic studies. Am J Psychiatry, 1970;127(5):698–703.

Bacon F, Rawley W. Sylva sylvarum; or, A naturall historie. In ten centuries ... London: Printed by J.H. for William Lee; 1626.

Baez S, Fittipaldi S, de la Fuente LA, Carballo M, Ferrando R, García-Cordero I, Gonzalez Campo C, Garcia AM, Sedeño L, Ibáñez A. Empathy deficits and their behavioral, neuroanatomical, and functional connectivity correlates in smoked cocaine users. Prog Neuropsychopharmacol Biol Psychiatry 2021; 110:110328.

Bahji A, Stephenson C, Tyo R, Hawken ER, Seitz DP. Prevalence of cannabis withdrawal symptoms among people with regular or dependent use of cannabinoids: a systematic review and meta-analysis. JAMA Network Open. 2020;3(4): e202370.

Ballenger JC, Post RM. Kindling as a model for alcohol withdrawal syndromes. Br J Psychiatry. 1978; 133:1–14.

Ban TA. Conditioning Behavior and Psychiatry. New Brunswick, N.J.: Aldine Transaction; 2008.

Bancroft HH. The native races of the Pacific states of North America. San Francisco: A.L. Bancroft & Co. 1874.

Bandura A, Walters RH. Social learning and personality development. New York: Holt, Rinehart and Winston; 1963.

Bardo MT, Neisewander JL, Kelly TH. Individual differences and social influences on the neurobehavioral pharmacology of abused drugs. Pharmacol Rev. 2013; 65(1):255.

Barinaga M. Pot, heroin unlocks new areas for neuroscience. Science. 1992;258(5090):1882-4.

Bartholomaeus A. De proprietatibus rerum; 2010.

Batson CD. These things called empathy: eight related but distinct phenomena. In: Decety J, Ickes WJ, editors. The Social Neuroscience of Empathy. Cambridge (MA); London: The MIT Press; 2011.

Battey LL, Heyman A, Patterson JL Jr. Effects of ethyl alcohol on cerebral blood flow and metabolism. J Am Med Assoc. 1953; 152(1):6-10.

Baumblatt JAG, Wiedeman C, Dunn JR, Schaffner W, Paulozzi LJ, Jones TF. High-risk use by patients prescribed opioids for pain and its role in overdose deaths. JAMA Intern Med 2014; 174:796–801.

Baxter BL. Comparison of the behavioral effects of electrical or chemical stimulation applied at the same brain loci. Exp Neurol 1967;19(4):412–32.

Beach LR, Shoenberger RW. Event salience and response frequency on a ten-alternative probability-learning situation. J Exp Psychol. US: American Psychological Association. 1965; 69(3):312-6.

Beaton C, Buckle R (editor). Self portrait with friends: the selected diaries of Cecil Beaton, 1926-1974. New York: Times Books; 1979.

Bebbington PE. The Efficacy of Alcoholics Anonymous: The Elusiveness of Hard Data. Br J Psychiatry. 1976;128(6):572-80.

Bechara A, Damasio H, Tranel D, Damasio AR. Deciding advantageously before knowing the advantageous strategy. Science, 1997;275(5304):1293.

Beckington T, Williams G. Memorials of the reign of King Henry VI: Official correspondence of Thomas Bekynton, secretary to King Henry VI., and bishop of Bath and Wells. London: Longman. 1872.

Bedford T. The sinne unto death ... a sermon preached at Pauls Crosse ... London: Sheffard; 1621.

Begleiter H, Porjesz B, Bihari B & Kissin B. Event-related brain potentials in boys at risk for alcoholism. Science 1984; 225(4669):1493.

Benaroyo L, Widdershoven G. Competence in mental health care: a hermeneutic perspective. Health Care Anal 2004;12(4):295–306.

Bennett AE, Dot LT, Mowrey GE. The value of electroencephalography in alcoholism. J Nerv Ment Dis. 1956; 124:27–31.

Benningfield MM, Dietrich MS, Jones HE, Kaltenbach K, Heil SH, Stine SM, Coyle MG, Arria AM, O'Grady KE, Fischer G, Martin PR. Opioid dependence during pregnancy: relationships of anxiety and depression symptoms to treatment outcomes. Addiction. 2012; 107(S1):74-82.

Benson H. Yoga for drug abuse. N Engl J Med. 1969;281(20):1133–1133.

Benson H, Herd J, Morse W, Kelleher R. Behavioral induction of arterial hypertension and its reversal. Am J Physiol. 1969;217(1):30–4.

Benson H, Marzetta B, Rosner B, Klemchuk H. Decreased blood-pressure in pharmacologically treated hypertensive patients who regularly elicited the relaxation response. Lancet. 1974;303(7852):289–91.

Benson H, Shapiro D, Tursky B, Schwartz GE. Decreased systolic blood pressure through operant conditioning techniques in patients with essential hypertension. Science 1971;173(3998):740–2.

Bejerot N. A theory of addiction as an artificially induced drive. Am J Psychiatry 1972; 128(7):842–6.

Bentham J. An introduction to the principles of morals and legislation. Printed in the year 1780, and now first published. By Jeremy Bentham... London: Printed for T. Payne, and Son; 1789.

Bentley KW. Sir Robert Robinson – his contribution to alkaloid chemistry. Nat Prod Rep 1987; 4:13–23.

Berecz JM. Superiority of a low-contrast smoking cessation method. Addict Behav. 1984; 9(3):273-8.

Berger FM. The pharmacological properties of 2-methyl-2-N-propyl-1,3-propanediol dicarbamate (Miltown), a new interneuronal blocking agent. J Pharmacol Exp Ther. 1954;112(4):413-23.

Berglund M, Ingvar DH. Cerebral blood flow and its regional distribution in alcoholism and in Korsakoff's psychosis. J Stud Alcohol. 1976;37(5):586–97.

Bernfeld S. Freud's studies on cocaine, 1884–1887. J Am Psychoanal Assoc, 1953;1:581–613.

Berglund M, Ingvar DH. Cerebral blood flow and its regional distribution in alcoholism and in Korsakoff's psychosis. J Stud Alcohol. 1976; 37(5):586-97.

Berglund M, Prohovnik I, Risberg J. Regional cerebral blood flow during alcoholic blackout. Psychiatry Res. 1989; 27(1):49-54.

Berman RM, Cappiello A, Anand A, Oren DA, Heninger GR, Charney DS, Krystal JH. Antidepressant effects of ketamine in depressed patients. Biological Psychiatry 2000; 47, 351-4.

Bernadt MW, Taylor C, Mumford J, Smith B, Murray RM. Comparison of questionnaire and laboratory tests in the detection of excessive drinking and alcoholism. Lancet. 1982;319(8267):325–8.

Bernard C, Atlee WF, Robin Ch. Notes of M. Bernard's lectures on the blood with an appendix. Philadelphia: Lippincott, Grambo; 1854.

Berridge KC, Robinson TE. Liking, wanting, and the incentive-sensitization theory of addiction. Am Psychol. 2016; 71(8):670-9.

Besant W. The demoniac. N.Y.: U.S. Book Co.; 1890.

Bett WR. The paradox of William Stewart Halsted. Proc R Soc Med, 1952;45(8):561–2.

Bezzegh A, Nyuli L, Kovács GL. α-Atrial natriuretic peptide, aldosterone secretion and plasma renin activity during ethanol withdrawal: a correlation with the onset of delirium tremens? Alcohol. 1991;8: 333–6.

Bhatnagar S, Bell ME, Liang J, Soriano L, Nagy TR, Dallman MF. Corticosterone Facilitates Saccharin Intake in Adrenalectomized Rats: Does Corticosterone Increase Stimulus Salience? J Neuroendocrinol. 2000; 12(5):453-60.

Bierer LM, Bader HN, Daskalakis NP, Lehrner A, Provençal N, Wiechmann T, Klengel T, Makotkine I, Binder EB, Yehuda R. Intergenerational Effects of Maternal Holocaust Exposure on FKBP5 Methylation. Am J Psychiatry 2020;177(8):744–53.

Bierut LJ. 2018 Langley Award for Basic Research on Nicotine and Tobacco: Bringing Precision Medicine to Smoking Cessation. Nicotine Tob Res. 2020;22(2):147–51.

Bishop ES. Narcotic addiction — a systemic disease condition. JAMA 1913; 60: 431-4.

Bixler EO, Scharf MB, Soldatos CR, Mitsky DJ, Kales A. Effects of hypnotic drugs on memory. Life Sci. 1979; 25(16):1379-88.

Björkqvist SE. Clonidine in alcohol withdrawal. Acta Psychiatr Scand. 1975;52::56–63.

Blair RJ. Neurocognitive models of aggression, the antisocial personality disorders, and psychopathy. J Neurol Neurosurg Psychiatry, 2001;71(6):727–31.

Blair RJR. Traits of empathy and anger: implications for psychopathy and other disorders associated with aggression. Philos Trans R Soc B Biol Sci 2018;373(1744):20170155.

Blalock A. William Stewart Halsted and his influence on surgery. Proc R Soc Med, 1952;45(8):555–61.

Blanco C, Hanania J, Petry NM, Wall MM, Wang S, Jin CJ, Kendler KS. Towards a compre-hensive developmental model of pathological gambling. Addiction, 2015;110(8):1340–51.

Blankaart S. A physical dictionary; in which all the terms relating either to anatomy, chirurgery, pharmacy, or chymistry, are very accurately explain'd. London: Printed by J.D. and are to be sold by John Gellibrand at the Golden-Ball in St. Paul's Churchyard; 1684.

Blass JP, Gibson GE. Abnormality of a thiamine-requiring enzyme in patients with Wernicke-Korsakoff syndrome. N Engl J Med. 1977;297(25):1367–70.

Blejer-Prieto H. Coca leaf and cocaine addiction--some historical notes. Can Med Assoc J, 1965;93(13):700–4.

Bliss TVP, Collingridge GL. A synaptic model of memory: long-term potentiation in the hippocampus. Nature 1993;361(6407):31–9.

Bliss TVP, Lømo T. Long-lasting potentiation of synaptic transmission in the dentate area of the anaesthetized rabbit following stimulation of the perforant path. J Physiol 1973;232(2):331–56.

Blount T. Glossographia, or, A dictionary: interpreting all such hard words, whether Hebrew, Greek, Latin, Italian, Spanish, French, Teutonick, Belgick, British or Saxon; as are now used in our refined English tongue. Also, the terms of divinity, law, physick, mathematicks, heraldry, anatomy, war, musick, architecture; and of several other arts and sciences explicated. With etymologies, definitions, and historical observations on the same. Very useful for all such as desire to understand what they read. London: Printed by Tho. Newcomb, and are to be sold by Humphrey Moseley, and George Sawbridge; 1656.

Bohus B. Effects of ACTH-like neuropeptides on animal behavior and man. Pharmacology. 1979; 18(3):113-22.

Boivin JR, Piscopo DM, Wilbrecht L. Brief cognitive training interventions in young adulthood promote long-term resilience to drug-seeking behavior. Neuropharmacology. 2015; 97:404-13.

Bonde W. Here begynneth a deuout treatyse in Englysshe, called the Pylgrimage of perfection: very p[ro]fitable for all christen people to rede: and in especiall, to all relygious p[er]sons moche necessary. London: [In Fletestrete, besyde saynt Dunstans churche, by Richarde Pynson, pri[n]ter to the kynges noble grace. Cu[m] priuilegio]; 1526.

Bonet T. A guide to the practical physician: shewing, from the most approved authors, both ancient and modern, the truest and safest way of curing all diseases, internal and external, whether by medicine, surgery, or diet. Published in Latin by the learn'd Theoph. Bonet, physician at Geneva. And now rendred into English, with an addition of many considerable cases, and excellent medicines for every disease. Collected from Dr. Waltherus his Sylva medica. by one of the Colledge of Physicians, London. To which is added. The office of a physician, and perfect tables of every distemper, and of any thing else considerable. Licensed, November 13h. 1685. London: printed for Thomas Flesher, at his house over against Distaff Lane in the Old Change; 1686.

Bonhoeffer Karl. Die akuten Geisteskrankheiten der Gewohnheitstrinker : eine klinische Studie. Jena: G. Fischer; 1901.

Bonhoeffer Karl. Der Korsakowsche symptomenkomplex in Seinen beizeitungen zu den verschiedenen kankheitsformen. Allg Z Psychiat. 1904; 61:744–52.

Bordia T, Zahr NM. The inferior colliculus in alcoholism and beyond. Front Syst Neurosci. 2020; 14:606345–606345.

Bose KC. Cocaine intoxication and its demoralizing effects. Br Med J, 1902;1(2156):1020–2.

Bosworth FH. Is Cocaine an Enslaving Drug? Trans Am Climatol Assoc, 1895;11:136–40.

Bőthe B, Bartók R, Tóth-Király I, Reid RC, Griffiths MD, Demetrovics Z, Orosz G. Hypersexuality, gender, and sexual orientation: a large-scale psychometric survey study. Arch Sex Behav 2018;47(8):2265–76.

Bőthe B, Tóth-Király I, Potenza MN, Griffiths MD, Orosz G, Demetrovics Z. Revisiting the role of impulsivity and compulsivity in problematic sexual behaviors. J Sex Res 2019;56(2):166–79.

Botticelli MP, Koh HK. Changing the language of addiction. JAMA, 2016; 316, 1361-1362.

Boublik JH, Quinn MJ, Clements JA, Herington AC, Wynne KN, Funder JW. Coffee contains potent opiate receptor binding activity. Nature. 1983; 301(5897):246-8.

Bowen S, Witkiewitz K, Clifasefi SL, Grow J, Chawla N, Hsu SH, Carroll HA, Harrop E, Collins SE, Lustyk MK, Larimer ME. Relative efficacy of mindfulness-based relapse prevention, standard relapse prevention, and treatment as usual for substance use disorders: a randomized clinical trial. JAMA Psychiatry 2014;71(5):547–56.

Bowlby J. Maternal care and mental health: a report prepared on behalf of the World Health Organization as a contribution to the United Nations programme for the welfare of homeless children. Geneva: World Health Organization; 1966.

Bowlby J. Attachment and loss. New York: Basic Books; 1969.

Bradley J. The China Mirage: The Hidden History of American Disaster in Asia. Little, Brown and Company; 2015.

Breitbart W, Feldstein M. A randomized clinical trial of alprazolam versus progressive muscle relaxation in cancer patients with anxiety and depressive symptoms. J Clin Oncol. 1991;9(6):1004–11.

Brewer JA, Worhunsky PD, Gray JR, Tang Y-Y, Weber J, Kober H. Meditation experience is associated with differences in default mode network activity and connectivity. Proc Natl Acad Sci 2011;108(50):20254.

Brezinová V, Oswald I. Sleep after a bedtime beverage. Br Med J. 1972; 2(5811):431–3.

British National Formulary. British Medical Association, Pharmaceutical Society of Great Britain. London; 1986.

British National Formulary. British Medical Association, Pharmaceutical Society of Great Britain. London; 1996.

Bristowe JS. A treatise on the theory and practice of medicine. London: Smith; 1878.

Brook K, Bennett J, Desai SP. The chemical history of morphine: an 8000-year journey, from resin to de-novo synthesis. J Anesth Hist 2017; 3:50–5.

Brower KJ. Alcohol's effects on sleep in alcoholics. Alcohol Res Health; 2001; 25(2):110–25.

Brower KJ, Perron BE. Sleep disturbance as a universal risk factor for relapse in addictions to psychoactive substances. Med Hypotheses. 2010; 74(5):928–33.

Brown GL, Goodwin FK, Ballenger JC, Goyer PF, Major LF. Aggression in humans correlates with cerebrospinal fluid amine metabolites. Psychiatry Res, 1979;1(2):131–9.

Brown GW, Harris TO. Aetiology of anxiety and depressive disorders in an inner-city population. 1. Early adversity. Psychol Med. 1993; 23(1):143–54.

Brown-Sequard E. Course of Lectures on the Physiology and Pathology of the Central Nervous System, Delivered before the Royal College of Surgeons of England, in May 1858. Br Foreign Medico-Chir Rev. 1859;24(47):1–36.

Browne T. Pseudodoxia epidemica: or, Enquiries into very many received tenets, and commonly presumed truths. London: Printed by J.R. for N. Ekins; 1672.

Browne AS, Coffey E. Treponemal serologic tests; experiences of the Bacteriology Laboratory, California State Department of Public Health. Calif Med. 1958;88(4):300–4.

Brownstein MJ. A brief history of opiates, opioid peptides, and opioid receptors. Proc Natl Acad Sci USA 1993; 90:5391–3.

Brun G. Mechanism of the vasoconstrictor action of ephedrine; interaction between ephedrine and adrenaline. Acta Pharmacol Toxicol (Copenh), 1947;3(3):239–51.

Brunschwig H. Chirurgia, das ist, Handwerken der Wundartzney M. Hieronymi Braunschweig ... wie er die von vil erfarnen Artzeten gelernet, und in seiner Practica l blich gebraucht hat. Mit sonderm Fleyss von newem wider aussgangen. Augspurg, Alexander Weyssenhorn; 1539.

Buchanan A. Mental capacity, legal competence and consent to treatment. J R Soc Med 2004;97(9):415–20.

Buchowski MS, Meade NN, Charboneau E, Park S, Dietrich MS, Cowan RL, Martin PR. Aerobic exercise training reduces cannabis craving and use in non-treatment seeking cannabis-dependent adults. PloS ONE. 2011; 6(3): e17465.

Budney AJ, Hughes JR. The cannabis withdrawal syndrome. Curr Opin Psychiatry. 2006;19(3):233-8.

Bullokar J. An English expositor teaching the interpretation of the hardest words vsed in our language; with svndry explications, descriptions, and discourses. London; 1616.

Bunney W, Murphy D, Goodwin F, Borge G. The switch process from depression to mania: relationship to drugs which alter brain Lancet. 1970; 295(7655):1022-7.

Burgess AW, Holmstrom LL. Rape trauma syndrome. Am J Psychiatry. 1974; 131(9):981–6.

Burn JH, Tainter ML. An analysis of the effect of cocaine on the actions of adrenaline and tyramine. J Physiol, 1931;71(2):169–93.

Burney F, Hemlow J. Journals and letters. France 1803-1812. Letters 550-631 6 6. Oxford, Clarendon Press; 1972.

Burroughs WS. Junkie: [confessions of an unredeemed drug addict]. New York: ACE Books; 1953.

Burrows GM. A Reply to Messieurs Esquirol's and Falret's Objections to Dr. Burrows' Comparative Proportions of Suicides in Paris and London. Lond Med Phys J. 1822; 48(286):483-7.

Burt KB, Whelan R, Conrod PJ, Banaschewski T, Barker GJ, Bokde ALW, Bromberg U, Büchel C, Fauth-Bühler M, Flor H, Galinowski A, Gallinat J, Gowland P, Heinz A, Ittermann B, Mann K, Nees F, Papadopoulos-Orfanos D, Paus T, Pausova Z, Poustka L, Rietschel M, Robbins TW, Smolka MN, Ströhle A, Schumann G, Garavan H, the IMAGEN Consortium. Structural brain correlates of adolescent resilience. J Child Psychol Psychiatry. 2016; 57(11):1287-96.

Burton R. The Anatomy of Melancholy. John Lichfield and James Short, for Henry Cripps; 1621.

Bush B, Shaw S, Cleary P, Delbanco TL, Aronson MD. Screening for alcohol abuse using the cage questionnaire. Am J Med. 1987;82(2):231–5.

Busto U, Sellers EM, Naranjo CA, Cappell H, Sanchez-Craig M, Sykora K. Withdrawal reaction after long-term therapeutic use of benzodiazepines. N Engl J Med. 1986;315(14):854–9.

Butler S. The way of all flesh. Washington: National Home Library Foundation. 1903.

Butters N, Cermak LS. Alcoholic Korsakoff's Syndrome. Academic Press; 1980.

Byck R. Cocaine use and research: three histories. In: Fisher Seymour, Raskin A, Uhlenhuth EH, editors. Cocaine: Clinical and Biobehavioral Aspects. New York: Oxford University Press; 1987.

Cadet JL. Epigenetics of stress, addiction, and resilience: Therapeutic implications. Mol Neurobiol. 2016; 53(1):545-60.

Cahill L, Prins B, Weber M, McGaugh JL. β-Adrenergic activation and memory for emotional events. Nature. 1994; 371(6499):702–4.

Caine D, Halliday GM, Kril JJ, Harper CG. Operational criteria for the classification of chronic alcoholics: identification of Wernicke's encephalopathy. J Neurol Neurosurg Psychiatry. 1997;62(1):51–60.

Cale JJ. Cocaine. Shelter; 1977.

Calvin J, Pagit E, Fetherstone C. A harmonie vpon the three euangelists, Matthew, Mark and Luke with the commentarie of M. Iohn Caluine. Londini: Impensis G. Bishop. 1584.
Cameron DE. David Kennedy Henderson (1884-1965). Am J Psychiatry. 1965; 122(4):467–9.

Cannon WB. Bodily changes in pain, hunger, fear and rage: an account of recent researches into the functions of emotional excitement. New York; London: D. Appleton; 1920.

Carlen P, Wortzman G, Holgate R, Wilkinson D, Rankin J. Reversible cerebral atrophy in recently abstinent chronic alcoholics measured by computed tomography scans. Science. 1978;200(4345):1076.

Carlson ET, Simpson MM. Opium as a tranquilizer. American Journal of Psychiatry. 1963; 120, 112-117.

Carlyle JW, Carlyle T, Froude JA. Letters and Memorials of Jane Welsh Carlyle. London: Longmans, Green; 1893.

Carnes P. Don't Call it Love: Recovery from Sexual Addiction. Bantam;1992.

Carter G. Alcohol and the Motorist: Alcoholic Concentration in Urine as a Test of Intoxication. Br Med J. 1927; 2(3477):333–5.

Carvalho M, Carmo H, Costa VM, Capela JP, Pontes H, Remião F, Carvalho F, Bastos M de L. Toxicity of amphetamines: an update. Arch Toxicol, 2012;86(8):1167–231.

Cassidy CM, Carpenter KM, Konova AB, Cheung V, Grassetti A, Zecca L, Abi-Dargham A, Martinez D, Horga G. Evidence for dopamine abnormalities in the substantia neuromelanin-sensitive MRI. Am J Psychiatry, 2020, pp. 1038-1047. appi.ajp.2020.20010090.

Castellucci V, Pinsker H, Kupfermann I, Kandel ER. Neuronal Mechanisms of Habituation and Dishabituation of the Gill-Withdrawal Reflex in Aplysia. Science. 1970;167(3926):1745.

Cavicchioli M, Movalli M, Maffei C. The clinical efficacy of mindfulness-based treatments for alcohol and drugs use disorders: a meta-analytic review of randomized and nonrandomized controlled trials. Eur Addict Res 2018;137–62.

Celsus AC, Spencer WG. De medicina. Cambridge, Mass: Harvard University Press; London: W. Heinemann, Ltd; 1935.

Centers for Disease Control and Prevention. Public health consequences among first responders to emergency events associated with illicit methamphetamine laboratories--selected states, 1996-1999. MMWR Morb Mortal Wkly Rep, 2000;49(45):1021–4.

Centerwall BS, Criqui MH. Prevention of the Wernicke-Korsakoff Syndrome. N Engl J Med. 1978;299(6):285–9.

de Cervantes Saavedra M. The history of the renown'd Don Quixote de la Mancha. London: Printed for Sam. Buckley; 1700.

Chamberlain SR, Grant JE. Efficacy of pharmacological interventions in targeting decision-making impairments across substance and behavioral addictions. Neuropsychol Rev 2019;29(1):93–102.

Chambers E. Cyclopaedia : or, An universal dictionary of arts and sciences : containing an explication of the terms, and an account of the things signify'd thereby, in the several arts both liberal and mechanical, and the several sciences, human and divine ... London: Printed for J. & J. Knapton; 1728.

Charboneau EJ, Dietrich MS, Park S, Cao A, Watkins TJ, Blackford JU, Benningfield MM, Martin PR, Buchowski MS, Cowan RL. Cannabis cue-induced brain activation correlates with drug craving in limbic and visual salience regions: Preliminary results. Psychiatry Res Neuroimaging. 2013; 214(2):122–31.

Charcot JM. Clinical lectures on diseases of the nervous system: delivered at the Infirmary of La Salpetriere. London: New Sydenham Society; 1889.

Charland LC. A Puzzling anomaly: decision-making capacity and research on addiction. In: Iltis AS, MacKay D, editors. Oxford Handbook Research Ethics. Oxford University Press; 2020.

Charlet K, Rosenthal A, Lohoff FW, Heinz A, Beck A. Imaging resilience and recovery in alcohol dependence. Addiction. 2018; 113(10):1933-50.

Charleton W. The Ephesian Matron. London: Printed for Henry Herringman at the Anchor in the Lower walke in the new exchange. 1659.

Chartrand TL, Lakin JL. The antecedents and consequences of human behavioral mimicry. Annu Rev Psychol. 2013; 64(1):285-308.

Chatzittofis A, Boström ADE, Ciuculete DM, Öberg KG, Arver S, Schiöth HB, Jokinen J. HPA axis dysregulation is associated with differential methylation of CpG-sites in related genes. Sci Rep 2021;11(1):20134.

Chaucer G. The booke of the Duchesse. Lexington, KY: Anvil Press; 1954.

Chaucer G. The Nun's Priest's Tale. 2013.

Chaucer G, Coghill N, Tolkien C. The Man of Law's Tale. London; 1904.

Chaudron CD, & Wilkinson DA, editors. Theories on Alcoholism. Toronto: Canada: Addiction Research Foundation; 1988.

de Chauliac G. La Grande Chirurgie de M. Guy de Chauliac ...restituée nouvellement à sa dignité par M. Laurent Joubert... Lyon: J. Ollier; 1659.

Chen ACH, Manz N, Tang Y, Rangaswamy M, Almasy L, Kuperman S, Nurnberger Jr J, O'Connor SJ, Edenberg HJ, Schuckit MA, Tischfield J, Foroud T, Bierut LJ, Rohrbaugh J, Rice JP, Goate A, Hesselbrock V, Porjesz B. Single-nucleotide polymorphisms in corticotropin releasing hormone receptor 1 gene (CRHR1) are associated with quantitative trait of event-related potential and alcohol dependence. Alcohol. Clin. Exp. Res. 2010;34(6):988–96.

Chen GS. Enkephalin, drug addiction and acupuncture. Am J Chin Med. 1977; 05(01):25-30.

Chen J. History of pain theories. Neurosci Bull. 2011; 27(5):343.

Chen J. Empathy for distress in humans and rodents. Neurosci Bull 2018;34(1):216–36.

Chen KK, Schmidt CF. The action of ephedrine, the active principle of the Chinese drug Ma Huang. J Pharmacol Exp Ther, 1924;24(5):339.

Chen KK. A study of ephedrine. Br Med J. 1927; 2(3482):593.

Cheng SB, Ding LK. Practical application of acupuncture analgesia. Nature. 1973;242(5400):559–60.

Childress AR, Mozley PD, McElgin W, Fitzgerald J, Reivich M, O'Brien CP. Limbic activation suring cue-induced cocaine craving. Am J Psychiatry. 1999; 156(1):11-8.

Chistiakov DA, Kekelidze ZI, Chekhonin VP. Endophenotypes as a measure of suicidality. J Appl Genet. 2012; 53(4):389-413.

Chiu J, Storm L. Personality, perceived luck and gambling attitudes as predictors of gambling involvement. J Gambl Stud, 2010;26(2):205–27.

Chlouverakis C. Dietary and medical treatments of obesity: An evaluative review. Addict Behav. 1975; 1(1):3–21.

Christopher PP, Anderson B, Stein MD. Comparing views on civil commitment for drug misuse and for mental illness among persons with opioid use disorder. J Subst Abuse Treat 2020; 113:107998.

Churchill JM. A treatise on acupuncturation: being a description of a surgical operation originally peculiar to the Japanese and Chinese, and by them denominated Zin-king, now introduced into European practice, with directions for its performance, and cases illustrating its success. London: Simpkin and Marshall; 1821.

Clark EV, Clark HH. When Nouns Surface as Verbs. Language. 1979;55(4):767-811.

Clark L. Disordered gambling: the evolving concept of behavioral addiction. Ann N Y Acad Sci, 2014;1327(1):46–61.

Clendinning J. Observations on the medicinal properties of the Cannabis Sativa of India. Medico-Chir Trans. 1843; 26:188-210.

Cloninger CR. Neurogenetic adaptive mechanisms in alcoholism. Science 1987;236(4800): 410-6.

Cloninger CR, Christiansen KO, Reich T, Gottesman II. Implications of sex differences in the prevalences of antisocial personality, alcoholism, and criminality for familial transmission. Arch Gen Psychiatry, 1978;35(8):941–51.

Clouston TS. Observations and experiments on the use of opium, bromide of potassium, and Cannabis Indica in insanity, especially in regard to the effects of the two latter given together. Br Foreign Medico-Chir Rev. John Churchill & Sons; 1870;46(92):493-511.

Coccaro EF. Intermittent explosive disorder as a disorder of impulsive aggression for DSM-5. Am J Psychiatry, 2012;169(6):577–88.

Coccaro EF, Lee R, Kavoussi RJ. Aggression, suicidality, and intermittent explosive disorder: serotonergic correlates in personality disorder and healthy control subjects. Neuropsychopharmacology, 2010;35(2):435–44.

Cocker BF. Moral government: its two postulates--the freedom of man and the personality of God. The Princeton Review. 1879;3(pt. 1):55–77.

Cohen S. Therapeutic aspects. In: Petersen R, editor. Marihuana Res Find 1976. Rockville, MD: U.S. Department of Health, Education, and Welfare, Public Health Service, Alcohol, Drug Abuse, and Mental Health Administration; 1977; pp. 194-225.

Collett B. Female monastic life in early Tudor England with an edition of Richard Fox's translation of the Benedictine rule for women, 1517. London: Routledge; 2016.

Collins JE. Effects of restraint, monitoring, and stimulus salience on eating behavior. Addict Behav. 1978; 3(3):197-204.

Connell PH. Amphetamine dependence. Proc R Soc Med, 1968;61(2):178–81.

Connolly GN, Alpert HR, Wayne GF, Koh H. Trends in nicotine yield in smoke and its relationship with design characteristics among popular US cigarette brands, 1997–2005. Tob Control. 2007;16(5): e5.

Contrepois K, Wu S, Moneghetti KJ, Hornburg D, Ahadi S, Tsai M-S, Metwally AA, Wei E, Lee-McMullen B, Quijada JV, Chen S, Christle JW, Ellenberger M, Balliu B, Taylor S, Durrant MG, Knowles DA, Choudhry H, Ashland M, Bahmani A, Enslen B, Amsallem M, Kobayashi Y, Avina M, Perelman D, Schüssler-Fiorenza Rose SM, Zhou W, Ashley EA, Montgomery SB, Chaib H, Haddad F, Snyder MP. Molecular choreography of acute exercise. Cell. 2020; 181(5):1112-30. e16.

Cooper JC, Knutson B. Valence and salience contribute to nucleus accumbens activation. NeuroImage. 2008; 39(1):538-47.

Cooperman NA, Hanley AW, Kline A, Garland EL. A pilot randomized clinical trial of mindfulness-oriented recovery enhancement as an adjunct to methadone treatment for people with opioid use disorder and chronic pain: Impact on illicit drug use, health, and well-being. J Subst Abuse Treat 2021; 127:108468.

Cotgrave R, Hollyband C, Sherwood R. A dictionarie of the French and English tongues. Compiled by Randle Cotgrave. Whereunto is also annexed a most copious dictionarie, of the English set before the French. By R.S. L. London: Printed by Adam Islip; 1632.

Courtney KE, Ray LA. Methamphetamine: An update on epidemiology, pharmacology, clinical phenomenology, and treatment literature. Drug Alcohol Depend, 2014;143:11–21.

Courville CB. Effects of Alcohol on the Nervous System of Man. Oxford, England: San Lucas Press; 1955.

Covington HE, Maze I, Sun H, Bomze HM, DeMaio KD, Wu EY, Dietz DM, Lobo MK, Ghose S, Mouzon E, Neve RL, Tamminga CA, Nestler EJ. A role for repressive histone methylation in cocaine-induced vulnerability to stress. Neuron. 2011; 71(4):656-70.

Covington III H, Newman E, Leonard M, Miczek K. Translational models of adaptive and excessive fighting: an emerging role for neural circuits in pathological aggression. F1000Research, 2019;8(963).

Cowen J. The First And Last Days Of Alcohol The Great, In The Empire Of Nationolia: Or, Manxman's Records Of The Temperance Revolution... BT Albro, Printer; 1848.

Craddock D. Anorectic drugs: use in general practice. Drugs. 1976; 11(5):378–93.

Cristofani C, Sesso G, Cristofani P, Fantozzi P, Inguaggiato E, Muratori P, Narzisi A, Pfanner C, Pisano S, Polidori L, Ruglioni L, Valente E, Masi G, Milone A. The role of executive functions in the development of empathy and its association with externalizing behaviors in children with neurodevelopmental disorders and other psychiatric comorbidities. Brain Sci 2020;10(8):489.

Cullen W. Synopsis of methodical nosology. Edinburgh: Printed for Maclachlan & Stewart; 1830.

Cutshall BJ. The Saunders-Sutton syndrome: an analysis of delirium tremens. Q J Stud Alcohol. 1965;26::423–48.

Da Costa J. On irritable heart; a clinical study of a form of functional cardiac disorder and its consequences. Am J Med Sci. 1871; 61(121):44–61.

Dale H. Pharmacology and nerve-endings (Walter Ernest Dixon Memorial Lecture). Proc R Soc Med, 1935;28(3):319–32.

Dale HCA. Subjective probability, gambling and intelligence. Nature, 1958;181(4605):363–4.

Dale HH. Walter Bradford Cannon, 1871-1945. Obit Not Fellows R Soc. Royal Society; 1947; 5(15):407-23.

Dallenbach KM. Pain: history and present status. Am J Psychol. 1939; 52(3):331-47.

Darwin C. The Origin of Species. Castle Books; 1859. Barrough P. The methode of phisicke conteyning the causes, signes, and cures of invvard diseases in mans body from the head to the foote. Whereunto is added, the forme and rule of making remedies and medicines, which our phisitians commonly vse at this day, with the proportion, quantitie, & names of ech [sic] medicine. London: Thomas Vautroullier dwelling in the Blackefriars by Lud-gate;1583.

Darwin C, Fitzroy R, King PP. Narrative of the surveying voyages of His Majesty's Ships Adventure and Beagle: between the years of 1826 and 1836 describing their examination of the southern shores of South America and Beagle's circumnavigation of the Globe. London: H. Colburn; 1839.

Dawson DA, Grant BF, Stinson FS, Chou PS. Estimating the effect of help-seeking on achieving recovery from alcohol dependence. Addiction 2006;101(6):824–34.

Defalque RJ, Wright AJ. Methamphetamine for Hitler's Germany: 1937 to 1945. Bull Anesth Hist, 2011;29(2):21–32.

Denber HCB. Anxiolytics, neuroleptics, and other drugs in the treatment of anxiety. Am J Psychother. 1982;36(3):304–17.

Deneau G, Yanagita T, Seevers MH. Self-administration of psychoactive substances by the monkey. Psychopharmacologia. 1969;16(1):30–48.

De Quincey T. Selections Grave and Gay Vol. 5 Confessions of an Opium-eater. Edinburgh: James Hogg; 1856.

Derefinko KJ, Salgado García FI, Talley KM, Bursac Z, Johnson KC, Murphy JG, McDevitt-Murphy ME, Andrasik F, Sumrok DD. Adverse childhood experiences predict opioid relapse during treatment among rural adults. Addict Behav. 2019; 96:171–4.

Descartes R, Haldane ES, Ross GRT. The philosophical works. C.U.P. 1912.

Detwiler SR. Anatomy as a science. Science. 1929;70(1824):563–6.

Devane WA, Dysarz FA, Johnson MR, Melvin LS, Howlett AC. Determination and characterization of a cannabinoid receptor in rat brain. Mol Pharmacol. 1988;34(5):605-13.

Devane W, Hanus L, Breuer A, Pertwee R, Stevenson L, Griffin G, Gibson D, Mandelbaum A, Etinger A, Mechoulam R. Isolation and structure of a brain constituent that binds to the cannabinoid receptor. Science. 1992;258(5090):1946-9.

Devin CJ, Lee DS, Armaghani SJ, Bible J, Shau DN, Martin PR, Ehrenfeld JM. Approach to pain management in chronic opioid users undergoing orthopaedic surgery. J Am Acad Orthop Surg. 2014; 22(10):614-22.

De Wardener HE, Lennox B. Cerebral beriberi (Wernicke's encephalopathy): review of 52 cases in a Singapore prisoner-of-war hospital. The Lancet. 1947;249(6436):11–7.

DiFranza JR, Norwood BD, Garner DW, Tye JB. Legislative efforts to protect children from tobacco. JAMA. 1987; 257(24):3387-9.

Dixon WE. The selective action of cocaine on nerve fibres. J Physiol, 1904;32(1):87–94.

Dixon WE, Hoyle JC. Studies in the pulmonary circulation: II. The action of adrenaline and nicotine. J Physiol. 1929;67(1):77–86.

Dodwell CR, Clemoes P. Rosenkilde og Bagger (Firm), British Museum. The Old English illustrated Hexateuch. British Museum Cotton Claudius B. IV. Copenhagen: Rosenkilde and Bagger; 1974.

Dole VP, Nyswander M. A medical treatment for diacetylmorphine (heroin) addiction: A clinical trial with methadone hydrochloride. JAMA 1965; 193:646–50.

Dollard J, Miller NE, Doob LW, Mowrer OH, Sears RR. Frustration and Aggression. New Haven, CT, US: Yale University Press; 1939. p. viii, 213.

Domingo-Rodriguez L, Ruiz de Azua I, Dominguez E, Senabre E, Serra I, Kummer S, Navandar M, Baddenhausen S, Hofmann C, Andero R, Gerber S, Navarrete M, Dierssen M, Lutz B, Martín-García E, Maldonado R. A specific prelimbic-nucleus accumbens pathway controls resilience versus vulnerability to food addiction. Nat Commun. 2020; 11(1):782.

Don Michel. Ayenbite of Inwyt. 1866.

Dornette WH. The anatomy of acupuncture. Bull N Y Acad Med. 1975;51(8):895–902.

Dossett ML, Fricchione GL, Benson H. A new era for mind–body medicine. N Engl J Med 2020;382(15):1390–1.

Dostoevsky F. The gambler. New York: Bantam Books; 1964.

Dowden CW, Bradbury JT. Eosinophil response to epinephrine and corticotropin: studies in alcoholics and non-alcoholics. JAMA. 1952;149: 725–8.

Drake LR, Scott PJH. DARK Classics in chemical neuroscience: cocaine. ACS Chem Neurosci, 2018;9(10):2358–72.

Draps M, Kowalczyk-Grębska N, Marchewka A, Shi F, Gola M. White matter microstructural and compulsive sexual behaviors disorder – diffusion tensor imaging study. J Behav Addict 2021;10(1):55–64.

Driver J, Frackowiak RSJ. Neurobiological measures of human selective attention. Neuropsychologia. 2001; 39(12):1257-62.

Drummond C, Edwards G, Glanz A, Glass I, Jackson P, Oppenheimer E, Sheehan M, Taylor C, Thom B. Rethinking drug policies in the context of the acquired immunodeficiency syndrome. Bull. Narc. 1987;39(2):29–35.

Dryden J. Fables ancient and modern: translated into verse, from Homer, Ovid, Boccace, and Chaucer: with original poems. By Mr. Dryden. London: Printed for T. Davies, B. White, C. Say, B. Law, S. Crowder; 1774.

Duan G, He Q, Pang Y, Chen W, Liao H, Liu H, Tan L, Liu Y, Tao J, Zhang J, Wei X, Sun P, Liu P, Deng D. Altered amygdala resting-state functional connectivity following acupuncture stimulation at BaiHui (GV20) in first-episode drug-Naïve major depressive disorder. Brain Imaging Behav. 2020;14(6):2269–80.

Dube SR, Anda RF, Felitti VJ, Edwards VJ, Croft JB. Adverse childhood experiences and personal alcohol abuse as an adult. Addict Behav. 2002; 27(5):713–25.

Dudley WHC, Williams JG. Electroconvulsive therapy in delirium tremens. Compr Psychiatry. 1972; 13:357–60.

Due DL, Huettel SA, Hall WG, Rubin DC. Activation in mesolimbic and visuospatial neural circuits elicited by smoking cues: evidence from functional magnetic resonance imaging. Am J Psychiatry. 2002; 159(6):954–60.

Duncan DF, Nicholson T. Dutch drug policy: a model for America? J Health Soc Policy. 1997; 8(3):1-15.

Dundar Y, Boland A, Strobl J, Dodd S, Haycox A, Bagust A, Bogg J, Dickson R, Walley T. Newer hypnotic drugs for the short-term management of insomnia: a systematic review and economic evaluation. Health Technol Assess. 2004; 8(24).

Dunglison R. On the Rational Treatment of Delirium Tremens. Edinburgh Med J. 1860; 5:923–5.

DuPuy WA. Uncle Sam, detective. New York, McKinlay Stone & Mackenzie; 1916.

Dykman RA, Gantt WH. Relation of experimental tachycardia to amplitude of motor activity and intensity of the motivating stimulus. Am J Physiol 1956;185(3):495–8.

Dynes JB. Objective method for distinguishing sleep from the hypnotic trance. Arch Neurol Psychiatry. 1947; 57(1):84–93.

Ebbinghaus H. Memory: a contribution to experimental psychology. New York City: Teachers College, Columbia University; 1913.

Eckardt MJ, Martin PR. Clinical assessment of cognition in alcoholism. Alcohol Clin Exp Res. 1986;10(2):123–7.

Eckardt MJ, Rawlings RR, Martin PR. Biological correlates and detection of alcohol abuse and alcoholism. Prog Neuropsychopharmacol Biol Psychiatry. 1986;10(2):135–44.

Eddy NB, Isbell H. Addiction liability and narcotics control. Public Health Rep. 1959;7 4(9):755-63.

Edeleano L. Ueber einige Derivate der Phenylmethacrylsäure und der Phenylisobuttersäure. Berichte der deutschen chemischen Gesellschaft. 1887;20(1):616–22.

Edwards G, Gross MM. Alcohol dependence: provisional description of a clinical syndrome. British Medical Journal 1976;1(6017), 1058–61.

Edwards G, Hensman C, Hawker A, Williamson V. Who goes to Alcoholics Anonymous? Lancet. 1966;2(7459):382-4.

Ekpu VU, Brown AK. The economic impact of smoking and of reducing smoking prevalence: review of evidence. Tobacco Use Insights. 2015;14(8):1-35.

Elliott TR. The action of adrenalin. J Physiol, 1905;32(5–6):401–67.

Engel G. The need for a new medical model: a challenge for biomedicine. Science. 1977; 196(4286):129.

Engel GL, Webb JP, Ferris EB. Quantitative electroencephalographic studies of anoxia in humans; comparison with acute alcoholic intoxication and hypoglycemia. J Clin Invest. 1945; 24(5):691-7.

Engel J. The legacy of Frank Morrell. Int Rev Neurobiol 2001; 45:571–90.

Engen HG, Singer T. Empathy circuits. Macrocircuits 2013;23(2):275–82.

Enoch M-A. Genetic and environmental influences on the development of alcoholism. Ann N Y Acad Sci. 2006; 1094(1):193-201.

Epel ES, Blackburn EH, Lin J, Dhabhar FS, Adler NE, Morrow JD, Cawthon RM. Accelerated telomere shortening in response to life stress. Proc Natl Acad Sci U S A 2004;101(49):17312–5.

Epel ES, Puterman E, Lin J, Blackburn EH, Lum PY, Beckmann ND, Zhu J, Lee E, Gilbert A, Rissman RA, Tanzi RE, Schadt EE. Meditation and vacation effects have an impact on disease-associated molecular phenotypes. Transl Psychiatry 2016;6(8): e880.

Erasmus D, Udall N. Apophthegmes of Erasmus. Boston: Lincolnshire, Roberts; 1877.

Erickson PG. The law in addictions: principles, practicalities and prospects. In: Erickson PG, Kalant H, editors. Windows on Science. Toronto, Canada: Addiction Research Foundation. 1992, pp. 125-60.

Erskine J. An Institute of the Law of Scotland. Edinburgh. 1773.

Essig CF, Jones BE, Lam RC. The effect of pentobarbital on alcohol withdrawal in dogs. Arch Neurol. 1969; 20:554–8.

Estienne C, Liebault J, Surflet R. Maison Rustique, or the Countrie Farme. London: E. Bollifant; 1600.

Estill M, Ribeiro E, Francoeur NJ, Smith ML, Sebra R, Yeh S-Y, Cunningham AM, Nestler EJ, Shen L. Long read, isoform aware sequencing of mouse nucleus accumbens after chronic cocaine treatment. Sci Rep 2021;11(1):6729.

Everard G. De herba panacea, quam alii tabacum, alii petum, aut nicotianam vocant, breuis commentariolus. Quo admirandæ ac prorsus diuinæ huius Peruanæ stirpis facultates & vsus explicantur. Antuerpiae: Apud Ioannem Bellerum; 1587.

Everett D. The middle English prose psalter of Richard Rolle of Hampole. Cambridge: Cambridge University Press; 1922.

Everitt BJ, Robbins TW. Neural systems of reinforcement for drug addiction: from actions to habits to compulsion. Nat Neurosci. 2005; 8(11):1481-9.
Ewart RB, Priest RG. Methaqualone addiction and delirium tremens. Br Med J. 1967; 3:92-3.

Ewing AC. Evolutionary Ethics. By J. S. Huxley. (Oxford University Press, 1943. Pp. 84. Price 2s. net.). Philosophy. 1944;19(73):170–1.

Ewing JA. Detecting alcoholism: the CAGE questionnaire. JAMA. 1984;252(14):1905–7.

Fabing HD. Frenquel, a blocking agent against experimental LSD-25 and mescaline psychosis. Neurology. 1955;5(5):319-28.

Fagerström K-O. Measuring degree of physical dependence to tobacco smoking with reference to individualization of treatment. Addict Behav. 1978;3(3):235–41.

Fairchild MD, Alles GA. The central locomotor stimulatory activity and acute toxicity of the ephedrine and norephedrine isomers in mice. J Pharmacol Exp Ther. 1967; 158(1):135.

Falk DE, O'Malley SS, Witkiewitz K, Anton RF, Litten RZ, Slater M, Kranzler HR, Mann KF, Hasin DS, Johnson B, Meulien D, Ryan M, Fertig J for the Alcohol Clinical Trials Initiative (ACTIVE) Workgroup. Evaluation of drinking risk levels as outcomes in alcohol pharmacotherapy trials: a secondary analysis of 3 randomized clinical trials. JAMA Psychiatry 2019;76(4)374-381.

Falk JL. Production of polydipsia in normal rats by an intermittent food schedule. Science. 1961; 133(3447):195.

Farah A. Coffee. Consumption and health implications. Royal Society of Chemistry; 2019.

Farah A, de Paulis T, Moreira DP, Trugo LC, Martin PR. Chlorogenic acids and lactones in regular and water-decaffeinated Arabica coffees. J Agric Food Chem. 2006; 54(2):374-81.

Farah MJ, Illes J, Cook-Deegan R, Gardner H, Kandel E, King P, Parens E, Sahakian B, Wolpe PR. Neurocognitive enhancement: what can we do and what should we do? Nat Rev Neurosci, 2004;5(5):421–5.

Farokhnia M, Grodin EN, Lee MR, Oot EN, Blackburn AN, Stangl BL, Schwandt ML, Farinelli LA, Momenan R, Ramchandani VA, Leggio L. Exogenous ghrelin administration increases alcohol self-administration and modulates brain functional activity in heavy-drinking alcohol-dependent individuals. Mol Psychiatry. 2018; 23(10):2029-38.

Faulkner AB. On the degree to which exercise should be carried in some varieties of dyspepsia. Edinb Med Surg J. 1806; 2(5):5–8.

Fauth-Bühler M, Mann K. Neurobiological correlates of internet gaming disorder: Similarities to pathological gambling. Addict Behav, 2017;64:349–56.

Ferrier D. The Functions of the Brain. New York: G P Putnam's Sons; 1876.

Field T, Diego M, Sanders CE. Exercise is positively related to adolescents' relationships and academics. Adolescence. 2001; 36(141):105.

Figueiro MG, Plitnick B, Roohan C, Sahin L, Kalsher M, Rea MS. Effects of a tailored lighting intervention on sleep quality, rest–activity, mood, and behavior in older adults with Alzheimer disease and related dementias: A randomized clinical trial. J Clin Sleep Med. 2019; 15(12):1757–67.

Finlayson AJR, Macoubrie J, Huff C, Foster DE, Martin PR. Experiences with benzodiazepine use, tapering, and discontinuation: an Internet survey. Therap Adv Psychopharmacol; 2022; 12:1-10.

Finlayson AJR, Sealy J, Martin PR. The differential diagnosis of problematic hypersexuality. Sex Addict Compulsivity 2001;8(3–4):241–51.

Finnegan JK, Larson PS, Haag HB. The role of nicotine in the cigarette habit. Science. 1945;102(2639):94–6.

Fischer E, von Mering J. Über eine neue Klasse von Schlafmitteln. Ther Ggw. 1903; 44:97–101.

Fischer EF, Victor B, Robinson D, Farah A, Martin PR. Coffee consumption and health impacts: a brief history of changing conceptions. Coffee Consumption Health Implications. The Royal Society of Chemistry; 2019, pp. 1-19.

Fish EW, De Bold JF, Miczek KA. Aggressive behavior as a reinforcer in mice: activation by allopregnanolone. Psychopharmacology (Berl), 2002a;163(3):459–66.

Fish EW, De Bold JF, Miczek KA. Repeated alcohol: behavioral sensitization and alcohol-heightened aggression in mice. Psychopharmacology (Berl), 2002b;160(1):39–48.

Fisher ML, Pauly JR, Froeliger B, Turner JR. Translational research in nicotine addiction. Cold Spring Harb Perspect Med. 2021;11: a039776doi:10.1101/cshperspect. a039776.

Flanagan J, Chatzittofis A, Boström ADE, Hallberg J, Öberg KG, Arver S, Jokinen J. High plasma oxytocin levels in men with hypersexual disorder. J Clin Endocrinol Metab 2022; dgac015.

Fleming R, Tillotson KJ. Further Studies on the Personality and Sociological Factors in the Prognosis and Treatment of Chronic Alcoholism. N Engl J Med. 1939;221(19):741–5.

Fletcher G. Israel Redux: or the restauration of Israel. London: Hancock; 1677.

Fletcher JC. Cases of delirium tremens rapidly cured by hydrate of chloral. Br Med J. 1870; 2:62.

Flink EB, Stutzman FL, Anderson AR, Konig T, Fraser R. Magnesium deficiency after prolonged parenteral fluid administration and after chronic alcoholism complicated by delirium tremens. J Lab Clin Med. 1954; 43:169–83.

Flint A. The source of muscular power, as deduced from observations upon the human subject under conditions of rest and of exercise. J Anat Physiol. 1877; 12(Pt 1):91–141.

Fontaine KR, Redden DT, Wang C, Westfall AO, Allison DB. Years of life lost due to obesity. JAMA. 2003; 289(2):187–93.

Forney RB. Toxicology of marihuana. Pharmacol Rev. 1971;23(4):279-84.

Fox KCR, Dixon ML, Nijeboer S, Girn M, Floman JL, Lifshitz M, Ellamil M, Sedlmeier P, Christoff K. Functional neuroanatomy of meditation: A review and meta-analysis of 78 functional neuroimaging investigations. Neurosci Biobehav Rev 2016; 65:208–28.

France CJ. The Gambling Impulse. Am J Psychol. University of Illinois Press, 1902;13(3):364–407.

Francis D, Diorio J, Liu D, Meaney MJ. Nongenomic transmission across generations of maternal behavior and stress responses in the rat. Science, 1999; 286, 1155.

Frank DW, Cinciripini PM, Deweese MM, Karam-Hage M, Kypriotakis G, Lerman C, Robinson JD, Tyndale RF, Vidrine DJ, Versace F. Toward precision medicine for smoking cessation: developing a neuroimaging-based classification algorithm to identify smokers at higher risk for relapse. Nicotine Tob Res. 2020;22(8):1277–84.

Fraser HF, Wikler A, Eisenman AJ, Isbell H. Use of N-allylnormorphine in treatment of methadone poisoning in man: report of two cases. J Am Med Assoc 1952; 148:1205–7.

Fraser JD. Withdrawal symptoms in cannabis-indica addicts. The Lancet. 1949;254(6582):747-8.

Freedman ND, Park Y, Abnet CC, Hollenbeck AR, Sinha R. Association of coffee drinking with total and cause-specific mortality. N Engl J Med. 2012; 366(20):1891-904.

Freud S. Ueber Coca. Wien: Verlag von Moritz Perles; 1884.

Freud S. Instincts and their vicissitudes. The Standard Edition of the Complete Psychological Works of Sigmund Freud, Volume XIV. London: Vintage Press; 2001.

Freud S, Brill AA. Three Contributions to the Sexual Theory; 1910.

Freund G. Chronic central nervous system toxicity of alcohol. Annu Rev Pharmacol. 1973;13(1):217–27.

Friedman M. Studies concerning the etiology and pathogenesis of neurocirculatory asthenia: III. The cardiovascular manifestations of neurocirculatory asthenia. Am Heart J. 1945; 30(5):478–91.

Frommel E, Fleury C, Schmidt-Ginzkey J, Beguin M. On the pharmacodynamic action of new tranquilizing agent: methaminodiazepoxide or Librium. Experimental study. Therapie. 1960; 15:1233–44.

Gaedcke F. Ueber das Erythroxylin, dargestellt aus den Blättern des in Südamerika cultivirten Strauches Erythroxylon Coca Lam. Arch Pharm (Weinheim), 1855;132(2):141–50.

Gaito J. The kindling effect. Physiol Psychol 1974;2(1):45–50.

Galaj E, Ranaldi R. Neurobiology of reward-related learning. Neurosci Biobehav Rev 2021; 124:224–34.

Galanter M. Alcoholics anonymous and twelve-step recovery: A model based on social and cognitive neuroscience. Am J Addict 2014;23(3):300–7.

Ganczarek J, Hünefeldt T, Olivetti Belardinelli M. From "Einfühlung" to empathy: exploring the relationship between aesthetic and interpersonal experience. Cogn Process 2018;19(2):141–5.

Garber J, Fencil-Morse E, Rosellini RA, Seligman MEP. 'Abnormal fixations' and 'learned helplessness': Inescapable shock as a weanling impairs adult discrimination learning in rats. Behav Res Ther. 1979; 17(3):197-206.

Gates S, Smith L, Foxcroft D. Auricular acupuncture for cocaine dependence. Cochrane Database Syst Rev. 2006;(1):CD005192.

Gaw AC, Chang LW, Shaw L-C. Efficacy of acupuncture on osteoarthritic pain. N Engl J Med. 1975;293(8):375–8.

Gawin FH, Kleber HD. Abstinence symptomatology and psychiatric diagnosis in cocaine abusers: clinical observations. Arch Gen Psychiatry, 1986;43(2):107–13.

Gay GR, Inaba DS, Sheppard CW, Newmeyer JA, Rappolt RT. Cocaine: history, epidemiology, human pharmacology, and treatment. A perspective on a new debut for an old girl. Clin Toxicol, 1975;8(2):149–78.

Gayet M. Affection encephalique (encephalite diffuse probable) localisee aux etages superieurs des pedoncules cerebraux et aux couches optiques, ainsi qu'au plaincher du quatrieme ventricule et aux parois lat6rales du troisieme. Arch Physiol Norm Pathol. 1875; 7:341–51.

Gendel MH. Forensic and medical legal issues in addiction psychiatry. Addict Disord 2004;27(4):611–26.

Gent WL (translator). Virgil's Eclogues. London: Printed by William Iones, dwelling in Red-crosse-street, 1628.

Giacobini E, Izikowitz S, Wegmann A. Urinary norepinephrine and epinephrine excretion in delirium tremens. Arch Gen Psychiatry. 1960; 3:289–96.

Giacobini E, Salum I. Treatment of delirium tremens. A comparative study of different therapeutic methods in 434 cases. Acta Psychiatr Scand. 1961; 37:198–208.

Girard P, Garde A, Devic M. Considérations terminologiques, étiologiques, anatomiques et cliniques concernant l'encéphalopathie de Gayet-Wernicke; ses rapports avec le syndrome de Marchiafava-Bignami et la psychose de Korsakow. Rev Neurol Paris. 1953;88(4):236–48.

Goddard GV. Development of epileptic seizures through brain stimulation at low intensity. Nature 1967;214(5092):1020–1.

Goddard GV, Douglas RM. Does the engram of kindling model the engram of normal long term memory? Can J Neurol Sci J Can Sci Neurol 1975;2(4):385–94.

Goddard GV, McIntyre DC, Leech CK. A permanent change in brain function resulting from daily electrical stimulation. Exp Neurol 1969;25(3):295–330.

Godfrey R. Various injuries and abuses in chymical and galenical physick committed both by Physicians and Apothecaries, detected, etc. London; 1674.

Goeders N, Smith J. Cortical dopaminergic involvement in cocaine reinforcement. Science. 1983; 221(4612):773.

Goel V, Dolan RJ. Reciprocal neural response within lateral and ventral medial prefrontal cortex during hot and cold reasoning. NeuroImage. 2003; 20(4):2314-21.

Gola M, Draps M. Ventral striatal reactivity in compulsive sexual behaviors. Front Psychiatry 2018; 9:546–546.

Goldberg MF. Cocaine: the first local anesthetic and the "third scourge of humanity": A centennial melodrama. Arch Ophthalmol, 1984;102(10):1443–7.

Goudriaan AE, Oosterlaan J, de Beurs E, Van den Brink W. Pathological gambling: a comprehensive review of biobehavioral findings. Neurosci Biobehav Rev, 2004;28(2):123–41.

Gover R. Here goes Kitten. New York: Grove; 1964.

Golden SA, Jin M, Heins C, Venniro M, Michaelides M, Shaham Y. Nucleus accumbens Drd1-expressing neurons control aggression self-administration and aggression seeking in mice. J Neurosci, 2019;39(13):2482–96.

Goldsmith O. An history of the earth, and animated nature. London: J. Nourse; 1774.

Goldstein A, Lowney LI, Pal BK. Stereospecific and nonspecific interactions of the morphine congener levorphanol in subcellular fractions of mouse brain. Proc Natl Acad Sci USA 1971;68(8):1742–7.

Goodman A. Sexual addiction: an Integrated Approach. Madison, Conn.: International Universities Press; 1998.

Goodwin DW, Crane JB, Guze SB. Phenomenological Aspects of the Alcoholic "Blackout." Br J Psychiatry 1969; 115(526):1033-8.

Goodwin DW, Othmer E, Halikas JA, Freemon F. Loss of Short Term Memory as a Predictor of the Alcoholic "Blackout." Nature 1970; 227(5254):201-2.

Goodwin DW, Powell B, Bremer D, Hoine H, Stern J. Alcohol and Recall: State-Dependent Effects in Man. Science. 1969; 163(3873):1358.

Gordis L. Consumption of methylxanthine-containing beverages and risk of pancreatic cancer. Cancer Lett. 1990; 52(1):1–12.

Gorwood P, Limosin F, Batel P, Hamon M, Adès J, Boni C. The A9 allele of the dopamine transporter gene is associated with delirium tremens and alcohol-withdrawal seizure. Biol Psychiatry. 2003; 53:85–92.

Grafton ST, Fadiga L, Arbib MA, Rizzolatti G. Premotor cortex activation during observation and naming of familiar tools. NeuroImage 1997;6(4):231–6.

Grahame-Smith DG. Self-medication with mood changing drugs. J Med Ethics. 1975;1(3):132-7.

Grahn R. The association between history of civil commitment for severe substance use and future imprisonment: A Swedish registry study. J Subst Abuse Treat 2021;108613.

Grant BF. Comorbidity between DSM-IV drug use disorders and major depression: Results of a national survey of adults. J Subst Abuse, 1995;7(4):481–97.

Grant BF, Hasin DS, Chou SP, Stinson FS, Dawson DA. Nicotine dependence and psychiatric disorders in the United States: results from the National Epidemiologic Survey on Alcohol and Related Conditions. Arch Gen Psychiatry. 2004;61(11):1107–15.

Grant BF, Shmulewitz D, Compton WM. Nicotine use and DSM-IV nicotine dependence in the United States, 2001–2002 and 2012–2013. Am J Psychiatry. 2020;177(11):1082-1090.

Grant S, London ED, Newlin DB, Villemagne VL, Liu X, Contoreggi C, Phillips RL, Kimes AS, Margolin A. Activation of memory circuits during cue-elicited cocaine craving. Proc Natl Acad Sci U S A. 1996; 93(21):12040-5.

Graves RJ. A System of Clinical Medicine. Dublin: Fannin; 1843.

Greenblatt DJ, Shader RI. Meprobamate: a study of irrational drug use. Am J Psychiatry; 1971; 127(10):1297–303.

Griner PF, Mayewski RJ, Mushlin AI, Greenland P. Selection and interpretation of diagnostic tests and procedures. Principles and applications. Ann Intern Med. 1981;94(4 Pt 2):557–92.

Grinker RR, Spiegel JP. Men Under Stress. Philadelphia: Blakiston; 1945.

Gross MM, Tobin M, Kissin B, Halpert E, Sabot L. Evoked Responses to clicks in delirium tremens: A preliminary report. Ann N Y Acad Sci. 1964;112: 543-6.:

Gross EG, Schiffrin MJ. Clinical Analgetics. Springfield, C.C. Thomas;1955.

Grollman A. Pharmacology and Therapeutics: A Textbook for Students and Practitioners of Medicine. Philadelphia: Lea & Febiger; 1951.

Gruber CM, Kohlstaedt KG, Moore RB, Peck FB. A study of the effects of Valmid, a non-barbiturate central nervous system depressant, in humans. J Pharmacol Exp Ther. 1954; 112(4):480.

Guillemin C, Provençal N, Suderman M, Côté SM, Vitaro F, Hallett M, Tremblay RE, Szyf M. DNA methylation signature of childhood chronic physical aggression in T cells of both men and women. PloS One, 2014;9(1): e86822–e86822.

Gulland JM, Robinson R. The morphine group. Part I. A discussion of the constitutional problem. J Chem Soc 1923; 123:980–8.

Guze SB, Woodruff RA Jr, Clayton PJ. Psychiatric disorders and criminality. JAMA, 1974;227(6):641–2.

Hagedorn JC, Encarnacion B, Brat GA, Morton JM. Does gastric bypass alter alcohol metabolism? Surg Obes Relat Dis. 2007; 3(5):543–8.

Hakluyt R, Goldsmid Edmund. The principal navigations, voyages, traffiques and discoveries of the English nation. Vol. I Edinburgh: E. & G. Goldsmid; 1885.

Hald J, Jacobsen E. A drug sensitising the organism to ethyl alcohol. The Lancet. 1948;252(6539):1001–4.

Halikas JA, Crosby RD, Pearson VL, Graves NM. A randomized double-blind study of carbamazepine in the treatment of cocaine abuse. Clin Pharmacol Ther 1997;62(1):89–105.

Hall GS. Senescence: the Last Half of Life. London; New York N.Y.: D. Appleton. 1922.

Hall K, Appelbaum P. The origins of commitment for substance abuse in the United States. J Am Acad Psychiatry Law Online 2002;30(1):33.

Hammett D. The Dain Curse. New York: Alfred A. Knopf; 1929.

Han J-S. Acupuncture: neuropeptide release produced by electrical stimulation of different frequencies. Trends Neurosci. 2003;26(1):17–22.

Handel AE, Ramagopalan SV. Is Lamarckian evolution relevant to medicine? BMC Med Genet. 2010; 11(1):73.

Hare EH, Dominian J, Sharpe L. Phenelzine and dexamphetamine in depressive illness. British Medical Journal 1962; 1: 9-12.

Hargrove EA, Ford FR. Acute and chronic barbiturate intoxication recent advances in therapeutic management. Calif Med. 1952; 77(6):383-6.

Harlow HF, Zimmermann RR. Affectional responses in the infant monkey; orphaned baby monkeys develop a strong and persistent attachment to inanimate surrogate mothers. Science. 1959;130(3373):421-32.

Harper C. The incidence of Wernicke's encephalopathy in Australia--a neuropathological study of 131 cases. J Neurol Neurosurg Psychiatry. 1983;46(7):593–8.

Hart E. Diet in disease: IV.-Stimulants: The coca of Peru-coca wine. Hospital (Rio J). Scientific Press; 1892; 13(317):51–2.

Hart J. The Anatomie of Vrines... Or, the Second Part of our Discourse of Vrines. London; 1625.

Harrison W. Harrison's Description of England in Shakespere's youth. Being the second and third books of his Description of Britaine and England. London: Pub. for the New Shakespere Society by N. Trubner; 1877.

Hartzler B, Fromme K. Fragmentary and en bloc blackouts: similarity and distinction among episodes of alcohol-induced memory loss. J Stud Alcohol. 2003; 64(4):547-50.

Harvey G. A discourse of the plague: containing the nature, causes, signs, and presages of the pestilence in general, together with the state of the present contagion: also most rational preservatives for families, and choice curative medicines both for rich and poor, with several waies for purifying the air in houses, streets, etc. London: Printed for Nath. Brooke; 1665.

Hasin DS, Johnson B, Meulien D, Ryan M, Fertig J. Evaluation of drinking risk levels as outcomes in alcohol pharmacotherapy trials: a secondary analysis of 3 randomized clinical trials. JAMA Psychiatry 2019;76(4):374-381.

Hatzfeld A, Darmesteter A. Dictionnaire général de la langue francaise du commencement du 17ieme siècle jusqu'à nos jours. Paris: Delagrave; 1964.

Hayman M. What psychiatrists think about alcoholism. Calif Med. 1955;83(6):435-40.

Heath CW. Differences between smokers and nonsmokers. AMA Arch Intern Med. 1958;101(2):377–88.

Hebb DO, Penfield W. Human behavior after extensive bilateral removal from the frontal lobes. Arch Neurol Psychiatry 1940;44(2):421–38.

Hebb DO. The Organisation of Behavior: A Neuropsychological Theory. New York: Wiley and Sons; 1949.

Hedegaard H, Miniño A, Warner M. Drug overdose deaths in the United States, 1999–2017. Hyattsville, MD, National Center for Health Statistics; 2018.

Heilig M, Epstein DH, Nader MA, Shaham Y. Time to connect: bringing social context into addiction neuroscience. Nat Rev Neurosci. 2016; 17(9):592-9.

Heller EA, Cates HM, Peña CJ, Sun H, Shao N, Feng J, Golden SA, Herman JP, Walsh JJ, Mazei-Robison M, Ferguson D, Knight S, Gerber MA, Nievera C, Han M-H, Russo SJ, Tamminga CS, Neve RL, Shen L, Zhang HS, Zhang F, Nestler EJ. Locus-specific epigenetic remodeling controls addiction- and depression-related behaviors. Nat Neurosci 2014; 17(12):1720-9.

Hemmingsen R, Vorstrup S, Clemmesen L, Holm S, Tfelt-Hansen P, Sørensen AS, Hansen C, Sommer W, Bolwig TG. Cerebral blood flow during delirium tremens and related clinical states studied with xenon-133 inhalation tomography. Am J Psychiatry. 1988; 145:1384–90.

Henderson DK, Gillespie RD. A Text-Book of Psychiatry. Oxford Medical Publications; London; 1927.

Henry. A glasse of the truthe. [London]: [By Thomas Berthelet]; 1532.

Heresbach C, Googe B. Foure Bookes of Husbandry, collected by M.C. Heresbachius ... Conteyning the whole arte and trade of Husbandry, with the antiquitie and commendation thereof. Newely Englished, and increased, by B. Googe, Esquire. B.L. R. Watkins: London; 1577.

Herodotus, Rawlinson G, Blakeney EH. The histories of Herodotus. London; New York: Dent; Dutton; 1970.

Heyes C. Empathy is not in our genes. Neurosci Biobehav Rev 2018; 95:499–507.

Heyes MP, Garnett ES, Coates G. Nigrostriatal dopaminergic activity is increased during exhaustive exercise stress in rats. Life Sci. 1988; 42(16):1537–42.

Higley JD, Hasert MF, Suomi SJ, Linnoila M. Nonhuman primate model of alcohol abuse: effects of early experience, personality, and stress on alcohol consumption. Proc Natl Acad Sci. 1991; 88(16):7261.

Hindley G, Beck K, Borgan F, Ginestet CE, McCutcheon R, Kleinloog D, Ganesh S, Radhakrishnan R, D'Souza DC, Howes OD. Psychiatric symptoms caused by cannabis constituents: a systematic review and meta-analysis. Lancet Psychiatry. 2020;7(4):344-53.

Hingson R, Zha W, Simons-Morton B, White A. Alcohol-induced blackouts as predictors of other drinking related harms among emerging young adults. Alcohol Clin Exp Res. 2016; 40(4):776–84.

Hinsie LE, Campbell RJ. Psychiatric Dictionary. New York: Oxford Univ. Pr.; 1960.

Ho A, Dole VP. Pain perception in drug-free and in methadone-maintained human ex-addicts. Proc Soc Exp Biol Med. 1979; 162(3):392-5.

Hofmann SG, Sawyer AT, Witt AA, Oh D. The effect of mindfulness-based therapy on anxiety and depression: A meta-analytic review. J Consult Clin Psychol 2010;78(2):169–83.

Holden C. "Behavioral" Addictions: Do They Exist? Science. 2001; 294(5544):980.

Holland JC, Morrow GR, Schmale A, Derogatis L, Stefanek M, Berenson S, Carpenter PJ,

Hollister LE. The present status of tranquilizing drugs. Calif Med. 1958;89(1):1–6.

Hollister LE. Chemical Psychoses. Annu Rev Med. 1964;15(1):203-14.

Hollister LE. Health aspects of cannabis. Pharmacol Rev. 1986;38(1):1-20.

Hopf FW, Martin M, Chen BT, Bowers MS, Mohamedi MM, Bonci A. Withdrawal from intermittent ethanol exposure increases probability of burst firing in VTA neurons in vitro. J Neurophysiol. 2007; 98(4):2297-310.

Horstmann C. The early south-English legendary, or lives of saints: mss. Laud, 108 in the Bodleian Library. London. 1887.

Hsu LKG, Benotti PN, Dwyer J, Roberts SB, Saltzman E, Shikora S, Rolls BJ, Rand W. Nonsurgical factors that influence the outcome of bariatric surgery: a review. Psychosom Med. 1998; 60(3).

Huarte J, Carew R. Examen de ingenios. The examination of mens wits. In which, by discouering the varietie of natures, is shewed for what profession each one is apt, and how far he shall profit therein. By Iohn Huarte. Translated out of the Spanish tongue by M. Camillo Camilli. Englished out of his Italian, by R.C. Esquire. London: printed by Adam Islip, for Thomas Adams; 1616.

Hughes J, Smith TW, Kosterlitz HW, Fothergill LA, Morgan BA, Morris HR. Identification of two related pentapeptides from the brain with potent opiate agonist activity. Nature 1975; 258:577–9.

Hume D. Essays and Treatises on Several Subjects. London; 1777.

Hunt L. The Seer: or, Common-places refreshed. London: E. Moxon; 1840.

Hunt WA, Barnett LW, Branch LG. Relapse rates in addiction programs. J. Clin. Psychol. 1971;27(4):455–6.

Huss M. Alcoholismus chronicus, eller Chronisk Alkoholssjukdom; est bidrag till dyskrasiernas kännedom, etc. Stockholm; 1849.

Hutt C, Bhavnani R. Predictions from play. Nature, 1972;237(5351):171–2.

Hutten U von., Turner Daniel. De morbo Gallico: publ. above 200 years past ... A treatise of the French disease. London: Clarke; 1730.

Huxley A. Brave new world. 1st ed. after the printing of two hundred and fifty deluxe copies. Garden City, N.Y: Doubleday, Doran & Co.; 1932.

Hyman SE, Malenka RC, Nestler EJ. Neural mechanisms of addiction: the role of reward-related learning and memory. Annu Rev Neurosci. 2006;29(1):565–98.

Insel TR, Young LJ. The neurobiology of attachment. Nat Rev Neurosci. 2001;2(2):129-36.

Institute of Medicine (US) Committee on Treatment of Alcohol Problems. Broadening the Base of Treatment for Alcohol Problems. Washington, DC: The National Academies Press; 1990.

Isbell H, Fraser HF, Wikler A, Belleville RE, Eisenman AJ. An experimental study of the etiology of "rum fits" and delirium tremens. Q J Stud Alcohol. 1955; 16:1–33.

Israelsson M, Nordlöf K, Gerdner A. European laws on compulsory commitment to care of persons suffering from substance use disorders or misuse problems- a comparative review from a human and civil rights perspective. Subst Abuse Treat Prev Policy 2015 Aug 28;10:34.

Iversen LL. Medical uses of marijuana? Nature. 1993;365(6441):12-3.

Izquierdo I, Izquierdo JA. Effects of drugs on deep brain centers. Annu Rev Pharmacol. 1971;11(1):189–208.

Jackson RH, Manaugh TS, Wiens AN, Matarazzo JD. A method for assessing the saliency level of areas in a person's current life situation. J Clin Psychol. 1971; 27(1):32-9.

Jaffe J. Drug addiction and drug abuse. In: Goodman LS, Gilman A, editors. Pharmacological Basis of Therapeutics. New York; London: Macmillan; Collier-Macmillan; 1970, p. 276–313.

Jaffe JH. Drug addiction and drug abuse. In: Goodman LS, Gilman A, Gilman AG, Koelle GG, editors. The Pharmacological Basis of Therapeutics Fifth ed., New York, NY: McMillan Publishing Co. Inc. 1975.

Jain A, Christopher P, Appelbaum PS. Civil commitment for opioid and other substance use disorders: does it work? Psychiatr Serv 2018;69(4):374–6.

Jain A, Christopher PP, Fisher CE, Choi CJ, Appelbaum PS. Civil commitment for substance use disorders: a national survey of addiction medicine physicians. J Addict Med 2021;15(4).

James H. The American. Boston, MA: James R. Osgood and Co. 1877.

James O, Day C. Non-alcoholic steatohepatitis: another disease of affluence. The Lancet. 1999; 353(9165):1634–6.

James W. Psychological literature: Abnormal. Psychol Rev. 1894; 1(2):199.

Jamison KR. Suicide and bipolar disorder. J Clin Psychiatry. 2000; 61(suppl 9):47-51.

Janal MN, Colt EWD, Clark WC, Glusman M. Pain sensitivity, mood and plasma endocrine levels in man following long-distance running: Effects of naloxone. Pain. 1984; 19(1):13–25.

Jasinski DR, Pevnick JS, Griffith JD. Human pharmacology and abuse potential of the analgesic buprenorphine: a potential agent for treating narcotic addiction. Arch Gen Psychiatry 1978; 35: 501–16.

Jasinski DR, Preston KL. Evaluation of mixtures of morphine and d-amphetamine for subjective and physiological effects. Drug Alcohol Depend. 1986; 17(1):1-13.

Jellinek EM. The disease concept of alcoholism. New Haven: College and University Press in association with Hillhouse Press; 1960.

Jenkins MA, Langlais PJ, Delis D, Cohen R. Learning and memory in rape victims with posttraumatic stress disorder. Am J Psychiatry. 1998; 155(2):278–9.

Jiao C, Wang T, Peng X, Cui F. Impaired empathy processing in individuals with internet addiction disorder: an event-related potential study. Front Hum Neurosci 2017; 11:498.

Jin X-T, Tucker BR, Drenan RM. Nicotine self-administration induces plastic changes to nicotinic receptors in medial habenula. eNeuro. 2020;7(4): ENEURO.0197-20.2020.

Joffe A, Yancy WS. Legalization of marijuana: potential impact on youth. Pediatrics. 2004; 113(6): e632.

John B, Lewis KR. Chromosome variability and geographic distribution in insects. Science. 1966; 152(3723):711-21.

Johnson G. The physiology and pathology of the circulation. Br Med J, 1871;1(542):524–5.

Johnson J. On syncope angens. Medico-Chir J Rev. 1817; 3(14):101-8.

Johnson RE, Chutuape MA, Strain EC, Walsh SL, Stitzer ML, Bigelow GE. A comparison of levomethadyl acetate, buprenorphine, and methadone for opioid dependence. N Engl J Med. 2000; 343:1290-7.

Johnson S. Lives of the Most Eminent English Poets. [Place of publication not identified]: Gale Ecco, Print Editions; 2018.

Johnson S. Bruce R, editor. The letters of Samuel Johnson Vol. III: 1777 – 1781. Oxford: Clarendon; 1992.

Jolly F. Ueber die psychischen Stoerungen bei Polyneuritis. Charite-Ann. 1897; 22:579–612.

Jones J. The arte and science of preseruing bodie and soule in healthe, wisedome, and Catholike religion: phisically, philosophically, and diuinely deuised: by Iohn Iones phisition. Right profitable for all persones: but chiefly for princes, rulers, nobles, byshoppes, preachers, parents, and them of the Parliament house. London: Henrie Bynneman; 1579.

Jones RH. Physical indices and clinical assessments of the nutrition of schoolchildren. J R Stat Soc. 1938;101(1):1–52.

Josselyn SA, Tonegawa S. Memory engrams: Recalling the past and imagining the future. Science. 2020;367(6473): eaaw4325.

Joyce EM. Aetiology of alcoholic brain damage: alcoholic neurotoxicity or thiamine malnutrition? Br Med Bull. 1994;50(1):99–114.

Kafka MP. Hypersexual disorder: a proposed diagnosis for DSM-V. Arch Sex Behav 2010;39(2):377–400.

Kagan J. New views on cognitive development. J Youth Adolesc. 1976; 5(2):113-29.

Kalant H, Kalant OJ. Death in amphetamine users: causes and rates. Can Med Assoc J. 1975; 112(3):299-304.

Kalant H, LeBlanc AE, Gibbins RJ. Tolerance to, and dependence on, some non-opiate psychotropic drugs. Pharmacological Reviews 1971; 23, 135-191.

Kalant OJ. The Amphetamines : Toxicity and Addiction. Toronto, Canada: Addiction Research Foundation, University of Toronto Press; 1973.

Kalivas PW, Volkow ND. The neural basis of addiction: a pathology of motivation and choice. Am J Psychiatry 2005;162(8):1403–13.

Kandel D. Stages in adolescent involvement in drug use. Science. 1975; 190(4217):912–4.

Kane HH. Rapid and easy cure of a case of morphine habit of twelve years' standing. Amount used sixteen grains per day. The Medical and Surgical Reporter. Philadelphia, PA; 1881;650.

Karatsoreos IN, Bhagat S, Bloss EB, Morrison JH, McEwen BS. Disruption of circadian clocks has ramifications for metabolism, brain, and behavior. Proc Natl Acad Sci. 2011; 108(4):1657–62.

Karler R, Calder LD, Sangdee P, Turkanis SA. Interaction between delta-9-tetrahydro-cannabinol and kindling by electrical and chemical stimuli in mice. Neuropharmacology 1984;23(11):1315–20.

Kassel JD, Shiffman S. What can hunger teach us about drug craving? A comparative analysis of the two constructs. Urges Cravings. 1992; 14(3):141-67.

Kataoka N, Shima Y, Nakajima K, Nakamura K. A central master driver of psychosocial stress responses in the rat. Science. 2020; 367(6482):1105-12.

Katz RL. Empathy: Its Nature and Uses. New York: Free Press of Glencoe; 1963.

Keefe FJ, Somers TJ. Psychological approaches to understanding and treating arthritis pain. Nat Rev Rheumatol. 2010; 6(4):210-6.

Keefe PR. Empire of Pain. The secret history of the Sackler dynasty. New York: Doubleday; 2021.

Kellam SG, Ensminger ME, Simon MB. Mental health in first grade and teenage drug, alcohol, and cigarette use. Drug Alcohol Depend. 1980;5(4):273–304.

Kellam SG, Rebok GW, Ialongo N, Mayer LS. The course and malleability of aggressive behavior from early First Grade into Middle School: results of a developmental epidemiologically-based preventive trial. J Child Psychol Psychiatry. 1994; 35(2):259-81.

Kelly JF. Is Alcoholics Anonymous religious, spiritual, neither? Findings from 25 years of mechanisms of behavior change research. Addiction. 2017;112(6):929-36.

Kelly JF, Greene MC, Bergman BG. Beyond Abstinence: Changes in indices of quality of life with time in recovery in a nationally representative sample of U.S. adults. Alcohol. Clin. Exp. Res. 2018;42(4):770–80.

Kelly JF, Westerhoff CM. Does it matter how we refer to individuals with substance-related conditions? A randomized study of two commonly used terms. Int J Drug Policy. 2010;21(3):202–7.

Kendler KS, Ohlsson H, Sundquist J, Sundquist K. A contagion model for within-family transmission of drug abuse. Am J Psychiatry 2019;176(3):239–48.

Kendler KS, Prescott CA. Caffeine intake, tolerance, and withdrawal in women: A population-based twin study. Am J Psychiatry. 1999; 156(2):223-8.

Kermani EJ, Castaneda R. Psychoactive substance use in forensic psychiatry. Am J Drug Alcohol Abuse. 1996;22(1):1–27.

Kerr NS. Inebriety, or narcomania; its etiology, pathology, treatment, and jurisprudence. Edinburgh Med J. 1894;40(3):242–243.

Kersey John. Dictionarium Anglo-Britannicum. London; H. Rhodes; and J. Taylor: Printed by J. Wilde, for J. Phillips; 1708.

Kessler RC, Sonnega A, Bromet E, Hughes M, Nelson CB. Posttraumatic Stress Disorder in the National Comorbidity Survey. Arch Gen Psychiatry. 1995; 52(12):1048–60.

Kety SS. Biochemical theories of schizophrenia. Science 1959; 129: 1528-1532.

Khantzian, EJ, Mack JE, Schatzberg AF. Heroin use as an attempt to cope: clinical observations. Am J Psychiatry. 1974; 131:160-164.

Khatami M, Rush JA. A one-year follow-up of the multimodal treatment for chronic pain. Pain. 1982; 14(1):45-52.

Kim YH, Zhao RJ, Lee SM, Kim MS, Lim SC, Kim JS, Lee HJ, Yang CH, Kim HY, Lee YK, Lee BH. Acupuncture inhibits reinstatement of intravenous methamphetamine self-administration via gamma aminobutyric acid pathway. NeuroReport. 2020;31(4):352-8.

Kimble GA, Hilgard ER (Ernest R. Hilgard and Marquis' Conditioning and learning. New York, NY: Appleton-Century Company; 1940.

Kilty J, Lorang D, Amara S. Cloning and expression of a cocaine-sensitive rat dopamine transporter. Science, 1991;254(5031):578.

King DL, Wölfling K, Potenza MN. Taking gaming disorder treatment to the next level. JAMA Psychiatry. JAMA Psychiatry, 2020;77(8):869-70.

Kinglake R. On dyspepsia. Med Phys J. Printed for R. Phillips; 1802; 7(39):425–9.

Kinglake R. On sedative efficiency. Med Phys J. 1802;7(40):522–8.

Kinsey AC Pomeroy, Wardell B, Martin, Clyde E. Sexual Behavior in the Human Male. Philadephia; London: W. B. Saunders Company; 1948.

Klag S, O'Callaghan F, Creed P. The use of legal coercion in the treatment of substance abusers: an overview and critical analysis of thirty years of research. Subst Use Misuse 2005;40(12):1777–95.

Klatsky AL, Armstrong MA. Alcohol, smoking, coffee, and cirrhosis. Am J Epidemiol. 1992; 136(10):1248-57.

Knoll J. Enhancer regulation/endogenous and synthetic enhancer compounds: a neurochemical concept of the innate and acquired drives. Neurochem Res. 2003;28(8):1275–97.

Kolla NJ, Bortolato M. The role of monoamine oxidase A in the neurobiology of aggressive, antisocial, and violent behavior: A tale of mice and men. Prog Neurobiol, 2020;194:101875.

Koo C, Wati Y, Lee CC, Oh HY. Internet-addicted kids and South Korean government efforts: boot-camp case. Cyberpsychology Behav Soc Netw, 2011;14(6):391–4.

Koob GF. The Dark Side of Addiction: The Horsley Gantt to Joseph Brady Connection. J Nerv Ment Dis. 2017;205(4):270–2.

Koob GF, Colrain IM. Alcohol use disorder and sleep disturbances: a feed-forward allostatic framework. Neuropsychopharmacology. 2020; 45(1):141–65.

Koob GF, Le Moal M. Neurobiology of addiction. Amsterdam; Boston: Elsevier/Academic Press; 2006.

Kornetsky C, Esposito RU. Reward and detection thresholds for brain stimulation: dissociative effects of cocaine. Brain Res 1981;209(2):496–500.

Korsakoff SS. Psychic disorder in conjunction with multiple neuritis: (Psychosis polyneuritica s. cerebropathia psychica toxaemica). Neurology. 1955;5(6):396–406.

Kosobud A, Crabbe JC. Ethanol withdrawal in mice bred to be genetically prone or resistant to ethanol withdrawal seizures. J Pharmacol Exp Ther. 1986; 238:170.

Kosten TR, Rounsaville BJ, Babor F, Spitzer RL, Williams JB. Substance use disorders in DSM-III-R: evidence for the dependence syndrome across different psychoactive substances. British Journal Psychiatry, 1987; 151, 834-843.

Krafft-Ebing R von. Psychopathia sexualis: mit besonderer Berucksichtigung der contraren Sexualempfindung ; eine klinisch-forensische Studie. Stuttgart: Enke; 1892.

Kranaster L, Aksay SS, Bumb JM, Janke C, Sartorius A. The "Forgotten" Treatment of alcohol withdrawal delirium with eectroconvulsive therapy: Successful use in a very prolonged and severe case. Clin Neuropharmacol. 2017; 40:183–4.

Kraus SW, Voon V, Potenza MN. Should compulsive sexual behavior be considered an addiction? Addiction 2016;111(12):2097–106.

Krut LH, Perrin MJ, Bronte-Stewart B. Taste perception in smokers and non-smokers. Br Med J. 1961;1(5223):384–7.

Krystal H. The physiological basis of the treatment of delirium tremens. Am J Psychiatry. 1959; 116:137–47.

Kubena RK, Barry H. Interactions of Δ^1-tetrahydrocannabinol with barbiturates and methamphetamine. J Pharmacol Exp Ther. 1970; 173(1):94.

Kühn S, Gallinat J. Neurobiological Basis of Hypersexuality. Zahr NM, Peterson ET, editors. Int Rev Neurobiol 2016; 129:67–83.

Kuhn SM. The Vespasian psalter. Ann Arbor: U. of Michigan P.; 1965.

Kwako LE, Schwandt ML, Ramchandani VA, Diazgranados N, Koob GF, Volkow ND, Blanco C, Goldman D. Neurofunctional Domains Derived from Deep Behavioral Phenotyping in Alcohol Use Disorder. Am J Psychiatry. 2019; 176(9)744-53.

Labonté B, Abdallah K, Maussion G, Yerko V, Yang J, Bittar T, Quessy F, Golden SA, Navarro L, Checknita D, Gigek C, Lopez JP, Neve RL, Russo SJ, Tremblay RE, Côté G, Meaney MJ, Mechawar N, Nestler EJ, Turecki G. Regulation of impulsive and aggressive behaviours by a novel lncRNA. Mol Psychiatry, 2020;10.1038/s41380-019-0637-4.

Laghi F, Bianchi D, Pompili S, Lonigro A, Baiocco R. Cognitive and affective empathy in binge drinking adolescents: Does empathy moderate the effect of self-efficacy in resisting peer pressure to drink? Addict Behav 2019; 89:229–35.

Lamm C, Rütgen M, Wagner IC. Imaging empathy and prosocial emotions. Neurosci Lett 2019; 693:49–53.

Langley JN, Dickinson WL. Action of various poisons upon nerve-fibres and peripheral nerve-cells. J Physiol, 1890;11(suppl):509–27.

Langley JN. The autonomic nervous system. Brain, 1903;26(1):1–26.

Langley JN. Sketch of the progress of discovery in the eighteenth century as regards the autonomic nervous system. J Physiol, 1916;50(4):225–58.

Lappalainen J, Long JC, Eggert M, Ozaki N, Robin RW, Brown GL, Naukkarinen H, Virkkunen M, Linnoila M, Goldman D. Linkage of antisocial alcoholism to the serotonin 5-HT1B receptor gene in 2 populations. Arch Gen Psychiatry, 1998;55(11):989–94.

Larson PS, Haag HB, Silvette H. Tobacco: Experimental and clinical studies: A comprehensive account of the world literature. Baltimore, MD: Williams and Wilkins; 1968.

Lasker GW. Human biological adaptability. Science. 1969; 166(3912):1480.

Lasswitz K. Ueber psychophysische Energie und ihre Factoren. Philos Rev 1895;4(6):665–79.
Le Berre A-P. Emotional processing and social cognition in alcohol use disorder. Neuropsychology 2019;33(6):808–21.

Lau MA, Bishop SR, Segal ZV, Buis T, Anderson ND, Carlson L, Shapiro S, Carmody J, Abbey S, Devins G. The Toronto Mindfulness Scale: development and validation. J Clin Psychol 2006;62(12):1445–67.

Lawson-Wood D. Chinese system of healing; an introductory handbook to Chinese massage treatment at the Chinese acupuncture points for influencing the psyche; with diagrams, repertories, and indexes. Grayshott, Eng.: Health Science Press; 1959.

Lawrence AJ, Luty J, Bogdan NA, Sahakian BJ, Clark L. Problem gamblers share deficits in im-pulsive decision-making with alcohol-dependent individuals. Addiction, 2009;104(6):1006–15.

Lazar SW, Kerr CE, Wasserman RH, Gray JR, Greve DN, Treadway MT, McGarvey M, Quinn BT, Dusek JA, Benson H, Rauch SL, Moore CI, Fischl B. Meditation experience is associated with increased cortical thickness. Neuroreport 2005;16(17):1893–7.

LeDain G. Interim report of the Commission of Inquiry into the Non-medical Use of Drugs. Ottawa: Information Canada; 1970.

Lee B, Kim B-K, Kim H-J, Jung IC, Kim A-R, Park H-J, Kwon O-J, Lee J-H, Kim J-H. Efficacy and safety of electroacupuncture for insomnia disorder: a multicenter, randomized, assessor-blinded, controlled trial. Nat Sci Sleep. 2020; 12:1145–59.

Leigh J, Bowen S, Marlatt GA. Spirituality, mindfulness and substance abuse. Addict Behav 2005;30(7):1335–41.

Lepack AE, Werner CT, Stewart AF, Fulton SL, Zhong P, Farrelly LA, Smith ACW, Ramakrishnan A, Lyu Y, Bastle RM, Martin JA, Mitra S, O'Connor RM, Wang Z-J, Molina H, Turecki G, Shen L, Yan Z, Calipari ES, Dietz DM, Kenny PJ, Maze I. Dopaminylation of histone H3 in ventral tegmental area regulates cocaine seeking. Science. 2020; 368(6487):197.

Lerner CA, Sundar IK, Yao H, Gerloff J, Ossip DJ, McIntosh S, Robinson R, Rahman I. Vapors produced by electronic cigarettes and e-juices with flavorings induce toxicity, oxidative stress, and inflammatory response in lung epithelial cells and in mouse lung. PloS One. 2015;10(2): e0116732–e0116732.

Lesieur HR. Chase - Career of the Compulsive Gambler. Garden City, N.Y.: Anchor Press; 1977.

Lesieur HR. Editor's introduction. J Gambling Stud, 1985;1:3–7.

Lesieur HR, Rosenthal RJ. Pathological gambling: A review of the literature (prepared for the American Psychiatric Association task force on DSM-IV committee on disorders of impulse control not elsewhere classified). J Gambling Stud, 1991;7:5–39.

Lesch OM, Kefer J, Lentner S, Mader R, Marx B, Musalek M, Nimmerrichter A, Preinsberger H, Puchinger H, Rustembegovic A, Walter H, Zach, E. Diagnosis of chronic alcoholism – classificatory problems. Psychopathology 1990;23(2):88–96.

Leshner AI. Addiction is a brain disease, and it matters. Science 1997;278(5335): 45.

L'Estrange R. Fables of AEsop, and other eminent mythologists with morals and reflexions. London: London: Printed for R. Sare, T. Sawbridge, B. Took, M. Gillyflower, A. & J. Churchill, and J. Hindmarsh, 1692.

Lette K. Girl's night out. New York: W. Morrow. 1989.

Levin HS, Peters BH, Hulkonen DA. Early Concepts of Anterograde and Retrograde Amnesia. Cortex. 1983; 19(4):427-40.

Lewy J. Limited to no responsibility: addiction, alcoholism and the law in modern Germany. Hist Psychiatry 2012;23(2):169–81.

Li W, Howard MO, Garland EL, McGovern P, Lazar M. Mindfulness treatment for substance misuse: A systematic review and meta-analysis. J Subst Abuse Treat 2017; 75:62–96.

Liebig J. Ueber die Verbindungen, welche durch die Einwirkung des Chlors auf Alkohol, Aether, ölbildendes Gas und Essiggeist entstehen. Annalen der Pharmacie. 1832;1(2):182–230.

Liljestrand G. Carl Koller and the development of local anesthesia. Acta Physiol Scand, 1967;71(s299):1–30.

Linden MA, Sheldon RD, Meers GM, Ortinau LC, Morris EM, Booth FW, Kanaley JA, Vieira-Potter VJ, Sowers JR, Ibdah JA, Thyfault JP, Laughlin MH, Rector RS. Aerobic exercise training in the treatment of non-alcoholic fatty liver disease related fibrosis. J Physiol. 2016; 594(18):5271–84.

Lindner GA, De Garmo C. Manual of Empirical Psychology as an Inductive Science. Boston: Heath; 1890.

Lindner RM. The psychodynamics of gambling. Ann Am Acad Pol Soc Sci, 1950;269:93–107.

Linnoila M, Mefford I, Nutt D, Adinoff B. NIH conference. Alcohol withdrawal and noradrenergic function. Ann Intern Med. 1987; 107:875–89.

Linnoila M, Virkkunen M, Scheinin M, Nuutila A, Rimon R, Goodwin FK. Low cerebrospinal fluid 5-hydroxyindoleacetic acid concentration differentiates impulsive from nonimpulsive violent behavior. Life Sci, 1983;33(26):2609–14.

Lishman WA. Cerebral disorder in alcoholism syndromes of impairment. Brain. 1981;104(1):1–20.

Liu L, Potenza MN, Lacadie CM, Zhang J-T, Yip SW, Xia C-C, Lan J, Yao Y-W, Deng L-Y, Park SQ, Fang X-Y. Altered intrinsic connectivity distribution in internet gaming disorder and its associations with psychotherapy treatment outcomes. Addict Biol, 2021;26:e12917.

Liu S, Wang Z-F, Su Y-S, Ray RS, Jing X-H, Wang Y-Q, Ma Q. Somatotopic organization and intensity dependence in driving distinct NPY-expressing sympathetic pathways by electroacupuncture. Neuron. 2020;108(3):436-50.

Locke J. An Essay concerning humane understanding. Printed for Tho. Basset, and sold by Edw. Mory: London; 1690.

Locke J. An essay concerning humane understanding. London; And Samuel Manship, at the Ship in Cornhill, near the Royal Exchange: Printed for Thomas Dring, at the Harrow, over-against the Inner-Temple Gate in Fleet-street; 1694.

Lofft C. Self-formation: or the history of an individual mind. London: Knight. 1837.

Lomax P, Schönbaum E. Body temperature: regulation, drug effects, and therapeutic implications. New York: M. Dekker; 1979.

Lømo T. The discovery of long-term potentiation. Philos Trans R Soc Lond B Biol Sci 2003;358(1432):617–20.

Lord H. A display of two forraigne sects in the East Indies vizt: the sect of the Banians the ancient natiues of India and the sect of the Persees the ancient inhabitants of Persia08 together with the religion and maners of each sect collected into two bookes by Henry Lord sometimes resident in East India and preacher to the Hoble Company of Merchants trading thether. Imprinted at London: [By T. and R. Cotes] for Francis Constable and are to be sold at his shoppe in Paules Church yard at the signe of the Crane; 1630.

Loomis AL, Harvey EN, Hobart G. Potential rhythms of the cerebral cortex during sleep. Science. 1935; 81(2111):597.

Lopez-Quintero C, Hasin DS, de los Cobos JP, Pines A, Wang S, Grant BF, Blanco C. Probability and predictors of remission from life-time nicotine, alcohol, cannabis or cocaine dependence: results from the National Epidemiologic Survey on Alcohol and Related Conditions. Addiction 2011;106(3):657–69.

Lovinger D, White G, Weight F. Ethanol inhibits NMDA-activated ion current in hippocampal neurons. Science. 1989; 243:1721.

Lucas WL. Predicting initial use of marijuana from correlates of marijuana use: assessment of panel and cross-sectional data 1969-1976. Int J Addict. 1978; 13(7):1035-47.

Lydgate J, Bergen H. Lydgate's Fall of Princes. [Place of publication not identified]: Carnegie Institution of Washington; 1923.

Lydgate J, Colonne G delle, Benoît de S-M, Bergen H, Furnivall FJ. Lydgate's Troy Book. A.D. 1412-20. 1906.

MacAndrew C, Edgerton RB. Drunken Comportment: A Social Explanation. Chicago: Aldine Pub. Co.; 1969.

MacDonald PW. Observations on some of the new hypnotics. Bristol Medico-Chir J 1883. J.W. Arrowsmith; 1887; 5(18):257–63.

MacLean PD, Delgado JMR. Electrical and chemical stimulation of frontotemporal portion of limbic system in the waking animal. Electroencephalogr Clin Neurophysiol 1953;5(1):91–100.

MacMahon B, Yen S, Trichopoulos D, Warren K, Nardi G. Coffee and cancer of the pancreas. N Engl J Med. 1981; 304(11):630-3.

MacNeill GP, editor. Thomas of Erceldoune. Printed for the Society by W. Blackwood and Sons, 1886.

Macrae-Gibson OD, editor. Of Arthour and of Merlin. Oxford, London and Toronto, Oxford University Press (Early English Text Society. Original Series, 268 and 279), 1973-1979.

Maddison A. Contours of the world economy, 1-2030 AD: essays in macro-economic history. Oxford, Oxford Univ. Press; 2013.

Madsen K. Theories of Motivation. In: Wolman BB, Pomeroy LR, Helson Harry, editors. Handbook of General Psychology. Englewood Cliffs: Prentice-Hall; 1973. p. 673-706.

Maehle A-H. "Receptive substances": John Newport Langley (1852-1925) and his path to a receptor theory of drug action. Med Hist Medical History, 2004;48(2):153–74.

Maes M, Vandoolaeghe E, Degroote J, Altamura C, Roels C, Hermans P. Linear CT-scan measurements in alcohol-dependent patients with and without delirium tremens. Alcohol. 2000; 20:117–23.

Magendie F. A formulary for the preparation and medical administration of certain new remedies. London; 1835.

Magliozzi JR, Kanter SL, Csernansky JG, Hollister LE. Detection of marijuana use in psychiatric patients by determination of urinary delta-9-tetrahydrocannabinol-11-oic acid. J Nerv Ment Dis. 1983;171(4).

Mainzer F, Krause M. Nicotinic acid in delirium tremens. Br Med J. 1939; 2:331–2.

Malan DH, Bacal HA, Heath ES, Balfour FHG. A study of psychodynamic changes in untreated neurotic patients: I. Improvements that are questionable on dynamic criteria. Br. J. Psychiatry. 1968;114(510):525–51.

Malandain L, Blanc J-V, Ferreri F, Thibaut F. Pharmacotherapy of sexual addiction. Curr Psychiatry Rep 2020;22(6):30.

Mann F. Acupuncture analgesia: Report of 100 experiments. Br J Anaesth. 1974;46(5):361–4.

Mann JJ, Waternaux C, Haas GL, Malone KM. Toward a Clinical Model of Suicidal Behavior in Psychiatric Patients. Am J Psychiatry. 1999; 156(2):181-9.

Manson MP. A psychometric determination of alcoholic addiction. Am J Psychiatry. 1949;106(3):199–205.

Marangos PJ, Boulenger JP. Basic and clinical aspects of adenosinergic neuromodulation. Neurosci Biobehav Rev. 1985; 9(3):421–30.

Mardones J, Segovia N, Onfray E. Relationship between the dose of factor N and the alcohol intake of rats under self-selection conditions. Arch Biochem. 1946; 9:401–6.

Marfaing-Jallat P, Larue C, Le Magnen J. Alcohol intake in hypothalamic hyperphagic rats. Physiol Behav. 1970; 5(3):345-51.

Marino EN, Fromme K. Early onset drinking predicts greater level but not growth of alcohol-induced blackouts beyond the effect of binge drinking during emerging adulthood. Alcohol Clin Exp Res. 2016; 40(3):599-605.

Marlatt GA. Buddhist philosophy and the treatment of addictive behavior. Cogn Behav Pract. 2002;9(1):44–50.

Marlatt GA, Baer JS, Donovan DM, Kivlahan DR. Addictive behaviors: etiology and treatment. Annu Rev Psychol. 1988; 39(1):223-52.

Marlatt GA, Gordon JR. Relapse prevention : maintenance strategies in the treatment of addictive behaviors. New York; London: Guilford Press; 1985.

Martensen-Larsen O. Treatment of alcoholism with a sensitising drug. The Lancet. 1948;252(6539):1004–5.

Martin PR. The human genetics of alcoholism. Subst Alcohol Actions Misuse. 1981; 2:389-406.

Martin PR, Adinoff B, Eckardt MJ, Stapleton JM, Bone GAH, Rubinow DR, Lane EA, Linnoila M. Effective pharmacotherapy of alcoholic amnestic disorder with fluvoxamine: preliminary findings. Arch Gen Psychiatry. 1989;46(7):617–21.

Martin PR, Adinoff B, Weingartner H, Mukherjee AB, Eckardt MJ. Alcoholic organic brain disease: nosology and pathophysiologic mechanisms. Prog Neuropsychopharmcol Biol Psychiatry. 1986;10(2):147–64.

Martin PR, Bhushan CM, Kapur BM, Whiteside EA, Sellers EM. Intravenous phenobarbital therapy in barbiturate and other hypnosedative withdrawal reactions: a kinetic approach. Clin Pharmacol Ther. 1979;26(2):256–64.

Martin PR, Finlayson AJR. Pharmacopsychosocial treatment of opioid dependence: harm reduction, palliation, or simply good medical practice? Düşünen Adam J Psychiatry Neurol Sci, 2012;25:1–7.

Martin PR, Gibbs SJ, Nimmerrichter AA, Riddle WR, Welch LW, Willcott MR. Brain proton magnetic resonance spectroscopy studies in recently abstinent alcoholics. Alcohol Clin Exp Res. 1995;19(4):1078–82.

Martin PR, Lovinger D, Breese G. Alcohol and other abused substances. In: Munson P, Mueller R, Breese G, editors. Princ Pharmacol Basic Concepts Clin Appl. New York: Chapman & Hall; 1995. p. 417–52.

Martin PR, Patel S. Pharmacology of drugs of abuse. In: Golan DE, Armstrong EJ, Armstrong AW, editors. Principles of Pharmacology: The Pathophysiologic Basis of Drug Therapy (Fourth ed., pp. 308-334). Philadelphia: Wolters Kluwer Health. 2017.

Martin PR, Petry NM. Are non-substance-related addictions really addictions? Am J Addict, 2005;14(1):1–7.
Martin PR, Rio D, Adinoff B, Johnson, JL, Bisserbe JC, Rawlings RR, Rohrbaugh JW, Stapleton JM, Eckardt MJ. Regional cerebral glucose utilization in chronic organic mental disorders associated with alcoholism. J Neuropsychiatry Clin Neurosci. 1992;4(2):159–67.

Martin PR, Singleton CK, Hiller-Sturmhöfel S. The role of thiamine deficiency in alcoholic brain disease. Alcohol Res Health. 2003;27(2):134–42.

Martin PR, Weinberg BA, Bealer BK. Healing Addiction: An Integrated Pharmacopsychosocial Approach to Treatment. Hoboken, New Jersey: John Wiley & Sons, Inc. 2007.

Martin WR. Opioid antagonists. Pharmacol Rev 1967; 19:463.

Martin WR, Jasinski DR. Physiological parameters of morphine dependence in man—Tolerance, early abstinence, protracted abstinence. J Psychiatric Res. 1969; 7: 9-17.

Marx K, Stenning HJ: Selected essays. New York, International Publishers; 1926.

Maugham WS. Of Human Bondage: A Novel. London; 1915.

May ME, Kennedy CH. Aggression as positive reinforcement in mice under various ratio- and time-based reinforcement schedules. J Exp Anal Behav, 2009;91(2):185–96.

Mayfield FH, Schwemlein GX, Hawkins JR. Howard Douglas Fabing. Feb. 21, 1907-July 29, 1970. Neurology. 1971;21(3):310-1.

Mayfield D, Mcleod G, Hall P. The CAGE questionnaire: validation of a new alcoholism screening instrument. Am J Psychiatry. 1974;131(10):1121–3.

Mayne RG, Sedgwick LW, Power H. The New Sydenham Society's Lexicon of Medicine and the Allied Sciences: (based on Mayne's Lexicon). London: The Society; 1881.

Mayo-Smith MF, Beecher LH, Fischer TL, Gorelick DA, Guillaume JL, Hill A, Jara G, Kasser C, Melbourne J, for the Working Group on the Management of Alcohol Withdrawal Delirium PGC American Society of Addiction Medicine. Management of Alcohol Withdrawal Delirium: An Evidence-Based Practice Guideline. Arch Intern Med. 2004; 164:1405–12.

McBain RK, Wong EC, Breslau J, Shearer AL, Cefalu MS, Roth E, Burnam MA, Collins RL. State medical marijuana laws, cannabis use and cannabis use disorder among adults with elevated psychological distress. Drug Alcohol Depend. 2020; 215:108191.

McDougall W. An introduction to social psychology. London: Methuen; 1908.

McEwen BS. Physiology and neurobiology of stress and adaptation: central role of the brain. Physiol Rev. 2007; 87(3):873-904.

McGaugh JL. Drug facilitation of learning and memory. Annu Rev Pharmacol. 1973;13(1):229–41.

McLellan AT, Grossman DS, Blaine JD, Haverkos HW. Acupuncture treatment for drug abuse: A technical review. J Subst Abuse Treat. 1993;10(6):569–76.

McLellan AT, Lewis DC, O'Brien CP, Kleber HD. Drug dependence, a chronic medical illness: implications for treatment, insurance, and outcomes evaluation. JAMA. 2000;284(13):1689–95.

McLellan AT, Luborsky L, Woody GE, O'Brien CP. An improved diagnostic evaluation instrument for substance abuse patients: the Addiction Severity Index. J Nerv Ment Dis. 1980;168(1).

McLellan AT, Woody GE, O'Brien CP. Development of psychiatric illness in drug abusers. N Engl J Med. 1979;301(24):1310-4.

McClernon FJ, Kozink RV, Lutz AM, Rose JE. 24-h smoking abstinence potentiates fMRI-BOLD activation to smoking cues in cerebral cortex and dorsal striatum. Psychopharmacology (Berl). 2009; 204(1):25-35.

McClintick MN, Grant KA. Aggressive temperament predicts ethanol self-administration in late adolescent male and female rhesus macaques. Psychopharmacology (Berl), 2016;233(23-24):3965-3976.

McClintick JN, Xuei X, Tischfield JA, Goate A, Foroud T, Wetherill L, Ehringer MA, Edenberg HJ. Stress–response pathways are altered in the hippocampus of chronic alcoholics. Alcohol. 2013; 47(7):505-15.

McCool BA, Plonk SG, Martin PR, Singleton CK. Cloning of human transketolase cDNAs and comparison of the nucleotide sequence of the coding region in Wernicke-Korsakoff and non-Wernicke-Korsakoff individuals. J Biol Chem. 1993;268(2):1397–404.

McEwen BS. Physiology and neurobiology of stress and adaptation: central role of the brain. Physiol Rev. 2007; 87(3):873–904.

McLuhan M. Understanding Media: the Extension of Man. London: New American Library; 1964.

Meaney MJ. Maternal care, gene expression, and the transmission of individual differences in stress reactivity across generations. Annu Rev Neurosci. 2001; 24(1):1161-92.

Mechoulam R, Gaoni Y. A Total synthesis of dl-Δ1-Tetrahydrocannabinol, the active constituent of hashish. J Am Chem Soc. American Chemical Society; 1965;87(14):3273-5.

Mechoulam R, Gaoni Y. The absolute configuration of δ1-tetrahydrocannabinol, the major active constituent of hashish. Tetrahedron Lett. 1967;8(12):1109-11.

Medakovic M, Banic B. The action of reserpine and α-methyl-m-tyrosine on the analgesic effect of morphine in rats and mice. J Pharm Pharmacol. 1964; 16(3):198-206.

Medicus. Remarks on the history and use of tobacco. Med Phys J. 1810;24(142):445–60.

Meerloo JA. Addiction abstention, acute deprivation, starvation, shock, withdrawal of chronic medication: A study in experimental adaptation. J Nerv Ment Dis. 1954; 120(1-2):46-55.

Mehta ND, Stevens JS, Li Z, Gillespie CF, Fani N, Michopoulos V, Felger JC. Inflammation, reward circuitry and symptoms of anhedonia and PTSD in trauma-exposed women. Soc Cogn Affect Neurosci. 2020; 15; nsz100.

Meier IM, van Honk J, Bos PA, Terburg D. A mu-opioid feedback model of human social behavior. Neurosci Biobehav Rev 2021; 121:250–8.

Meister RK, Miller HE. The dynamics of non-directive psychotherapy. J Clin Psychol 1946;2(1):59–67.

Mello N. Schedule-induced polydipsia and oral intake of drugs. Pharmacol Rev. 1975; 27(4):489-98.

Mello N, Mendelson J. Buprenorphine suppresses heroin use by heroin addicts. Science. 1980; 2076:657-9.

Melsens L. Note sur la nicotine. Ann Chim Phys. 1843; 9:465–79.

Melzack R, Torgerson WS. On the language of pain. Anesthesiol J Am Soc Anesthesiol. 1971; 34(1):50-9.

Melzack R, Wall PD. Pain mechanisms: a new theory. Science. 1965; 150(3699):971.

Mendelson JH, Wexler D, Kubzansky PE, Harrison R, Leiderman G, Solomon P. Physicians' attitudes toward alcoholic patients. Arch Gen Psychiatry. 1964;11(4):392–9.

Menninger KA. Man, Against Himself. New York: Harcourt, Brace and Company. 1938.

Meritt HD. Old English glosses (a collection). New York; London: Modern Language Association of America; Oxford University Press; 1945.

Mesmer FA. Mesmer's aphorisms and instructions, by M. Caullet de Veaumore, physician to the household of Monsieur, his most Christian majesty's brother. London: Printed and sold at the Glass Warehouse, Coventry-Street, near the Hay-Market; 1785.

Miles CP. Conditions predisposing to suicide: a review. J Nerv Ment Dis. 1977; 164(4):231-46.

Miller G. Learning to forget. Science. 2004; 304(5667):34.

Miller H. The Colossus of Maroussi. Norfolk, Conn.; 1941.

Miller NS, Flaherty JA. Effectiveness of coerced addiction treatment (alternative consequences): A review of the clinical research. J Subst Abuse Treat 2000;18(1):9–16.

Miller NS, Gold MS, Belkin BM, Klahr AL. Family history and diagnosis of alcohol dependence in cocaine dependence. Psychiatry Res. 1989;29(2):113–21.

Miller WR. Motivational interviewing with problem drinkers. Behav Psychother. 1983;11(2):147–72.

Miller WR. Spirituality: the silent dimension in addiction research. The 1990 Leonard Ball oration. Drug Alcohol Rev 1990;9(3):259–66.

Miller WR, Moyers TB. The forest and the trees: relational and specific factors in addiction treatment. Addiction 2015;110(3):401–13.

Milne-Edwards H, Vavasseur P, Togno Joseph, Durand E. A manual of materia medica and pharmacy, comprising a concise description of the articles used in medicine. Philadelphia: Carey, Lea & Carey; 1829.

Mitchell W, Bhatia R, Zebardast N. Retrospective cross-sectional analysis of the changes in marijuana use in the USA, 2005-2018. BMJ Open. 2020;10(7): e037905.

Mitford MR, L'Estrange AGK, Harness W. The life of Mary Russell Mitford ... related in a selection from her letters to her friends. London: R. Bentley; 1870.

Moeller FG, Dougherty DM, Lane SD, Steinberg JL, Cherek DR. Antisocial personality disorder and alcohol-induced aggression. Alcohol Clin Exp Res, 1998;22(9):1898–902.

Molina T de. The Trickster of Seville and the stone guest. El burlador de Sevilla y el convidado de piedra. Warminster: Aris and Phillips; 1986.

Moner SE. Acupuncture and addiction treatment. J Addict Dis. 1996;15(3):79–100.

Monier-Williams M. Buddhism. London; 1889.

Moore M. Alcoholism: Some Contemporary Opinions. N Engl J Med. 1941;224(20):848–57.

Monardes N. Historia medicinal. Pts. 1-2. Dos libros, el uno que trata de todas las cosas que traen de nuestras Indias Occidentales que siruen al uso de la medicina y el otro que trata de la piedra bezaar. Sevilla: Hernando Diaz; 1569.

Monardes N. The three bookes written in the Spanishe tonge. London: Norton; 1577.

Morand J. Mémoire sur l'acupuncture: suivi d'une série d'observations recueillies sous les yeux de M. Jules Cloquet. Paris: Crevot; 1825.

Moreau JL, Pieri L, Prud'hon B. Convulsions induced by centrally administered NMDA in mice: effects of NMDA antagonists, benzodiazepines, minor tranquilizers and anticonvulsants. Br J Pharmacol. 1989;98(3):1050–4.

Morey L, Martin PR. Assessment of alcoholism and substance abuse. In: Wetzler S, editor. Measuring Mental Illness: Psychometric Assessment for Clinicians. Washington, DC: American Psychiatric Press; 1989. p. 161–81.

Moriguchi S, Inagaki R, Yi L, Shibata M, Sakagami H, Fukunaga K. Nicotine rescues depressive-like behaviors via α7-type Nicotinic Acetylcholine Receptor activation in CaMKIV null mice. Mol Neurobiol. 2020; 57:4929–4940.

Morrell F. Lasting changes in synaptic organization produced by continuous neuronal bombardment. In: Delafresnaye JF, editor. Brain Mech Learn Symp. Blackwell Scientific; 1961. pp. 375–92.

Morrell F. Graham Goddard: An Appreciation. Epilepsia 1987;28(6):717–20.

Morris R. Cursor mundi: A Northumbrian poem of the 14th century; in four variations, two of them Midland = (The Cursor of the world). Pt. 1 Pt. 1. London: Trübner; 1874.

Morris RGM, Anderson E, Lynch GS, Baudry M. Selective impairment of learning and blockade of long-term potentiation by an N-methyl-D-aspartate receptor antagonist, AP5. Nature 1986;319(6056):774–6.

Mortimer WG. Peru: history of coca "the divine plant" of the Incas. New York: J.H. Vail & Co.; 1901.

Morton T. A preamble vnto an incounter with P.R. the author of the deceitfull treatise of mitigation: concerning the Romish doctrine both in question of rebellion and aequiuocation: by Thomas Morton. Published by authoritie. London, Printed by Melch. Bradwood for Iohn Bill and Edmond Weauer; 1608.

Moskowitz HR, Gerbers CL. Dimensional salience of odors. Annals of the New York Academy of Sciences. 1974; 237:1-16.

Motto AL, Clark JR. Seneca On Drunkenness. Riv Cult Class E Medioev. Accademia Editoriale; 1990; 32(1/2):105-10. Jelliffe SE. Drug addictions. Preliminary report of the Committee in Section on Nervous and Mental Diseases. Journal of the American Medical Association. 1906; XLVI (9):643–4.

Mueller GC, Fleming MF, LeMahieu MA, Lybrand GS, Barry KJ. Synthesis of phosphatidylethanol--a potential marker for adult males at risk for alcoholism. Proc Natl Acad Sci. 1988;85(24):9778.

Mukherjee AB, Svoronos S, Ghazanfari A, Martin PR, Fisher A, Roecklein B, Rodbard D, Staton R, Behar D, Berg CJ. Transketolase abnormality in cultured fibroblasts from familial chronic alcoholic men and their male offspring. J Clin Invest. 1987;79(4):1039–43.

Musci RJ, Fairman B, Masyn KE, Uhl G, Maher B, Sisto DY, Kellam SG, Ialongo NS. Polygenic score × intervention moderation: an application of discrete-time survival analysis to model the timing of first marijuana use among urban youth. Prev Sci. 2018; 19(1):6-14.

Musser RD, Bird JG. Modern pharmacology and therapeutics. New York: Macmillan; 1961.

Myerson A. Effect of Benzedrine sulfate on mood and fatigue in normal and in neurotic persons. Arch Neurol Psychiatry, 1936;36(4):816–22.

Nagai N. Kanyaku maou seibun kenkyuu seiseki (zoku). Yakugaku Zasshi. 1893; 127:832–60.

Nathan PE, Conrad M, Skinstad AH. History of the concept of addiction. Annual Review of Clinical Psychology, 2016; 12, 29-51.

National Academies of Sciences, Engineering, and Medicine. The Health Effects of Cannabis and Cannabinoids: The Current State of Evidence and Recommendations for Research. Washington, DC: The National Academies Press; 2017.

National Council Against Health Fraud. Acupuncture: the position paper of the National Council Against Health Fraud. Clin J Pain. 1991;7(2):162–6.

Nehlig A. Are we dependent upon coffee and caffeine? A review on human and animal data. Neurosci Biobehav Rev. 1999; 23(4):563-76.

Nelson EC, Heath AC, Bucholz KK, Madden PAF, Fu Q, Knopik V, Lynskey MT, Whitfield JB, Statham DJ, Martin NG. Genetic Epidemiology of Alcohol-Induced Blackouts. Arch Gen Psychiatry 2004; 61(3):257-63.

Nestoros J. Ethanol specifically potentiates GABA-mediated neurotransmission in feline cerebral cortex. Science. 1980; 209:708.

Neumann J, Beck O, Helander A, Böttcher M. Performance of pethanol compared with other alcohol biomarkers in subjects presenting for occupational and pre-employment medical examination. Alcohol Alcohol. 2020;55(4):401–8.

Neve RL, Shen L, Zhang HS, Zhang F, Nestler EJ. Locus-specific epigenetic remodeling controls addiction- and depression-related behaviors. Nat Neurosci, 2014;17(12):1720-7.

Ngo H-VV, Born J. Sleep and the balance between memory and forgetting. Cell; 2019; 179(2):289–91.

Nicolas NH. The privy purse expenses of King Henry the Eighth, from November MDXXIX to December MDXXII: with introductory remarks and illustrative notes. London: Pickering; 1827.

Nicolas NH. A history of the Royal Navy, from the earliest times to the wars of the French Revolution 1. 1. London: Bentley; 1847.

Nicoll RA. A Brief History of Long-Term Potentiation. Neuron 2017;93(2):281–90.

Niemann A. Ueber eine neue organische Base in den Cocablättern. Arch Pharm (Weinheim), 1860;153(2):129–55.

Norris R, Carroll D, Cochrane R. The effects of aerobic and anaerobic training on fitness, blood pressure, and psychological stress and well-being. J Psychosom Res. 1990; 34(4):367–75.

Nugent T. The Life of Benvenuto Cellini, a Florentine Artist: Containing a Variety of Curious and Interesting Particulars Relative to Painting, Sculpture and Architecture, and the History of His Own Time. London: Printed for T. Davies; 1771.

Nurco DN, DuPont RL. A preliminary report on crime and addiction within a community-wide population of narcotic addicts. Drug Alcohol Depend, 1977;2(2):109–21.

Nutt D, King L, Saulsbury W, Blakemore C. Development of a rational scale to assess the harm of drugs of potential misuse. Lancet. 2007;369(9566):1047-53.

O'Brien CP. Experimental analysis of conditioning factors in human narcotic addiction. Pharmacol Rev 1975;27(4):533.

Ogden CL, Carroll MD, Curtin LR, McDowell MA, Tabak CJ, Flegal KM. Prevalence of overweight and obesity in the United States, 1999-2004. JAMA. 2006; 295(13):1549–55.

Ogston F. Phenomena of the more advanced stages of intoxication, with cases and dissections. Edinburgh Med Surg J. 1833; 40(117):276-95.

O'Hollaren P, Wellman WM. Hidden alcoholics. Calif Med. 1958;89(2):129–31.

Ohashi K, Anderson CM, Bolger EA, Khan A, McGreenery CE, Teicher MH. Susceptibility or resilience to maltreatment can be explained by specific differences in brain network architecture. Biol Psychiatry. 2019; 85(8):690–702.

Oikonomou MT, Arvanitis M, Sokolove RL. Mindfulness training for smoking cessation: A meta-analysis of randomized-controlled trials. J Health Psychol 2017;22(14):1841–50.

Okajima I, Akitomi J, Kajiyama I, Ishii M, Murakami H, Yamaguchi M. Effects of a tailored brief behavioral therapy application on insomnia severity and social disabilities among workers with insomnia in Japan: a randomized clinical trial. JAMA Network Open. 2020; 3(4): e202775.

Olch PD. William S. Halsted and local anesthesia: contributions and complications. Anesthesiology, 1975;42(4):479–86.

Olds, J. Self-stimulation of the brain. Science, 1958; 127, 315.

Olds J, Milner P. Positive reinforcement produced by electrical stimulation of septal area and other regions of rat brain. J Comp Physiol Psychol. 1954; 47(6):419-27.

Olds J, Olds ME. Positive reinforcement produced by stimulating hypothalamus with iproniazid and other compounds. Science, 1958;127(3307):1175.

Oliver G, Schäfer EA. The physiological effects of extracts of the suprarenal capsules. J Physiol, 1895;18(3):230–76.

Omenn GS, Motulsky AG. A biochemical and genetic approach to alcoholism. Annals of the New York Academy of Sciences 1972;197(1):16–23.

Oquendo MA, Galfalvy H, Russo S, Ellis SP, Grunebaum MF, Burke A, Mann JJ. Prospective study of clinical predictors of suicidal acts after a major depressive episode in patients with major depressive disorder or bipolar disorder. Am J Psychiatry. 2004; 161(8):1433-41.

Orford J. Hypersexuality: implications for a theory of dependence. Br J Addict Alcohol Other Drugs1978;73(3):299–310. Malvaez M, Barrett RM, Wood MA, Sanchis-Segura C. Epigenetic mechanisms underlying extinction of memory and drug-seeking behavior. Mammalian Genome, 2009; 20, 612-623.

Oscar-Berman M, Ruiz SM, Marinkovic K, Valmas MM, Harris GJ, Sawyer KS. Brain responsivity to emotional faces differs in men and women with and without a history of alcohol use disorder. PloS ONE 2021;16(6): e0248831.

Öst L-G, Götestam KG. Behavioral and pharmacological treatments for obesity: An experimental comparison. Addict Behav. 1976; 1(4):331–8.

Osterman E, Bellander-Lofvenberg S, Lassenius B. S.C.T.Z., a new sedative and hypnotic related to thiamine. Acta Psychiatr Scand Suppl. 1959; 34:56–61.

Ostrovsky YuM. Endogenous ethanol—Its metabolic, behavioral and biomedical significance. Alcohol. 1986; 3:239–47.

Oswald I. Drugs and sleep. Pharmacol Rev. 1968; 20(4):273.

Page RL, Allen LA, Kloner RA, Carriker CR, Martel C, Morris AA., Piano MR., RanaS., Saucedo JF, American Heart Association Clinical Pharmacology Committee and Heart Failure and Transplantation Committee of the Council on Clinical Cardiology, Council on Basic Cardiovascular Sciences, Council on Cardiovascular and Stroke Nursing, Council on Epidemiology and Prevention, Council on Lifestyle and Cardiometabolic Health, Council on Quality of Care and Outcomes Research. Medical marijuana, recreational cannabis, and cardiovascular health: a scientific statement from the American Heart Association. Circulation. 2020; 142(10): e131-e152.

Palazzolo DL. Electronic cigarettes and vaping: a new challenge in clinical medicine and public health. A literature review. Front Public Health. 2013; 1:56–56.

Palsgrave J. Lesclarcissement de la langue françoyse: 1530. Genève: Slatkine reprints; 1972.

Pascoe MC, Thompson DR, Ski CF. Yoga, mindfulness-based stress reduction and stress-related physiological measures: A meta-analysis. Psychoneuroendocrinology 2017;86:152–68.

Pavlov IP, Gantt WH. Lectures on conditioned reflexes: twenty-five years of objective study of the higher nervous activity (behaviour) of animals. London: Lawrence & Wishart; 1928.

Park A, Tran T, Scheuermann EA, Smith DP, Atkinson NS. Alcohol potentiates a pheromone signal in flies. Elife, 2020;9: e59853.

Parks MH, Dawant BM, Riddle WR, Hartmann SL, Dietrich MS, Nickel MK, Price RR, Martin PR. Longitudinal brain metabolic characterization of chronic alcoholics with proton magnetic resonance spectroscopy. Alcohol. Clin. Exp. Res. 2002;26(9):1368–80.

Parsons OA. Neuropsychological deficits in alcoholics: facts and fancies. Alcohol Clin Exp Res. 1977;1(1):51–6.

Paul S, Marangos P, Skolnick P. The benzodiazepine--GABA--chloride ionophore receptor complex: common site of minor tranquilizer action. Biol Psychiatry. 1981;16(3):213–29.

Paul IA, Nowak G, Layer RT, Popik P, Skolnick P. Adaptation of the N-methyl–D–aspartate receptor complex following chronic antidepressant treatments. Journal of Pharmacology and Experimental Therapeutics 1994; 269, 95-102.

de Paulis T, Commers P, Farah A, Zhao J, McDonald MP, Galici R, Martin PR. 4-Caffeoyl-1,5-quinide in roasted coffee inhibits [3H]naloxone binding and reverses anti-nociceptive effects of morphine in mice. Psychopharmacology (Berl). 2004; 176(2):146-53.

de Paulis T, Schmidt DE, Bruchey AK, Kirby MT, McDonald MP, Commers P, Lovinger DM, Martin PR. Dicinnamoylquinides in roasted coffee inhibit the human adenosine transporter. Eur J Pharmacol. 2002; 442(3):215-23.

Paulus MP, Schuckit MA, Tapert SF, Tolentino NJ, Matthews SC, Smith TL, Trim RS, Hall SA, Simmons AN. High versus low level of response to alcohol: evidence of differential reactivity to emotional stimuli. Subst Abuse Psychos. 2012;72(10):848–55.

Payne TJ, Schare ML, Levis DJ, Colletti G. Exposure to smoking-relevant cues: Effects on desire to smoke and topographical components of smoking behavior. Addict Behav. 1991; 16(6):467-79.

Peary D. Cult movies: a hundred ways to find the reel thing. London: Vermilion; 1982.

di Pellegrino G, Fadiga L, Fogassi L, Gallese V, Rizzolatti G. Understanding motor events: a neurophysiological study. Exp Brain Res 1992;91(1):176–80.

Pendergrast M. Uncommon Grounds: the History of Coffee and how it Transformed our World. 2019.

Pendery M, Maltzman I, West L. Controlled drinking by alcoholics? New findings and a reevaluation of a major affirmative study. Science 1982;217(4555):169.

Penfield W. Oriental Renaissance in education and medicine. Science. 1963;141(3586):1153.

Penfield W, Erickson TC, Jasper HH, Harrower M. Epilepsy and cerebral localization: a study of the mechanism, treatment and prevention of epileptic seizures. Springfield: C.C. Thomas; 1941.

Penfield W, Milner B. Memory deficit produced by bilateral lesions in the hippocampal zone. AMA Arch Neurol Psychiatry 1958;79(5):475–97.

Perkins KA. Effects of tobacco smoking on caloric intake. Br J Addict. 1992;87(2):193–205.

Perl ER. Ideas about pain, a historical view. Nat Rev Neurosci. 2007; 8(1):71-80.

Pert CB, Snyder SH. Opiate receptor: demonstration in nervous tissue. Science 1973; 179:1011–14.

Petry NM. Patterns and correlates of Gamblers Anonymous attendance in pathological gamblers seeking professional treatment. Addict Behav, 2003;28(6):1049–62.

Pfefferbaum A, Sullivan EV, Rosenbloom MJ, Shear PK, Mathalon DH, Lim KO. Increase in brain cerebrospinal fluid volume is greater in older than in younger alcoholic patients: A replication study and CT/MRI comparison. Psychiatry Res Neuroimaging. 1993;50(4):257–74.

Phelps AE. Evaluation of cardiac and circulatory stimulants for surgical patients. Ann Surg, 1930;91(1):24–8.

Philanthropus. On the use of stimulants in burns. Med Phys J, 1809;21(123):386–9.

Pictet A, Rotschy A. Synthese des Nicotins. Berichte Dtsch Chem Ges. 1904;37(2):1225–35.

Piersol GM. The recognition and treatment of neurocirculatory asthenia in civil life. Trans Am Climatol Clin Assoc Am Climatol Clin Assoc. 1925; 41:123–34.

Pihl RO, Smith M, Farrell B. Individual characteristics of aggressive beer and distilled beverage drinkers. Int J Addict, 1984;19(6):689–96.

Piker P. On the relationship of the sudden withdrawal of alcohol to delirium tremens. Am J Psychiatry. 1937; 93:1387–90.

Pinner A. Ueber Nicotin. Die Constitution des Alkaloïds. Berichte Dtsch Chem Ges. 1893;26(1):292–305.

Pittis W. Dr. Radcliffe's life, and letters. London; 1716.

Plato, Jowett B. The dialogues of Plato. Oxford: Clarendon Press; 1875.

Plinius Secundus C. Naturalis historia. Berolini; 1866.

Pluvinage R. Les atrophies cérébrales des alcooliques [Cerebral atrophy in alcoholics]. Bull Mem Soc Med Hop Paris. 1954; 70:524–6.

Poggiogalle E, Jamshed H, Peterson CM. Circadian regulation of glucose, lipid, and energy metabolism in humans. Metabolism 2018; 84:11–27.

Pond DA. Psychological effects in depressive patients of the marihuana homologue synhexyl. J Neurol Neurosurg Psychiatry. 1948;11(4):271-9.

Posselt W, Reimann L. Chemische Untersuchung des Tabaks und Darstellung eines eigenthümlich wirksamen Prinzips dieser Pflanze. Mag Für Pharm. 1828;6(24):138–61.

Post RM. Use of the anticonvulsant carbamazepine in primary and secondary affective illness: clinical and theoretical implications. Psychol Med. 2009/07/09 ed. Cambridge University Press 1982;12(4):701–4.

Post R, Kopanda R. Cocaine, kindling, and reverse tolerance. The Lancet 1975;305(7903):409–10.

Post RM, Uhde T, Putnam FW, Ballenger JC, Berrettini WH. Kindling and Carbamazepine in Affective Illness. J Nerv Ment Dis 1982;170(12).

Post RM, Weiss SRB, Smith M, Li H, McCann U. Kindling versus quenching. Ann N Y Acad Sci 1997;821(1):285–95.

Potenza MN. Review. The neurobiology of pathological gambling and drug addiction: an overview and new findings. Philos Trans R Soc Lond B Biol Sci, 2008;363(1507):3181–9.

Preller KH, Hulka LM, Vonmoos M, Jenni D, Baumgartner MR, Seifritz E, Dziobek I, Quednow BB. Impaired emotional empathy and related social network deficits in cocaine users. Addict Biol 2014;19(3):452–66.

Preston T. A Lamentable Tragedy Mixed Ful of Pleasant Mirth, Conteyning the Life Of Cambises King Of Percia, From the Beginning Of His Kingdome Vnto His Death, His One Good Deed Of Execution, After That Many Wicked Deeds and Tirannous Murders, Committed By and Through Him, and Last Of All, His Odious Death By Gods Iustice Appointed. Doon In Such Order As Foloweth. By Thomas Preston. London: Imprinted ... by Iohn Allde; 1569.

Preston SD, de Waal FBM. Empathy: Its ultimate and proximate bases. Behav Brain Sci 2002;25(1):1–20.

Prochaska JO, DiClemente CC. Stages and processes of self-change of smoking: toward an integrative model of change. J Consult Clin Psychol. 1983;51(3):390–5.

Prickett CO. The effect of a deficiency of vitamin B1 upon the central and peripheral nervous systems of the rat. Am J Physiol-Leg Content. 1934;107(2):459–70.

Project MATCH Research Group. Matching Alcoholism Treatments to Client Heterogeneity: Project MATCH Three-Year Drinking Outcomes. Alcohol Clin Exp Res. 1998;22(6):1300-11.

Psederska E, Savov S, Atanassov N, Vassileva J. Relationships between alexithymia and psychopathy in heroin dependent individuals. Front Psychol 2019; 10:2269.

Purchas S, Hakluyt R. Hakluytus posthumus or Purchas his Pilgrimes: Contayning a history of the world, in sea voyages, & lande-trauells. London: Imprinted for H. Fetherston; 1625.

Quarles F. Argalus and Parthenia. [In verse]. J. Marriott: London; 1629.

Quinn PD, Fromme K. Individual differences in subjective alcohol responses and alcohol-related disinhibition. Exp Clin Psychopharmacol. 2016/02/11 ed. 2016;24(2):90–9.

Rabin RA, Parvaz MA, Alia-Klein N, Goldstein RZ. Emotion recognition in individuals with cocaine use disorder: the role of abstinence length and the social brain network. Psychopharmacology 2021.

Ragan PW, Martin PR. The psychobiology of sexual addiction. Sex Addict Compulsivity, 2000;7(3):161–75.

Ramsden E. Making animals alcoholic: shifting laboratory models of addiction. J Hist Behav Sci. 2015; 51(2):164-94.

Ramsey GR. Two sides to the prevention equation — demand reduction vs. supply reduction. J Sch Health. 1986; 56(9):418.

Rankine WJM. A Manual of applied mechanics, by William John Macquorn Rankine. London and Glasgow: R. Griffin; 1858.

Raskind MA, Peskind ER, Kanter ED, Petrie EC, Radant A, Thompson CE, Dobie DJ, Hoff D, Rein RJ, Straits-Tröster K, Thomas RG, McFall MM. Reduction of nightmares and other PTSD symptoms in combat veterans by prazosin: a placebo-controlled study. Am J Psychiatry. 2003; 160(2):371–3.

Rasmussen N. America's first amphetamine epidemic 1929-1971: a quantitative and qualitative retrospective with implications for the present. Am J Public Health. 2008/04/29 ed. American Public Health Association, 2008;98(6):974–85.

Rechtschaffen A, Kales A, editors. A Manual of Standardized Terminology, Techniques and Scoring System for Sleep Stages of Human Subjects. U. S. National Institute of Neurological Diseases and Blindness, Neurological Information Network; 1968.

Redlich FC. Value of electroencephalography in differential diagnosis of epilepsy and fainting. Dis Nerv Syst. 1946; 7(12):362-7.

Reed PL, Anthony JC, Breslau N. Incidence of drug problems in young adults exposed to trauma and posttraumatic stress disorder: Do early life experiences and predispositions matter? Arch Gen Psychiatry. 2007; 64(12):1435-42.

Regier DA, Farmer ME, Rae DS, Locke BZ, Keith SJ, Judd LL, Goodwin FK. Comorbidity of mental disorders with alcohol and other drug abuse: results from the Epidemiologic Catchment Area (ECA) Study. JAMA. 1990;264(19):2511-8.

Reich MS, Dietrich MS, Finlayson RAJ, Fischer EF, Martin PR. Coffee and Cigarette Consumption and perceived effects in recovering alcoholics participating in Alcoholics Anonymous in Nashville, Tennessee. Alcohol Clin Exp Res. 2008; 32(10):1799-806.

Reich MS, Dietrich MS, Martin PR. Temporal sequence of incident cigarette, coffee, and alcohol use among AA participants. Am J Drug Alcohol Abuse. 2011; 37(1):27-36.

Reichard JD. Addiction: some theoretical considerations as to its nature, cause, prevention and prevention. Am J Psychiatry. 1947; 103(6):721-30.

Reid-Varley W-B, Ponce Martinez C, Khurshid KA. Sleep disorders and disrupted sleep in addiction, withdrawal and abstinence with focus on alcohol and opioids. J Neurol Sci; 2020; 411.

Renton AH. Case of Delirium tremens treated by local blood-letting and purgatives previous to the administration of opium. Edinb Med Surg J. 1829; 31:312–3.

Reuter J, Raedler T, Rose M, Hand I, Gläscher J, Büchel C. Pathological gambling is linked to reduced activation of the mesolimbic reward system. Nat Neurosci, 2005;8(2):147–8.

Rich SJ, Martin PR. Co-occurring psychiatric disorders and alcoholism. In: Sullivan EV, Pfefferbaum A, editors. Handbook of Clinical Neurology. Alcohol and the Nervous System (Volume 125). Amsterdam: Elsevier; 2014, pp. 573-88.

Richter CP. Alcohol, beer and wine as foods. Q J Stud Alcohol. 1953; 14(4):525-39.

Richter CP, Holt LE, Barelare B. Vitamin B1 craving in rats. Science. 1937; 86(2233):354.

Ritchie C. On diagnosis. Edinb Med Surg. 1820;16(62):53–62.

Ritter A, Cameron J. A review of the efficacy and effectiveness of harm reduction strategies for alcohol, tobacco and illicit drugs. Drug Alcohol Rev. 2006; 25(6):611-24.

Ritter K, Lookatch SJ, Schmidt MR, Moore TM. The impact of history of aggression and alcohol use on aggressive: responding in the laboratory. Subst Abuse, 2019;13:1178221819884328.

Ritz MC, Kuhar MJ. Relationship between self-administration of amphetamine and monoamine receptors in brain: comparison with cocaine. J Pharmacol Exp Ther, 1989;248(3):1010.

Ritz M, Lamb R, Goldberg, Kuhar M. Cocaine receptors on dopamine transporters are related to self-administration of cocaine. Science, 1987;237(4819):1219.

Roberts JM, Arth MJ, Bush RR. Games in culture. Am Anthropol, 1959;61(4):597–605.

Roberts W. Looker-on. Period Pap. Whitehall [London]: Printed for T. and J. Egerton; 1792.

Robins E, Gassner S, Kayes J, Wilkinson RH, Murphy GE. The communication of suicidal intent: a study of 134 consecutive cases of successful (completed) suicide. Am J Psychiatry. 1959; 115(8):724-33.

Robinson TE, Berridge KC. The neural basis of drug craving: An incentive-sensitization theory of addiction. Brain Res Rev. 1993; 18(3):247-91.

Rodrigues SM, Schafe GE, LeDoux JE. Molecular mechanisms underlying emotional learning and memory in the lateral amygdala. Neuron. 2004; 44(1):75–91.

Romero K, Daniels CW, Gipson CD, Sanabria F. Suppressive and enhancing effects of nicotine on food-seeking behavior. Behav Brain Res. 2018; 339:130–9.

Ronsley C, Nolan S, Knight R, Hayashi K, Klimas J, Walley A, Wood E, Fairbairn N. Treatment of stimulant use disorder: A systematic review of reviews. PloS ONE. 2020;15(6): e0234809.

Ropper AH. Neurosyphilis. N Engl J Med. 2019;381(14):1358–63.

Rounsaville BJ, Spitzer RL, Williams JB. Proposed changes in DSM-III substance use disorders: description and rationale. Am J Psychiatry. 1986; 143:463-8.

Roy A. Genetic and biologic risk factors for suicide in depressive disorders. Psychiatr Q. 1993; 64(4):345-58.

Rudgley R. The Lost Civilizations of the Stone Age. New York, NY, Free Press; 1999.

Rupp CI, Junker D, Kemmler G, Mangweth-Matzek B, Derntl B. Do social cognition deficits recover with abstinence in alcohol-dependent patients? Alcohol Clin Exp Res 2021;45(2):470–9.

Runge FF. Neueste phytochemische Entdeckungen zur Begründung einer wissenschaftlichen Phytochemie 1. Anleitung zu einer bessern Zerlegungsweise der Vegetabilien. - 1820. 1. Anleitung zu einer bessern Zerlegungsweise der Vegetabilien. - 1820. Berlin: Reimer; 1820.

Rutter M. Resilience in the face of adversity: Protective factors and resistance to psychiatric disorder. Br J Psychiatry. 1985; 147(6):598-611.

Rush B, Thomas I, Andrews ET. An Inquiry into the Effects of Spirituous Liquors on the Human Body: to which is Added, a Moral and Physical Thermometer. Printed at Boston: By Thomas and Andrews; at Faust's Statue, no. 45, Newbury Street; 1790.

Rush B. Medical Inquiries and Observations on the Diseases of the Mind. Philadelphia: B. & T. Kite; 1812.

Ryback RS. The continuum and specificity of the effects of alcohol on memory: A review. Q J Stud Alcohol. 1971; 32(4, Pt. A):995-1016.

Ryback RS, Eckardt MJ, Rawlings RR, Rosenthal LS. Quadratic discriminant analysis as an aid to interpretive reporting of clinical laboratory tests. JAMA. 1982;248(18):2342–5.

Rynd F. Neuralgia - introduction of fluid to the nerve. Dublin Medical Press. 1845; 13:167–8.

Saitz R, Miller SC, Fiellin DA, Rosenthal RN. Recommended Use of Terminology in Addiction Medicine. J Addict Med. 2021;15(1).

Sancho M, De Gracia M, Rodríguez RC, Mallorquí-Bagué N, Sánchez-González J, Trujols J, Sánchez I, Jiménez-Murcia S, Menchón JM. Mindfulness-based interventions for the treatment of substance and behavioral addictions: a systematic review. Front Psychiatry 2018; 9:95.

Sander T, Harms H, Rommelspacher H, Hoehe M, Schmidt LG. Possible allelic association of a tyrosine hydroxylase polymorphism with vulnerability to alcohol-withdrawal delirium. Psychiatr Genet. 1998; 8:13–7.

Sandys E. A relation of the state of religion: and with what hopes and pollicies it hath beene framed and is maintained in the several states of these westerne parts of the world. London: Printed for Simon Waterson dwelling in Paules Churchyard at the signe of the Crowne; 1605.

Sandys G. A Relation of a Journey begun An. Dom. 1610: 4 Bookes, Containing a description of the Turkish Empire, of Aegypt, of the Holy Land, of the Remote parts of Italy, and Ilands adioyning. London, Barren; 1615.

Sanfey AG, Rilling JK, Aronson JA, Nystrom LE, Cohen JD. The neural basis of economic decision-making in the Ultimatum Game. Science, 2003;300(5626):1755.

Sapolsky RM. Why stress is bad for your brain. Science. 1996; 273(5276):749.

Savard J, Öberg KG, Chatzittofis A, Dhejne C, Arver S, Jokinen J. Naltrexone in compulsive sexual behavior disorder: a feasibility study of twenty men. J Sex Med 2020;17(8):1544–52.

Schenker S, Henderson GI, Hoyumpa AM Jr, McCandless DW. Hepatic and Wernicke's encephalopathies: current concepts of pathogenesis. Am J Clin Nutr. 1980;33(12):2719–26.

Schiff M, Zweig HH, Benbenishty R, Hasin DS. Exposure to terrorism and Israeli youths' cigarette, alcohol, and cannabis use. Am J Public Health. 2007;97(10):1852-8.

Schorlemmer C. A manual of the chemistry of the carbon compounds, or, Organic chemistry. London: Macmillan; 1874.

Schuckit MA. Self-rating of alcohol intoxication by young men with and without family histories of alcoholism. J Stud Alcohol, 1980;41(3):242–9.

Schuckit MA, Rayses V. Ethanol ingestion: differences in blood acetaldehyde concentrations in relatives of alcoholics and controls. Science 1979; 203, 54-55.

Schulkin J, Rozin P, Stellar E. Curt P. Richter - February 20, 1894-December 21, 1988. Biogr Mem Natl Acad Sci. 1994; 65:311-20.

Schuster CR, Thompson T. Self-administration of and behavioral dependence on drugs. Annu Rev Pharmacol. 1969;9(1):483-502.

Schutte NS, Malouff JM. A meta-analytic review of the effects of mindfulness meditation on telomerase activity. Psychoneuroendocrinology 2014; 42:45–8.

Schutte NS, Malouff JM, Keng S-L. Meditation and telomere length: a meta-analysis. Psychol Health 2020;35(8):901–15.

Schwartz RH. Urine testing in the detection of drugs of abuse. Arch Intern Med. 1988;148(11):2407–12.

Scoville WB, Milner B. Loss of recent memory after bilateral hippocampal lesions. J Neurol Neurosurg Amp Psychiatry 1957;20(1):11.

Scripture EW. Consciousness under the influence of Cannabis Indica. 1893;22(560):233-4.

Scriver CR, Clow CL. Phenylketonuria: epitome of human biochemical genetics. New England Journal of Medicine, 1980; 303, 1336-1342.

Seay B, Hansen E, Harlow HF. Mother-infant separation in monkeys. J Child Psychol Psychiatry. 1962; 3:123-32.

Seidell JC. Obesity, insulin resistance and diabetes – a worldwide epidemic. Br J Nutr. 2000; 83(S1): S5-8.

Sellers EM, Kalant H. Alcohol intoxication and withdrawal. N Engl J Med. 1976; 294:757–62.

Selye H. The significance of the adrenals for adaptation. Science. 1937; 85:247–8.

Serturner FWA. J Pharm F Arzte Apoth Chem 1806; 14:47–93.

Shah A, Hayes CJ, Martin BC. Characteristics of Initial Prescription Episodes and Likelihood of Long-Term Opioid Use — United States, 2006–2015. MMWR Morb Mortal Wkly Rep 2017; 66:265–269.

Shakespeare W. The second part of Henrie the Fourth, continuing to his death, and coronation of Henrie the Fift : with the humours of Sir John Falstaffe, and swaggering Pistoll, as it hath been sundrie times publikely acted by the Right Honourable, the Lord Chamberlaine his seruants. London: Printed by V.S. for Andrew Wise and William Aspley; 1600.

Shakespeare W. The tragicall historie of Hamlet, Prince of Denmarke. London: L[ing]; 1604.

Shaw B. Bernard Shaw's letters to Granville Barker. London: Phoenix House; 1956.

Sheldon R. Certain general reasons, proving the lawfulnesse of the oath of allegiance ... Whereunto is added, the treatise of ... Mr. William Barclay, concerning the temporall power of the Pope ... London; 1611.

Shrady GF. Proceedings of the fifteenth annual meeting of the Association of Medical Superintendents of American Institutions for the Insane. Am J Psychiatry 1860;17(1):32–73.

Shulman R. Psycogenic illness with physical manifestations and the other side of the coin: a practical approach. The Lancet. 1977; 309(8010):524-6.

Sieveking EH. Observations on the etiology of pain. Brit Med J. 1867; 1(319):131-5.

Silva AR, Magalhães R, Arantes C, Moreira PS, Rodrigues M, Marques P, Marques J, Sousa N, Pereira VH. Brain functional connectivity is altered in patients with Takotsubo Syndrome. Sci Rep. 2019; 9(1):4187–4187.

Simard D, Olesen J, Paulson OB, Lassen NA, Skinhøj E. Regional cerebral blood flow and its regulation in dementia. Brain 1971; 94(2):27388.

Sinclair JD. Drugs to decrease alcohol drinking. Ann Med. 1990; 22(5):357-62.

Singleton CK, Martin PR. Molecular mechanisms of thiamine utilization. Curr Mol Med. 2001;1(2):197–207.

Sinha R. How does stress increase risk of drug abuse and relapse? Psychopharmacology (Berl). 2001; 158(4):343-59.

Sinke C, Engel J, Veit M, Hartmann U, Hillemacher T, Kneer J, Kruger THC. Sexual cues alter working memory performance and brain processing in men with compulsive sexual behavior. NeuroImage Clin 2020; 27:102308–102308.

Skeat WW. Alexander and Dindimus, or The letters of Alexander to Dindimus, King of the Brahmans, with the replies of Dindimus. London: Published for the Early English Text Society, by N. Trübner & Co; 1878.

Skinner BF. Two Types of Conditioned Reflex: A Reply to Konorski and Miller. J Gen Psychol. 1937;16(1):272–9.

Skinner HA, Holt S, Schuller R, Roy J, Israel Y. Identification of alcohol abuse using laboratory tests and a history of trauma. Ann Intern Med. 1984;101(6):847–51.

Smart R, Pacula RL. Early evidence of the impact of cannabis legalization on cannabis use, cannabis use disorder, and the use of other substances: Findings from state policy evaluations. Am J Drug Alcohol Abuse. 2019;45(6):644-63.

Smiles S. Self-Help. John Murry, London; 1859.

Smith E. On the influence of exercise over respiration and pulsation; with comments. Edinb Med J. 1859; 4(7):614–23.

Smith H. The Tin Trumpet. Bradbury, Evans & Company. 1869.

Smith J. The True travels, adventures, and observations of Captaine Iohn Smith, in Europe, Asia, Affrica, and America, from anno Domini 1593. to 1629. His accidents and sea-fighte in the Straights, his services and stratagems of warre in Hungaria, Transilvania, Wallachia, and Moldavia; Together with a continuation of his Generall history of Viginia, Summer-Iles, New England, and their proceedings, since 1624 to this preent 1629. London: J.H. for Thomas Slater; 1630.

Smith J. A compleat practice of physick. Wherein is plainly described, the nature, causes, differences, and signs, of all diseases in the body of man. With the choicest cures for the same. London: Printed by J. Streater, for Simon Miller at the Star in S. Pauls Church-yard; 1656.

Smith JA. Methods of treatment of delirium tremens. J Am Med Assoc. 1953; 152:384–7.

Smith JF, Howitt W. John Cassell's Illustrated History of England. The text, to the Reign of Edward I., by J.F. Smith; and from that period by W. Howitt. London; 1856.

Smith JT, Smith LT. English gilds: the original ordinances of more than one hundred early English gilds: together with Ye olde usages of ye cite of Winchester; The ordinances of Worcester; The office of the mayor of Bristol; and the costomary of the manor of Tettenhall-Regis, from original mass of the fourteenth and fifteenth centuries. Published for the Early English Text Society, by Trübner; 1870.

Smith KE, Porges EC, Norman GJ, Connelly JJ, Decety J. Oxytocin receptor gene variation predicts empathic concern and autonomic arousal while perceiving harm to others. Soc Neurosci 2014;9(1):1–9.

Smith MA, Chick J, Kean DM, Douglas RHB, Singer A, Kendell RE, Best JJK. Brain water in chronic alcoholic patients measured by magnetic resonance imaging. Lancet 1985; 1:1273–4.

Solomon RL. The opponent-process theory of acquired motivation: the costs of pleasure and the benefits of pain. Am Psychol. 1980; 35(8):691-712.

Snell JE, Rosenwald RJ, Robey A. The wifebeater's wife: a study of family interaction. Arch Gen Psychiatry, 1964;11(2):107–12.

Snow HL. Some remarks on the condition of the cerebral circulation produced by stimulants and hypnotics. Br Med J, 1875;2(770):424–424.

Snow J. On the Mode of Communication of Cholera. (2nd ed.) London: John Churchill; 1855.

Snyder SH, Banerjee, SP, Yamamura HI, Greenberg D. Drugs, neurotransmitters, and schizophrenia. Science 1974; 184, 1243.

Snyder SH. Opiate receptor in normal and drug altered brain function. Nature. 1975;257(5523):185–9.

Sobell MB, Sobell LC. The aftermath of heresy: A response to Pendery et al.'s (1982) critique of "Individualized behavior therapy for alcoholics." Behav Res Ther. 1984;22(4):413–40.

Society Proceedings: Société d'électroencéphalographie et de neurophysiologie clinique de langue francaise Secretary: Dr. G.C. Lairy Hôpital Henri-Rousselle, 1, rue Cabanis, Paris 14 (France). Electroencephalograph Clin Neurophysiol. 1962;14(5):774–84.

Sotres-Bayon F, Bush DEA, LeDoux JE. Emotional Perseveration: An Update on Prefrontal-Amygdala Interactions in Fear Extinction. Learn Mem. 2004;11(5):525–35.

Soyka M. Psychopathological characteristics in alcohol hallucinosis and paranoid schizophrenia. Acta Psychiatr Scand. 1990; 81:255–9.

Sox HC. Diagnostic decision: probability theory in the use of diagnostic tests. Ann Intern Med. 1986;104(1):60–6.

Spain DM, Bradess VA, Eggston AA. Alcohol and violent death: a one-year study of consecutive cases in a representative community. J Am Med Assoc, 1951;146(4):334–5.

Spence DW, Kayumov L, Chen A, Lowe A, Jain U, Katzman MA, Shen J, Perelman B, Shapiro CM. Acupuncture increases nocturnal melatonin secretion and reduces insomnia and anxiety: a preliminary report. J Neuropsychiatry Clin Neurosci. 2004;16(1):19–28.

Squire LR. Memory and Brain. Oxford University Press; 1987.

Squire LR, Davis HP. The pharmacology of memory: a neurobiological perspective. Annu Rev Pharmacol Toxicol. 1981; 21(1):323–56.

Stancliffe (Dr). Of sleep, its utility, causes, its varieties, perturbances, defect, excess; of their irregularities, and of the rationale, and cause of dreams; translated from Dr. Gregory's Conspectus Medicinæ. Med Phys J. 1810; 24(140):279–85.

Starzer MSK, Nordentoft M, Hjorthøj C. Rates and predictors of conversion to schizophrenia or bipolar disorder following substance-induced psychosis. Am J Psychiatry 2017;175(4):343–50.

Stein L, Berger BD. Paradoxical fear-increasing effects of tranquilizers: evidence of repression of memory in the rat. Science. 1969;166(3902):253-6.

Steinbeck J. Tortilla Flat. New York: Modern Library; 1935.

Steinglass P, Weiner S, Mendelson JH. A systems approach to alcoholism: A model and its clinical application. Arch Gen Psychiatry. 1971; 24(5):401-8. Rayer PFO. Mémoire sur le delirium tremens. Paris: Baillière; 1819.

Stephens JM. (1933). Punishment and reward in learning. Science. 1933;78(2012):60.

Stern W, Spoerl HD. General psychology from the personalistic standpoint. New York: Macmillan. 1938.

Sternbach LH, Fryer RI, Keller O, Metlesics W, Sach G, Steiger N. Quinazolines and 1,4-Benzodiazepines. X.1 Nitro-Substituted 5-Phenyl-1,4-benzodiazepine Derivatives. J Med Chem. 1963; 6(3):261–5.

Stienen MN, Scholtes F, Samuel R, Weil A, Weyerbrock A, Surbeck W. Different but similar: personality traits of surgeons and internists—results of a cross-sectional observational study. BMJ Open. 2018;8(7): e021310.

Stolerman I. Drugs of abuse: behavioural principles, methods and terms. Trends Pharmacol Sci. 1992; 13:170–6.

Storr Anthony. Human Aggression. Harmondsworth, Mddx.: Penguin; 1968.

Stripling JS, Ellinwood EH. Augmentation of the behavioral and electrophysiologic response to cocaine by chronic administration in the rat. Exp Neurol 1977;54(3):546–64.

Styron W. Darkness Visible: A Memoir of Madness. London: Jonathan Cape; 1991.

Sutton T. Tracts on Delirium Tremens, on Peritonitis, and on Some Other Internal Inflammatory Affections, and on the Gout. London: Underwood; 1813.

Swanson JA, Lee JW, Hopp JW. Caffeine and nicotine: a review of their joint use and possible interactive effects in tobacco withdrawal. Addict Behav. 1994; 19(3):229-56.

Sweatt JD. Neural plasticity and behavior—sixty years of conceptual advances. Journal of Neurochemistry, 2016; 139, 179-199.

Sychla H, Gründer G, Lammertz SE. comparison of clomethiazole and diazepam in the treatment of alcohol withdrawal syndrome in clinical practice. Eur Addict Res. 2017; 23:211–8.

Sydenham T, Pechey J. Whole works of that excellent practical physician Dr. Thomas Sydenham: wherein not only the history and cures of acute diseases are treated of, after a new and accurate method: but also, the shortest and safest way of curing most chronical diseases. London: Printed for J. Darby for M. Poulson; 1722.

Szasz TS. The ethics of addiction. Am J Psychiatry. 1971;128(5):541-6.

Talland GA. Deranged Memory. New York: Academic Press; 1965.

Tallman JF, Thomad JW, Gallager DW. GABAergic modulation of benzodiazepine binding site sensitivity. Nature. 1978;274(5669):383–5.

Tang Y-Y, Hölzel BK, Posner MI. The neuroscience of mindfulness meditation. Nat Rev Neurosci 2015;16(4):213–25.

Tang Y-Y, Lu Q, Geng X, Stein EA, Yang Y, Posner MI. Short-term meditation induces white matter changes in the anterior cingulate. Proc Natl Acad Sci 2010;107(35):15649.

Tang Y-Y, Ma Y, Wang J, Fan Y, Feng S, Lu Q, Yu Q, Sui D, Rothbart MK, Fan M, Posner MI. Short-term meditation training improves attention and self-regulation. Proc Natl Acad Sci U S A 2007;104(43):17152–6.

Tamminga CA. The Anatomy of Fear Extinction. Am J Psychiatry. 2006;163(6):961–961.

Tanaka T, Takeshita H, Kawahara R, Hazama H. Chemical kindling with Met-enkephalin and transfer between chemical and electrical kindling. Epilepsy Res 1989;3(3):214–21.

Tarter RE, Hegedus AM, Goldstein G, Shelly C, Alterman AI. Adolescent sons of alcoholics: neuropsychological and personality characteristics. Alcohol. Clin. Exp. Res. 1984;8(2):216–22.

Tarter RE, Schneider DU. Blackouts: Relationship with memory capacity and alcoholism history. Arch Gen Psychiatry 1976; 33(12):1492-6.

Tatum AL, Seevers MH, Collins KH. Morphine addiction and its physiological interpretation based on experimental evidences. J Pharmacol Exp Ther. 1929;36(3):447.

Taylor AS, Hartshorne E. Medical jurisprudence. Philadelphia: Blanchard & Lea; 1856.

Tennyson AL. History and mechanism of international and national control of drugs of addiction. Symp Drug Addict. 1953; 14(5):578-85.

Tettenhall-Regis, from original mass of the fourteenth and fifteenth centuries. London: Published for the Early English Text Society, by Trübner; 1870.

Thackeray WM. Vanity Fair. Leipzig: Tauchnitz; 1848.

Thackeray WM. The four Georges sketches of manners, morals, court and town life. London: Smith, Elder and Co.; 1861.

Thévenot J de, Archibald L. The travels of Monsieur de Thévenot into the Levant in three parts, viz. into I. Turkey, II. Persia, III. the East-Indies. London: H. Faithorne. 1687.

Thiele TE, Navarro M, Sparta DR, Fee JR, Knapp DJ, Cubero I. Alcoholism and obesity: overlapping neuropeptide pathways? Neuropeptides. 2003; 37(6):321-37.

Thimann J. The Conditioned Reflex as a Treatment for Abnormal Drinking: Its Principle, Technic and Success. N Engl J Med. 1943;228(11):333–5.

Thoma KH. William T. G. Morton at the Massachusetts General Hospital. J Am Dent Assoc. 1946; 33(23):1519-21.

Thomas DW, Freedman DX. Treatment of the alcohol withdrawal syndrome: Comparison of promazine and paraldehyde. JAMA. 1964;188(3):316–8.

Thomson AD, Cook CCH, Touquet R, Henry JA. The Royal College of Physicians Report on Alcohol: Guidelines for Managing Wernicke's Encephalopathy in the Accident and Emergency Department. Alcohol Alcohol. 2002;37(6):513–21.

Thomson T. A system of chemistry: in four volumes. 1817.

Thompson T. The acts of the Lords Auditors of Causes & Complaints. [1466-1494]. Edinburgh: Scotland, Lords Auditors; 1839.

Thompson TI. Visual reinforcement in Siamese fighting fish. Science, 1963;141(3575):55.

Thorndike EL. The Elements of Psychology. New York: A.G. Seiler; 1905.

Thorndike EL. Biographical memoir of Granville Stanley Hall. National Academy of Sciences Biographical Memoirs. Washington, DC: National Academies Press. 1925.

Titchener EB. Lectures on the experimental psychology of the thought-processes. New York: Macmillan; 1909.

Tomei A, Besson J, Grivel J. Linking empathy to visuospatial perspective-taking in gambling addiction. Psychiatry Res 2017; 250:177–84. Rado S. Narcotic bondage. Am J Psychiatry. 1957;114(2):165-70.

Tomlinson MF, Brown M, Hoaken PNS. Recreational drug use and human aggressive behavior: A comprehensive review since 2003. Aggress Violent Behav, 2016;27:9–29.

Tori ME, Larochelle MR, Naimi TS. Alcohol or benzodiazepine co-involvement with opioid overdose deaths in the United States, 1999-2017. JAMA Network Open. 2020; 3(4):e202361.

Trana AD, Mannocchi G, Pirani F, Maida NL, Gottardi M, Pichini S, Busardò FP. A Comprehensive HPLC–MS-MS screening method for 77 new psychoactive substances, 24 classic drugs and 18 related metabolites in blood, urine and oral fluid. J Anal Toxicol. 2020; bkaa103.

Trento MMS, Moré AOO, Duarte ECW, Martins DF. Peripheral receptors and neuromediators involved in the antihyperalgesic effects of acupuncture: a state-of-the-art review. Pflüg Arch - Eur J Physiol. 2021; 473(4):573-593.

Treveris P. The grete Herball. London; 1529.

Trice HM, Staudenmeier WJ. A sociocultural history of Alcoholics Anonymous. In: Galanter M, editor. Recent Dev Alcohol Treat Res. Boston, MA: Springer; 1989. p. 11-35.

Trotter T. An Essay, Medical, Philosophical, and Chemical, on Drunkenness, and its Effects on the Human Body. London: Printed for TN Longman and O Rees, 1804.

Tseung YK. Acupuncture for drug addiction. The Lancet. 1974;304(7884):839.

Tubbs F. Historical Notes: Centenary of the death G. M. Burrows 1771-1846. Br Med Bull. 1947; 5(1):83.

Turner D. De Morbis Cutaneis. A Treatise of Diseases Incident to the Skin. London: Printed for R. Bonwicke, J. Walthoe, R. Wilkin, T. Ward, and S. Tooke; 1723.

Turner RJ, Lloyd DA. Cumulative adversity and drug dependence in young adults: racial/ethnic contrasts. Addiction. 2003; 98(3):305–15.

Tyrrell IR. Sobering up: from temperance to prohibition in ante-bellum America, 1800-1860. Westport, Conn: Greenwood Press; 1979.

Ungless MA, Whistler JL, Malenka RC, Bonci A. Single cocaine exposure in vivo induces long-term potentiation in dopamine neurons. Nature 2001;411(6837):583–7.

Unna K. Antagonistic effect of N-allylnormorphine upon morphine. J Pharmacol Exp Ther 1943; 79:27–31.

United States Surgeon General. The Health Consequences of Smoking -- 50 Years of progress: A Report of the Surgeon General: (510072014-001). 2014.

Unzer JA. The Principles of Physiology. Sydenham Society Edition. 1851, p. 53.

Ussher M, Taylor A, Faulkner G. Exercise interventions for smoking cessation. Cochrane Database Syst Rev. 2008;(4).

Vaillant GE. Twelve-year follow-up of New York narcotic addicts. N Engl J Med. 1966; 275(23):1282-8.

Vaillant GE. An empirically derived hierarchy of adaptive mechanisms and its usefulness as a potential diagnostic axis. Acta Psychiatr Scand. 1985; 71(S319):171-80.

van Linschoten JH. Iohn Hvighen van Linschoten : his discours of voyages into ye Easte & West Indies, divided into foure bookes. London: Printed by Iohn Wolfe. 1598.

Van Rensburg KJ, Taylor A, Hodgson T. The effects of acute exercise on attentional bias towards smoking-related stimuli during temporary abstinence from smoking. Addiction. 2009; 104(11):1910-7.

Van Zee A. The promotion and marketing of oxycontin: commercial triumph, public health tragedy. Am J Public Health 2009; 99:221–7.

Vashchinkina E, Panhelainen A, Aitta-aho T, Korpi ER. GABA$_A$ receptor drugs and neuronal plasticity in reward and aversion: focus on the ventral tegmental area. Front Pharmacol. 2014; 5:256.

Vaughan B. The sins of society: words spoken by Father Bernard Vaughan of the Society of Jesus, in the Church of the Immaculate Conception, Mayfair, during the season 1906. Toronto, Canada: Musson; 1906.

Veith I. Acupuncture therapy—past and present. Verity or delusion. JAMA. 1962;180(6):478–84.

Veith I. Huang Ti nei ching su wên. (The Yellow Emperor's Classic of Internal Medicine.) Berkeley: University of California Press; 1966.

Venniro M, Zhang M, Caprioli D, Hoots JK, Golden SA, Heins C, Morales M, Epstein DH, Shaham Y. Volitional social interaction prevents drug addiction in rat models. Nat Neurosci. 2018; 21(11):1520-9.

Vespucci A, Medici L di P de'. Alberic[us] Vespucci[us] Laure[n]tio Petri Francisci de Medicis salutem plurima[m] dicit. Paris: Felix Baligault and Jehan Lambert; 1503.

Victor M, Adams RD, Collins GH. The Wernicke-Korsakoff Syndrome: A Clinical and Pathological Study of 245 Patients, 82 with Post-mortem Examinations. Philadelphia: F. A. Davis; 1971.

Victor M, Yakovlev PI. S.S. Korsakoff's psychic dysphoric disorder in conjunction with peripheral neuritis; a translation of Korsakoff's original article with comments on the author and his contribution to clinical medicine. Neurology 1955; 5(6):394-406.

Vincent S, Curtis FR. Adrenin and the splanchnic nerve. J Physiol, 1927;63(2):151–4.

Vingilis E, Smart RG. Effects of raising the legal drinking age in Ontario. Br J Addict. 1981; 76(4):415-24.

Virkkunen M. Alcohol as a factor precipitating aggression and conflict behaviour leading to homicide. Br J Addict Alcohol Other Drugs, 1974;69(2):149–54.

Vischer R. Uber das optische Formgefühl ein Beitrag zur Aesthetik. Leipzig: Credner; 1873.

Vives JL, Morison R, Paynell T, Berthelet T, Taverner R, Erasmus D, Elyot T, Agapetos. Introduction to wisedome : Blanket of sapience. Preceptes of Agapetus. [Imprinted at London]: [In Fletestrete, in the hous of Tho. Berthelet]; 1550.

Voegtlin WL. The treatment of alcoholism by establishing a conditioned reflex. Am J Med Sci. 1940; 199:802–9.

Volkow ND. Stigma and the toll of addiction. N Engl J Med. 2020;382(14):1289–90.

Volkow ND, Fowler JS, Wang G-J. The addicted human brain: insights from imaging studies. J Clin Invest. 2003; 111(10):1444–51.

Volkow ND, Fowler JS, Wang G-J, Goldstein RZ. Role of dopamine, the frontal cortex and memory circuits in drug addiction: insight from imaging studies. Neurobiol Learn Mem. 2002; 78(3):610-24.

Volkow ND, Morales M. The brain on drugs: from reward to addiction. Cell. 2015;162(4):712–25.

Volkow ND, Wise RA. How can drug addiction help us understand obesity? Nat Neurosci. 2005; 8(5):555–60.

Volkow ND, Wise RA, Baler R. The dopamine motive system: implications for drug and food addiction. Nat Rev Neurosci. 2017; 18(12):741-52.

Von Euler US. A specific sympathomimetic ergone in adrenergic nerve fibres (Sympathin) and its relations to adrenaline and nor-adrenaline. Acta Physiol Scand, 1946;12(1):73–97.

Vonmoos M, Eisenegger C, Bosch OG, Preller KH, Hulka LM, Baumgartner M, Seifritz E, Quednow BB. Improvement of emotional empathy and cluster B personality disorder symptoms associated with decreased cocaine use severity. Front Psychiatry 2019; 10:213.

Von Neumann J, Morgenstern O. Theory of games and economic behaviour. Oxford: Oxford University Press; 1947.

de Waal FBM, Preston SD. Mammalian empathy: behavioural manifestations and neural basis. Nat Rev Neurosci 2017;18(8):498–509.

Waddington CH. The epigenotype. International Journal of Epidemiology, 2012; 41, 10-13.

Wadstein J, Skude G. Does hypokalaemia precede delirium tremens? Lancet. 1978; 312:549–50.

Wallace RK. Physiological effects of transcendental meditation. Science 1970;167(3926):1751–4.

Waller PF. Challenges in motor vehicle safety. Annu Rev Public Health. 2002; 23(1):93-113.

Wang G-J, Volkow ND, Chang L, Miller E, Sedler M, Hitzemann R, Zhu W, Logan J, Ma Y, Fowler JS. Partial recovery of brain metabolism in methamphetamine abusers after protracted abstinence. Am J Psychiatry, 2004;161(2):242–8.

Wang Y, Storr CL, Green KM, Zhu S, Stuart EA, Lynne-Landsman SD, Clemans KH, Petras H, Kellam SG, Ialongo NS. The effect of two elementary school-based prevention interventions on being offered tobacco and the transition to smoking. Drug Alcohol Depend. 2012; 120(1):202-8.

Warburton DER, Nicol CW, Bredin SSD. Health benefits of physical activity: the evidence. Can Med Assoc J. 2006; 174(6):801.

Ware J. Remarks on the history and treatment of delirium tremens. Lond Med Phys J. 1832; 120:280–91.

Walpole H, Wright J, Dover GA-E. The letters of Horace Walpole, earl of Orford: including numerous letters now first published from the original manuscripts. London, R. Bentley; 1846.

Ward E: The London spy. For the month of August, 1699. Part x. London, Printed and sold by J. How, in the Ram-Head-inn-yard in Fanchurch-street; 1699.

Watkins LR, Mayer DJ. Organization of endogenous opiate and nonopiate pain control systems. Science. 1982;216(4551):1185–92.

Watson JB, Rayner R. Conditioned emotional reactions. J Exp Psychol. 1920;3(1):1–14.

Watson R. Akolouthos or A second faire warning to take heed of the Scotish discipline, in vindication of the first, (which the Rt. Reverend Father in God, the Ld. Bishop of London Derrie published Ao 1649.) Against a schismatical & seditious reviewer R.B.G. one of the bold commissioners from the rebellious Kirke in Scotland to His Sacred Majestie K. Charles the Second when at the Hage, by Ri. Watson chaplane to the Rs. [sic] Hoble. the Lord Hopton. Hagh: printed by Samuel Broun, English bookseller; 1651.

Wee S-L, Hernández JC. Despite Trump's Pleas, China's Online Opioid Bazaar Is Booming. New York Times, Nov. 10, 2017, Section A, p. 8.

Wei S, Wang D, Wei G, Wang J, Zhou H, Xu H, Xia L, Tian Y, Dai Q, Zhu R, Wang W, Chen D, Xiu M, Wang L, Zhang XY. Association of cigarette smoking with cognitive impairment in male patients with chronic schizophrenia. Psychopharmacology (Berl). 2020.

Wei L, Wu G-R, Bi M, Baeken C. Effective connectivity predicts cognitive empathy in cocaine addiction: a spectral dynamic causal modeling study. Brain Imaging and Behavior 2021; 15:1553–61

Weijlard J, Erickson A. N-Allylnormorphine. J Am Chem Soc 1942; 64:869–70.

Weiner B, White W. The Journal of Inebriety (1876–1914): history, topical analysis, and photographic images. Addiction 2007;102(1):15–23.

Weingartner H, Grafman J, Boutelle W, Kaye W, Martin PR. Forms of memory failure. Science. 1983;221(4608):380-382.

Weinstein DD, Martin PR. Psychiatric implications of alcoholism and traumatic brain injury. Am J Addict. 1995; 4:285–96.

Weissman MM, Slobetz F, Prusoff B, Mezritz M, Howard P. Clinical depression among narcotic addicts maintained on methadone in the community. Am J Psychiatry. 1976; 133(12):1434-8.

Welch LW, Nimmerrichter A, Kessler R, King D, Hoehn R, Margolin R, Martin PR. Severe global amnesia presenting as Wernicke–Korsakoff syndrome but resulting from atypical lesions. Psychological Medicine. 1996;26(2):421–5.

Wernicke K. Die akute, hämorrhagische Polioencephalitis superior. Lehrb Gehirnkrankheiten. Kassel: Theodor Fischer; 1881. p. 229–42.

Westcott BF. Christian Aspects of Life. London; New York: Macmillan; 1897.

Wetherill RR, Castro N, Squeglia LM, Tapert SF. Atypical neural activity during inhibitory processing in substance-naïve youth who later experience alcohol-induced blackouts. Drug Alcohol Depend. 2013; 128(3):243-9.

Wetherill RR, Schnyer DM, Fromme K. Acute alcohol effects on contextual memory BOLD response: differences based on fragmentary blackout history. Alcohol Clin Exp Res. 2012; 36(6):1108-15.

Whately R. Introductory lessons on morals, and Christian evidences. Cambridge [Mass.]: J. Bartlett Ann Arbor, Michigan: University of Michigan Library; 1857.

White NM. Reward or reinforcement: What's the difference? Neural Basis Reward Reinforcement: A Conference in Honour of Peter M Milner. Neuroscience & Biobehavioral Reviews 1989;13(2):181–6.

Whitehead CS, Hoff CA, Stoll JJ. Ethical sex relations: or, The new eugenics: a safe guide for young men - young women. Chicago; Toronto: The John A. Hertel Co.; 1928.

Whitehead PC. Notes on the association between alcoholism and suicide. Int J Addict. 1972; 7(3):525-32.

Wikler A. Recent progress in research on the neurophysiologic basis of morphine addiction. Am J Psychiatry. 1948;105(5):329–38.

Wikler A. Pharmacologic dissociation of behavior and EEG "sleep patterns" in Dogs: morphine, N-Allylnormorphine, and atropine. Proc Soc Exp Biol Med. 1952; 79(2):261–5.

Wikler A. On the nature of addiction and habituation. Br J Addict Alcohol Other Drugs. 1961; 57(2):73-9.

Wikler A. Dynamics of drug dependence: implications of a conditioning theory for research and treatment. JAMA Psychiatry. 1973;28(5):611–6.

Wilkinson DA, Carlen PL. Relationship of neuropsychological test performance to brain morphology in amnesic and non-amnesic chronic alcoholics. Acta Psychiatr Scand. 1980;62(s286):89–101.

Willcox WH, Pickworth FA, Young HM. The clinical and pathological effects of hypnotic drugs of the barbituric acid and sulphonal groups. Proc R Soc Med. 1927; 20(9):1479–506.

Willis T, Pordage S, Loggan D, Van Dyke R. The remaining medical works of that famous and renowned physician Dr Thomas Willis of Christchurch in Oxford, and Sidley Professor of Natural Philosophy in the famous University: viz. I. Of fermentation. II. Of feavours. III. Of urines. IV. Of the accension of the bloud. V. Of muscular motion. VI. Of the anatomy of the brain. VII. Of the description and use of the nerves. VIII. Of convulsive diseases; with large alphabetical tables for the whole, and an index for the explaining all the hard and unusual words and terms of art, derived from the Latine, Greek, or other languages, for the benefit of the meer English reader, and meanest capacity; with eighteen copper plates. London: Printed for T. Dring, C. Harper, J. Leigh, and S. Martyn, and are to be sold by Robert Clavell, at the Peacock in St Paul's Church-yard; 1681.

Wilner DM, Kassebaum GC, editors. Narcotics. New York: McGraw-Hill Book Company, Inc. (Blakiston):1965.

Willstätter R, Ettlinger F. Synthese der Hygrinsäure und der α-Pyrrolidincarbonsäure. Justus Liebigs Ann Chem. John Wiley & Sons, Ltd, 1903;326(1-2):91–128.

Wilson B. Alcoholics Anonymous: The Story of How Many Thousands of Men and Women Have Recovered from Alcoholism. Works Publishing Company, New York City. 1939.

Wilson C. The pathology of drunkenness; a view of the operation of ardent spirits in the production of disease; founded on original observation, and research. Edinburgh: A. & C. Black; 1855.

Wise RA. The role of reward pathways in the development of drug dependence. Pharmacol Ther. 1987; 35(1):227-63.

Wise RA. Addictive drugs and brain stimulation reward. Annu Rev Neurosci 1996;19(1):319–40.

Witkiewitz K, Falk DE, Litten RZ, Hasin DS, Kranzler HR, Mann KF, O'Malley SS, Anton RF. Maintenance of World Health Organization risk drinking level reductions and posttreatment functioning following a large alcohol use disorder clinical trial. Alcohol Clin Exp Res. 2019; 43(5):979-87.

Witkiewitz K, Vowles KE. Alcohol and opioid use, co-use, and chronic pain in the context of the opioid epidemic: a critical review. Alcohol Clin Exp Res. 2018; 42(3):478-88.

Witt ED, Goldman-Rakic PS. Intermittent thiamine deficiency in the rhesus monkey. I. Progression of neurological signs and neuroanatomical lesions. Ann Neurol. 1983;13(4):376–95.

Woermann FG, van Elst LT, Koepp MJ, Free SL, Thompson PJ, Trimble MR, Duncan JS. Reduction of frontal neocortical grey matter associated with affective aggression in patients with temporal lobe epilepsy: an objective voxel by voxel analysis of automatically segmented MRI. J Neurol Neurosurg Psychiatry, 2000;68(2):162–9.

Wolpe J. Conditioned inhibition of craving in drug addiction: A pilot experiment. Behav Res Ther. 1964; 2(2):285-8.

Wood HC Jr. A treatise on therapeutics: comprising materia medica and toxicology, with especial reference to the application of the physiological action of drugs to clinical medicine. Philadelphia: J.B. Lippincott & Co.; 1874.

Wood P. Da Costa's Syndrome: Aetiology. Lecture III. Br Med J. 1941; 1(4196):845–51.

Wood S, Sage JR, Shuman T, Anagnostaras SG. Psychostimulants and cognition: a continuum of behavioral and cognitive activation. Pharmacol Rev. 2014; 66(1):193.

Woodward SB. Essays on Asylums for Inebriates. Worcester, Mass, 1838.

Woolf SH, Schoomaker H. Life expectancy and mortality rates in the United States, 1959-2017. JAMA. 2019; 322(20):1996-2016.

Wordsworth W, Coleridge ST. Lyrical ballads, with other poems: two volumes. London: Printed for T.N. Longman and O. Rees, Paternoster-Row, by Biggs and Co. Bristol; 1800.

Work TS, Bergel F, Todd AR. The active principles of Cannabis indica resin. I. Biochem J. 1939;33(1):123-7.

World Health Organization. Alcohol and alcoholism: report of an Expert Committee [meeting held in Geneva from 27 September to 2 October 1954]. World Health Organization Technical Report Series, 94, 955.

World Health Organization. Mental disorders: Glossary and guide to their classification in accordance with the Ninth Revision of the International Classification of Diseases. Geneva: World Health Organization; 1978.

World Health Organization. International statistical classification of diseases and related health problems. Geneva, Switzerland; 2016.

World Health Organization. International standards for the treatment of drug use disorders: revised edition incorporating results of field-testing. Geneva: World Health Organization and United Nations Office on Drugs and Crime; 2020.

Wortis H, Bueding E, Stein MH, Jolliffe N. Pyruvic acid studies in the Wernicke syndrome. Arch Neurol Psychiatry. 1942;47(2):215–22.

Wright T, Halliwell-Phillipps JO. Reliquiae antiquae scraps from ancient manuscripts, illustrating chiefly early English literature and the English language 1 1. London: R. Smith; 1845.

Wright T, Wülcker RP. Anglo-Saxon and Old English vocabularies. London: Trübner; 1884.

Xiao Z, Lee T, Zhang JX, Wu Q, Wu R, Weng X, Hu X. Thirsty heroin addicts show different fMRI activations when exposed to water-related and drug-related cues. Drug Alcohol Depend. 2006; 83(2):157-62.

Yang F, Yao L, Wang S, Guo Y, Xu Z, Zhang C-H, Zhang K, Fang Y, Liu Y. Current Tracking on effectiveness and mechanisms of acupuncture therapy: a literature review of high-quality studies. Chin J Integr Med. 2020;26(4):310–20.

Yehuda R, Keefe RS, Harvey P, Levengood R, Gerber D, Geni J, Siever L. Learning and memory in combat veterans with posttraumatic stress disorder. Am J Psychiatry. 1995; 152(1):137–9.

Yehuda R, Schmeidler J, Wainberg M, Binder-Brynes K, Duvdevani T. Vulnerability to Posttraumatic Stress Disorder in adult offspring of Holocaust survivors. Am J Psychiatry. 1998; 155(9):1163-71.

Yentis SM, Vlassakov KV. Vassily von Anrep, Forgotten Pioneer of Regional Anesthesia. Anesthesiology, 1999;90(3):890–5.

Yerkes RM, Dodson JD. The relation of strength of stimulus to rapidity of habit-formation. J Comp Neurol Psychol. 1908; 18(5):459–82.

Yerkes RM, Morgulis S. The method of Pawlow in animal psychology. Psychol Bull. 1909;6(8):257–73.

Yi JP, Vitaliano PP, Smith RE, Yi JC, Weinger K. The role of resilience on psychological adjustment and physical health in patients with diabetes. Br J Health Psychol. 2008; 13(2):311-25.

Yip SW, Scheinost D, Potenza MN, Carroll KM. Connectome-based prediction of cocaine abstinence. Am J Psychiatry, 2019;176(2):156-64.

Young T. A course of lectures on natural philosophy and the mechanical arts. London: Printed for J. Johnson by W. Savage; 1807.

Young PT. Motivation of Behavior. New York: J. Wiley & Sons, Inc.; 1936.

Yu J, Min D, Bai Y, Qu L, Zou T, Wang S. Electroacupuncture alleviates Parkinson disease and regulates the expression of brain-gut peptides. Exp Anim. 2020;69(4):448–60.

Yu K-C, Wei H-T, Chang S-C, Huang K-Y, Hsu C-H. The efficacy of combined electroacupuncture and auricular pressure on sleep quality in patients receiving methadone maintenance treatment. Am J Addict. 2021;30(2):156–63.

Yuan N, Chen Y, Xia Y, Dai J, Liu C. Inflammation-related biomarkers in major psychiatric disorders: a cross-disorder assessment of reproducibility and specificity in 43 meta-analyses. Transl Psychiatry. 2019; 9(1):233.

Yules RB, Freedman DX, Chandler KA. The effect of ethyl alcohol on man's electroencephalographic sleep cycle. Electroencephalogr Clin Neurophysiol. 1966; 20(2):109–11.

Zale EL, Maisto SA, Ditre JW. Interrelations between pain and alcohol: An integrative review. Clin Psychol Rev. 2015; 37:57-71.

Zhang D, Lee EKP, Mak ECW, Ho CY, Wong SYS. Mindfulness-based interventions: an overall review. Br Med Bull 2021;138(1):41–57.

Zhang R, Volkow ND. Brain default-mode network dysfunction in addiction. NeuroImage. 2019; 200:313-31.

Zhong Y-M, Luo X-C, Chen Y, Lai D-L, Lu W-T, Shang Y-N, Zhang L-L, Zhou H-Y. Acupuncture versus sham acupuncture for simple obesity: a systematic review and meta-analysis. Postgrad Med J. 2020;96(1134):221–7.

Zhu M. The Medical Classic of the Yellow Emperor. Beijing, China: Foreign Languages Press; 2001.

Acknowledgements

I wish to thank Dr. Thomas Ban who encouraged me to begin this journey and stimulated me to continue my travels even during the challenging period of the COVID-19 pandemic. In many ways he helped me through regular discussions until I found my own way so I could carry on when he passed. Additionally, my good friend Dr. Reid Finlayson was a constant sounding board about various aspects of addiction and psychiatry both on and off the tennis courts. Finally, my wife Barbara and son Alec continue to inspire, love and support me.

I also want to acknowledge the expert editorial contribution of Olaf Fjetland who was rigorous and demanding but very helpful. My colleagues at INHN Publishing, Dr. Carlos Morra and Ms. Lucrecia Alvarez were eager to offer their assistance as needed and without their important contributions it would have been impossible to publish this volume. Finally, I want to thank the other members of INHN who made the effort to comment on my entries on the INHN website—Jose de Leon (Coffee), Carlos R. Hojaij (Exercise), Louis C. Charland (Addiction) and Hector Warnes (Wernicke-Korsakoff and Empathy). Special thanks to Johan Schioldann whose very short but to the point comment led to substantive revision of the Opium entry. All comments and my responses thereto have been included in an Appendix for the interest of the reader.

APPENDIX. Posting Interactions

Louis C. Charland's comment on Addiction

I am writing to offer praise and a comment for reflection on Peter R. Martin's remarks on the history of the term "addiction" in his Historical Vocabulary of Addiction (Martin 2016).

Martin's brief historical comments on the origins of the medical meaning of "addiction" go well beyond what is common in contemporary state of the art medical discussions on the history of the term "addiction" (Maddux and Desmon 2000). This is to be commended. In particular, citing detailed examples, Martin skillfully draws our attention to the manner in which very early usages of the term begin to branch out from a more generic meaning of the term to more specific usages that point directly to specific substances known for their neuropsychopharmacological properties. Addiction *to* alcohol is his first example.

Before making this point about early medical usages of the term, Martin commendably mentions an earlier generic use of the term "addiction," which centers around "dedication, devotion to a thing or an activity" (Martin 2016). Yet he does not appear to mention an important feature of this generic use of the term, which might be of interest to medical practitioners and scholars interested in addiction. This is that "addiction" in this prior generic sense of 'devotion' occurs with sometimes very different – even paradoxical – social evaluations of the practices with which it is identified.

Devotional addictions can occur when there are no substances with neuropsychopharmacological properties: for example, addictions to God, or to a person who is loved. These can develop into extreme forms (sometimes called "passions"), where agency and "agentive selfhood" are severely compromised and there are harms to self and/or others, even though the addiction itself is still viewed as a laudable social practice. Evidently, progressive "loss of selfhood" and "loss of control" in addiction are not new notions and are not limited to addictions directed at substances with neuropsychopharmacological properties.

There are a variety of examples like these in the history of addiction in the early modern period, which highlight the manner in which some addictions can be viewed as positive, even though they also lead to negative consequences, including physical harms, compromised agency and loss of self (Lemon 2018). The point is that addictive practices are subject to social evaluations that vary, and their positive or negative character is not an objective feature of the practices themselves, but instead a result of social contextual factors. In sum:

The history of addiction in the early modern period teaches us that addiction is a paradoxical human phenomenon that offers rich possibilities for positive action and development, though these are inextricably bound and inseparable from risks that may lead to negative outcomes. This provides a helpful contrast to current discourse on addiction, which is often paralyzed with the oversimplifications imposed by the adoption of false dichotomies, especially the view that the term "addiction" refers to a phenomenon that is exclusively either good or bad (Charland 2020).

It is interesting that even practices such as excessive individual participation in community "health drinking" (to the point of complete inebriation) in the early modern era, which was clearly understood to sometimes lead to harmful compulsive drinking in the individual over time, was often excused and even lauded, despite its harmful consequences (Lemon 2018). The reason is that the addiction was socially appraised according to a higher ethical ideal of devotion to community bonding, where the health of the individual drinker is secondary.

Indeed, in these early uses of the term "addiction," addictions apparently have a paradoxical feature built into them. Submitting or surrendering to a passion always carries an inherent risk of coming to a point where one loses oneself in an addiction, with all the negative consequences that may come with this. And yet this can still ultimately be declared a good thing! One could attempt to stipulate and redefine "addiction" in such a way that it carries no inherent risk of paradox of this sort. But that would arguably represent an impoverishment of the original meaning and conceptual dynamics of the term – and the human (all too human) realties it was developed to capture and contend with. The view that medical addictions to substances with neuropsychopharmacological properties are pathological should probably always be understood with this nuance in mind.

References:

Charland LC. A puzzling anomaly: Decision-Making Capacity and Research on Addiction. In: Iltis A, MacKay D, editors. Oxford Handbook of Research Ethics. Oxford: Oxford University Press; 2020

Lemon R. Addiction and Devotion in Early Modern England. Philadelphia: University of Pennsylvania Press; 2018

Maddux JF, Desmon DP. Addiction or dependence? Addiction 2000;95(5):661–5.

Martin P. Addiction. Historical Vocabulary of Addiction. inhn.org.ebooks. November 24, 2016.

Peter Martin's response to Louis C. Charland's comment

I thank Louis C. Charland for his thoughtful comments concerning my note on the history of the word "addiction" in the *Historical Vocabulary of Addiction* (HVA) (Martin 2016).

Charland rightly identifies a meaning that was only just mentioned in my analysis of the term "addiction", which pertains to "devotion", and he discusses how such can occur without neuropsychopharmacological agents and thus are sometimes called "passions." The discussion comes essentially from Charland's excellent contribution on compromise of decision-making capacity in addiction (Charland 2020).

This is an important topic to which I have not yet attended in great detail, in part, because I do not possess Charland's command of ethics and philosophy. I do hope to address this topic in a subsequent entry in HVA, as this issue is really very important, particularly when one considers newer areas of research such as behavioral addictions, wherein no neuropsychopharmacological agent is involved, yet decision making can be profoundly compromised.

I refer the reader to another entry in HVA wherein I raise some of the issues Charland discusses in his comment.   In the analysis of the word "opium" (Martin 2019) there is some discussion of meanings of this word that go well beyond physiology and medicine. These concepts of "opium" extend to historical, social, and political philosophy, perhaps most notably expressed by Karl Marx (Marx and Stenning 1926): "Religion is the moan of the oppressed creature, the sentiment of a heartless world, as it is the spirit of spiritless conditions. It is the opium of the people." In this quotation, "passion" and "addiction" are utterly confounded linguistically within the understood meaning of the neuropsychopharmacological agent "opium," perhaps the primal addictive substance used by Man. Conceivably, such subtle distinctions might not be possible, as behavioral and neuropsychopharmacological effects in the brain are made of some of the same "stuff"?

References:

Charland LC. A Puzzling Anomaly: Decision-Making Capacity and Research on Addiction. In: Iltis AS, MacKay D, editors. Oxf Handb Res Ethics. Oxford University Press; 2020.

Martin PR. Addiction. Peter R. Martin: Historical Vocabulary of Addiction. inhn.org.ebooks. November 24, 2016.

Martin PR. Opium. Peter R. Martin: Historical Vocabulary of Addiction. inhn.org.ebooks. July 4, 2019.

Marx K, Stenning HJ. Selected essays. New York: International Publishers; 1926.

Jose de Leon's comment on Coffee

I found the history of coffee use very helpful, and I learned a lot from it. The section on the interactions of caffeine use with tobacco and alcohol use may be strengthened by focusing on the pharmacokinetic and pharmacodynamic mechanisms as they appear to be important, according to our caffeine studies in schizophrenia.

The polycyclic aromatic hydrocarbon (PAH) compounds from tobacco smoke induce caffeine metabolism by increasing the expression of cytochrome P450 1A2 (CYP1A2). This induction is probably mediated by the aryl hydrocarbon receptor (AhR) (de Leon 2015). Heavy smokers need two to three times higher caffeine intake to get the same serum caffeine concentrations as non-smokers (de Leon, Diaz, Rogers et al., 2003). The inductive effects of smoking can confound the association studies; we first thought that caffeine use may be greater in outpatients with schizophrenia (Gurpegui, Aguilar, Martínez-Ortega et al. 2004; Gurpegui, Aguilar, Martínez-Ortega et al. 2006). However, in further studies including inpatients (Arrojo-Romero, Armas Barbazán, López-Moriñigo et al. 2015), we found that schizophrenia does not appear to be consistently associated with increased prevalence of caffeine use and the increased prevalence of high caffeine intake in caffeine users does not stand up when controlling for confounders. Future epidemiological studies, preferably using serum concentrations, will need to establish whether caffeinism (defined as >700 mg/day of caffeine) is particularly prevalent in schizophrenia or not and determine the contribution of inducers in caffeinism (Arrojo-Romero, Armas Barbazán, López-Moriñigo et al. 2015).

Our schizophrenia outpatients had access to alcohol and demonstrated that alcohol and caffeine use were significantly associated. In caffeine users, alcohol was associated with less frequent high caffeine consumption among non-smokers, probably because alcohol may potentiate caffeine brain pharmacodynamic effects (Gurpegui, Aguilar, Martínez-Ortega et al., 2006). Chronic alcohol intake decreases adenosine tone (Ferré and O'Brien 2011), suggesting that alcohol users may have decreased need for higher caffeine intake since lower caffeine intake may have the same effects in the brain for a chronic alcohol user as high caffeine intake has for a non-alcohol user. As our inpatients had no access to alcohol (Arrojo-Romero, Armas Barbazán, López-Moriñigo et al. 2015), we could not replicate the possibility of this pharmacodynamic interaction between alcohol and caffeine in non-smokers (Gurpegui, Aguilar, Martínez-Ortega et al., 2006).

References:

Arrojo-Romero M, Armas Barbazán C, López-Moriñigo JD, Ramos-Ríos R, Gurpegui M, Martínez-Ortega JM, Jurado D, Diaz FJ, de Leon J. Caffeine consumption in a long-term psychiatric hospital: Tobacco smoking may explain in large part the apparent association between schizophrenia and caffeine use. Schizophrenia Research 2015; 164:234-41.

de Leon J. The effects of antiepileptic inducers in neuropsychopharmacology, a neglected issue. Part II: Pharmacological issues and further understanding. Revista de Psiquiatría y Salud Mental 2015; 8:167-88.

de Leon J, Diaz FJ, Rogers T, Browne D, Dinsmore L, Ghosheh OH, Dwoskin LP, Crooks PA. A pilot study of plasma caffeine concentrations in a US sample of smoker and nonsmoker volunteers. Progress in Neuropsychopharmacology & Biological Psychiatry 2003; 27:165-71.

Ferré S, O'Brien MC. Alcohol and caffeine: the perfect storm. J. Caffeine Research 2011; 1:153-62.

Gurpegui M, Aguilar MC, Martínez-Ortega JM, Diaz FJ, de Leon J. Caffeine intake in outpatients with schizophrenia. Schizophrenia Bulletin 2004; 30:935-45.

Gurpegui M, Aguilar MC, Martínez-Ortega JM, Jurado D, Diaz FJ, Quintana HM, de Leon J. Fewer but heavier caffeine consumers in schizophrenia: a case-control study. Schizophrenia Research 2006; 86:276-83.

Peter R. Martin's response to Jose de Leon's comment

I thank Jose de Leon for his thoughtful comments. He raises some very interesting issues about the pharmacokinetic (smoking and caffeine consumption) and pharmacodynamic (alcohol and caffeine) interactions among these widely available psychoactive substances that tend to be used together. He examined these interactions in inpatient, outpatient, and controls to better understand pathogenesis and clinical features of schizophrenia.

Caffeine biotransformation has been used for decades to probe cytochrome P450 activity *in vivo* and it is now well accepted that smoking induces the microsomal metabolism of many compounds including caffeine (Axelrod and Reichenthal 1953; Conney 1967; Parsons and Neims 1978). Nevertheless, as summarized by Nehlig (2018) in her recent review on caffeine metabolism and coffee consumption: "it appears that consumption of coffee/caffeine would rather be driven by the functional consequences of caffeine than by the rate at which the methylxanthine is metabolized." Moreover, tolerance to the behavioral effects of caffeine/coffee is of relatively low magnitude and incomplete compared to other drugs of abuse (Fredholm, Bättig, Holmén et al. 1999). This suggests that the pharmacodynamic interactions between alcohol and caffeine that Jose de Leon describes in his comments are theoretically possible but in fact the opposite typically occurs in life - alcohol consumption, smoking and coffee drinking have seemed to go hand in hand in the history of the western world, acquired developmentally in the individual and culturally in society (Reich, Dietrich and Martin 2011; Fischer, Victor, Robinson et al. 2019).

One of the major issues I wanted to raise in my contribution is that coffee is not only caffeine, although these two words are often confused and used interchangeably in common parlance as they were by Jose de Leon. The very widely consumed beverage coffee contains a myriad of biologically active molecules which account for many of its health benefits (Farah, de Paulis, Moreira et al. 2006; Freedman, Park, Abnet et al. 2012; van Dam, Hu and Willett 2020). In fact, the interactions between coffee and alcohol consumption alluded to by Jose de Leon are even more compelling because coffee consumption seems to be *protective* against development of alcoholic cirrhosis, cancer, obesity and even suicide/depression that are major causes of morbidity and mortality in alcoholism. Additionally, most of these and other health benefits associated with coffee consumption are related to non-caffeine components of coffee rather than caffeine. Therefore, unravelling the mechanisms involved are challenging and distinct from the pharmacology of caffeine *per se* and have become an emerging area of ongoing research.

References:

Axelrod J, Reichenthal J. The fate of caffeine in man and a method for its estimation in biological material. J Pharmacol Exp Ther 1953;107(4):519.

Conney AH. Pharmacological implications of microsomal enzyme induction. Pharmacol Rev 1967;19(3):317.

Farah A, de Paulis T, Moreira DP, Trugo LC, Martin PR. Chlorogenic acids and lactones in regular and water-decaffeinated Arabica coffees. J Agric Food Chem 2006;54(2):374–81.

Fischer EF, Victor B, Robinson D, Farah A, Martin PR. Coffee consumption and health impacts: a brief history of changing conceptions. Coffee: Consumption and Health Implications. The Royal Society of Chemistry; 2019. pp. 1–19.

Fredholm BB, Bättig K, Holmén J, Nehlig A, Zvartau EE. Actions of caffeine in the brain with special reference to factors that contribute to its widespread use. Pharmacol Rev 1999;51(1):83.

Freedman ND, Park Y, Abnet CC, Hollenbeck AR, Sinha R. Association of coffee drinking with total and cause-specific mortality. N Engl J Med 2012;366(20):1891–904.

Nehlig A. Interindividual differences in caffeine metabolism and factors driving caffeine consumption. Alexander SPH, editor. Pharmacol Rev 2018;70(2):384.

Parsons WD, Neims AH. Effect of smoking on caffeine clearance. Clinical Pharmacology & Therapeutics 1978;24(1):40–5.

Reich MS, Dietrich MS, Martin PR. Temporal sequence of incident cigarette, coffee, and alcohol use among AA participants. The American Journal of Drug and Alcohol Abuse 2011;37(1):27–36.

van Dam RM, Hu FB, Willett WC. Coffee, caffeine, and health. N Engl J Med 2020;383(4):369–78.

Hector Warnes' comment on Empathy

My congratulations to Peter Martin for his brilliant narrative on Empathy and its relationship with Sympathy, its neurophysiological basis and the addictive disorders.

I would like to pay tribute to Heinz Kohut (1913-1981) who transformed psychoanalytic technique by introducing Self-psychology (beyond Ego Psychology) (Kohut 1959).

In the analytic practice of Self psychology, you are likely to evoke three types of transference particularly in those patients with "deficit disorders," dissolution of the Self, limitation of interpersonal bonds and short-coming of the capacity for introspection and empathy during human interactions, e.g., mirroring, idealizing and twinship/alter-ego transference. An empathic connectedness is a kind of "projective identification," or as Peter Martin puts it, a person or analyst projects one's personality... identifying himself with the object of contemplation. Martin further argues, "Probably, the first manifestation of this interconnectedness in humans is the mother-child bond," a statement supported by Bowlby's extensive research on attachment behavior with emphasis on maternal care in primates and Spitz's observations on early maternal deprivation in babies (Hospitalism).

Clinical Psychoanalysis has uncovered the False Self, which is the Image one projects of oneself, and the authentic sense of Self. The latter comes about through countless empathic contacts with significant other humans which, according to Heinz Kohut (1971), are internalized as Self-objects. Of course, the starting point is having experienced a "good enough mothering."

Henry Krystal (1988) found in drug-dependent persons an affective disturbance consisting of affect de-differentiation, de-verbalization, and re-somatization. Not unlike the alexithymic person, these patients were not able to put their emotions into words and often somatized them. They experienced a sense of painful emptiness which was transiently alleviated by the use of drugs.

Bartels and Zeki, using f-MRI scan, in 2004 wrote about the neural correlates of maternal and romantic love while mothers viewed pictures of their own and/or acquainted children. Both types of attachment behavior activate regions in the brain's reward system, particularly the dopaminergic circuits and the oxytoxin-vasopressin receptors.

References:

Bartels A, Zeki S. The neural correlates of maternal and romantic love. Neuroimage 2004;21(3):1155-66.

Kohut H. Introspection, empathy, and psychoanalysis. An Examination of the Relationship between Mode of Observation and Theory. Journal of the Amer Psychoanalytic Assoc 1959;3(3):459-83.

Kohut H. The Analysis of the Self. A Systematic Approach to the Psychoanalytic Treatment of Narcissistic Personality Disorders. New York: International Universities Press; 1971.

Krystal H. Integration and Self-Healing. Affect, Trauma and Alexithymia. Hillsdale, NJ: The Analytic Press; 1988.

Peter R. Martin's response to Hector Warnes' comment

Hector Warnes adds a very worthwhile perspective with his analysis of my essay on Empathy. His viewpoint is likely based on a comprehensive working knowledge of human interactions gained through clinical observations of the interconnectedness of human beings using psychoanalytic techniques. Conceptualization of human bonds within the framework of psychoanalysis, a uniquely human construct, adds to and can be complemented by those of neuroscience and evolutionary study of these phenomenon in other species. Merging these perspectives by reflecting on the contributions of Kohut, Bowlby, Spitz and Krystal who have observed these phenomena in man throughout the stages of development in health and in disease are valuable.

I particularly appreciate Hector Warnes acknowledging the epistemological linkages between neuroscientific methods embodied in neuroimaging/neuroendocrinology and psychoanalytic concepts via a demonstrated relationship between "maternal and romantic love while mothers viewed pictures of their own and/or acquainted children" and "the brain's reward system, particularly the dopaminergic circuits and the oxytoxin-vasopressin receptors." This, of course, elegantly summarizes the vital role of empathy (or lack thereof) in the pathophysiology, phenomenology, and treatment of the very human disease of addiction.

Carlos R. Hojaij's comment on Exercise

Peter Martin goes into "exercise's" etymology and historical citations demonstrating the importance of a proper diet to maintain an equilibrium between body and mind. His erudite paper leading to contemporaneous scientific findings allows him to conclude that "the multiple relationship between exercise and behavioral/alcohol/drug addictions suggest a potential evolutionary role of physical activity in maintenance of physical and emotional health that has been dislocated by our affluent society. More important, these observations point to the importance of exercise to help recreate the level of activity that is required to maintain health and vitality… we appear to have lost in the 'developed' world."

This paper stimulated me to revisit our most relevant cultural heritage: the classical Greek and its pragmatical Roman culture.

1. In "Carmides" Plato (1979) describes Socrates visiting gymnasiums to meet people, young and old, and engage them is his famous dialogues. It is known that the Greeks of that time practice gymnastic and sport completely naked. Metaphorically, a gymnasium would be a place where the body, the soul or ideas could freely be disposed, for any kind censorship was not present. The gymnasium would be a place of excellence for the practice (exercise) of physical activity and philosophy. Coincidence or not, maybe the most famous philosophical schools in the world, the Academy (Plato) and the Liceum (Aristotle), are the names of two Athena's gymnasium (Jaeger 2013).

2. In "Fedro" Plato (1979) mentions Socrates in a dialogue with Fedro citing Herodico: "go from Athens to the walls of Megara and return (a 80 km walking)." Herodico de Salimbria, a Greek doctor from the V century, Hippocrates's tutor, is considered the first one to propose physical exercise for treatment of medical diseases and maintenance of heath, what currently could be called Sports Medicine (Georgoulis, Kiapidou, Velogianni et al. 2007).

3. Gymnastics (together with music) was an essential part of the classical Greek education, once more composing elements of body and soul. Of course, physical exercises were imperative for a better preparation of the citizens, taking into account the common battles between the Greek

states and its neighbors. However, in terms of education, the force was not the major point, but the dexterity of movements, harmony, equilibrium and the beauty of the body.

4. Before the classical period, in 776 BC the Greek states decided to homage Zeus every four years with a festival including disputes comprising several sports. As it is well known, the importance of the Olympiads was so high that all states suspended any kind disagreement and battles for the time of the festival. It was time to honor the heroes of all cities.

5. The Greek philosophy is based on the principle of isomerism: no prevalence of one force. This principle is applied to the Hippocratic medicine: a state of health would be achieved by the equilibrium (harmony) between the needs of the body and a diet: the necessary amount of food would be dictated by the need of the body in specific situation (Hippocrates' empiricism). Equally, the sense of measurement (limit) was applied to the mind to permit adequate actions. Icarus is the famous example where the measurement failed.

6. Jaeger (2013) analyses several aspects of Da *Dieta*, written by an unknown author, probably prior to Hippocrates. The author could well be a philosopher and/or a doctor because incorporated in the text are Hippocratic principles and philosophical aspects. It is interesting to cite: "The diagnosis is linked to gnosis, knowledge of the whole nature. In sequence, comes the knowledge of details, to start from foods and their effects on different constitutions, as well in reference to physical efforts. This last aspect is so important as it is an adequate diet… proposing a systematic and conscious balance to the opposite effects from food and physical efforts." Here we realize the symmetric principle applied to the relationship between nutrition and physical exercises. In this regard there is a similarity to Herodico, who attributed to exercises the first place in a diet.

7. It was a Roman writer, the satiric Decimus Junius Juvenalis (Juvenal), living in the I-II centuries who created the aphorism: *mens sana in corpore sano*. Analyzing this Juvenal expression, I understand the initial (primordial) importance is given to the body. If you don't have a healthy body, you are unlikely to have a healthy mind. Of course, the mind is able to influence the body, but up to a certain point. I don't need to go further on this matter. On the other hand, the mind is able to influence the body, again up to a certain point. That is what Peter Martin claims for

regular exercise, to help to suppress addiction, a concept going back to Herodico and Hippocrates's medicine.

8. Peter Martin writes: "…we appear to have lost in the 'developed world' the appetite to regular exercise." Indeed, the governments and the big monopolies are promoting, "If you want something, press the keyboard." Smartly, this has created a technical dependence on computers and phones, a new fanaticism almost replacing all religions. The well corrupt and conducted media promotes a society heavily dependent on fast food, stimulating laziness and self-indulgence. There are announcements for food everywhere, all the time. Currently, there is no further need to seduce; the population has become, if not addicted, entirely "regulated" to constantly eat. It is this cocktail of "be yourself, do yourself pressing the key, enjoy yourself, take it easy, be part of the modern world," that institutionalizes the sacred obesity and a new aphorism: "be fatty, but happy." For sure, in this regard there is an epidemic addiction to food, maybe much worse than the one caused by the international Corona Virus-19; the viral epidemic will pass, but not the food addiction, because at least at the beginning it offers just pleasure.

9. Wall Disney Pictures launched in 2008 a movie initially dedicated to children called "Wall-E" (Waste Allocation Load Lifter-Earth Class). Wall-E is a robot from our time, but his presence in the movie relates to 700 years ahead, let us say 2700. At that time, the Earth is literally covered by mountains of garbage. Wall-E survived all these years and continually keeps doing his task: collect garbage and remove it to a specific area. Wall-E had the peculiar characteristic of collecting for itself objects directly linked to the humans that he knew centuries before. One object was a TV, still working. During pauses, Wall-E enjoys watching the humans in romantic scenes, dancing, touching each other, kissing, etc. - a nostalgic robot. Wall-E also has a small insect, the only life left in the planet Earth. One day he is surprised by an intense tremor and terrifying noise. It is a space shuttle just deploying a robot conducted to investigate possible signs of life. The story goes on… important here is to say that the world from where the new robot was coming was a planet inhabited by humans who migrated from Earth due to the destruction provoked by their antecedents. This new world is commanded by a master machine, supervised by an army of robots. The humans had one representative to dialogue with the master machine and evidently follow its orders. The world is entirely automatized, the humans just need to sleep and during the day sit down in their personal electric car and be conducted around the

city, always the same route. There is no need to stand up for anything. It they want a sandwich or a soft drink, they only must press a button and a robot immediately approaches with the order. They are all fatty, happy people with no concerns whatsoever. They could not walk anymore, because they did not need to walk. They don't touch each other anymore, for the machines provide all sensations. There are no more moments of doubt and reflection, because the screens installed everywhere anticipate all the answers, etc. Of course, Wall-E was not a movie for kids, but a satirical description of the human world that is already coming, a world with infantilized and superficialized beings: people lacking a sense of identity, personality; they are absent of affective experiences, inter-contact; they miss sense of time, perspective of death; they are no more surrounded by nature to be observed and experienced offering the perception of life in movement. They are obese in body and flat in mind: happy stupid.

10. Peter Martin well realized his task is gigantic, titanic, for having to deal not just with psychiatric disease, but also to take into consideration a generalized poor education, culture of consumerism, individualism, hedonism, immediatism, all tending to anarchy; an anarchy that seems will be "corrected" by the big brother.

(In Central America and South America lives an animal genetically disposed to live in trees [it sleeps holding branches with long arms and relatively enormously curved slot claws] evidently to survive. It is called *bicho preguiça* (sloth). *Bicho preguiça* has 8-9 cervical vertebrae and can rotate its little head 270 degrees, again a genetic modification for protection, because on land it cannot move faster than 4m per minute; swimming it reaches 13m per minute. Slow movement, slow metabolism; being a vegetarian, it accumulates many leaves (plenty of water) in the stomach and evacuates feces once a week; it sleeps up to 14 hours per day. Most of the time it gives the impression of being in a torporous state. It is heterothermic, frequently exposed to sun to increase body temperature; heart beats around 40 per minute. *Bicho preguiça* is a small animal, its size varies between 60 to 80 cm, and weighs from 3 to 8 kg. As consequence of all these biological elements, its very low level of exercise is the clue to reduced energy consumption and survival. Life span: around 20 years).

References:

Carmides. In: Platon, Obras Completas. Aguilar s.a. de ediciones. Madrid; 1979.

Fedro. In: Platon, Obras Completas. Aguilar s.a. de ediciones. Madrid; 1979.

Georgoulis AD, Kiapidou I-S, Velogianni L, Stergiou N, Boland A. Herodicus, the father of sports medicine. Knee Surg Sports Traumatol Arthrosc 2007;15(3):315-8.

Jaeger W. Paideia. The Formation of the Greek Man. 6th Edition. Editora Martins Fontes, SãoPaulo; 2013.

Johan Schioldann's comment on Opium

I have read Peter Martin's interesting entry on Opium in his Historical Vocabulary of Addiction and would like to note that the word "Opium" comes from the Greek: opion, a dim. of opos, meaning plant juice.

Peter R. Martin's response to Johan Schioldann's comment

I greatly appreciate Johan Schioldann's informed etymologic comment. The origins of the word *opium* should be sought prior to the era to which it was attributed in the original entry. The word was not first described by Caius Plinius Secundus (23/24 – 79), or Pliny the Elder, the Roman author, naturalist and natural philosopher, in his *Naturalis Historia* (Plinius Secundus 1866). Rather, as Johan Schioldann indicates, we must begin the history of the word in Ancient Greece.

According to OED, the noun *opium* originated from the Hellenistic Greek ὄπιον (poppy juice, opium), which in turn, was from the ancient Greek ὀπός (vegetable juice) in combination with the diminutive suffix *-ιον*. The true importance of opium to the ancient Greeks is perhaps best reflected by the fact that such a simple generic term as "**vegetable juice**" (in its diminutive form, no less) denoted the thickened dried latex of the unripe capsules of the opium poppy *Papaver somniferum* and that the ancients knew with some clarity its meaning from amongst the many other vegetables that were available to them.

Reference:

Caius Plinius Secundus. Naturalis Historia. Berolini; 1866-1882.

Hector Warnes' comment on Wernicke-Korsakoff Syndrome

Peter Martin's vignette is an excellent summary of the successive changes of the definition, etiology and outcome of the syndrome which came to be known as the Wernicke-Korsakoff'. Of the three cases published by Wernicke in 1881 only two were chronic alcoholics. One was a 20- year-old seamstress whose brain stem neurological lesions (which necropsy showed mainly a "polioencephalitis haemorrhagica superioris") were induced by an overdose of sulphuric acid. Wernicke's accurate clinical observations are still valid (confusional delirium which can lead to a comatose state, gait ataxia, horizontal nystagmus, unequal pupils, lateral rectus and gaze palsies).

Korsakoff published in 1887 and 1890-1891 cases of chronic alcoholics who developed an amnestic syndrome with confabulations (pseudo-reminiscence) and polyneuritis without disturbances of consciousness. At the time Wernicke published his textbook of psychiatry neither Korsakoff nor Wernicke associated the two disorders. Korsakoff's patients suffered amnestic psychosis seen in chronic alcoholics; Wernicke's cases were cases of delirium frequently seen in alcoholics but almost invariably fatal until thiamine was part of the treatment (neuropathic beriberi). It was later discovered, as Peter Martin pointed out, that malnutrition, hyperemesis, malabsorption and multiple deficiencies were involved particularly pyridoxine and pantothenic acid.

It was also found that although different etiological factors caused the same illness mostly Korsakoff's psychosis was due to chronic alcoholism along with malnutrition, polyneuritis, severe gastritis or esophagitis, hepatic failure and an amnestic syndrome. Another related disorder rarely observed in chronic alcoholics were those addicted to red wine in Italy (Marchiafava-Bignami disease) with finding at necropsy of necrosis and demyelination of the corpus callosum and axonal degeneration. More cases who were not chronic alcoholics were found to be associated with Wernicke's encephalopathy (hyperemesis gravidarum, starvation, chronic hemodialysis, pyloric stenosis, cancer chemotherapy, bariatric surgery, disseminated tuberculosis, hepatic failure, gastric malignancy, digitalis poisoning and so on).

The classical textbook on this syndrome was published in its second edition in 1989 after 18 years of its first edition by Victor, Adams and Collins. They observed 245 patients with Wernicke-Korsakoff Syndrome with detailed brain pathological findings of 82 post-mortem cases. In its second edition the authors updated the findings including new cases and outcome of treatment.

The other classical textbook on the subject was published by David W. McCandless in 2009 which encompassed animal studies and metabolic encephalopathies in general. McDowell and LeBlanc published more specifically on the computed tomographic findings in Wernicke-Korsakoff syndrome as well as another publication on imagenology by Chanraud and Bernard in 2015.

References:

Chanraud S, Bernard C. Neuroimagerie de l'alcoolisme chronique. In: Annales Médico-psychologiques. vol. 173, Elsevier; 2015, pp. 249-54.

McCandless DW. Metabolic Encephalopathy. Springer, New York; 2009

McDowell JR, LeBlanc C. Computed Tomographic findings in Wernicke-Korsakoff syndrome. Arch. Neurol 1984; 41:453-4.

Korsakoff SS. Über eine besondere Form psychischer Störung kombiniert mit multipler neuritis. Arch. Psychiatr. Bd 21; 1890.

Korsakoff SS. Über Erinnerung-Störungen (Pseudo-reminiscenzen) by poly-neuritischen psychosen. Allgem. Zeitschr. Psychiat. Bd 47; 1891.

Victor M, Adams RD, Collins G. The Wernicke-Korsakoff and related Neurological Disorders due to alcoholism and malnutrition. Philadelphia: F.A. Davis Co; 1989.

Wernicke C. Lehrbuch der Gehirnkrankheiten für Aerzte und Studierende. Kassel Theodor Fisher, Edit. Berlin; 1881, pp. 229-42.

Peter Martin's response to Hector Warnes' comment

I greatly appreciate Hector Warnes' comprehensive comment concerning my essay on Wernicke-Korsakoff's syndrome (WKS) which is a chapter in my Historical Vocabulary of Addiction. It is always gratifying when someone with Hector Warnes' detailed understanding of the history of Psychiatry concurs with what one has written. Accordingly, my response will be appropriately brief as we are in agreement on the majority of Warnes' comments.

I would like to correct Warnes' point that "multiple [nutritional] deficiencies were involved particularly pyridoxine and pantothenic acid" in pathogenesis of WKS. This is an important point, the sine qua non for the neuropathological findings of WKS is thiamine deficiency, often but not always, enhanced by the metabolic effects of chronic alcohol consumption (De Wardener and Lennox 1947; Martin, Singleton and Hiller-Sturmhöfel 2003; Victor, Adams and Collins 1971). Accordingly, the following statement by Warnes is probably incorrect: "It was also found that although different etiological factors caused the same illness mostly Korsakoff's psychosis was due to chronic alcoholism."

I was not familiar with the term "pseudo-reminiscence" that Warnes employed for denoting the more commonly used confabulation, but admit I like the sound of the word and may start using it to be less monotonous in my writing.

Warnes rightly mentions Marchiafava-Bignami disease, which is likely a variant of WKS "with finding at necropsy of necrosis and demyelination of the corpus callosum and axonal degeneration" which can be due to alcoholism but also nonalcoholic causes. However, both require thiamine treatment as recommended by colleagues in Norway, where preferences for the source of alcohol tends to beer, vodka or Akvavit, quite different from that in Italy (Hillbom Saloheimo, Fujioka et al. 2014).

Finally, I would like to strongly concur with Warnes about the importance of the volume published by Victor, Adams and Collins (1971) which played an immense role in inspiring my own research on the role of thiamine deficiency in brain injury in alcoholics.

References:

De Wardener HE, Lennox B. Cerebral beriberi (Wernicke's encephalopathy): Review of 52 cases in a Singapore prisoner-of-war hospital. The Lancet 1947;249(6436):11–17.

Hillbom M, Saloheimo P, Fujioka S, Wszolek ZK, Juvela S, Leone MA. Diagnosis and management of Marchiafava-Bignami disease: A review of CT/MRI confirmed cases. Journal of Neurology, Neurosurgery, and Psychiatry 2014);85(2):168–73.

Martin PR, Singleton CK, Hiller-Sturmhöfel S. The role of thiamine deficiency in alcoholic brain disease. Alcohol Research & Health 2003;27(2):134–42.

Victor M, Adams RD, Collins GH. The Wernicke-Korsakoff Syndrome: A Clinical and Pathological Study of 245 Patients, 82 with Post-mortem Examinations. Contemp Neurol Ser 1971; 7:1-206.

Hector Warnes reply to Peter Martin's response to his comment

I am most grateful to Peter Martin for his outstanding review of the Wernicke-Korsakoff syndrome. I have seen many cases admitted to psychiatric hospitals with partial remission in spite of high doses of Thiamine which can be monitored by the resolution of the ophthalmoplegia and ataxia (though truncal ataxia may also persist) but not necessarily of other neurological and cognitive deficits. The patients were also given Magnesium which is a co-factor for Thiamine transketolase activity; thiamine should be given prior to glucose loading for dehydration. It is estimated that more than 50% of people with Wernicke encephalopathy also get Korsakoff's syndrome. Wernicke encephalopathy may clear with Thiamine treatment or may be followed by a Korsakoff Psychosis (Dementia) which consists of an amnestic-confabulatory state without delirium.

I did not emphasize the unique role of Thiamine because most patients with this encephalopathy have other co-morbidities and lately neuroscientists have shown synergies of thiamine (B1), pyridoxine (B6) and cyanocobalamin (B12) in the integrity of the Central Nervous System. The deficiency of only one factor Thiamine was found in an animal model (Beriberi in chickens with polyneuritis). The hydrosoluble vitamins of the B group act on the myelin and neurotransmitter synthesis.

Peter Martin's response to Hector Warnes' reply to his comment

This insightful comment by Hector Warnes demonstrates the wealth of his clinical experience and his translational thinking. He identifies one of the most important issues in the pathogenesis of Wernicke-Korsakoff syndrome — the interindividual differences in susceptibility to the disorder among individuals who are exposed to alcoholism and malnutrition. Why do only a fraction of those with Wernicke's encephalopathy progress to Korsakoff's psychosis? This enigma remains to be answered yet.

We have proposed to explain interindividual differences in susceptibility to brain injury in alcoholics based on various aspects of thiamine metabolism (Martin, Singleton and Hiller-Sturmhöfel 2003), although it seems that other issues may also be relevant as Warnes points out, especially comorbid medical illnesses such as liver disease, head trauma, and premorbid brain functioning among many other factors.

Additionally, I would like to emphasize that Korsakoff's Psychosis is quite distinct from dementia in its clinical presentation and neuropsychological characteristics and has been so classified in most diagnostic systems. For example, patients with Korsakoff's Psychosis can be demonstrated to have a different structure of neuropsychological deficits compared to those diagnosed with Alzheimer's disease (Weingartner, Grafman, Boutelle et al. 1983).

References:

Martin PR, Singleton CK, Hiller-Sturmhöfel S. The role of thiamine deficiency in alcoholic brain disease. Alcohol Res Health 2003;27(2):134–42.

Weingartner H, Grafman J, Boutelle W, Kaye W, Martin PR. Forms of memory failure. Science 1983;221(4608):380-2.

IN MEMORIAM. Prof. Thomas A. Ban.
(1929 – 2022)